INTERNATIONAL STUDIES

The Totalitarian Party

INTERNATIONAL STUDIES

PUBLISHED FOR THE CENTRE FOR
INTERNATIONAL STUDIES, LONDON SCHOOL
OF ECONOMICS AND POLITICAL SCIENCE

The Centre for International Studies at the London
School of Economics was established in 1967 with
the aid of a grant from the Ford Foundation. Its
aim is to promote research and advanced training
on a multi-disciplinary basis in the general field
of International Studies, particular emphasis
being given initially to contemporary China, the
Soviet Union and Eastern Europe and the
relationship between these areas and the outside
world. To this end the Centre offers research
fellowships and studentships and, in collaboration
with other bodies (such as the Social Science
Research Council), sponsors research projects
and seminars.

The Centre is undertaking a series of
publications in International Studies, of which
this volume is the fourth.

*Whilst the Editorial Board accepts responsibility for recom-
mending the inclusion of a volume in the series, the author
is alone responsible for the views and opinions expressed.*

ALSO IN THIS SERIES

BLIT: The Origins of Polish Socialism
STEINER: The Slovak Dilemma
VAN CREVELD: Hitler's Strategy 1940–1941: The Balkan Clue

THE TOTALITARIAN PARTY

PARTY AND PEOPLE IN NAZI GERMANY
AND SOVIET RUSSIA

ARYEH L. UNGER
The Hebrew University, Jerusalem

CAMBRIDGE UNIVERSITY PRESS

Published by the Syndics of the Cambridge University Press
Bentley House, 200 Euston Road, London NW1 2DB
American Branch: 32 East 57th Street, New York, N.Y. 10022

© Cambridge University Press 1974

Library of Congress Catalogue Card Number: 73–92786

ISBN: 0 521 20427 5

First published 1974

Printed in Great Britain by
Western Printing Services Ltd,
Bristol

CONTENTS

1827146

PREFACE	vii
ABBREVIATIONS	ix
INTRODUCTION	1
1 THE PARTY AND THE MASSES	6
2 TOTALITARIAN PROPAGANDA	32
3 TOTALITARIAN ORGANIZATION	61
4 POLITICAL AGITATION IN NAZI GERMANY	83
The Role of the Rank and File	83
The Nazi Block Leader	99
5 POLITICAL AGITATION IN SOVIET RUSSIA	105
The Role of the Rank and File	105
The Agitator	112
The Politinformator	150
6 INDIRECT PROPAGANDA: THE USURPATION OF LEISURE AND RITUAL	167
7 PROPAGANDA OF THE DEED: WELFARE	204
8 REPORTING PUBLIC OPINION	221
9 CONCLUDING REMARKS	263
LIST OF SOURCES	272
INDEX	281

To the memory of my parents, Max and Rosa Unger,
and my sister, Hannele

PREFACE

The subject of this book is the role of the Nazi and Soviet parties
in relation to the peoples under their rule. My concern is with
some of the functions which the two parties performed in their
respective political systems rather than with their internal structure, discipline, training, membership, etc. I have tried, as far as
possible, to pursue party activities down to the grass-roots, the
points at which they impinge upon the lives of ordinary men and
women. This has occasionally involved somewhat lengthy quotations from Nazi and Soviet sources which deal with party affairs
at this level. Readers familiar with either or both regimes may
find some of this material rather tedious. But I believe it is important for others, who are not thus familiar, to understand
not only what the totalitarian party does but also how it communicates about it.

I have approached my subject without an explicit 'conceptual
framework'. To admit this is not, of course, to imply that I have
approached it without preconceptions. I have read the works of
others and have been influenced by them, and I have absorbed
some of the diffuse notions and prejudices that are inseparable
from membership in any culture.

The extent to which different party activities could be covered
was in part determined by the availability of material. In some
cases I have thought it advisable to explore certain activities, on
which evidence was relatively abundant, more thoroughly than
others on which evidence was relatively sparse, rather than aim
at a balanced presentation. For Nazi Germany much of the
evidence comes from the German archives captured by the
Allies at the end of World War II. For the Soviet Union, I have
necessarily had to rely largely on published sources available in
libraries in the West. An apparent inconsistency in citing articles
from Nazi and Soviet party journals may require clarification:
full bibliographical details are provided in the footnotes only
where the subject under discussion was a principal theme of the

article, or where I felt that the title of the article was itself a significant piece of information; in all other cases the name of the author and the title of the articles are omitted.

While I am alone responsible for its shortcomings this book is, like others of its kind, very much the product of collective effort. Among my unwitting collaborators I must mention first my teachers, colleagues and students at the Hebrew University. They have contributed more than they might wish to recall. I owe a similar tribute to the knowledgeable and unfailingly courteous keepers of the records; if they must go unnamed it is because they are too numerous to be identified here. More specific acknowledgements are due to several persons and institutions. Professor Leonard Schapiro guided my first steps in the study of totalitarian government and has continued to give me the benefit of his erudition unstintingly and unobtrusively ever since. My gratitude to him is profound. I would also like to express my appreciation to Professor Geoffrey Goodwin and Professor George L. Mosse for their helpful suggestions and encouragement. The Friends of the Hebrew University provided generous support at an early stage of my research. My thanks go especially to Dr Walter Zander, former Secretary of the Friends in London, for his warm personal interest no less than for his invaluable help. A travel grant from the Astor Foundation enabled me to consult materials located in the United States and as a Research Fellow of the Centre for International Studies at the London School of Economics and Political Science I enjoyed a year's freedom to write in an exceptionally rewarding environment. I am also grateful to the editors of *Journal of Social History*, *Osteuropa*, *The Public Opinion Quarterly* and *Soviet Studies* for permission to reprint in revised form material from articles previously published in these journals.

To my wife, Chava, I owe apologies as well as thanks: apologies because the writing of this book imposed upon her and upon our children a burden of sacrifices that would have been excessive even for a much weightier tome; thanks because she bore that burden cheerfully throughout.

Jerusalem, Israel   A.U.
December 1973

ABBREVIATIONS

CC	Central Committee of the CPSU
CPSU	Communist Party of the Soviet Union
Gestapo	Geheime Staatspolizei (Secret State Police)
Komsomol	Kommunisticheskii Soyuz Molodezhi (Communist Youth League)
NEP	Novaya Ekonomicheskaya Politika (New Economic Policy)
NKVD	Narodnyi Komissariat Vnutrennykh Del (People's Commissariat of Internal Affairs)
NSDAP	Nationalsozialistische Deutsche Arbeiterpartei (National Socialist German Workers' Party)
NSV	Nationalsozialistische · Volkswohlfahrt (National Socialist People's Welfare)
OKW	Oberkommando der Wehrmacht (Supreme Command of the Armed Forces)
RSHA	Reichssicherheitshauptamt (Main Security Office of the Reich)
SD	Sicherheitsdienst (Security Service)
WHW	Winterhilfswerk (Winter Help Project)

INTRODUCTION

Shortly after World War II a German scholar declared: 'The total state is *the* political phenomenon of the 20th Century.'[1] Over two decades later an American scholar described the concept of totalitarianism as 'a conceptual harlot of uncertain parentage, belonging to no one but at the service of all'.[2] To juxtapose these two statements is to obtain a measure of the frustration that has dogged the study of totalitarianism to this day: the apparent importance of the phenomenon, on the one hand; the apparent impotence of social science to arrive at a reasonably clear conception of it, on the other.

I do not propose to enter into the continuing debate about the proper definition of 'totalitarianism', nor to stipulate a definition of my own. A clearer conception of the phenomenon can only be reached through the close study of political systems labelled 'totalitarian'. There are no definitional shortcuts. What is needed, it seems to me, at least at this stage of our very partial knowledge of such systems, is a concept to delineate the subject area of inquiry. And for this the widely accepted meaning of 'totalitarianism' as a system of rule in which public power is concentrated in the hands of a single ruler or small ruling group, as in other forms of autocratic government, and also 'totalist', in the sense of aspiring to be all-pervasive, seems quite adequate. To be sure, various writers have sought to refine this notion by extending the connotation of the term, and some have tried to 'define' the phenomenon itself, in the familiar manner of a Platonic search for the 'essence' of the thing. But even the most implacable critics of totalitarianism as a valid concept do not deny that the autocratic concentration of power at the summit

[1] G. Leibholz in a BBC broadcast of 1946, reprinted in his *Strukturprobleme der modernen Demokratie*, Karlsruhe, 1958, p. 225. (Emphasis in the original.)
[2] B. R. Barber, 'Conceptual Foundations of Totalitarianism', in C. J. Friedrich, M. Curtis and B. R. Barber, *Totalitarianism in Perspective: Three Views*, London, 1969, p. 19.

1

of the political system together with its totalist expansion throughout the society constitute the common denominators of the great
majority of definitions whether 'nominal' or 'real'.

That the concept remains vague cannot be denied. The relevant question, however, is not whether it is vague, but whether
it is useful. As here defined 'totalitarianism' is associated with
two structural and therefore relatively observable dimensions of
power, i.e. its distribution and its scope. To say 'relatively observable' is not to allege that we are able to measure power along
either of the two scales, or that other effective means for 'opera-
tionalizing' the concept are ready at hand. It is, however, to
suggest that the defining characteristics facilitate reliable identification; that the relevant data are fairly accessible to observation,
and, in particular, that objective observers are likely to agree on
their interpretation, or, at least, are more likely to agree than
they would be in the case of many other significant aspects of a
political system. To this extent, therefore, observation is at a
maximum and evaluation is at a minimum. Conceivably, too,
it is not beyond the ingenuity of political science to devise a set
of indicators that would greatly enhance the reliability of the
concept. But even without such indicators there can be little
doubt that instances of totalitarianism, including the two regimes
which form the subject of this study, can be identified on the
scene of 20th century politics.

Similarly, it should require little argument that the two attributes of totalitarianism can be connected with many others which
political scientists have long regarded as central features of
political systems – the rights and freedoms of the individual, the
forms and limits of group action, the diffusion of information and
knowledge, opportunities for discussion and dissent, the stability
of legal norms, etc. To apply the categories of what has come
to be known as 'the functional approach to comparative politics',
totalitarianism bears directly on all the major functions of a
political system: its capabilities, its conversion processes and
its system maintenance and adaptation functions. Precisely what
rights the individual enjoys (if any) in a particular totalitarian
polity or just how responsive the political system is to the demands of the society (if at all), remains to be established by appropriate investigation. But from what we already know about
politics it is a reasonable hypothesis that individual rights will
be severely circumscribed and that the responsive capability of
the system will be rather low. In other words, to classify a poli-

tical system as totalitarian is to characterize it in a way that to
the student of politics holds out the promise of significance. The
defining characteristics of totalitarianism point to, are 'sure
marks' of, its accompanying characteristics, and polities designated as totalitarian are likely to resemble one another in regard
to attributes other than those constituting the original criteria
of classification. In as much as it 'generates' a cluster of em-
pirically associated attributes, the classification instituted by the
concept of totalitarianism is therefore a 'natural' rather than an
'artificial' one, 'carving at nature's joints', as it were.[3]

These all too brief remarks cannot pretend to encompass a
complex and controversial topic. They may suffice, however, to
indicate that the concept is here intended not as a 'generalization
in disguise',[4] but as a classificatory device which should enable
us to group together things that seem 'to belong' together, to
compare them and ultimately and hopefully to explain them. It
does not imply that these things are alike in all 'essentials'. If
they were, they would for all practical purposes be identical and
it obviously makes no sense whatever to embark upon a comparison of things that are *a priori* assumed to be identical. Nor
does it imply that they are 'basically alike',[5] which presumably
means that they share their more important features, for such a
judgment, to be at all credible, would require at the very least
an explicit statement of the criteria on which it was based. Certainly one could argue that Nazi Germany and Soviet Russia
differed in aspects which by any standard of evaluation were
fairly important to each of them: their respective traditional
cultures, for one, their respective attitudes to the socio-economic
status quo, for another; the drive towards industrialization –
surely a basic feature of the Soviet system, but absent from
Germany; or racialism – surely equally basic to the latter in a way
not even remotely attributable to the former. Instead, the sole
implication is that the things classified, i.e. totalitarian systems,

[3] See A. Kaplan, *The Conduct of Enquiry*, San Francisco, 1967, pp. 50ff
and C. G. Hempel, *Aspects of Scientific Explanation*, New York and
London, 1965, pp. 146ff.
[4] R. Bendix, 'Concepts and Generalizations in Comparative Sociological
Studies', *Amer. Sociological Review*, 1963, no. 4, pp. 533ff.
[5] This is claimed in C. J. Friedrich and Z. K. Brzezinski, *Totalitarian Dictatorship and Autocracy*, Cambridge, Mass., 1956, pp. 5 and 7. In the
second edition of this work, revised by Friedrich alone, the assertion is
qualified to refer to structure, institutions and processes of rule. (1965, p.
19.)

are alike in some features which to the political scientist are significant and which, because they are significant, are likely to lead to the discovery of other, possibly more important, resemblances. The defining characteristics are derived on the basis of import and not of importance; import is inter-subjectively verifiable, importance is very much in the eyes of the beholder.

In every context of inquiry, after all, we begin with rather vague notions, or 'imageries',[6] and as we progress these are gradually refined into increasingly precise tools serviceable for successive stages of the scientific enterprise. That our notion of totalitarianism is still in the 'imagery' stage doubtless accounts for much, though by no means all, of the general dissatisfaction with the concept, causing some writers, particularly in recent years, to demand that it be discarded from our conceptual toolbox. But an 'imagery' is not necessarily a chimera. Somewhere 'out there' in the external world a real phenomenon may still be beckoning, even though it is at present beyond the range of our comprehension. Totalitarianism is such a phenomenon. It deserves to be studied and it deserves a name.

This book will deal with some of the functions of one totalitarian institution – the party – in the two totalitarian polities of Nazi Germany and Soviet Russia. Contemporary political science is rich in universal categories denoting functions which parties are said to perform in all political systems. I have no quarrel here with these categories. They were for the most part extended from the politics of Western democracy, and I have not generally used them in this study. Doubtless if the level of generality is pegged high enough, many of them can be made to apply in entirely dissimilar political situations. Thus, both democratic and totalitarian parties may be regarded as instruments of political participation, socialization, communication, mobilization, integration, adaptation, aggregation, representation, legitimation, recruitment, goal specification, goal attainment, and all the rest. However, in the service of the cross-cultural studies which have provided so much of the impetus behind the new comparative politics of the past two decades, these categories are sometimes employed at such rarefied heights that their scientific utility is considerably im-

6 P. F. Lazarsfeld, 'Concept Formation and Measurement in the Behavioral Sciences: Some Historical Observations', in G. J. DiRenzio, ed., *Concepts, Theory and Explanation in the Behavioral Sciences*, New York, 1966, p. 187.

paired. This is particularly true in comparisons between democratic and totalitarian parties. The distinction between the two-party or multi-party systems of democracies and the single-party systems of totalitarian regimes cuts across all party functions. Democratic parties exist to organize the competition for political power. Totalitarian parties exist to organize a monopoly of political power; they are permanent ruling parties. The two purposes are fundamentally opposed to one another, and such common functions as parties may perform in both kinds of systems are crucially affected by this opposition. It has often been pointed out that 'single party' is a marriage of incompatibles because the very term 'party' implies the presence of other 'parts'. The problem is not, of course, one of semantic incompatibility alone. As one author put it: 'Where there is only one "party", all party life ceases, just as, if there were only one "sex", all "sex" life would cease.'[7]

If there is a single universal category under which the functions of the Nazi and Soviet parties vis-à-vis the people may be subsumed, it is that of mobilization. The latter concept is now widely employed with regard to single-party systems in developing countries but also with regard to the politics of advanced industrial societies. Note, however, that it entered the discourse of modern politics from the dictionary of the totalitarians who, in turn, derived it from military terminology. Those who apply it to democratic politics therefore do so by a process of 'reversed extrapolation'.[8] Unlike such terms as 'participation', 'representation', 'aggregation', etc., which are primarily drawn from democratic experience, the natural habitat of 'mobilization', or 'mobilization of the masses', to give the authentic totalitarian version, is so much part of totalitarian reality that it is often listed as one of its principal characteristics. The meaning of the concept in general social science literature is far from uniform. In this book it refers to any process by which totalitarian regimes seek to activate their peoples in support of official norms and goals. It involves changes in opinion, attitude and behaviour; it involves executing the tasks set by the leadership; above all it involves control. It is an organized, directed process, part of the purposive exercise of totalitarian power.

[7] B. D. Wolfe, *Communist Totalitarianism*, 2nd rev. ed., Boston, 1961, p. 266.
[8] G. Sartori, 'Concept Misformation in Comparative Politics', *Amer. Pol. Science Review*, 1970, no. 4, p. 1051.

1: THE PARTY AND THE MASSES

The political and social doctrines in the service of which the Bolsheviks and the Nazis each purported to make their respective revolutions were mutually exclusive. They issued from different moral and philosophical assumptions, they appealed to different scientific or pseudo-scientific disciplines for their theoretical insights, and they arrived at different conclusions on almost all questions affecting the desirable or 'necessary' development of human society. Yet they formulated and consistently upheld an attitude towards the masses that was identical in both its essential ingredients. It contained on the one hand a near-mystical affirmation of the positive life-force residing in the 'toiling masses' or the *Volk*,[1] and on the other, expressed the undisguised conviction that by themselves the masses were unable to perceive and exploit the potentialities which History or Nature had bestowed upon them. The relationship of the party to the masses which grew out of this creed could not but mirror its innate dualism. Each party was charged to remain in close contact with the masses in order to partake in the elemental, history-making force that emanated from them at the same time as it was urged to keep itself aloof from the masses in order to retain a firm hold on the ultimate vision, to ensure, as Lenin once put it, that 'the regular troops will not be overwhelmed by the crowd but stand at the head of the crowd'.[2]

Both doctrines never ceased to avow their faith in the potentialities lying dormant in the masses and their conviction that it was only by activating these potentialities that their cause could be brought to victory. 'Marxism', Lenin wrote,

---

1 The term *Volk* (people), especially as used by the Nazis, contains overtones of an 'essential unity', spiritual and biological, which, strictly speaking, render the term untranslatable into English. I have nevertheless occasionally translated it as 'people', when it seemed unduly pedantic to adhere to the original German term.

2 V. I. Lenin, *Polnoe Sobranie Sochinenii*, 5th ed., 55 vols., Moscow, 1967–1970, vol. VI, p. 175.

differs from all other social theories by its remarkable combination of a complete, sober, scientific analysis of the objective state of affairs and the objective course of evolution, and the most resolute recognition of the importance of revolutionary energy, revolutionary creativity and revolutionary initiative of the masses.[3]

Neither of these two distinctive features claimed for Marxism has been eclipsed by the progress of time, but both are on the contrary said to have developed further with the aid of the practical experience gained in the building of socialism and the attendant growth in the consciousness of the masses. Even at the height of the personality cult Soviet spokesmen did not fail to pay their respects to the 'living creativity' of the masses.[4] That the party must 'heed the voice of the masses and rely on their creative experience', that the masses are 'the genuine makers of history', that 'the party believes profoundly in the reason and the wisdom of the people', these are perennial refrains of Soviet ideological pronouncements.

National socialism regarded the biologically determined community of the people, the *Volk*, or *Volksgemeinschaft*, as the mainspring of historical progress. The 'natural *Volk*' matured under the impact of 'historical experience' and inspired by the call of its 'historical mission' as embodied in the national socialist idea, grows into the 'political *Volk*'. Nazi doctrine taught that the 'concept of a political *Volk* implies that the *Volk* itself proceeds to active, creative action'.[5] Where the Bolsheviks directed their efforts towards the development of the 'living creativity' of the masses, the 'appeal of national socialism was from the first to the heroic instincts of the people'.[6] But the emphasis on the need to awaken and develop the slumbering capacities residing in the broad masses is equally marked in both doctrines.

These affirmations of their belief in the creative potentialities of the masses did not, however, suffice to conceal the attitude of

---

[3] *Ibid.*, vol. xvi, p. 23.

[4] See, e.g. *Pravda*, 22 August 1949.

[5] E. R. Huber, *Das Verfassungsrecht des Grossdeutschen Reichs*, Hamburg, 1939, p. 154; see also A. Rosenberg, *Der Mythus des XX Jahrhunderts*, Munich, 1930, p. 253.

[6] Hitler at the 1934 Party Congress, *Frankfurter Zeitung*, 12 September 1934.

suspicion and even contempt with which the two doctrines regarded the mass of the people, an attitude which was no less openly – though perhaps less frequently – expressed than its populist counterpart. Despite their many protestations to the contrary both doctrines invariably viewed every manifestation of 'heroic instinct' or 'living creativity' that was not firmly guided and controlled by the party with the utmost distrust. Already in *What is to be Done?* (1902), the first systematic exposition of his ideas on the party and the masses, Lenin formulated his famous dictum according to which the 'history of all countries shows that the working class exclusively by its own efforts is able to develop only trade union consciousness'.[7] The central thesis of the book is the imminent need to combat the 'fundamental error' of 'subservience to spontaneity' in the ranks of Russian Social Democracy.[8] The consciousness necessary for the all-round struggle against Tsardom, a struggle that was to be conducted on all planes but above all on the political plane, must, according to Lenin, be brought to the working class from without. On their own the workers were fundamentally incapable of acting in a manner compatible with their true class interests. Lenin never deviated from this belief, whatever else he may have said or written at different times concerning the capacity of the Russian proletariat to take over the government of Russia. Nearly twenty years later and over three years after the establishment of 'proletarian class rule' he told the 10th Congress of the party:

> Marxism teaches – and this tenet ... has also been confirmed in practice by our revolution – that only the political party of the working class, i.e., the Communist Party, is capable of unifying, educating and organizing a vanguard of the proletariat and of the whole mass of the working people that alone will be capable of withstanding the inevitable petty-bourgeois vaccilations of this mass and the inevitable traditions and relapses of narrow craft unionism or craft prejudices among the proletariat, i.e. of leading it politically and through it the whole mass of the working people. Without this the dictatorship of the proletariat is impossible.[9]

The attitude of suspicion towards spontaneity in all its manifestations has remained one of the most enduring aspects of

---

[7] Lenin, *Pol. Sob. Soch.*, vol. VI, p. 30.
[8] *Ibid.*, p. 52.
[9] *Ibid.*, vol. XLIII, p. 94.

Lenin's teaching. Notwithstanding the intensive propaganda conducted among the masses over many years, the victorious conclusion of the internal class struggle and the establishment of the
'moral-political unity of the Soviet people' which are said to have
marked the steady progress of Soviet society towards communism,
the ferments that are constantly at work in the midst of the masses
have apparently lost none of their potency. 'We must not forget',
reads a *Pravda* editorial, 'that where we Communists do not
carry on political work among the masses conditions are created
for the penetration of the influence of foreign bourgeois ideology,
for the revival of the remnants of capitalist notions in the midst
of the Soviet people.'[10] Indulgence in what Soviet spokesmen
describe as 'the "theory" and practice of spontaneous development, of drift', is still among the greatest of sins.[11] Khrushchev
once referred to it as the party's 'most terrible foe' in the struggle
for the communist transformation of Soviet society,[12] and his
successors have had occasion to point out that 'socialist democracy has nothing in common with anarchic strong-headedness
and spontaneity, with disregard for discipline. It means that the
responsibility of each worker for the realization of the tasks and
plans becomes greater.'[13] There is probably no other facet of the
official doctrine that has been as often stated or as unequivocally
implemented as that for the Soviet people 'the Communist Party
was, is, and will be the only ruler of thought, the inspirer of ideas
and aspirations', the 'sovereign of their minds', the 'collective
reason', etc.[14]

Hitler, too, maintained in *Mein Kampf* that 'the political understanding of the broad masses is not at all sufficiently developed
to enable them to arrive on their own at a definite general political view'.[15] Indeed, the book is unique among the writings of
practising politicians in that it makes no attempt to hide its
author's contemptuously manipulative attitude towards the
masses; it abounds in expressions such as 'the granite stupidity of
mankind', 'voting cattle', and the 'ingrained inertia of the

---

[10] *Pravda*, 29 January 1958.
[11] *Kommunist*, 1958, no. 6, p. 31; 1970, no. 16, pp. 83–4.
[12] *Plenum Tsentral'nogo Komiteta Kommunisticheskoi Partii Sovetskogo
   Soyuza, 15–19 dekabrya 1958 g. Stenograficheskii otchet*, Moscow, 1958,
   p. 452.
[13] *Politicheskoe samoobrazovanie*, 1968, no. 6, p. 78.
[14] *Pravda*, 6 July 1956; 12 January 1965; *Partiinaya zhizn'*, 1971, no. 6,
   p. 4.
[15] A. Hitler, *Mein Kampf*, Munich, 1930, p. 92.

mass'.[16] Goebbels repeatedly emphasized that 'the masses are for us unformed stuff. Only in the hands of the political artist do the masses become a people and the people a nation.'[17] His appraisal of the masses was such that he felt compelled to place limitations even on what could be achieved by the 'political artist', a species, of whom he clearly – and not unjustly – regarded himself as an outstanding representative. 'The mass', he declared, 'is a weak, lazy, cowardly majority of people. The broad mass can never be entirely won. Its best components must be so brought into shape that they are able at the end to assemble for their victory march.'[18] Finally, Robert Ley, the leader of the German Labour Front who was also in charge of internal party organization and training, urged, like *Pravda*, the need for unremitting supervision over the masses, notwithstanding the fact that the Nazis, too, had long before proclaimed their version of 'national solidarity'. 'The people', he wrote in 1942,

> are like a big child. A child believes and has confidence but can also be naughty and cause many troubles. It must be constantly educated and guarded, and likewise the people want protection; they will not think for themselves but wish someone to think for them. They will not act for themselves but want to see will-power and energy and deeds.[19]

The role of the party as conceived by both Nazis and Bolsheviks fitted logically into this view of the character of the masses. If the masses were themselves organically incapable of fulfilling their class or racial-national mission an organization was necessary which would think and act for them, and the party was assigned to fill that role. It was constructed to be both the brain and the brawn of the masses; it was to constitute that organization which, standing outside and above the masses, would bring them the necessary 'revolutionary consciousness' and implant in them that 'definite general political view' without which the

16 *Ibid.*, pp. 86, 414, 544, 617. For Hitler's privately voiced views on the masses, see H. Picker, *Hitlers Tischgespraeche im Fuehrerhauptquartier 1941–42*, edited by P. E. Schramm *et al.*, Stuttgart, 1963, p. 159: 'How fortunate for governments that people do not think. There is no thinking except in giving and executing commands. If it were otherwise human society could not exist.' Also *The Goebbels Diaries*, edited and translated by L. P. Lochner, London, 1948, p. 172; H. Rauschning, *Hitler Speaks*, London, 1939, *passim*.
17 J. Goebbels, *Der Kampf um Berlin*, Munich, 1934, p. 40.
18 J. Goebbels, *Signale der neuen Zeit*, Munich, 1934, p. 51.
19 *Der Angriff*, 9 April 1942.

revolution was doomed to failure. The party's task was to point out the revolutionary goals, to mobilize the masses for the revolutionary struggle, and to lead that struggle as their vanguard. Although they insistently protested their faith in the masses as the fount of all progress, both doctrines looked to the party as the real guarantor of that progress. Without the party to lead and organize the masses their revolutionary energy was bound to exhaust itself in a series of futile outbursts. 'In its struggle for power', wrote Lenin in 1904,

> the proletariat has no other weapon but organization. Disunited by the rule of anarchic competition ... ground down by forced labour ... constantly thrust back to the 'lower depths' of utter destitution and desperation, the proletariat can become, and inevitably will become, an invincible force only when its ideological unification by the principles of Marxism is consolidated by the material unity of an organization that will weld millions of workers into an army of the working class.[20]

Hitler similarly emphasized the importance of organization when he wrote:

> Every *Weltanschauung*, be it a thousand times right and of the greatest use to mankind, will remain without significance for the practical development of a people's life so long as its principles have not become the platform of a fighting movement ... The translation of a general, ideologically-determined, ideal conception of the highest truth into a firmly limited, rigidly organized political community of faith and combat, united in spirit and will, is the most significant achievement, the successful solution of which alone makes the victory of the idea possible.[21]

Organization, in both conceptions, implied a degree of unity in thought and action such as could only be achieved by centralized leadership from above and unquestioning discipline from below. The practical differences between the 'democratic centralism' of the Soviet party and the *Fuehrerprinzip* of the Nazi party were minor and ephemeral. Both parties were constructed to ensure strict centralization and strict discipline. Just as Lenin fom the beginning insisted on 'building the party from the top downwards',[22] so Hitler refused to countenance the formation

[20] Lenin, *Pol. Sob. Soch.*, vol. viii, pp. 403–4.
[21] *Mein Kampf.*, pp. 418–19.
[22] Lenin, *Pol. Sob. Soch.*, vol. viii, p. 189.

of new party branches before their subordination to the central authority had been assured beyond all doubt.[23] For Lenin it was axiomatic that 'the less wavering there is *within* the party, the broader, the more varied, the richer and more fertile will be the influence of the party on the working-class *masses* surrounding it and guided by it'.[24] His design for a highly centralized party of dedicated and disciplined 'professional revolutionaries' embodies this belief. Hitler's vision encompassed a party of 'political apostles and combatants, who then as obedient officers, true to their duty, will serve their movement'.[25] It was founded on the conviction that 'the strength of an organization in no way lies in the greatest possible and independent intellectual capacity of its individual members, but rather in the disciplined subordination with which the members follow the spiritual leadership'.[26]

[23] Hitler, *Mein Kampf*, pp. 381–2. The construction of the 'Fuehrer party' in the years prior to the assumption of power is the subject of an important recent study by W. Horn, *Fuehrerideologie und Parteiorganisation (1919–1933)*, Duesseldorf, 1972.

[24] Lenin, *Pol. Sob. Soch.*, vol. viii, p. 244. (Emphasis in the original.)

[25] Speech at the 1934 Party Congress, *Frankfurter Zeitung*, 12 September 1934.

[26] Hitler, *Mein Kampf*, p. 510. Hitler sometimes explained the need for utmost discipline by the argument that only thus could the party hope to stand up to the superior organization and militant tactics of the left-wing parties in the Weimar Republic. (*Ibid.*, pp. 423, 509–10.) In fact, of course, the *Fuehrerprinzip* was neither devised to meet the temporary exigencies of the struggle for power, nor was it confined to the organization of the party alone; after 1933 it became the ruling principle of all social organization in Nazi Germany.

Lenin, too, in *What is to be Done?*, argued the case for centralization, discipline and professionalism in the party among others by reference to the conditions in which the revolutionary struggle against Tsarist autocracy had to be waged. It was a struggle in which, according to Lenin, secrecy was all-important and the need for conspiratorial organization and action outweighed all other considerations. But in his next important work, *One Step Forward, Two Steps Back*, written two years later and devoted to the defence of the stand Lenin took at the 2nd Party Congress, the paramount need for secrecy, derived from the specific conditions of autocratic Russia, is no longer advanced. Instead, Lenin's views on party organization are seen to be determined by his fundamental conception of the relationship between party and masses and their respective roles in the revolutionary process. 'If it is to be a conscious spokesman *in fact*,' he wrote, 'the party must work out such organizational relations as will *ensure a definite level* of consciousness and systematically raise this level.' (Lenin, *Pol. Sob. Soch.*, vol. viii, p. 260. Emphasis in the original.) Stalin's *Short Course* was right for once when it referred to *What is to be Done?* as 'Lenin's plan for the creation of a party of the working class in autocratic Tsarist Russia', while it said of *One Step Forward, Two Steps Back*, that its 'historic significance

It was around this conception of the party that a veritable party cult evolved in due course. In Lenin's celebrated phrase the Bolshevik party was 'the mind, the honour and the conscience of our epoch'.[27] Hitler's characterization of the NSDAP as 'the political conception, the political conscience and the political will' was less well-known but equally magniloquent.[28] Clearly, these were not parties in the accepted sense of the term, as, indeed, their spokesmen never wearied of pointing out. The Bolsheviks formed 'a party of a new type' – in the words of the Party History, 'Lenin was the first Marxist to see that the working class needed a party of a new type.'[29] The Nazis made the same claim to historical uniqueness for the NSDAP, rejecting all attempts 'of the liberal to bring this new phenomenon within his own conceptual framework, because he would not understand it otherwise'.[30] They were particularly conscious of the fact that the term 'party' did not do justice to the NSDAP and often preferred to speak of 'movement' (*Bewegung*); only its outward organizational form, it was said, was that of a party, 'its inner core remained always that of a movement'.[31]

lies in the fact that in it Lenin for the first time in the history of Marxism elaborated the *doctrine of the party* as the leading *organization* of the proletariat, as the principal *weapon* of the proletariat, without which the dictatorship of the proletariat cannot be won'. (*Short History of the Communist Party of the Soviet Union (Bolsheviks)*, London, 1943, pp. 30 and 45. Emphasis in the original.)

[27] Lenin, *Pol. Sob. Soch.*, vol. xxxiv, p. 93.

[28] Speech in Reichstag, *Voelkischer Beobachter*, 21 February 1938. It was perhaps more usual for these lofty attributes to be reserved for Hitler himself. As the party organizational manual put it: 'Political conception, political conscience and political will are embodied in the person of the Fuehrer.' (*Organisationsbuch der NSDAP*, Munich, 1943, p. 148.) But then national socialist doctrine identified the party with its Fuehrer who was 'necessarily bound to the party . . . as the priesthood is bound to the Church . . . exactly as the individual king is rooted in the institution of the monarchy'. (H. Mehringer, *Die NSDAP als politische Ausleseorganisation*, Munich, 1938, p. 114.) Hitler also claimed that 'the Fuehrer is the party and the party is the Fuehrer. Just as I feel myself to be part of this party so the party feels itself to be part of me.' (*Voelkischer Beobachter*, 18 September 1938.)

[29] *Istoriya Kommunisticheskoi Partii Sovetskogo Soyuza*, Moscow, 1962, p. 52.

[30] Mehringer, *NSDAP*, p. 50; see also W. Sommer, 'Die NSDAP als Verfassungstraegerin', in H. H. Lammers and H. Pfundtner, eds., *Die Verwaltungsakademie. Ein Handbuch fuer den Beamten im Deutschen Staat*, 4 vols., Berlin and Vienna, 1936–9, vol. i, no. 12, p. 23.

[31] W. Ruthe, *Der Nationalsozialismus in seinen Programmpunkten, Organisationsformen und Aufbaumassnahmen*, Frankfurt, 1936, p. 11. According

Neither the Nazis nor the Bolsheviks equated the 'victory of the idea' with the seizure of political power. The doctrine of the indispensable party, leading, teaching and organizing the masses, was evolved in the period of struggle for power and generally rationalized by the need to activate the masses for revolution. Once power was attained, however, it was rapidly transformed into a permanent constitutional principle – probably the only truly abiding political norm – of both systems.

Hitler knew that 'the conquest of power is a never-ending process',[32] and that revolutions in the past had failed because they had not realized that 'the essential thing is not the assumption of power, but the education of men'.[33] He saw in the party 'a mighty safeguard' for the continued success of the national socialist revolution. For the party was to be that 'great school of education towards a life in common',[34] which would 'stamp the new *Weltanschauung* upon Germany so durably that it would become the element of cohesion in the German people'.[35] But this was not to say that once the *Weltanschauung* was 'durably stamped' upon the people, the party would become redundant. Goebbels put the argument succinctly when he declared that 'even if a whole people thinks militantly, there is still need for an army'.[36] Hitler himself repeatedly affirmed the party's immortality. The NSDAP would remain in existence for 'a thousand years', he told a British newspaper correspondent in 1935;[37] several months later he predicted to an audience of the party Old Guard: 'This movement will never perish!'[38] And his lieutenants were in no doubt that the future of the Reich was inseparably linked to

to Rauschning, Hitler realized that 'the term "party" is a misnomer. I should prefer "order" myself.' (Rauschning, *Hitler Speaks*, p. 198.) At least one Nazi theorist, however, justified the application of the term 'party' on the grounds that 'the single-party, too, is only a part of the people ... though not a part among equivalent parts with which it shares power; but the select, highest-grade part of the people ... It rightfully bears the name "party": it is the one thing it has in common with the liberal multi-parties.' (G. Neesse, 'Die Verfassungsrechtliche Gestaltung der Ein-Partei', *Zeitschrift fuer die gesamte Staatswissenschaft*, 1938, no. 4, p. 678, n. 1.)

32 Speech at the 1935 Party Congress, *Voelkischer Beobachter*, 9 September 1935.
33 Speech at Reichenhall, *ibid.*, 3 July 1933.
34 Speech at Gera, *Ibid.*, 17 June 1934.
35 Speech at Godesburg, *ibid.*, 22 August 1933; also 18 September 1935.
36 *Ibid.*, 14 February 1934.
37 Interview with Vernon Bartlett, *News Chronicle*, 25 June 1935.
38 *Voelkischer Beobachter*, 1 February 1936.

that of the party. Even Frick, who as Minister of the Interior was often involved in jurisdictional disputes with the party on behalf of the civil service, declared that the 'German Reich cannot exist without the party. If the party falls... then the Reich, too, collapses and the German dream will have ended for ever.'[39] Certainly for the men of the party apparatus, such as *Gauleiter* Paul Giesler, the last regional party leader of Munich, it was an 'unalterable truth that the party, the Fuehrer's own creation, bears in its hands the fate of Germany'.[40]

To Lenin, too, the party was clearly as necessary after the revolution as before it, for the corrosive influence of the past was hard to eradicate. 'The dictatorship of the proletariat', he wrote in 1920,

is a persistent struggle – bloody and bloodless, violent and peaceful, military and economic, educational and administrative – against the forces and traditions of the old society. The force of habit of millions and tens of millions is a most terrible force. Without an iron party tempered in the struggle, without a party enjoying the confidence of all that is honest in the given class, without a party capable of watching and influencing the mood of the masses, it is impossible to conduct such a struggle successfully.[41]

And Stalin, asserting the obvious truth – 'it scarcely needs proof' – that without the party it would have been impossible to establish the proletarian dictatorship, declared in 1924: 'But the proletariat needs the party not only to achieve the dictatorship;

---

[39] Quoted in H. Volz, ed., *Von der Grossmacht zur Weltmacht 1937*, Berlin, 1938, p. 280. (This is vol. III of P. Meier-Benneckenstein, ed., [later F. A. Six] *Dokumente der deutschen Politik*, 8 vols., Berlin, 1935–1943.)

[40] *Voelkischer Beobachter*, 9–10 April 1944.

[41] Lenin, *Pol. Sob. Soch.*, vol. XLI, pp. 26–7. The above passage, cited from '*Left-Wing' Communism – An Infantile Disorder*, was written to counter what Lenin called 'the repudiation of the party principle and of party discipline'. Characteristically, it is his appraisal of the immaturity of the masses and their vulnerability to the 'petty-bourgeois atmosphere, which permeates and corrupts the proletariat and causes constant relapses among the proletariat into petty-bourgeois spinelessness, disunity, individualism, and alternate moods of exaltation and dejection' that justifies in Lenin's eyes both the 'party principle' itself and the need for discipline within the party. 'The strictest centralization and discipline are required within the political party of the proletariat in order to counteract this, in order that the *organizational* role of the proletariat (and that is its principal role) may be exercised correctly, successfully, victoriously.' (*Ibid.*, p. 26. Emphasis in the original.)

it needs it still more to maintain the dictatorship, to consolidate and expand it in order to achieve the complete victory of socialism.' At the same time Stalin predicted, in keeping with current orthodoxy, that since the party was 'an instrument of the dictatorship of the proletariat . . . it follows that when classes disappear and the dictatorship of the proletariat withers away, the party will also wither away'.[42] Since then socialism has been officially established in the Soviet Union and the dictatorship of the proletariat has become, in the words of the 1961 Party Programme, 'a state of the entire people, an organ expressing the interests and the will of the people as a whole'.[43] Yet the party remains as indispensable as ever. A prominent commentator on party affairs, V. Stepanov, put the case for the party in a manner reminiscent of Goebbels: 'The masses are the chief motive force of social progress in our century. But the masses carry through when they are organized and when they are guided by knowledge. The Communist Party gives them both organization and knowledge.'[44]

Indeed, far from withering away, the party has gone from strength to strength: according to the official formula its 'growing role' has become an 'objective necessity for the development of the life of society', i.e. 'an objective historical law'. The party itself has been transformed from a class instrument, the 'vanguard of the proletariat', into an instrument of the socialist, class-harmonious community, the 'vanguard of the toilers', or, since the 1961 Programme, the 'vanguard of the Soviet people'. As such it is implicitly independent of the existence of classes and there is nothing to prevent Soviet spokesmen from asserting that the importance of the party will increase in proportion as Soviet society evolves further towards communism and class distinctions are altogether obliterated. Khrushchev, under whose stewardship the metamorphosis of state and party into 'all-people' organs was accomplished, took care to enrich the ideological heritage by the addition of 'one of the most important principles of Leninism, namely, that in the process of building communist society the role of the party must grow stronger'.[45] It is thus no longer a question of linking the existence

---

[42] J. Stalin, *Problems of Leninism*, Moscow, 1954, pp. 104–5.
[43] *Programmy i ustavy KPSS*, Moscow, 1969, p. 176.
[44] *Pravda*, 12 January 1965.
[45] *Vneocherednoi XXI S'ezd Kommunisticheskoi Partii Sovetskogo Soyuza 27 yanvarya – 5 fevralya 1959 goda. Stenograficheskii otchet*, 2 vols.,

of the party to the class struggle or, indeed, to the immaturity of the masses. Instead, the enhancement of the party's role has by means of a not unfamiliar feat of dialectical reasoning, become a function of the very forces which were originally said to lead to its 'withering away'. If there had still been some doubts on this score, they were removed by the new Party Programme which listed the 'growth of the creative activity of the masses' and the 'further development of socialist democracy' – together with the greater complexity of communist construction and the increased importance of communist theory and propaganda – as the reasons justifying the party's growing role in Soviet society.[46] By the time Brezhnev came to sum up the party record fifty years after the October Revolution, he was voicing a commonplace when he declared that 'the party understands well that its role, its responsibility for the fate of the people, for the fate of the country, grows together with the increase in the scope of communist construction'.[47]

By way of reconciling the indispensable leadership function of the party with the 'creativity' of the masses, both doctrines have from the beginning conceded that the intimate contact of their parties with the masses was an essential requisite of their leadership status. Stalin, in the 1920s, was particularly fond of the

---

Moscow, 1959, p. 117. (This and all other Party Congress reports will hereafter be cited as *S'ezd*, preceded by a Roman numeral indicating the number of the relevant Congress.) Khrushchev distinguished between party and state as regards their future fate: whereas the state would gradually die off in proportion as coercion became unnecessary, the party derived 'from principals of a moral nature. And mankind will always need moral factors.' (Interview with the correspondent of *The Times* reproduced in *Pravda*, 16 February 1958.)

[46] *Programmy i ustavy KPSS*, p. 218.

[47] *Kommunist*, 1967, no. 16, p. 44. Because this is a subject of some ideological delicacy it should be pointed out that in the last years of Khrushchev's rule the prospect of the party's 'withering away' under full communism was again mooted in Soviet writings albeit very cautiously. Since Khrushchev's fall the question has once more disappeared into the limbo of non-theory. When the diminution of the party's functions is mentioned, it is usually in the context of the various intra-bloc political challenges – Chinese, Yugoslav and (in 1968) Czech – and then only to reject it out of hand as utter heresy, contrary to both the Leninist teaching and 'objective historical necessity'. (E.g., *Pravda*, 20 February 1967, 27 August 1968, 19 September 1968; *Kommunist*, 1967, no. 8, p. 21.) As Brezhnev put it at the 24th Congress, the question of the party's 'leading role' has become 'the key point in the struggle between Marxists–Leninists and representatives of various forms of revisionism'. (*XXIV S'ezd*, vol. i, p. 128.)

image of a party 'near and dear' to the masses: 'The party cannot lead the mass . . . if there is no bond between the party and the non-party masses, if these masses do not accept its leadership, if the party enjoys no moral and political credit among the masses.'[48] Other Soviet leaders have repeatedly made the same point. For Khrushchev, the party was 'flesh of the flesh and blood of the blood of the people'.[49] And Brezhnev, too, declared that the party 'draws its powerful energy and unshakeable will and strength from the inviolable unity with the people. This unity is the guarantee of all our successes, all our victories'.[50] There is hardly an article or speech on the subject of the party's place in Soviet society which does not insist on some variation of the unity theme: 'The party is bound by vital ties to the broad masses and is genuinely a peoples' party.' Or: 'Party and people are one. The thoughts of the party are the thoughts of the people. The word of the party is the word of the people.'[51]

The claims of national socialist doctrine were identical. The 'confidence' of the people in the party[52] and the party's 'deep roots in the body of the people'[53] formed an important and oft-stressed component of the Nazi party's legitimation for leadership. Like the Bolsheviks, the Nazis were constantly exhorted to guard their 'vital contact with the masses'.[54] The party was described as 'originating in the people and eternally striving towards it',[55] a 'live and sensitive mechanism continuously moving from the people towards the state'.[56] And Hitler, too, equated party and people when he said: 'For to one we may be a party, to another an organization, to a third something else, but in truth we are the German people.'[57]

In asserting the unity between party and people the Nazis had

[48] Stalin, *Problems of Leninism*, pp. 98 and 174.
[49] *Pravda*, 15 March 1958. This is a popular simile; see, e.g. *ibid.*, 4 January and 10 October 1967.
[50] *Ibid.*, 29 August 1970.
[51] A typical recitation of these avowals is I. V. Malyshev, 'Edinstvo partii i naroda – istochnik nesokrushimoi sily sovetskogo obshchestva', *Voprosy istorii KPSS*, 1972, no. 1, pp. 99–109.
[52] Hitler's speech at the 1933 Party Congress, *Voelkischer Beobachter*, 5 September 1933.
[53] Hitler, *Mein Kampf*, p. 364; also pp. 108–9.
[54] *Hoheitstraeger*, 1938, no. 4, p. 4.
[55] Mehringer, *NSDAP*, p. 48.
[56] Ruthe, *Nationalsozialismus*, p. 11.
[57] Speech at the 1934 Party Congress, *Voelkischer Beobachter*, 9 September 1934.

an initial advantage over the Bolsheviks. Unfettered by the ideological heritage of the class struggle, the Nazis could proclaim
the 'unification of the *Volk*'[58] as the immediate objective of their
political aspirations. Four months after coming to power Hitler
emphasized that in contrast to the class dictatorship of the Soviet
Union, national socialist Germany aimed at a 'dictatorship of the
Volk, the community',[59] and five years later he was ready to announce the 'achievement of national solidarity [*Geschlossenheit*]'.[60]

By contrast the Bolsheviks originated as a class party with the
declared objective of establishing proletarian class rule in Russia.
Admittedly, this had never prevented the party from claiming the
support of all the 'toiling masses'. Long before the 1917 revolution
Lenin had tirelessly argued for the need to mobilize all the 'dis-
contented' and called upon the party to become 'the vanguard
of revolution in our time' by 'uniting into one inseparable whole
the pressure upon the government in the name of the whole
people'.[61] The 'hegemony' of the proletariat over all other 'oppressed classes' in the struggle against the ruling power was an
old Social Democratic concept, whose validity in Russia was not
vitiated by the anticipation, at first fully shared by the Bolsheviks,
that the immediate objective of the revolutionary struggle was to
bring the bourgeoisie to power. This position was strengthened
by the transformation of the proletariat from the 'vanguard of
the oppressed classes' into the 'ruling class'. And yet, for as
long as the class struggle continued to be officially waged within
Soviet Russia the party could not properly claim to be at one
with the entire people. The unanimity of the popular base, the
monolithic *Geschlossenheit*, which became a relatively early
feature of Nazi pronouncements, was lacking while kulaks and
other 'remnants of the exploiter classes' still composed part of
Soviet society.

In 1936, in connection with the adoption of the new Constitution, Stalin announced 'the complete victory of the socialist
system' and the abolition of 'class antagonisms' in the Soviet

58 Hitler, *Mein Kampf*, p. 373.
59 Speech at the Congress of German Workers, quoted in A. Friedrichs,
   ed., *Die Nationalsozialistische Revolution*, Berlin, 1935, p. 154. (This is
   vol. I, of P. Meier-Benneckenstein, ed., *Dokumente der Deutschen
   Politik*.)
60 May Day Speech, *Frankfurter Zeitung*, 2 May 1938.
61 Lenin, *Pol. Sob. Soch.*, vol. VI, pp. 82ff.

Union.[62] It was now, after the class struggle had been officially terminated, that Soviet doctrine could launch its own full-blown unity myth. The 'liquidation of the exploiter class' had provided the 'foundation' for the 'moral-political unity' of Soviet society; and the party could become the 'higher expression and the living soul of the moral-political unity of our people'.[63] This is, of course, exactly what the Nazis had all along claimed as the distinctive feature of their own political system. It is not surprising, therefore, that when Soviet spokesmen affirm that 'the unity of party, state and people is one of the characteristics of the political life of a free country',[64] they should be echoing the words of their Nazi counterparts, who had earlier described the objective of the national socialist regime as the creation of 'a living organism in which people, state and party form an inner unity'.[65]

Although both doctrines thus postulated the existence of mass support for the party's leadership, neither regarded mass support as more than a secondary source of the party's legitimacy. The primary allegiance of both parties was always to the revolutionary doctrine whose sole guardians they claimed to be. In any conflict between the precepts of the doctrine and the wishes of the masses, it was the former which had the first claim upon the loyalty of the party. For Lenin there were no doubts that the interests of the revolution were 'above the interests of the proletariat'.[66] And Hitler, too, knew that 'a movement which wishes to conquer a world must not serve the moment but the future'.[67] Both doctrines had nothing but contempt for a party which limited its leadership to expressing the desires of the masses. This was implicit in the views which each held about the inability of the masses to perceive their true interests without party guidance. 'Tailism', as Lenin called it,[68] or merely 'registering what the masses of the working class feel and think', as Stalin wrote,[69] was submitting to spontaneity and sacrificing consciousness; a party content to follow in the tail of the spontaneous movement of the masses lost its right to existence, was no 'real party' in the Bolshevik conception. According to Lenin, the party

---

62 Stalin, *Problems of Leninism*, pp. 683 and 690.
63 *Pravda*, 26 February 1950.
64 *Sovetskoe gosudarstvo i pravo*, 1955, no. 8, p. 7.
65 Ruthe, *Nationalsozialismus*, p. 13.
66 Lenin, *Pol. Sob. Soch.*, vol. IV, p. 220.
67 Hitler, *Mein Kampf*, p. 521.
68 Lenin, *Pol. Sob. Soch.*, vol. VI, p. 52.
69 Stalin, *Problems of Leninism*, p. 97.

sees its mission 'not as reflecting the average condition of the masses but as leading the masses'.[70] Hitler expressed his own views rather more bluntly when he wrote: 'The NSDAP was not to be a weather vane of public opinion, but had to become its master. Not a servant shall it be to the mass, but its lord!'[71]

It is in the light of the interpretation which the two parties placed upon their dual loyalties, to the masses and to the revolutionary doctrine, that their claims of mass support must be seen. For when they asserted that 'the will of the party is the will of the people',[72] and that 'confidence is won only through persuasion',[73] they meant neither that it was the party's duty to ascertain and abide by the will of the people, nor that persuasion was the sole means by which it could influence the will of the people.[74] The claim to embody an infallible doctrine allowed the party to evolve a uniquely totalitarian interpretation for its function of persuading or teaching the masses. In particular, it conferred upon it authority not to delay action until the masses, sufficiently enlightened by the propaganda and education of the party, were ready to give their consent and active support to the measures proposed by the party.

It was in keeping with the professed priority of loyalties of the two parties as well as with their general appraisal of the character of the masses that they assumed that learning from experience was an essential part of the education of the masses,

---

[70] Lenin, *Pol. Sob. Soch.*, vol. xxxv, p. 94.

[71] Hitler, *Mein Kampf*, p. 521.

[72] Mehringer, *NSDAP*, p. 99.

[73] *Partiinaya zhizn'*, 1956, no. 6, p. 3.

[74] Elections were one of the means by which the party sought to mobilize the masses around the goals determined by the leadership. 'The Communist Party', wrote Kalinin, 'approaches the elections in order to throw before the masses its ideals, strivings and tasks ... to organize the masses around these ideals ... and nourish them on the striving to achieve communism; the party calls upon them, pushes them and organizes them for socialist construction.' (M. I. Kalinin, *Rechi i Stati: 1919–1935*, Moscow, 1936, p. 271.) And a prominent German theorist wrote: 'For the constitution of the Reich it is irrelevant to develop, as in parliamentary democracies, means and methods in order to ascertain the will of the people. What matters is to make everyone grasp it as the determining idea of the community of the *Volk* ... The party of the *Fuehrerstaat* has neither the task of emancipating truth and justice, nor of seeking it in public discussion. It bears and preserves the existing state idea [*Staatsidee*] which has the claim to be truth and justice because it has proved its legitimacy in revolution and evolution.' (H. P. Ipsen, 'Vom Begriff der Partei', *Zeitschrift fuer die gesamte Staatswissenschaft*, 1940, no. 4, pp. 496–9.)

that without seeing the results of the practical application of party policy the masses could not be convinced of its correctness. According to Lenin, for the masses to support the revolution, 'propaganda and agitation are not enough, for this the masses must have their own experience'. While he argued that it would 'not merely be folly but a crime' to throw the 'vanguard alone into the decisive battle', he was also content with 'at least ... benevolent neutrality' on the part of the broad masses.[75] He proceeded from the assumption that it was necessary to 'begin to build socialism, not with the human material invented by us, but with the human material bequeathed to us by capitalism', and asserted that the

> art of politics ... lies in correctly gauging the conditions and the moment when the vanguard of the proletariat can success-fully seize power, when it is able during and after the seizure of power, to obtain adequate support from adequately broad strata of the working masses, and when it is able thereafter to maintain, consolidate and extend its rule by educating, training and attracting ever broader masses of the working people.[76]

In this scheme, elaborated after the Bolshevik revolution, the order of priorities is quite clear. Although the ultimate objective of mass support is not lost sight of, the fundamental assumption is that mass support can and will follow the action of the van-guard, or at best will be forthcoming while the action is still in progress.

Nor was this merely a *post factum* rationalization of the cir-cumstances under which the October revolution had come about. The essence of Lenin's attitude towards mass opinion is perhaps nowhere more clearly expressed than in a passage written at the end of 1916, at a time when the prospect of revolution in Russia still seemed very remote to Lenin. Referring to the French revolution and the first Russian revolution, Lenin noted that the 'conscious, determined revolutionaries' had in both cases con-sisted of numerically insignificant minorities:

> They were only isolated individuals, composing at the utmost only one ten-thousandth or even one-hundred-thousandth of their class. And after a few years these same isolated indi-viduals, this same almost non-existing minority, stood at the head of millions and tens of millions. Why?

[75] Lenin, *Pol. Sob. Soch.*, vol. XLI, pp. 77–8.
[76] *Ibid.*, p. 34.

Lenin's reply to his rhetorical question lies at the root of the credo that animated the professional revolutionary:

> Because this minority actively represented the interests of the masses, because it believed in the coming revolution, because it was ready to serve it unreservedly. Numerical weakness? But since when have revolutionaries made their policies dependent on whether they were in a majority or in a minority.[77]

A group of dedicated men with boundless faith in the righteousness of their cause and an unlimited capacity for service, a minority that did not shrink, in the moment of history, from 'actively representing the interests of the masses', i.e. from irretrievably committing the majority to a course of action which it, the minority, knew to be the only correct one, this was for Lenin the sole indispensable prerequisite for successful revolution.

In the last turbulent days before the October revolution, when Lenin was engaged in a single-minded attempt to convince the leadership of the Bolshevik party that the chance of revolution would be lost unless immediately grasped, he again indicated the value to be attached to public opinion, when he told members of the Bolshevik Central Committee on 16 October 1917: 'One cannot be guided by the mood of the masses; that is changeable and unaccountable. We must be guided by an objective analysis and estimate of the revolution.'[78] In the 'objective analysis and estimate of the revolution', the presence or absence of mass support, was merely one of several circumstances determining the timing and tactics of revolution, but it could not by itself be decisive. Whether or not revolution was a feasible course of action at any one time depended upon a complex of circumstances

---

[77] *Ibid.*, vol. xxx, pp. 266–7.

[78] *Ibid.*, vol. xxxiv, p. 394. Lenin repeatedly denied that the Bolsheviks were Blanquists and as such 'in favour of the seizure of power by a minority'. (E.g., *ibid.*, vol. xxxi, p. 147.) He had, however, a highly flexible view of the manner in which majority opinion was to be gauged, and when the time for revolution seemed ripe he instructed his leading cadres that it would be 'naive to wait for a "formal" majority for the Bolsheviks; no revolution waits for that'. (*Ibid.*, vol. xxxiv, p. 241.) It was a similar sentiment which prompted Lenin to declare at the Extraordinary Congress of Peasant Deputies in November 1917, in reply to a speech by the Left SR, Kachinsky: 'As regards the Constituent Assembly, the speaker said that its work will depend on the mood of the country. But I say: Trust in the mood but don't forget your rifles.' (*Ibid.*, xxxv, p. 95.)

among which the active support of the broad masses ranked at best alongside such factors as the international situation, the solidarity of the non-revolutionary camp, the decisiveness and self-confidence of the government and the morale and deployment of the armed forces, each of which, if it favoured revolution, could be relied upon to make up for any inadequacy in the degree of popular enthusiasm for it. Lenin's frequent and perfectly genuine disclaimers of Blanquist aspirations for a conspiratorial coup must not be allowed to detract attention from the fact that he did not look upon mass support as an essential legitimizing pre-requisite of revolution, but rather as an important, i.e. useful, addition to the arsenal of revolutionary forces. Armed with the firm conviction that its actions were sanctioned by History itself, Lenin's party acted in the sure knowledge that the course which it followed would meet with the eventual approval of the masses who were as yet incapable of perceiving the correctness of the party's actions and the benefits they would ultimately derive from them.[79]

This ability not only to formulate and expound policies but to act upon them in a manner that would commit the masses, regardless of the initial degree of mass support, has become an integral component of the party's qualification for leadership. Indeed, it was only the acquisition of state power which afforded the party countless opportunities for displaying its leadership mettle in this way and on a scale far exceeding the capacities of an opposition party. Far from having been confined to the fateful decision of revolution it is continuously being tested anew on matters ranging from relatively trivial questions of production techniques to the great issues of state policy. That is what Lenin meant when he stated at the 8th Party Congress: 'While formerly we carried on propaganda by means of general truths, *we are now carrying on propaganda by our work.* That is also preaching but it is preaching in action . . .'[80] This conception has remained unaltered through the years. Everywhere the party 'leads by con-crete example'; it 'persuades' by erecting the milestones on the road to communism and as the milestones multiply so the con-

---

[79] I have tended to stress what seemed to me to be Lenin's operative ideas, i.e. those most clearly supported by his actions. Doubtless, the above treatment does not do justice to the ambivalence that can be found in Lenin's expressed views on the role of the masses in the revolutionary process. For a more comprehensive and more even-handed analysis of these views see A. G. Meyer, *Leninism*, Cambridge, Mass., 1957, ch. 2.

[80] Lenin, *Pol. Sob. Soch.*, vol. xxxiii, p. 198. (Emphasis in the original.)

fidence of the people in their party is said to increase, for 'the correctness of the party is clearly evident . . . in the achievements of Socialist construction'.[81]

The Nazis had a conception of their educational duties towards the masses that was even more pronouncedly activist. 'We do not talk, we act', was one of Hitler's proudest boasts.[82] The Nazis acted on the principle that 'the German people will follow you in ever-growing numbers when they see the fruit of your work firmly planted on German soil'.[83] 'Leadership', wrote one high-ranking party functionary, 'has to be earned by positive example, by actions which leave no doubt where the true source of leadership in the Reich lies. We must argue and convince, we must never cease to spread the truth of the national socialist idea among the people, but above all we must act.'[84] According to Otto Dietrich, Hitler's press chief, the Nazis had proceeded 'in line with the principle of creating practical life' before completing the 'scientific formulation' of their doctrine.[85] Another writer saw the strength of national socialism precisely in the 'courage with which it has responsibly taken German matters in hand. Forces which create, which intervene creatively in life and not only polemically . . . are also "true" . . . The idea justifies itself in its fertility.'[86]

It is this formula of 'preaching in action', of 'the idea justifying itself in its fertility', which has become one of the most outstanding characteristics of modern totalitarian systems. For while democracies generally attempt to preach before they act, and autocracies have been largely content to act without preaching, the totalitarian regime of the twentieth century insists upon combining the two in a single, uninterrupted process which leaves the borderline between word and deed sufficiently blurred to enable it to claim both the support of the people and the right to act solely in the light of its own conceptions.

Elitism, in one form or another, is deeply embedded in European thought and civilization, and to attempt an enumeration of the spiritual precursers of the totalitarian creed of the party and

[81] *Pravda*, 23 January 1955; also 23 February 1969.
[82] *Voelkischer Beobachter*, 15 September 1935.
[83] *Hoheitstraeger*, 1939, no. 3, p. 23.
[84] *Unser Wille und Weg*, 1940, no. 3, p. 82.
[85] O. Dietrich, *Die philosophischen Grundlagen des National Sozialismus*, Breslau, 1936, p. 7.
[86] Mehringer, *NSDAP*, pp. 20–1.

the masses would lead far beyond the confines of the present study. It may in any case be doubted whether it has ever before been joined to a sham veneration of the masses with quite so striking a disregard for intellectual consistency. The peculiar hybrid which has emerged seems an authentic innovation of the age of mass democracy.

The Nazis, for their part, acknowledged allegiance to none of the thinkers whose ideas charted the spiritual landscape of the twentieth century. To them Hitler was not only the founder and leader of a political movement; he was also the originator and undisputed arbiter of all its teachings. This is not to deny that national socialism received many of its immediate intellectual impulses from a variety of German and non-German theorists, ranging in time and originality from Johann Gottfried Herder to Houston Stewart Chamberlain. It is merely to recognize that it did not consider itself descendant from or bound by any one particular ideological lineage. Directly and indirectly German nationalism, romanticism, racialism and elitism were absorbed into the national socialist *Weltanschauung* – that 'gruesome medley of all the contemporary half-truths'.[87] They were part of the soil which fertilized national socialism and in turn fostered its malignant growth. But ultimately the only ideas that were considered 'valid' and binding on the Nazi movement were those which Hitler himself espoused or, at least, tolerated.

The case of Soviet doctrine is more complex, though not basically different. In all its incarnations – Leninist, Stalinist and contemporary – Soviet doctrine has persistently claimed Marxist ancestry and just as persistently disclaimed any other. In fact, as has often been noted, for many aspects of Soviet doctrine the line that leads from Marx and Engels to their Soviet heirs presumptive is highly questionable, and nowhere more so than in the matter of party and class (or 'toiling classes').

There can be no doubting Marx's and Engels' fundamental belief in the proletarian potential for self-emancipation, whatever unflattering comments they may have allowed themselves in private concerning the intellectual capacity and political sophistication of actual workers in their own time. In his preface to the German edition of the *Communist Manifesto* of 1890 Engels wrote: 'For the ultimate triumph of the ideas set forth in the Manifesto Marx relied solely and exclusively upon the intellectual

---

[87] R. Dahrendorf, *Gesellschaft und Demokratie in Deutschland*, Munich, 1966, p. 433.

development of the working class, as it necessarily had to ensue from united action and discussion.'[88] This is something of an overstatement. Nevertheless. it indicates the extent of the gulf that separated the founding fathers from Leninist orthodoxy.

Marx and Engels fully accepted the need to educate and organize the proletariat by means of a political party, complementary to the educational and organizational forces inherent in the historical process itself. The *Communist Manifesto* credited Communists with having 'over the great mass of the proletariat the advantage of clearly understanding the line of march, the conditions, and the ultimate general results of the proletarian movement'.[89] And in subsequent years Marx and Engels repeatedly referred to such a party as 'indispensable', 'the primary condition', 'a first step', etc.[90] However, their conception of the party was wholly unlike that of Lenin's narrow vanguard. They envisaged a broadly-based and loosely-organized mass movement that would be firmly rooted in the unity of party and class, and they invariably spoke of 'the organization of the proletariat as an independent political party', or 'the constitution of the proletariat into a political party'.[91] At one time Engels even went on record that the German proletariat 'no longer needs any official organization, either public or secret. The simple self-evident interconnection of like-minded class comrades suffices without any rules, boards, resolutions and other tangible forms to shake the whole German Empire to its foundations.'[92] There is nothing in the views of either Marx or Engels of that exclusiveness which was so crucial to Lenin's notion of the 'party of a new type'.

[88] K. Marx and F. Engels, *Selected Works*, 2 vols., Moscow, 1951, vol. i, p. 31.
[89] *Ibid.*, p. 46.
[90] *Ibid.*, pp. 389 and 614; K. Marx and F. Engels, *Letters to Americans*, New York, 1953, p. 163.   [91] *Ibid.*, vol. II, pp. 291 and 422.
[92] *On the History of the Communist League, ibid.*, vol. ii, pp. 322–3. In a footnote to this quotation the Soviet editors describe Engels' statement as an ironic challenge of Bismarck's policy to prohibit the proletarian party and strangle the workers' movement'. (See also P. Fedoseev, 'Vozrastanie roli partii', *Kommunist*, 1971, no. 15, p. 76.) Such an inference is neither warranted by the context – Engels went on to make a similar statement about the international working class movement – nor was it made in *Der Sozialdemokrat* (26 November 1885) in which Engels' article originally appeared, or, indeed, in a previous Soviet edition under the editorship of V. Adoratsky. (See English edition, London, 1942, vol. ii, p. 26; also K. Marx, *Enthuellungen ueber den Kommunisten Prozess zu Koeln*, introduced and annotated by F. Mehring, Berlin, 1914, p. 48.)

Perhaps the most incisive anticipatory condemnation of the Bolshevik conception of the party and class came from the pen of Marx himself. Referring to sectarian principles which he attributed to Lassalle's leadership of the German labour movement, Marx wrote to J. B. von Schweitzer in 1868: 'The sect sees its *raison d'être* in its *point d'honneur*, not in what it has in *common* with the class movement, but in the *special shibboleth* which distinguishes it from it.'[93] And in a letter to the German socialist F. Bolte, in the United States, he wrote three years later, in the same context, complaining this time of 'the notorious Schweitzer':

> The development of the system of socialist sects and that of the real workers' movement are always inversely proportional to each other. So long as the sects are (historically) justified, the working class is not yet ripe for an independent historic movement. As soon as it has attained this maturity all sects are essentially reactionary.[94]

Rather than deriving from the writings of Marx and Engels, Lenin's ideas on the relationship of party and class bear the influence of Russian Populism and, in particular, of its Jacobin tradition. The exaltation of the minority – resolute, dedicated, self-disciplined and supremely practical – destined to implant its revolutionary energy into the inert masses of Russia, was a widespread reaction of the Russian radical intelligentsia to the social and political conditions of Tsarist autocracy in the latter half of the nineteenth century. If the priggish protagonists of Chernyshevsky's didactic novel *What is to be Done?* became the heroes of generations of Russian radicals, the infusion of Jacobinism, notably represented in the writings of Tkachev, endowed them with that disdain for the will and the capacity of the masses to work out their own salvation, that single-minded emphasis on the virtues of authoritarian organization, and, above all, that terrible impatience to hasten the revolutionary process at any

---

93 K. Marx and F. Engels, *Werke*, 41 vols., Berlin, 1958–68, vol. xxxii, p. 569. Marx also warned in the letter of the German worker's ingrained predisposition to bureaucratic subordination and urged the need to teach him above all 'to walk by himself'. Note that the motto which Lenin prefixed to his *What is to be Done?* was taken not from Marx but from Lassalle.

94 Marx and Engels, *Selected Works*, vol. ii, p. 422. Charges of elitist sectarianism also figured prominently in Marx's and Engels' polemics against Bakunin. (*Werke*, vol. xviii, pp. 138, 346, 439 and *passim*.)

price, which were to be the hallmarks of the Leninist doctrine. To be sure, the various strains of Populist radicalism were anchored in moral indignation, and if the end justified the means, that, too, was because the future order would be infinitely more moral than the present. It was left to Lenin to provide the underpinning of 'scientific' certainty by wedding this outlook to Marxist determinism. It was a potent and, as it turned out, irresistible combination.

One may regard it as a measure of the Marxist orthodoxy of Lenin's views that their most scathing criticism came from the ranks of fellow Marxists. Indeed, the different conceptions of the party–class relationship were at the root of the split between Bolsheviks and Mensheviks at the 2nd Party Congress. Probably the sharpest condemnation of Lenin on this question was voiced not by his 'revisionist' or 'soft-line' opponents, the 'Economist' Akimov and the Menshevik leaders, including, at that time, Trotsky – all of whom were extremely critical and quite extraordinarily prescient about the implications of Lenin's elitist attitudes – but by Rosa Luxemburg, an orthodox, revolutionary Marxist, even by Lenin's standards. Writing in the columns of *Iskra* in 1904, she characterized Lenin's approach 'as something which in its essence is not informed with positive and creative spirit, but with the sterile spirit of the nightwatchman'.[95] It was a harsh judgment, indicative of the force with which Lenin's views struck at the susceptibilities of some of his fellow Marxists; if it was meant to impute conscious intention on Lenin's part, it was also unfair. But it went to the heart of the doctrine which Lenin bequeathed to the Bolshevik party.[96] The 'sterile spirit of the nightwatchman' survived the years of underground conspiracy and has since been perpetuated in countless institutional forms. Its shadow continues to lie over the lives of the Soviet people to the present day; certainly the frequent incantations of the bonds between the masses and their 'vanguard' party have not succeeded in banishing it.

It has been seen above that the party's uncompromising leadership of the masses is central to both Nazi and Soviet beliefs.

[95] R. Luxemburg, *Leninism or Marxism*, Glasgow, 1935, p. 15.
[96] We are, of course, concerned not with Lenin, the man, but with his political doctrine. On a purely personal and emotional level, Lenin felt profound sympathy for ordinary working people and was usually able to attain genuine rapport with working-class audiences.

However much their spokesmen acclaimed the 'unity' between the party and the masses and the 'creativity' of the latter, neither conceived of 'unity' on any but the party's terms and neither believed that 'creativity' could – or, for that matter, should – be generated spontaneously. Both, on the contrary, never wavered in their conviction that 'unity' and 'creativity' had to be perpetually mobilized by the party. The doctrine of the mobilization of the masses does not only reflect the totalitarian view of the masses as innately passive, the objects of manipulation from above rather than the subjects of spontaneous, constructive action from below; it also expresses the determination of the totalitarian regime not to content itself with the passive support of the people, but to bring about their active, indeed, enthusiastic, participation in the execution of its goals and policies. The theoretical assumption may well have been shared by the majority of autocratic rulers of all times, but the practical conclusion is one which clearly belongs to the socio-economic reality of the modern age. While all government involves a degree of voluntary compliance and co-operation on the part of the governed this has never been more true than in the twentieth century. A full-scale industrial society cannot be run for long with a subject people of sullen serfs; it requires a nation that is both technically literate and politically willing. The mobilization of the masses, whatever its ideological legitimation, is the totalitarian response to these twentieth-century realities.

Viewed in this light, it will not seem paradoxical that it is precisely the insistence of totalitarianism on mass support which has been responsible for some of its most oppressive features. For coupled, as it is, with an almost absolute distrust of every manifestation of individual or group spontaneity, it has given rise to a technique of government which has not hesitated to reach out to the innermost recesses of private life. Ultimately, the totalitarian mobilization of the masses is nothing less than an attempt to construct a system of 'positive' controls capable both of embracing every individual within its compass and of plumbing every layer of human experience. The attempt was perhaps too ambitious to be altogether successful. In making it, however, the Nazi and Soviet regimes have demonstrated the awesome potentiality of a form of despotism that is not content 'to make man do' but sets out 'to make him want to do'.

A German scholar has written of 'voluntary compulsion' with

reference to life in Nazi Germany.[97] It seems a singularly apt characterization of totalitarian mass mobilization in general. Certainly, Soviet people would have no difficulty in recognizing its applicability to life in the Soviet Union. They have long been familiar with the principle of *dobrovol'no–obyazatel'no* (voluntarily–obligatorily) from their own experience.

Much of the remainder of this book will show 'voluntary compulsion' in action. For now it will suffice to say that 'voluntary compulsion' is largely the product of totalitarian propaganda and totalitarian organization, and that both of these elements are supremely exemplified in the functions of the totalitarian party. The Nazis spoke of the party's role in the mobilization of the masses as that of *Menschenfuehrung* (literally, the leadership of men); the Soviets speak in the same context of the party's 'mass-political work' or 'work with people'. The outstanding feature common to both is the deliberate and continuous interaction between propaganda and organization. Indeed, the party's specific contribution to the totalitarian mobilization of the masses lies in its unique ability to organize the masses at the same time as it activates them. The party is more than an additional channel of communication through which official views and exhortations are passed downward from the leadership to the masses (and – on an incomparably more modest scale – popular reactions are passed upward). The principal advantage of both the Nazi party's *Menschenfuehrung* and the Soviet party's 'mass-political work' is that they contain those built-in organizational safeguards which not only extend the range and penetration of propaganda but also ensure that its effect is everywhere closely controlled. Activism, pure and simple, is anathema to the totalitarian ruler, for it is liable to break out in unexpected forms and in undesirable directions. The only kind of activism compatible with totalitarian government is controlled activism. It is the existence of the party above all which enables the regime to direct and control every stage of the process by which its propaganda slogans are directed into the heightened activism of the masses.

[97] F. von Hippel, *Die nationalsozialistische Herrschaftsordnung als Warnung und Lehre*, Tuebingen, 1946, p. 6.

2: TOTALITARIAN PROPAGANDA

Totalitarian propaganda must be viewed within the setting of totalitarian society. Coercion enters into it as much as it enters into every other sphere of social life and any attempt to disentangle the two elements would be not only arduous in the extreme but also futile.[1] The propaganda of totalitarian regimes cannot be measured with the yardstick of persuasion applied to non-totalitarian societies. Clearly one cannot speak of persuasion, as that concept is commonly understood, where those to be persuaded are *a priori* denied the freedom to hold contrary views. Yet it is possible to speak of a kind of 'persuasion' which retains sufficient attributes of that function to distinguish it from straightforward compulsion. It is this kind of 'coercive persuasion', inextricably linked with force yet by no means identical with it, which is meant by such terms as propaganda or agitation in their relation to the totalitarian scene. Only the absence of more apposite terms warrants the retention of conventional terminology.[2] Bearing in mind this reservation, the terms propaganda and agitation will henceforth be used interchangeably and, unless placed in quotation marks, should be interpreted in the loosest sense as activities concerned with the widest possible dissemination of ideas and symbols aimed at influencing opinion and conduct.

Soviet terminology is rather more specific. Following Plekhanov's famous maxim it distinguishes between 'propaganda'

[1] The role of force in totalitarian propaganda was stressed by E. Hadamovsky, the Nazi exponent of 'power propaganda' (*Machtpropaganda*), in his *Propaganda und nationale Macht: Die Organisation der oeffentlichen Meinung*, Oldenburg, 1933, pp. 22, 42ff. See also H. M. Pachter, 'National-Socialist and Fascist Propaganda in the Conquest of Power', in M. Beaumont *et al.*, *The Third Reich*, London, 1955, pp. 710ff; E. K. Bramsted, *Goebbels and National Socialist Propaganda 1925–1945*, East Lansing, 1965, p. 451f.
[2] An attempt to formulate a conceptual distinction between propaganda in totalitarian and democratic systems is M. Schuette, *Politische Werbung und totalitaere Propaganda*, Duesseldorf, 1968.

as the presentation 'of many ideas to a few persons' and 'agitation' as that 'of one or a few ideas ... to a mass of people'.[3] The distinction formulated by Plekhanov in quantitative terms is, of course, essentially one of quality. By 'propaganda' Soviet terminology has understood a more profound, intellectual elucidation in contrast to the easily comprehensible arguments and slogans of 'agitation'. The terms 'Marxist–Leninist', 'communist' or 'party propaganda' usually denote ideological indoctrination as distinct from the theoretical elucidation of other subjects.

The Nazis, too, at times distinguished between two forms of propaganda along very similar lines. What in Soviet terminology would resemble 'agitation' the Nazis described as 'propaganda' while they sometimes used the term 'enlightenment' (*Aufklaerung*) to mean something close to the Soviet understanding of 'propaganda'. Goebbels thus described the two national socialist interpretations:

> Political propaganda as a principle is an active, revolutionary element. It is in essence and purpose directed at the masses. It speaks the language of the people ... Its task is to simplify with the highest creative art the sometimes complicated events and circumstances of a political situation, so that they can also be grasped by the man in the street ... The concept of people's enlightenment is essentially different. It is basically defensive and evolutionary. It does not drum or hammer. It is of a more moderate kind and seeks to teach; it elucidates and explains ...[4]

On the whole, however, the Nazis did not take their distinction

---

[3] G. V. Plekhanov, *Sochineniya*, 8 vols., Moscow, 1923, vol. III, p. 397; see also Lenin, *Pol. Sob. Soch.*, vol. VI, p. 66.

[4] *Der Kongress zu Nuernberg vom 5. bis 10. September 1934. Offizieller Bericht ueber den Verlauf des Reichsparteitages mit saemtlichen Reden*, Munich, 1934, pp. 131–2. In *Mein Kampf* (p. 196) Hitler already affirmed of 'propaganda' that it 'must perennially address itself to the masses alone'. The term 'agitation', although it had no pejorative connotations in Nazi writings of the early years – e.g. *Mein Kampf*, p. 651 and J. Goebbels, *Vom Kaiserhof zur Reichskanzlei*, Munich, 1934, p. 46 – was later officially declared a 'negative' expression to be used only in reference to enemy propaganda. (See the confidential instructions to the German press at the YIVO Institute for Jewish Research in New York – File G 105.) One Nazi writer distinguished between 'propaganda' as a 'politically constructive function' and 'agitation' as 'the spreading of atrocity stories and lies ... born out of the Jewish spirit and applied with Jewish methods'. (F. Erhard, 'Propaganda und Agitation', *Unser Wille und Weg*, 1938, no. 1, pp. 5–10.)

too seriously, even in theory. Goebbels argued that in the final analysis 'means and methods are wholly irrelevant. What matters is the complete knowledge of and mastery over the soul and the mind, the bearing and the inner conviction of the people.'[5] Until recently at least Soviet doctrine has clung more rigidly to its distinction between 'propaganda' and 'agitation', and in practice the mass of the people has been largely by-passed by Soviet 'propaganda'. This much was admitted in a 1960 Central Committee decree 'On the Tasks of Party Propaganda in Contemporary Conditions', which most strongly deplored the fact that 'the fundamental direction of oral and printed propaganda is as before turned pre-eminently towards members and candidate-members of the party, the non-party *aktiv* and the intelligentsia.'[6] Plekhanov's formulation had, of course, implicitly restricted the application of 'propaganda' to the educationally advanced strata of the population, and this view was later explicitly endorsed by Lenin.[7] The 1960 Central Committee decree, however, declared that 'the mastering of a communist world outlook . . . of the foundations of Marxism–Leninism . . . is becoming a vital need for every Soviet person', and in the following year the new Party Programme called for 'the education of the population as a whole in the spirit of scientific communism'.[8] Official pronouncements throughout the 1960s have shown great concern over the need 'to broaden the framework of propaganda, to make it easier to understand and to give it a mass character'.[9] For a time, at

[5] *Voelkischer Beobachter*, 15 September 1936.
[6] The decree, which is the most comprehensive, formal party document on the subject in the post-Stalin period, will be found in *Spravochnik partii-nogo rabotnika*, Moscow, 1961, pp. 486–508.
[7] See below p. 40, n. 34.
[8] *Programmy i ustavy KPSS*, p. 196. Note, however, that the requirement that all people 'master the ideas of Marxism–Leninism' which had been included in the Draft Programme, as published in *Pravda* of 30 July 1961, was deleted from the final version adopted by the 22nd Party Congress. (See W. Leonhard, 'Adoption of the New Party Programme', in L. Schapiro, ed., *The USSR and the Future*, London and New York, 1963, p. 20.)
[9] *Pravda*, 27 June 1960; 4 August 1965; 21 January 1968. The party's political studies programme ('propaganda') was indeed greatly expanded under Khrushchev – from 6.2 million members in 1957–8 to over 36 million in 1964–5. An immediate and striking reduction took place after Khrushchev's fall with enrolment down to 12 million in 1964–5 and rising gradually to 15 million in 1968–9. (See E. Propper Mickiewicz, *Soviet Political Schools*, New Haven, 1967, p. 10, and the same author's article 'The Modernization of Party Propaganda in the USSR', *Slavic Review*, 1971, no. 2, p. 260.)

least, it seemed as if Soviet theory was moving away from the Plekhanov–Lenin distinction towards a more realistic 'fusion' of the two concepts on the Nazi model. Lenin himself, it was argued, had not erected 'a stone wall between propaganda and agitation' and as the educational and political level of the Soviet population rises so propaganda becomes 'more and more agitational, and agitation . . . increasingly takes on a propagandistic character'.[10]

In fact, the totalitarian propaganda beamed at the masses is action-oriented agitation aimed at their controlled manipulation in accordance with changing policy ends. Its principal objective is not the 'enlightenment' of the masses, ideological or otherwise, but their mobilization for action. For the Nazis 'every propaganda' was 'the preparation of political activities'.[11] 'Without it', as Goebbels knew, 'the implementation of great things has become well-nigh impossible in the century of the masses. It stands at the beginning of all practical work in public life.'[12]

Soviet propaganda, too, has been intimately bound up with the execution of practical policy. 'Concrete', 'operative', 'purposeful', 'close to life', these have been the categorical imperatives of Soviet propaganda ever since Lenin had in 1920 authoritatively declared that 'propaganda of the old type' which 'describes and illustrates what communism is . . . is useless, for we must show in practice how to build socialism'.[13] At the 20th Congress Khrushchev recalled Lenin's remarks in support of his own demand that propaganda be more closely wedded to 'the practice of communist construction'.[14] At the 21st Congress he emphasized that 'what is particularly needed now is concreteness and singleness of purpose . . . General talk and general appeals are of no use whatsoever.'[15] And at the 22nd Congress, he once again pointed out: 'Ideological work is not an end in itself, but the most important means of solving the fundamental tasks of communist

---

[10] A. G. Efimov and P. V. Pozdnyakov, *Nauchnye osnovy partiinoi propagandy*, Moscow, 1966, pp. 19–20. See also A. T. Kabanov, 'Leninskii printsip svyazi propagandy s zhiznyu', in I. I. Groshev *et al.*, eds., *Iz opyta ideologicheskoi raboty partiinykh organizatsii*, Moscow, 1965, p. 28, where the 'merging of propaganda and agitation' is described as a function of a then current (though short-lived) trend towards the specialization of agitation.

[11] Hadamovsky, *Propaganda und nationale Macht*, p. 45.

[12] *Kongress 1934*, p. 138.

[13] Lenin, *Pol. Sob. Soch.*, vol. XLI, p. 407; see also vol. XLV, pp. 417–18.

[14] *XX S'ezd*, vol. I, pp. 114–15.

[15] *XXI S'ezd*, vol. I, p. 113. Compare this with a similar statement by Lenin in *Pol. Sob. Soch.*, vol. XXXIX, p. 13.

construction. That is why high activism and effectiveness are the essential requirements of ideological–educational work in contemporary conditions.'[16] Lenin's proposition that 'the results of political enlightenment can only be measured in the improvement of the economy',[17] finds its echo in the above-quoted Central Committee decree of 1960 which declared that 'the effectiveness of party propaganda is manifested above all in concrete production results'. The same decree designated as the 'main shortcoming' of Soviet propaganda its 'estrangement from life', the fact that it 'frequently bears an abstract, purely enlightening character'.

Since Khrushchev's dismissal, the propaganda conducted under his aegis has been variously criticized, among other things, for its undue concentration on practical economic matters. The then head of the Agitation Section in the Propaganda Department of the Central Committee, M. A. Morozov, declared that the 'narrow-production approach caused great harm to agitation', and instead of bringing it 'closer to life' in fact removed it 'further from the real needs of the people'.[18] And the First Secretary of the Belorussian party organization, P. M. Masherov, writing of 'propaganda', criticized the 'simplistic approach' which had 'for a long while' reduced everything 'to two indices – the number of ideological measures carried out and the units of output. If a plant or collective farm fulfilled its sales plan, it was automatically assumed that the ideological work there was up to par . . .'[19]

However, both in their affirmations of the central purposes of propaganda and in their criticisms of its principal shortcomings the present leaders can hardly be said to have departed from Khrushchev's views. Brezhnev, too, reiterated at the 23rd Party Congress the conventional formula that 'all ideological work must be closely tied to life, to the practice of communist con-

---

16 *XXII S'ezd*, vol. I, p. 122.
17 Lenin, *Pol. Sob. Soch.*, vol. XLIV, p. 175.
18 *Agitator*, 1966, no. 1, p. 28; see also *Pravda*, 17 May 1965.
19 *Pravda*, 15 April 1970. Other sins laid at the door of Khrushchev's propaganda methods were 'idle talk', 'bragging', 'subjectivism' and 'projectionism'. The resultant gap 'between word and deed, promise and fulfilment, caused a feeling of irritation, resentment and a certain mistrust of propaganda'. (Yu. I. Tarasov, 'O edinstve ideologicheskoi i organizatorskoi raboty v kommunisticheskom vospitanii mass', in V. A. Smyshlyaev *et al.*, eds., *KPSS v period stroitel'stva kommunizma*, Leningrad, 1967, p. 77; also *Pravda*, 25 October 1964 and 18 September 1965; *Kommunist*, 1966, no. 2, p. 7.)

struction, for otherwise, as Lenin repeatedly stressed, it deteriorates into mere political phrasemongering'.[20] Two years later he was more specific:

> The level of work done by party organizations and the level of ideological work must be judged first and foremost by how production assignments are fulfilled, by how labour productivity is increasing, by the state of labour discipline and by how implacably the struggle against all manifestations of lack of organization and slackness is being waged.[21]

Criticisms, familiar from the Khrushchev era, namely that 'mass-political work is frequently divorced from the concrete tasks of the development of industry and agriculture' or that 'questions of theory are frequently presented in the abstract, divorced from practice' continue, as before, to be listed among the major failings of Soviet propaganda.[22]

Nor does the need 'to show how to build communism in practice' allow much scope for mass indoctrination in the teaching of Marxism–Leninism, much of which perforce bears 'an abstract, purely enlightening character' in Soviet conditions. Official references to propaganda have always featured such phrases as 'the communist education of the toilers', 'arming the masses with a scientific Marxist–Leninist ideology' and ensuring that 'every step taken by Soviet people is imbued with lofty ideological content', thus conveying an impression of constant preoccupation with ideological themes.[23] This is further strengthened by the stress that is placed upon 'ideological work' as a necessary requisite to the successful implementation of economic and technical tasks. In Stalin's time it used to be said: 'Stalin teaches us that the better the Marxist–Leninist training of the worker the more productive is his labour.'[24] Nowadays it is asserted that a bountiful grain harvest depends in large measure on 'the ideological upbringing of the corngrowers'.[25] Needless to say, whatever Stalin may have taught, neither he nor his successors acted on the belief that ideological erudition was

---

[20] *XXIII S'ezd*, vol. i, p. 102.
[21] *Pravda*, 29 March 1968; see also his speech at the October 1968 Central Committee plenum, *ibid.*, 31 October 1968.
[22] *Spravochnik partiinogo rabotnika*, 1968, pp. 291–2; *Pravda*, 11 September 1970.
[23] *Pravda*, 1 January 1950, 2 February 1959, 4 September 1967.
[24] *Ibid.*, 5 August 1949; see also 13 October 1949 and 4 April 1950.
[25] *Agitator*, 1969, no. 4, p. 3.

particularly conducive to labour productivity. Instead, the true thrust of Soviet propaganda has always been directed towards more worldly matters. Where it does not centre around economic or political issues of immediate relevance, it aims at the elimination of 'such vestiges of the past as an unconscious attitude towards labour, the plundering of socialist property, self-seeking, private-property views and morals, an incorrect attitude towards women, coarseness, drunkenness and hooliganism'.[26]

More positively, Soviet propaganda is geared to inculcating 'in every Soviet person a sense of responsibility for the tasks assigned to him', of 'conscious discipline' and respect for the law, and of what is usually bracketed together as 'Soviet patriotism and socialist internationalism'. Above all, so runs the official doctrine, Soviet man is formed in the process of work and Soviet 'ideological upbringing' is pre-eminently devoted to aiding this process. As an editorial in the party journal put it:

> The true ideological fibre of man is tested in the deed, in work for the benefit of society. That is why our party considers that *the most important component of idea-political work* is education towards a communist attitude to work and to social property, the development of the creative activeness of the working people, the strengthening of conscious discipline and organization. In the solution of these important and responsible tasks a most important role belongs to socialist competition as an effective method of economic construction and strengthening socialist relations among people.[27]

This is what official pronouncements term bringing 'the ideas of communist construction to the consciousness of the masses, through ... posing concrete tasks of economic and cultural construction', as distinct from the mere presentation of 'abstract propositions and general aspirations'. From time to time an editorial in the party press provides the necessary rationalization: 'In present-day conditions the solution of practical tasks of communist construction is simultaneously the solution of the cardinal theoretical problems of Marxism–Leninism ...'[28]

The Nazis were also fond of propaganda statements in which the term *Weltanschauung* figured prominently in one context or another. Yet such more or less permanent ideas as the new

---

26 *Pravda*, 8 August 1959; also *Agitator*, 1971, no. 9, p. 5.
27 *Partiinaya zhizn'*, 1971, no. 14, p. 8. (Emphasis in the original.)
28 *Pravda*, 6 April 1960.

Weltanschauung contained – the concept of 'eternal struggle', the 'leader principle', the regeneration of 'Germanic' qualities, of 'racial purity', 'soldierly bearing' and 'community spirit' – were literally 'hammered'[29] into the minds of the people, with little or no attempt at even that limited degree of theoretical exposition which the nature of Nazi doctrine allowed. The basic attitude of the Nazis was succinctly summarized by Ley, who, with a characteristic artlessness that often earned him the scorn of his more sophisticated colleagues,[30] declared before an audience of party functionaries: 'Although a *Weltanschauung* cannot be taught and cannot be learned, it can be drilled, it can be trained.'[31]

The fundamental purpose of national socialism was to set the nation in motion. To this end, what mattered was not the 'truth' of the *Weltanschauung*, still less the extent to which its teachings had been assimilated by the population at large, but its value as myth, more specifically, its potentiality as a lever to induce men to act as if it were true in pursuit of the goals set by the Leader. According to Hitler,

> It is not necessary that everyone who fights for this *Weltanschauung* should obtain full insight into and exact knowledge of the latest ideas and thought-processes of the leader of the movement. What is necessary is that a few very great viewpoints be indelibly impressed upon him so that he may be thoroughly imbued with the necessity of the victory of the movement and of its teaching.[32]

And it was Alfred Rosenberg, the man who saw himself in the role of national socialism's theoretician-in-chief, who declared in 1935: 'The German nation is now finally about to find its style of life . . . It is the style of a marching column, no matter where or for what purpose the marching column may be deployed.'[33]

The realization by totalitarian rulers that their propaganda resources are more productively employed when engaged upon matters of direct, tangible application to the practical problems

---

[29] *Hoheitstraeger*, 1934, no. 4, p. 8.

[30] Goebbels: 'Every time he opens his mouth he puts his foot in it.' (*Goebbels Diaries*, p. 150.)

[31] R. Ley, *Der Weg zur Ordensburg*, Der Reichorganisationsleiter (special publication for the party leadership corps – not on public sale) n.d., n.p., unpaged (sequence 26).

[32] *Mein Kampf*, p. 508.

[33] A. Rosenberg, *Gestaltung der Idee: Reden und Aufsaetze von 1933–1935*, Munich, 1936, p. 303.

of government rather than upon strictly ideological themes may be traced to several factors. It derives, firstly, from the irrelevance of much of the doctrine to the solution of practical issues and it is rationalized by the belief that the limited intellectual capacity of the masses in any case prevents them from understanding purely theoretical expositions.[34] In some cases, too, it is governed by a realistic precognition of popular reaction to a frank disclosure of ideological objectives. The wall of silence which surrounded the 'final solution' of the Jewish question in Nazi Germany and the suppression of the Communist *motif* in Soviet propaganda during World War II are prominent examples for this kind of 'adjustment' of propaganda to mass susceptibilities.

Finally, the reluctance of totalitarian regimes to acquaint the masses with their ideological precepts may be attributed to the desire to reduce the danger of conflict between loyalty to the cause and loyalty to the leadership. Its avowed adherence to ideological precepts obliges the leadership to attempt to show a minimum degree of accord between ideological promise and practical fulfilment. Yet totalitarian rulers, however much they may be personally convinced of the 'scientific' truth of the ideological promise and of the long-run efficacy of their policies in fulfilling that promise, are well aware that the realities of government occasionally necessitate measures which run counter to the ideological vision. In these circumstances, extensive knowledge of and undue loyalty to ideology may only too easily clash with the absolute obedience demanded by the leadership at all times.

The history of the Russian Marxist movement, from its inception until 1917, bears eloquent testimony to the inherent capacity of a radical ideology for causing or exacerbating disunity of opinion and action among its adherents. And the various opposition groups in the first decade of Soviet rule, from the 'Left Opposition' in 1918 to the 'Right Opposition' in 1929, reveal the extent to which ideological considerations sparked off or reinforced dissension within the ranks of the ruling party itself.[35]

---

34 That 'the broad mass of a people does not consist of philosophers' was at the root of the propaganda concepts which Hitler developed in *Mein Kampf* (p. 293). And Lenin in referring to Plekhanov's definition of the 'propagandist' wrote that 'he must present "many ideas", so many indeed that they will be understood by a (comparatively) few persons.' (*Pol. Sob. Soch.*, vol. VI, p. 66.)

35 'To each new situation', Trotsky wrote, 'the party adapted itself only by way of an inner crisis.' (L. Trotsky, *The History of the Russian Revolu-*

The Otto Strasser and Stennes affairs before the Nazi seizure of power, and the opposition within the SA which led to the Roehm purge of 1934, also contained elements of ideological disaffection flowing mainly from Hitler's unwillingness to implement the revolutionary ambitions of the movement and his increasingly evident disregard for the 'socialist' strands in national socialist doctrine. Goebbels' remark in 1931 to Lieutenant Scheringer, a then fairly prominent Nazi, who was about to desert to the Communists, that if he (Goebbels) had founded the party he would 'not have put up any programme at all',[36] illustrates both the Nazis' diagnosis of their internal troubles and their favourite therapy.

On the whole, however, the ideological fervour of the Nazis was of a relatively low intensity. Moreover, as has already been noted, Hitler, in contrast to the Bolshevik leaders, was able to add the authority of 'spiritual founder' of national socialism to that of party leader. And yet he, too, was not unaware of the dangers inherent in too zealous a preoccupation with ideological formulae. His insistence on doctrinal rigidity does not contradict but confirm this, for it rested on the premise that 'for the large number of followers the essence of our movement will lie not in the letter of our precepts, but rather in the meaning which we shall be able to give them'.[37] He rejected all attempts at assimilating the framework of Nazi doctrine to changing circumstances precisely because he feared that this

lution, 3 vols., London, 1932–3. vol. III, p. 139.) In a famous reference to machine guns Lenin illustrated the danger of ideological commitment in the face of practical 'retreat' such as that which the introduction of NEP implied: 'A retreat is a difficult matter, especially for revolutionaries who are accustomed to advance... Moved by the best Communist sentiments and aspirations, several of the comrades burst into tears because – oh horror! – the good Russian Communists were retreating ... During a victorious advance, even if discipline is relaxed, everybody presses forward on his own accord. During a retreat, however, discipline must be more conscious and a hundred times more necessary... When a real army is in retreat, machine guns are placed in the rear; and when an orderly retreat degenerates into a disorderly one, the command is given: "Fire!" and quite right.' (*Pol. Sob. Soch.*, vol. XLV, pp. 87–9.)

[36] Quoted from *Voessische Zeitung*, 4 July 1931, in K. D. Bracher, *Die Aufloesung der Weimarer Republik*, Stuttgart and Duesseldorf, 1955, p. 106. Lieutenant Scheringer was at that time in the public limelight because of his part in the Leipzig Trial of autumn 1930. (See A. Bullock, *Hitler. A Study in Tyranny*, rev. ed., London, 1962, pp. 164ff.)

[37] *Mein Kampf*, p. 514; See also Rauschning, *Hitler Speaks*, p. 188, and Picker, *Hitlers Tischgespraeche*, pp. 158–9.

would surrender to discussion something that should be un-
assailably firm ... would lead to endless discussion and general
confusion ... Thus the will and strength to fight for an idea
are renounced and the activism which should be turned out-
wards will be devoured by internal programmatic struggles.[38]

In fact, amid the overriding concern to foster 'the will and
strength to fight for an idea', characteristic of Soviet propaganda
no less than it was of its Nazi counterpart, the 'idea' itself has
been all but forgotten.

It would go too far to suggest that the ideological motivations
of totalitarian regimes become in the course of time among their
most closely guarded secrets – although this was certainly true
in the case of the more extreme of the Nazi racial beliefs – but
'indoctrination', in the sense of instilling an exclusive, all-
embracing body of doctrine, did not constitute part of either
Nazi or Soviet propaganda. Totalitarian rulers are not concerned
to bring about widespread ideological sophistication; they do not
require a nation of theologians, or 'Talmudists', as the Stalinist
idiom used to have it, but of believers.[39] The masses are not
expected to know the ideological scriptures, but to obey their
commandments as interpreted and transmitted by the leadership.
It is this purpose that the propaganda machine is intended to
serve.[40] Such indoctrination in the theoretical basis of their

---

[38] *Mein Kampf*, pp. 511–12. Gerhard Ritter reports that when Goerdeler,
then Lord Mayor of Leipzig, suggested to Ley in 1935 that the Labour
Front should foster popular political education the reply he received
was: 'We had better leave that alone, otherwise the workers will get too
clever.' (*The German Resistance*, London, 1958, p. 31.)

[39] Hitler knew that 'especially for the masses faith is frequently altogether
the sole basis for an ethical *Weltanschauung*', and Stalin did not disguise
his resentment of the 'exegetes and Talmudists ... [who] think that if
they learn these conclusions and formulae by heart and begin to quote
them here and there, then they will be able to solve any question whatsoever, in the belief that the memorized conclusions and formulae suit
them for all times and countries' (*Mein Kampf*, p. 293; I. Stalin, 'Otvet
tovarishcham', *Bol'shevik*, 1950, no. 14, p. 6.)

[40] In an attempt to place the shortcomings of Soviet propaganda at the door
of the personality cult one Soviet functionary affirmed that the 'duties
of propagandists and other workers on the ideological front had to a
large extent been reduced to popularizing what was said by Stalin'.
(*Kommunist*, 1956, no. 12, p. 27.) For an analysis of the progressive
contraction of Nazi propaganda themes to the single 'categorical imperative' that the Fuehrer was 'infinitely great and that unconditional
subordination was due to him in all circumstances', see von Hippel,
Nationalsozialistische Herrschaftsordnung, pp. 43–4.

respective ideologies as was conducted on behalf of the Soviet and Nazi regimes was as a rule disbursed in small doses, to a limited group of people and under conditions of maximum control. Above all the party, and particularly its corps of professional functionaries, constituting as it does the most organized and disciplined segment of the adult civilian population, is allowed some insight into the arcana of doctrine. The fact that it is in the party, more than in any other single group, that the persons with the greatest material stake in the survival of the regime are concentrated, furnishes an additional guarantee that its members will be more inclined than the rest of the population to view the inevitable disparities between ideology and reality in the 'correct' perspective.

Against this background the vital role of the party in the mobilization of the masses can be seen in full relief. Given the action-oriented, command character of totalitarian propaganda, the need to ensure that it does indeed lead to the action ordained, that the command is obeyed fully and promptly, assumes paramount importance. Other instruments, notably the mass media of press, radio and now television, are highly efficient in disseminating the goals and demands of the regime, and the organs of coercion, notably the secret police, are equally efficient in enforcing their fulfilment. But none is as qualified as the party to merge both functions into the single process that alone does justice to the preaching-in-action precept, none is as capable as the party of giving effect to the typically totalitarian phenomenon of 'voluntary compulsion'. It is the party which disposes over the million-strong army of 'political apostles' who by their diffused but organized presence among the masses are able both to stimulate and to supervise the desired pattern of conformist response throughout the land.

The propaganda conditions in which each of the two parties operated could hardly have been more dissimilar, especially during the formative stages of the Nazi and Soviet regimes. The NSDAP confronted a highly literate nation that was technically accessible to propaganda. The Germans read books, attended the theatre and cinema, listened to the radio and were accustomed to turn to their newspapers for information and direction in political matters. By contrast, the Bolshevik revolution found the Russian masses largely illiterate and almost entirely bereft of the cultural and informational media which bind the fabric of modern society.

Moreover, the Nazis assumed power with a party which in the last comparatively free elections to the *Reichstag* in March 1933 polled 43.9% of the total vote.[41] A little less than half the adult population of Germany could therefore already be counted as at least partly standing in the Nazi camp at the outset of the Third Reich. The Bolsheviks, on the other hand, could claim to represent no more than a quarter of the electorate on the solitary day on which the newly-elected Constituent Assembly met in session on 18 January 1918.

The difference was not only numerical. There can be little doubt that a substantial proportion of those who cast their votes for the Bolsheviks had little, if any, knowledge of the substance of Bolshevism, of its doctrines or of its leaders. They voted for the party with the slogan of 'Land, Bread and Peace!' and which by its determined, self-confident activism seemed to offer greater promise of its ability to implement these popular demands than its rivals. Under Tsarism the activities of the Bolsheviks had been largely clandestine and directed primarily at limited groups of industrial workers and the radical intelligentsia. In the countryside the party was almost completely unknown until the soldiers returning from the front brought its propaganda image to the villages. Awareness of the Nazi party in the Germany of 1933 was of a different order. Many of those who voted national socialism into power clearly did not suspect the full perversity of its ultimate objectives and many others may have had reservations about certain Nazi personalities and tactics, but few could have been completely ignorant of the Nazi programme or of the methods by which it was to be brought to fruition. Years of intense and open election campaigning had preceded the Nazi assumption of power, years in which, if not the entire population, at least those who came to vote for national socialism had ample opportunity to acquaint themselves with its essential character and aims.[42]

41 The elections were, of course, free only in the sense that other parties were still allowed to participate. Yet, though the Nazis, now in possession of state power, had no scruples about using every form of pressure available to them in order to deny success to their rivals, all the major parties except the Communists (against whom Nazi intimidation had been particularly severe and who lost a little over one million votes) maintained their absolute voting strength at the level of the pre-Nazi elections of November 1932.

42 This is the kind of statement that one is easily led to, perhaps too easily, when comparing Germany in 1933 with Russia in 1917; if one looks at the German situation in isolation it stands out as a greatly over-

In comparison with the Nazis the Bolsheviks did not only have a precariously narrow popular base at the beginning of their regime; they were also soon propelled towards policies which posed far greater problems for Soviet propaganda than those which its Nazi counterpart was called upon to solve. The forced march by which an entire nation was led from economic and social backwardness into the modern industrial age demanded a degree of sacrifice on the part of the people comparable only to that which the Germans experienced in the closing stages of the war. It demanded a concerted attack on mass illiteracy and the living habits of the millions who were brought from the country-side into the urban industrial centres and had to be equipped with the social and cultural requisites of an industrial civilization. And in the compulsory collectivization of agriculture it involved a direct clash between the regime and the majority of the popula-tion. With all this, the rapid mobilization of the country's under-developed human potential for the construction of an industrial economy and the alienation from the regime of vast sections of the peasantry which resulted from it, Soviet propaganda was expected to cope.

By contrast with the immensity of this task, that which con-fronted Nazi propaganda – at least until the last years of World War II – is almost negligible. The Germans lacked neither tech-nical skill nor the virtues of labour discipline. And although propaganda for such specific industrial aims as higher pro-ductivity and loyalty to the 'plant community' (*Betriebsgemein-schaft*) constituted part of the Nazi propaganda, its main effort could be concentrated on questions of more direct relevance to active, political support. Secondly, the two major practical tasks which the Nazis set themselves, the abolition of unemployment at home and the re-establishment of Germany's *grandeur* abroad, far from alienating sections of the population, served to broaden

simplified generalization, justifiable only on the somewhat dubious grounds that it 'saves heaps of explanations'. A conclusion from Allen's imaginative reconstruction of how Nazism was perceived (and enacted) in one small German town should temper this sufficiently: 'Hardly any-one in Thalburg in those days grasped what was happening. There was no real comprehension of what the town would experience if Hitler came to power, no real understanding of what Nazism was ... Each group saw one or the other side of Nazism, but none saw it in its full hideousness. Only later did this become apparent and even then not to everyone.' (W. S. Allen, *The Nazi Seizure of Power: The Experience of a Single German Town*, London, 1966, p. 281. The name of the town is dis-guised.)

the regime's popular support even further. It was only when the pursuit of these policies led to war, and particularly when it became clear that the war could not be won, that anything like significant dissatisfaction with Nazi policies developed.

This is not to say, of course, that the repressive measures of the Nazi regime, and especially those directed against the Churches, did not cause considerable resentment among the people. But such repressive measures were also a prominent part of the Soviet scene and, not unnaturally, their effect on the popular attitude to the regime was similarly negative. The point is that, whereas for the Bolsheviks one of the main measures in the realm of practical policy necessarily involved a clash with the numerically dominant class in the country, the Nazis were able to set themselves political objectives which were bound to meet with general approval as long as they were being successfully attained. In short, in important spheres of interest, Nazi propaganda needed only to enhance the popularity of policies that were intrinsically popular, while Soviet propaganda was called upon to create a measure of popularity for policies that were intrinsically unpopular.

There is, however, at least one respect in which the propaganda task of the Nazis was more difficult than that of the Bolsheviks. While the relatively high cultural level of the Germans enabled the Nazis to employ the technical potentialities of modern propaganda to the full, it also made higher demands on the quality and variety of its propaganda output. German society was highly stratified, with varying and often deep-rooted cultural interests and needs to which Nazi propaganda had to adjust itself, at least to some extent. The stereotyped monotony of Soviet press editorials and the declarative, almost naïve simplicity of its propaganda slogans would have carried little conviction in Germany. It is true, of course, that in line with the principles elaborated by Hitler in *Mein Kampf*, Nazi propaganda was 'adapted to the capacity of the least intelligent' and constant repetition was one of its main weapons.[43] Like Soviet propagandists the Nazis also revealed early on a particular fondness for certain words and phrases which whatever their initial propaganda appeal soon degenerated into hollow clichés. Yet significant differences remain. Nazi propagandists never lost their interest in the form in which propaganda themes were presented. They did not rely on arid affirmations of the kind that charac-

[43] *Mein Kampf*, pp. 197–8.

terizes much of Soviet propaganda to this day, but developed the manipulation of words and symbols into 'the highest creative art'.[44] They were forever preoccupied with rendering their propaganda attractive, an aim which, if it is not wholly absent from the mind of the Soviet propagandist, occupies a place of minor importance in his scale of values. A nation lying geographically and culturally in the heart of Europe had somewhat wider and more discerning intellectual appetites than the Russian masses who had been bypassed by the mainstream of modern civilization. Nor were the Nazis able to disrupt the innumerable ties which bound Germany to the rest of Europe with anything like the same thoroughness with which the Russians severed their tenuous connections. Consequently Nazi propaganda could not distort or exclude the reality of the outside world with the absolute impunity frequently attained in Soviet Russia.[45]

Finally, although the far-flung repression which accompanied the implementation of Bolshevik policy posed considerable propaganda tasks, it also 'supported' propaganda by physically eliminating large sections of the population hostile to the regime. The bloodletting and emigration of the Civil War, the decimation of the peasantry and the periodic purges did, in their own irrevocable manner, make a substantial contribution to 'the moral-political unity of the Soviet people'. Nazi propagandists also had this kind of support from their colleagues in the repressive agencies, but its application to 'racial' Germans never reached mass proportions on a scale comparable to Soviet experience. The avowed aim of 'national reconciliation' (*nationale Versoehnung*), symbolized at the very outset of Hitler's reign by the notorious ceremonial farce in the Potsdam Garrison Church, placed upon the shoulders of the propagandists the main burden of obtaining support from reluctant or critical sections of the

---

[44] Goebbels, see above p. 33.

[45] It was only with the outbreak of war that Nazi propaganda could begin to operate in conditions of near-complete immunity from outside influence. Even then, however – and this is indicative of the problems involved in imposing totalitarian propaganda upon a technically advanced and culturally alert people – Goebbels' demand that all radio sets be confiscated for the duration of the war was refused by the Reich Defence Council, and he had to be content with stringent regulations forbidding listening to foreign broadcasts (see below p. 248). It is understandable that Goebbels looked with some envy at Soviet Russia where 'the Kremlin has been clever enough to exclude the Russian people from receiving the great world broadcasts and to limit them to their local stations'. (*Goebbels Diaries*, p. 453.)

community. And among these there were many who had developed a degree of political sophistication and with it an attitude of scepticism towards political slogans, and some whose political convictions had become well defined and sharpened with hostility towards the Nazis in the intensity of the political conflicts which had marked the demise of the Weimar Republic.

To the differences in propaganda conditions must now be added the differences in propaganda resources which each party could contribute to the total effort. Two factors will have to be mentioned briefly – the size of each party at the outset of its rule and the sum total of its responsibilities. The Nazis assumed power with a membership of 1.1 million; the strength of the Bolsheviks at the time of the October revolution is said to have been 'around 350,000'.[46] It is not necessary to bear in mind the vast differences in population and area of each country to appreciate the disproportion in the propaganda forces which each party could place at the disposal of its leadership. Moreover, in Germany the party was effectively encouraged to steer clear of administrative responsibilities and the 'education' of the nation remained its main preoccupation. The wide experience which the party had gained during the election campaigns of the Weimar years and the propaganda machine it had constructed stood ready to serve the leadership in the enlarged arena of the totalitarian state. As one Nazi functionary put it, it was 'self-evident' that the responsibility for the spiritual welfare of the nation would be entrusted to that 'organization which had from the beginning been the bearer of national socialist propaganda and – it may be said – possesses the best propaganda apparatus in the world: the NSDAP'.[47]

The Bolsheviks, on the other hand, not only had relatively little experience in the field of open, large-scale mass persuasion when they set out to bring socialism to the Russian masses with the aid of state power, but immediately found themselves confronted with a variety of tasks, each of extreme urgency and each sufficient to test the moral and physical resources of the party's sparse ranks to breaking point. The exigencies of the Civil War,

[46] For Nazi party statistics see below pp. 83f. The exact size of the Bolshevik party in October–November 1917 cannot be established. Party statistics for the period are unreliable and for many years contradictory figures were cited in Soviet sources. But 'around 350,000' is now the official figure. (P. N. Pospelov *et al.*, eds., *Istoriya Kommunisticheskoi Partii Sovetskogo Soyuza*, 6 vols., Moscow, 1964–, vol. III, part I, pp. 243–4.)

[47] *Unser Wille und Weg*, 1936, no. 6, p. 165.

the problems of restoring a semblance of orderly administration and the tasks of economic reconstruction vied together with propaganda needs for the attention of the party. Clearly, amid the variety of functions which the party was called upon to perform immediately upon its accession to power the resources that were available for propaganda were extremely limited; they were certainly out of all proportion to those which the Nazi party could bring into play in 1933. With the consolidation of Soviet rule and the growth in party membership on the one hand, and the Nazi party's increasing involvement in matters outside the realm of *Menschenfuehrung* on the other, the gap was greatly reduced. Although a considerable share of the Soviet party's energy is still expended on direct and often trivial administrative duties, propaganda has come to occupy a place of special importance among its manifold functions. 'The work of party organizations may be many-sided', runs one article extolling the 'creative' aspects of party activity,

> but, it always has been and continues to be work with people. The party organization deals with the people who run the machines in the factories, with the people in the collective farms, with those who serve in the administration, with the producers of everything of material and intellectual value ... The education and organization of the masses is the main part of the party's work.[48]

In the more prosaic language of a province party secretary:

> Party committees are responsible for everything and that is right. We must answer for the work of the state apparatus and the economic organs. But this does not mean that we must have the same attitude towards the supply of potatoes and towards ideological work. There is someone to take care of the supply of potatoes, here only party control is needed. But in regard to education there is no one to whom we can pass it on. Here all must work, from the secretary to the rank-and-file communist.[49]

As will be seen below, notwithstanding the very dissimilar propaganda conditions obtaining in Nazi Germany and Soviet Russia, the manner of the party's deployment reveals several fundamental traits in common. These may be regarded as the totalitarian basis of the mobilization of the masses upon which

[48] *Kommunist*, 1954, no. 17, p. 29.
[49] *Partiinaya zhizn'*, 1956, no. 22, p. 39.

the superstructure of means and methods determined by the different conditions of the two countries was erected. Three features arising out of these differences are particularly relevant to this discussion, for they affected the role that each party could play. First, in the Soviet Union the inaccessibility of the mass of the people, and especially of the peasantry, to modern mass media has placed a premium on oral agitation. The concept of the party member as 'missionary to the heathen... [who] communicates the goals and demands of the ruling group into the farthest reaches of Soviet society'[50] has retained much of its validity to the present day, notwithstanding the rapid growth both in the number of cultural and informational media and in the rate of literacy that has taken place over the past fifty years. There are still sections of the rural population who are virtually cut off from the formal mass communications network, because of its quantitative or qualitative inadequacy, the cultural habits of the peasants or their ingrained distrust of official media.

This has rarely, if ever, been true in Nazi Germany. There the personal oral agitation of party members could at best augment the flow of formal propaganda. Nor could many rank-and-file party members be relied upon to provide the kind of propaganda which a relatively sophisticated populace required. In contrast to Soviet Russia where the average party member had a natural propaganda 'advantage' over the rest of the people, if only because his literacy gave him access to the official communications network, the average Nazi enjoyed no such superiority over his fellow-Germans. Nazi propaganda consequently tended to place greater stress on mass activities whose quality could be more easily controlled from the centre; the formal mass media could be manipulated by a small group of professionals and the requisite standards of political and psychological perfection could thus be ensured. The Nazis had great faith in the persuasive potentialities of the spoken word, but it was the huge mass rally at which the skilled orator played upon the emotions of the audience amid an elaborate stage setting, rather than the intimate group agitation, which they regarded as their 'strongest form of propaganda'.[51] These were the occasions on which 'the

---

50 M. Fainsod, *How Russia is Ruled*, 2nd ed., Cambridge, Mass., 1963, p. 216.
51 Hadamovsky, *Propaganda und nationale Macht*, p. 47; Hitler, *Mein Kampf*, p. 115. Almost every foreign observer has reported on the skilful *mise en scène* of Nazi mass meetings. A thoroughly researched

crowd was embraced by a single symphony of brotherhood' and on which, to the individual, 'the suggestive intoxication and enthusiasm of three to four thousand others ... [and] the visible success and acclamation of thousands confirm ... the correctness of the new teaching'.[52]

To be sure, the Nazi party no less than the Communist party expected its members to be active propagandists; yet this should not be allowed to obscure the fact that in comparison with Soviet Russia there was in Nazi Germany both less need and less scope for such personal agitation. It was only in the latter years of World War II that the regime was compelled to fall back on the party rank-and-file as a propaganda medium in its own right. But by then the situation in this as in many other respects had begun to approximate to that of Soviet Russia. For, although the mass media were still technically available – with the exception of the rallies which had been drastically curtailed owing to wartime conditions – they had become increasingly discredited in the eyes of the people and had thus forfeited a great deal of their former propaganda effectiveness.

The second feature that differentiated Soviet propaganda from that of the Nazis and had similar implications for the role of personal agitation was the Soviet emphasis on matters of economic production. This was, of course, a reflection of the state of economic development in each of the two countries, but apart from influencing the content of Soviet propaganda it also dictated its dominant form. Especially since the onset of industrialization and collectivization, when the attempt to transform the economic face of Russia was begun in earnest, Soviet propaganda has been largely an appendage of the production process. It was employed not only to exhort the masses to greater effort but to teach them the rudiments of industrial civilization. In the circumstances, the advantage of personal agitation over the more remote mass media were those which classroom teaching has over correspondence courses. Above all the agitator was on the spot. He could not only

account is K. Schmeer, *Die Regie des oeffentlichen Lebens im Dritten Reich*, Munich, 1956. The pageantry of the party congresses is described in H. T. Burden, *The Nuremberg Party Rallies: 1923–39*, London, 1967; see now also the memoirs of Speer who was closely associated with the design of the decor of the new Germany and still takes professional pride in some of the architectonic effects of the Nuremberg spectaculars. (A. Speer, *Inside the Third Reich*, London, 1971, p. 101.)

[52] *Unser Wille und Weg*, 1935, no. 12, p. 421; Hitler, *Mein Kampf*, p. 536; E. Dovifat, *Rede und Redner*, Leipzig, 1937, p. 48.

teach but demonstrate, supervise, correct and punish. As Inkeles has shown in his pioneering study, it was with the beginning of the Five-Year Plans in the late 1920s that the conception of the agitator–organizer as opposed to his predecessor, the agitator–popularizer, came to the fore.[53]

The Germans, it has already been noted, were not in need of industrial training. Agitation at the enterprise, which was the exclusive responsibility of the Labour Front, was largely confined to mass propaganda activities designed to foster the Nazi conception of labour–management relations. The most common forms were celebrations of one kind or another and the factory roll-calls (*Betriebsappelle*) at which the factory director usually held a short speech to the workers.[54] Similar activities with a similar end in view are also a feature of Soviet agitation. The Soviet factory-wide *sobranie* is a fairly close parallel of the Nazi *Betriebsappell*; it is held at regular intervals of approximately four to six weeks, is as a rule addressed by members of the managerial staff and is intended to foster 'the participation of the masses in the running of the enterprise'.[55] But the mainstay of Soviet agitation is the day-to-day 'work with people' conducted individually or in small groups which will form the subject of subsequent discussion.

Finally, the higher cultural level of the German people and the less urgent need to mobilize them for the solution of concrete tasks in the sphere of economic production both compelled and enabled the Nazi party to explore more thoroughly the channels of 'indirect propaganda', i.e. to elaborate communication activities in which the propaganda intent, though always present, is subdued or concealed.[56] In contrast, Soviet 'mass-political work' has for many years been content to rely on unadorned direct exhortation as its principal method. Given the comparative cultural and political apathy of a large proportion of the population

[53] A. Inkeles, *Public Opinion in Soviet Russia*, Cambridge, Mass., 1950, pp. 77ff. More recent studies of communication behaviour in underdeveloped societies have confirmed the effectiveness of face-to-face communication both for arousing interest in innovation and for teaching the related skills.

[54] See F. Irwahn, *Betriebsappell und Kameradschaftsabende*, Hamburg, 1936, pp. 18–32 and 68–71; W. Denkler, *Wie halte ich eine Betriebsversammlung ab oder einen Betriebsappell*, Berlin, n.d., pp. 7–16; also Th. Lueddecke, *Menschenfuehrung in den Betrieben*, Hamburg, 1934, *passim*.

[55] *Partiinaya zhizn'*, 1957, no. 15, p. 22; see also 1971, no. 20, pp. 67–70.

[56] On the concept of 'indirect propaganda' see below pp. 167ff.

on the one hand and the acute need for tangible success in the fulfilment of economic plans with which the party was so closely associated on the other, there seemed to be little point in experimenting with propaganda methods which at best had only indirect relevance to the immediate and practical problems which faced every party organization, and incidentally determined the survival of the party functionary in his position. In the conditions of the Soviet Union the direct call to action, suitably supplemented with the necessary technical information, seemed far and away the shortest road between the demands of the regime and their fulfilment by the people.

What has been said so far must now be qualified somewhat to take account of several post-Stalin developments. The differences between Nazi and Soviet propaganda noted above still hold true to a very large degree; but the social and political changes which the Soviet Union underwent in the past two decades have also had repercussions on propaganda policies, and as a result the differences are no longer as marked as they used to be. On the one hand, the abolition of mass terror made it necessary to reinforce alternative, 'persuasive' instruments of social control. On the other, the continuing modernization of Soviet society, and especially educational advancement, the development of communication media and greater knowledge of the world outside, created the opportunity and also accentuated the need not only for more, but also for better propaganda, more attractive, more sophisticated, more likely to appeal to different social strata, and more effective in countering the potentially subversive exposure to contacts with the West.

The characters of the top leaders have probably also played a part. Everything we know about Stalin, from the day of his entry into the ranks of the conspiratorial party to the day of his death, reveals him as a leader singularly devoid of both the ability and the inclination to move men by persuasion. He was a dedicated believer in power, i.e., in moving men to do his bidding, but it was not the power of the word which held him in thrall. By contrast, Khrushchev, ebullient, gregarious, and much given to histrionics when the occasion seemed to call for it, was the agitator *par excellence*. Though no mean practitioner of power himself, he seemed possessed of an almost naïve faith in his ability to harangue his listeners into submission, whether he was addressing a mass rally of farm workers in the virgin lands or meeting the world's statesmen in private conclave. It would have been surprising if the character differences of these two men did not influence the propaganda practices followed under their rule. The present leaders have so far appeared as more conventional and less colourful *apparatchiki* of the type that Stalin, and Khrushchev too for that matter, raised to run the various branches of the party–government hierarchy. Yet while they do not share their predecessor's personal propensity for propagandistic fireworks, they have continued to maintain and even to elaborate the machinery of mass agitation.

Considering the altered socio-political circumstances and the differences in leadership styles, the qualitative changes in Soviet propaganda since 1953 are remarkably few. Still, there were some attempts under Khrushchev, sponsored in part by his no less energetic and communication-conscious son-in-law, Aleksei Adzhubei, to enliven the mass media and develop new approaches that would be more attuned to the comparatively relaxed climate and greater cultural requirements of post-Stalin Russia.

More recently Soviet propaganda spokesmen have stressed the techniques of political communication, in place of the former, seemingly exclusive preoccupation with content; there is the beginning of an awareness in the thinking of agitprop specialists of the importance of the technical and psychological aspects of opinion formation, even though very little of that is as yet apparent in their propaganda output. Conferences of propaganda workers now attend lectures on such subjects as 'Problems of Social Psychology in the Formation of Personality and their Impact in Political Work',[57] and the party press carries articles with such titles as 'Psychological and Pedagogical Factors in Agitation'.[58] Increasingly, party officials are being urged to study 'the art of oratory',[59] and to remember that the effectiveness of propaganda depends 'to a large extent on understanding the mechanism of public opinion formation'.[60]

None other than the then head of the Central Committee Department for Propaganda, V. I. Stepakov, in a book published in 1967, deplored what he called the 'excessive "rationalism" in our propaganda', and demanded instead that Soviet propagandists develop 'the ability to combine the rational and the

---

[57] *Agitator*, 1968, no. 13, p. 48; *Partiinaya zhizn'*, 1969, no. 5, p. 66.
[58] *Voprosy istorii KPSS*, 1970, no. 10, pp. 96ff; *Agitator*, 1971, no. 9, pp. 46ff.
[59] *Pravda*, 17 January 1967.
[60] *Partiinaya zhizn'*, 1968, no. 4, p. 57.

emotional'.[61] He rejected 'the assertion, which can still be heard, that it is supposedly enough to have a profound knowledge of the content of the propaganda material and that method will come of its own accord',[62] and stressed the need to study not only social psychology in general but also the propaganda methods of the bourgeois enemy in particular: 'Their researches provide detailed descriptions of the ways of influencing people; on the basis of numerous questionnaires and observations over many years, practical recommendations are made as to the organization and methods of propaganda in different spheres of life.'[63] His own book did not indicate that he was familiar with any of these recommendations, but some of the recent writings of Soviet social scientists do reflect fairly extensive knowledge of the Western literature.[64]

Much of the aforesaid is the direct result of the broadening and, in part, the revival of social science research in the Soviet Union initiated in the 1950s. And while it has so far had little visible impact on the communication policies of the party, its long-run effect may well be to render Soviet propaganda more subtle and presumably also more formidable. At the very least, the application of social science methods, if allowed to continue, should help to ensure that propaganda practices will not fall behind changing audience requirements.

Perhaps one of the most important innovations of recent years has been the growing reliance on 'concrete' sociological surveys. The rehabilitation of sociology as a legitimate discipline after a quarter century of Stalinist proscription as a 'pseudo science', when 'even the word "sociology" was in effect banned [and] social research, like the study of facts in general, was neglected',[65] has already given rise to a spate of research projects on a fairly broad range of subjects – from the sociology of work to that of leisure, from social stratification to village life. Judging by the

---

[61] V. I. Stepakov, *Partiinoi propagande – nauchnye osnovy*, Moscow, 1967, pp. 86–7. For a perceptive analysis of recent Soviet preoccupations with propaganda methods, based largely on Stepakov's book, see David Wedgewood Benn, 'New Thinking in Soviet Propaganda', *Soviet Studies*, 1969, no. 1, pp. 52ff.

[62] Stepakov, *Partinoi propagande*, p. 283.

[63] *Ibid.*, pp. 265–6.

[64] See, e.g. the series edited by B. D. Datsyuk, *Voprosy teorii i praktiki massovykh sredstv propagandy*, Moscow, 1968 – of which four volumes have so far appeared; also V. N. Kol'banovskii and Yu. A. Shervokin, comp., *Problemy sotsial'noi psikhologii i propaganda*, Moscow, 1971.

[65] *Novyi mir*, 1965, no. 6, p. 272.

published evidence, public opinion studies have not as yet attracted a substantial share of the academically more respectable inquiries, but some apparently useful work has been done both in studying the effects of various communication measures, including the party's ideological work, and in surveying public opinion trends.

The mass media studies need not concern us here. As regards the party's ideological work, most, but not all, of the research appears to be conducted by special sociological groups or laboratories attached to party committees, at the centre and in the provinces, rather than by the formally independent scientific institutions.[66] Thus far relatively little meaningful information about this research has been made public; it is therefore difficult to form an opinion of its scope or quality. All that can be said with certainty is that this work is going on and that not only sociologists but also party functionaries continue to call for more and better studies. In view of the inherent limitations attending the study of social behaviour in a totalitarian system, especially when conducted under direct party auspices, and the shortage of formally trained professional sociologists in the Soviet Union, one may perhaps assume that the quality of this work still leaves much to be desired.[67] Certainly the party has until now shown little inclination to disseminate the fruit of this research in the party press for the benefit of its propagandists at large, but this may, of course, be due as much to the fact that it is considered politically unpalatable for the consumption of a broader public as

---

[66] However, it appears that individual members of the academic community often co-operate with the party's own establishments on a more or less permanent basis. Thus, e.g. the sociological group operating under the Moscow Province party committee was headed by Prof. G. V. Osipov, a deputy director of what was then the Institute for Concrete Social Research at the USSR Academy of Sciences, and one of the foremost Soviet sociologists. (*Partiinaya zhizn'*, 1969, no. 4, p. 49.)

[67] Much sociological research is still said to be in the hands of such people as 'geologists, mechanics, historians and former pilots'. (*Izvestiya*, 27 October 1969; see also the article by V. Peredentsev, a leading professional sociologist, in *Literaturnaya gazeta*, 18 March 1970, p. 12.) As regards quality, some projects are undertaken 'without a clear aim and elementary knowledge of methodology'. (Efimov and Pozdnyakov, *Nauchnye osnovy*, p. 9.) In one case a project to study the effectiveness of personal agitation in a Moscow collective designed a questionnaire comprising 'a chaotic selection of a large number of questions unconnected by an inner logic'. When asked for the aim of the research the author of the questionnaire was alleged to have replied that it would depend on the results of the inquiry. (*Partiinaya zhizn'*, 1969, no. 4, p. 48.)

to any doubts about its utility or methodological rigour. While accounts of ideological work in party journals have of late been increasingly laced with snippets of information purportedly derived from sociological surveys, the data adduced have generally been more revealing of the lack of sophistication of the research than of the subject matter under investigation.[68]

Of the opinion surveys a great deal more is known. The first 'opinion polls' were introduced in 1960 by *Komsomol'skaya pravda* which established its own Public Opinion Institute for this purpose. Since then many polls have been conducted by this as well as by other institutions. Controversial subjects, especially those of direct political relevance have been carefully avoided: a question such as 'Do you approve or disapprove of the actions of the Soviet Union in Czechoslovakia?' was as inconceivable in August 1968 as a similar question on the Molotov–Ribbentrop pact would have been in August 1939. The methodology employed, too, is often dubious with regard to questionnaire design, sampling, anonymity of the respondents, processing and analysis of data, and so forth.[69] And yet, while some of the polls have no doubt been conceived with an eye to their propaganda value, as 'concrete' confirmation of the official myths, others do reflect a desire on the part of the leadership to know the views of its subjects–citizens, particularly of the younger generation, on a variety of relatively innocuous, but socially important, topics such as career aspirations, living standards, consumer demands, leisure, family relations, etc.[70] Even at its best and most objective this

---

[68] For somewhat more extensive but still greatly inadequate summaries of such research findings see *Agitator*, 1973, no. 16, pp. 46–8 and no. 24, pp. 45–6.

[69] *Komsomol'skaya pravda*, 28 October 1966, on research in Novosibirsk: 'First, it does not always consider the influences governing the respondent's consciousness of a given problem at the time of the survey. For instance, questionnaires are sent out that are not anonymous (sometimes on very subtle and delicate topics), with the extremely categorical request: "Indicate name" or "Sign." Secondly, it is unable to process with technical competence all the answers received; this leads to a repetition, on a new "sociological" level, of the old "game with examples", whereby only the answers needed to confirm a preconceived hypothesis, scheme or dogma are selected and used. Thirdly, the results obtained are interpreted too broadly . . .'

[70] As an example of the former category, one may cite one of the earlier polls (on the characteristics and aspirations of Soviet youth) which enabled the then First Secretary of the Komsomol, Pavlov, to quote in evidence that 'Soviet youth unanimously . . . regards as the principal characteristics of the generation patriotism, devotion to the party, faith in communism, love of work, a feeling for the new.' (*XXII S'ezd*, vol.

kind of probing into latent, i.e. 'unpublic' opinion does not presage the strengthening of the input functions of 'potential interest groups' (in Truman's sense of the term).[71] But it has already helped to challenge the more extreme interpretations of 'moral-political unity' which had traditionally extended the unanimity of the 'socialist public' to all questions of social life.[72]

It is perhaps intriguing to speculate on the potential impact of the burgeoning sociological research on the Soviet system in general. Soviet sociological investigations are instrumental rather than critical, 'concrete' rather than truly empirical. But even within these limits they may well help to illuminate important aspects of Soviet life. Does this mean that the system itself will in due course become transformed as more and more of the 'facts in general' – so long 'neglected' – come to light? Does it mean that the processes and structures of policy-making will be fundamentally altered, and, in particular, that the role of the omniscient party allegedly guided by a 'scientific' ideology will be gradually but irrevocably eroded as sociological experts are allowed to pursue their researches and proffer their recommendations? Possibly it does, but on the record there is room for doubt. The Soviet leaders are past masters at handling both the experts and their facts; there is no reason to believe that they will allow

II, p. 145.) As an example of the latter category, see a poll on the leisure of youth in Smolensk Province which revealed among others that 'only 3% of those polled would like to engage in public activities'. (*Komsomol'skaya pravda*, 16 June 1965.) A detailed discussion of the polls conducted by the Institute of Public Opinion will be found in B. A. Grushin, 'K probleme kachestvennoi reprezentatsii v vyborochnom oprose', in G. E. Glezerman and V. G. Afanas'ev, eds., *Opyt i metodika konkretnykh sotsiologicheskikh issledovanii*, Moscow, 1965, pp. 61–107. For a sophisticated treatment of the methodology of public opinion research, including a recommendation for the establishment of a central institution (with branches in different parts of the country) which would collate and process public opinion information and also train the necessary researchers, see A. I. Prigozhin, 'Metodologicheskie problemy issledovaniya obshchestvennogo mnenya', *Voprosy filosofii*, 1969, no. 2, pp. 64–73.

71 D. B. Truman, *The Governmental Process: Political Interests and Public Opinion*, New York, 1951.

72 The significant differences between the older 'monistic' school of public opinion in the Soviet Union, represented by A. K. Uledov (*Obshchest-vennoe mnenie sovetskogo obshchestva*, Moscow, 1963), and the new 'pluralist' approach, evident in the work of the Soviet Union's leading opinion pollster, B. A. Grushin (*Mnenya o mire i mir mnenii*, Moscow, 1967), are discussed in R. Ahlberg, 'Theorie der oeffentlichen Meinung und empirische Meinungsforschung in der UdSSR', *Osteuropa*, 1969, no. 3, pp. 161–72.

themselves to be overwhelmed by sociologists any more than by military, scientific, economic or any other experts. Over the years, thousands of historians, writers, journalists and many others whose inherent respect for the 'facts in general' does not lag behind that of the new breed of sociologists have had to learn to adjust their work to the current official line, to distort or suppress as the occasion required.[73] There is nothing in the method of 'concrete' sociology which immunizes its practitioners to the pressures and temptations to which others searching for truth in the Soviet system have been exposed.

It is probably true that the development of sociological research, even under the familiar conditions of censorship (both self-imposed and party-imposed) presupposes a rather more tolerant attitude on the part of the leadership to the disclosure of the ills of Soviet society than has been the case in the past. But are such disclosures, published in a few esoteric journals or books, likely to shatter the self-image of a society that has heard a succession of its leaders denounce their predecessors, colleagues and subordinates for the gravest crimes and political errors? Are they likely to add significantly to the incongruence which Soviet citizens must experience constantly between the reality they know and the 'socialist reality' that is projected through the official media? One would have thought that most Soviet citizens, whatever their views about the basic soundness of the system, the desirability of the goals it has set for itself and its ability to achieve these goals, would not be greatly affected by the fact that sociological inquiries reveal some of the deficiencies, deviations or even regressions in the development of the society with somewhat greater precision than does their own experience.

Where the impact of the new sociology may make itself felt is in improving the quality of Soviet leadership and, in part at least, the quality of life of the ordinary citizen. By pinpointing the exact causes and true extent of crucial social problems it should enable the Soviet leaders to know their society better and consequently to rule it more rationally and efficiently. What effect this is likely to have on propaganda practices in particular it is impossible to predict. In this, as in other spheres of social life, the effect will depend upon the ability of Soviet sociologists to

---

[73] 'It is truly embarrassing to watch how some authors' work over a number of years offers mutually exclusive conceptions of the events of the war years, the end of collectivization and the role of certain individuals.' (*Pravda*, 18 August 1965.)

develop rigorous techniques of investigation, upon the relaxation of ideological–political restrictions on the scope of their investigations, and upon the willingness of Soviet policy-makers to act on their recommendations. As yet, only the fulfilment of the first of these three conditions may be posited with some certainty.[74]

74 It is worth bearing in mind that in the other communist countries of Eastern Europe where sociology is generally far more advanced, notably Poland and Yugoslavia, one still has to search hard for evidence of substantial change following empirical social inquiry. For a recent report on the state of sociology in these countries, see B. Denitch, 'Sociology in Eastern Europe', *Slavic Review*, 1971, no. 2, pp. 317–39. On p. 330, n. 20, the author quotes a remark by a Rumanian sociologist which might well have come from the mouth of a Russian colleague: 'Our leaders need a great deal of information about what is happening: the trouble is that many of them do not want to know.'

If the experience of Western sociologists with their own political decision-makers may dispose them to view such complaints with considerable sympathy, the following passage from a recent article by Prof. M. Rutkevich, the new director of the re-named Institute of Sociological Research at the USSR Academy of Sciences, will indicate something of the nature of the constraints faced by their Soviet colleagues: 'Sociology is a party science. The Marxist sociologist . . . cannot pose as a "disinterested researcher". Here the conception of the sociologist as a doctor allegedly called upon to cure society's ills cannot be considered correct. The researcher cannot confine himself to the study of negative phenomena; he must give special attention to the perception of what is new and advanced in all spheres of social life. In the Soviet land the social scientist . . . sees his highest aim in serving the people, in providing the process of administration with scientific knowledge.' (*Pravda*, 14 September 1973.)

3: TOTALITARIAN ORGANIZATION

'Power formations through pure propaganda are fluid', wrote the Nazi propagandist, Hadamovsky, 'and can suddenly disintegrate from one day to another, unless propaganda is joined by the force of organization.'[1] The controlled manipulation of large numbers of people requires an organizational frame by means of which the people can be reached and deployed. It is necessary that each individual knows his place within the larger collective, and, what is more important, that the leadership knows where to find each individual. In both Soviet Russia and Nazi Germany the party provided 'the force of organization' in two ways: indirectly through its control of the various associational groups – trade unions, professional societies, youth organizations, cultural and sport associations, etc., and directly, through its own network of primary organizations.

In the Soviet Union the associational groups are officially described as non-party (*nepartiiny*) and formally independent of the party, but their subordination to party control and direction is nonetheless real for that.[2] It is indicated in art. 126 of the

---

[1] *Propaganda und nationale Macht*, p. 21.

[2] The description of a 'mass non-party organization' is even applied to the Komsomol. How this label is officially interpreted may be seen from the following passage in a *Pravda* article of 18 October 1968:

The party takes the position that the Komsomol ... must be an independently acting organization in which youth can display maximum independent activity essential for its communist upbringing. It would, however, be a crass mistake to take this to mean an absolute, unlimited independence ... 'Absolute' independence may lead to the breaking away of the youth organization from the party, to spontaneity in the development of the communist youth movement. In the era of a sharp class struggle ... there are not, nor can there be any 'neutral' positions or 'no-man's land.' That is why communists cannot leave the youth movement to drift, especially in regard to its organizational construction and the working out of organizational forms.

Para. 61 of the Party Statutes refers to the Komsomol as 'an independently acting social organization of young people'. Para. 63 amplifies this: 'The Y.C.L. [Komsomol] acts under the leadership of the Communist

61

Soviet Constitution which defines the party as 'the leading core of all organizations of the working people both social and state', and is more explicitly reaffirmed in countless official references to their activities. In Lenin's famous phrase, these organizations represent the essential 'transmission belts' from the party to the masses; without them, 'it is impossible to exercise the dictatorship'.[3] The rationale of party dominance was expressed by Stalin in 1924, when he asked:

> ... who is to determine the line, the general direction, along which the work of all these organizations is to be conducted? Where is the central organization which is not only able, because it has the necessary experience, to work out such a general line, but in addition, is in a position, because it has sufficient prestige, to induce all these organizations to carry out the line so as to attain unity of leadership and to make hitches impossible?

The terseness of his reply stands in significant contrast to the rhetoric of the question: 'That organization is the party of the proletariat.'[4] From time to time Soviet spokesmen have felt the need to reaffirm that nothing has changed in this regard since then, as in the following recent *Pravda* article on 'questions of theory':

> Under socialism, there is no other political force that could take into consideration, combine and coordinate the interests of the working people, all classes and social groups, all nations and nationalities and all generations as fully and consistently as the party of the communists is capable of doing ... Without the directing activity of the party of communists, state and public organizations will inevitably act without coordination and run the risk of straying from the correct path.[5]

In view of the attempts of some Western analysts to develop a group or 'conflict' model of Soviet politics, it should perhaps be stressed that Soviet associational groups must not be understood as performing interest articulation functions comparable to those of similar groups in pluralist systems. The conflicts exist,

Party of the Soviet Union. The work of local Y.C.L. organizations is directed and controlled by the corresponding ... party organizations.' (*Programmy i ustavy KPSS*, p. 393.)

[3] Lenin, *Pol. Sob. Soch.*, vol. XLII, p. 205.
[4] *Problems of Leninism*, p. 102; also p. 168.
[5] *Pravda*, 25 May 1971.

of course, and so, presumably, do the underlying interests. But while one may recognize that a measure of incipient interest articulation takes place as the result of interaction that is inherent in organization, it is equally important to recognize that such interest conflict as has been visible on the surface of the Soviet scene has at no time been fought out by associational groups, at least not since the 1920s. The social forces that have contended for influence over policy-making since then were either institutional groups (in the armed forces, the secret police, the party and ministerial bureaucracies, etc.) or informal factions 'representing' broader non-associational interests, vaguely and sometimes misleadingly identified by such labels as 'liberal economic planners', 'conservative writers', 'metal-eaters', 'agricultural lobby', etc. The associational groups may have served at different times as power bases for individuals or cliques engaged in the intricate manoeuvres for ascendancy within the Kremlin's ruling circles; they have not so far entered the political arena on behalf of their own group interests. Needless to add, it is precisely in order to prevent the autonomous articulation of associational interests ('to make hitches impossible' and to avoid 'the risk of straying from the correct path') that party control is considered essential. From the viewpoint of the Soviet leadership, the function of the organized social groups is not to articulate their separate interests, but to facilitate the mobilization of the society as a whole in pursuit of a 'general interest' articulated by the leadership. There is nothing in recent Soviet history to support the belief that the leadership is no longer capable of imposing this viewpoint on the 'crypto-politics'[6] of the Soviet system.

Referring to hunting and fishing sports societies, one Soviet text had this to say: 'Their task is not only to attract the working people to the sport of hunting and fishing, but also to restore, to develop to the utmost and to utilize correctly hunting and fishing husbandry in accordance with the general tasks and plans for the development of the national economy.'[7] Statements such as this are ritualistic commonplaces and perhaps too much should not be made of them: it is not suggested that they mirror a reality in which Sunday morning anglers are required to co-ordinate their

---

[6] This particular felicitous description was applied by T. H. Rigby in an article under that title, *Survey*, 1964, January (no. 50), pp. 183–94.

[7] V. M. Chkhikvadze *et al.*, eds., *Politicheskaya organizatsiya sovetskogo obshchestva*, Moscow, 1967, p. 329.

catch with the current Gosplan projections. But they express that unity of interest and purpose which is said to underlie the actions of all Soviet citizens irrespective of their particular group affiliation. 'In the conditions of the Soviet system,' Khrushchev told the Supreme Soviet in July 1964, 'the interests of each member of the collective and the interests of the collective as a whole, the interests of each individual and the interests of the state, are merged into one.'[8] This, too, Soviet theorists hasten to add, must not be interpreted literally, for interest conflict, albeit 'non-antagonistic', persists during the socialist stage of the evolution towards full communism.[9] Nevertheless, it helps to provide the legitimizing myth which allows the party alone, in its all-embracing wisdom, to direct all collective endeavour in Soviet society: 'The party solves all these problems so as not to permit infringement of the interests of any social group . . .'[10]

Soviet man is now more organized than ever. It would be tedious to enumerate the many 'social' or 'public' organizations, all of them 'voluntary' but some more voluntary than others, which criss-cross Soviet society – from the amateur art groups (numbering some 23 million members)[11] to the Voluntary Society for Cooperation with the Armed Forces (DOSAAF – said to have 'tens of millions' of members organized in over 300,000 primary organizations)[12] and the trade unions (with 98 million members and 646,000 primary organizations).[13] Soviet spokesmen take pride in citing figures on their growing membership and expanding organizational coverage[14] (and indeed if associational membership is an index of modernity and overlapping membership a factor making for consensus then the Soviet Union can hold its own with the most modern and consensual of societies). The ultimate purpose of all this organizational abun-

---

8   *Pravda*, 13 July 1964.
9   G. M. Shtraks, *Sotsial'noe edinstvo i protivorechiya sotsialisticheskogo obshchestva*, Moscow, 1966, p. 103; T. A. Kuliev, *Problema interesov v sotsialisticheskom obshchestve*, Moscow, 1967, pp. 86ff. See also F. Griffiths, 'A Tendency Analysis of Soviet Policy-Making', in G. Skilling and F. Griffiths, eds., *Interest Groups in Soviet Politics*, Princeton, 1970, pp. 355–77, and the Soviet sources cited therein.
10 *Kommunist*, 1963, no. 7, p. 32.   11   *Pravda*, 4 June 1971.
12 *Agitator*, 1969, no. 10, p. 30; *Pravda*, 21 December 1971.
13 *Pravda*, 21 March 1972.
14 See, e.g. V. F. Klochko, *Partiya i massovye organizatsii trudyashchikhsya*, Moscow, 1967, *passim*; R. S. Shikov, 'Partiya i narod v period stroitel'stva kommunizma', in K. I. Suvorov *et al.*, *Partiya i massy*, Moscow, 1966, pp. 108ff.

dance is perhaps best stated in the words of former Central Committee Secretary, L. F. Ilyichev, who headed the party's propaganda apparatus in the last years of Khrushchev's rule: 'Communism is a highly organized society, a society of organized and therefore of strict discipline.'[15]

The official theory looks to some of these organizations not only to organize and control the activities of their members but also to combat manifestations of bureaucratic mismanagement in the society. This is the function that Khrushchev had in mind when he said in 1962 (referring to the party, the Komsomol and the trade unions): 'If we were to put all these forces into operation, to use them for the purposes of control, not even a gnat would be able to fly past without our noticing it.'[16] We need not dwell on the different institutions which in accordance with the Soviet conception of 'mass democracy' operate as instruments of 'popular control' over bureaucratic agencies – such as the so-called soviet *aktiv* (said to enlist over 25 million people) or the 'people's controllers' (now numbering some 9 million members).[17] Instead, attention must be turned briefly to two forms of mass participation established for the explicit purpose of strengthening public control over the lives of individual citizens. These are the comrades' courts and the people's guards (known as *druzhiny*), formed at the end of the 1950s as part of a campaign to transfer some of the punitive functions of state agencies to 'voluntary public organizations'.

Earlier versions of the comrades' courts had functioned under Lenin, when they were primarily concerned with labour discipline, and also, with somewhat broader jurisdiction, under Stalin. In the latter 1930s the comrades' courts fell increasingly into disuse and for all intents and purposes ceased to exist: at the height of the Stalinist terror there was clearly no role for 'comradely justice'. A half-hearted attempt to use comrades' courts for cases of labour absenteeism brought by management was made in 1951, but it was not until 1959 that a massive effort to resurrect the comrades' courts was launched. Following

---

[15] *Pravda*, 19 June 1963. Cf. Brezhnev: 'Comrades, what we are building is ... the most organized and most hard-working society in the history of mankind.' (*Ibid.*, 22 December 1972.)

[16] *Pravda*, 20 November 1962.

[17] *Ibid.*, 23 April 1969; *Partiinaya zhizn'*, 1973, no. 23, p. 27. The 'people's controllers' replaced the 'assistance groups' of Khrushchev's Party-State Control Committee, the predecessor of the present Committee of People's Control.

Khrushchev's speech at the 21st Party Congress, in which he made clear that their jurisdiction would not be confined to matters of labour discipline,[18] thousands of comrades' courts sprang up all over the country. Draft statutes were published later that year for 'public discussion' and a final decree, differing substantially from the draft proposals, was promulgated in 1961. As amended since then, it provides for the election of comrades' courts for a term of two years in both places of work (including educational institutions) and places of residence. Jurisdiction encompasses violations of labour discipline, minor cases of damage to or misuse of public property, petty theft, minor civil litigation, and a variety of infringements of 'the rules of socialist community life' such as hooliganism, drunkenness, neglect of family responsibilities, abuse, slander as well as 'other anti-social acts' not involving criminal liability, for example, card playing in residential hostels.

The penalties at the disposal of comrades' courts may be divided into two categories. One includes measures of 'moral influence' graded from public apology to public censure. The other consists of material sanctions which take the form of fines (up to 50 rubles) imposed by the comrades' court itself or of what may well be more consequential, though non-binding, recommendations to other agencies for the culprit's transfer, demotion or even dismissal from work, eviction from his flat, or criminal prosecution. There is no appeal to the regular state courts but a re-trial may be ordered by the appropriate trade union committee or local soviet. Soviet sources have repeatedly criticized the comrades' courts for abusing their authority to an extent that 'many people . . . are forced to haunt the threshholds of soviets, trade unions and other organizations with complaints against the comrades' courts'.[19] Petty denunciations by 'comrades' and neighbours, alongside charges brought by the police (militia) or by social organizations, often lead to arbitrary procedures without minimal safeguards for the rights of the accused. As a recent article, reporting one such case, put it: 'This is a wide door, and along with advanced views, backward and philistine attitudes gravitate towards it.'[20]

18 *XXI S'ezd*, vol. i, p. 104.
19 *Izvestiya*, 12 September 1965; also 1 November 1965.
20 *Ibid.*, 1 August 1970. A Western observer who attended some comrades' court trials in Moscow in the early 1960s and does not share these misgivings is G. Feifer, *Justice in Moscow*, London, 1964, pp. 111ff.

The people's guards, too, had their forerunners in Soviet history, such as the 'Brigades for Co-operation with the Militia' of the 1930s or the 'Groups for the Protection of Social Order', which operated during World War II. Unlike similar organs in the past, however, the people's guards are not subordinate to the militia but to 'public organizations', i.e. the party.[21] After some experiments apparently undertaken at local initiative in Leningrad in 1958, a joint Party–Government decree of 2 March 1959 brought a nation-wide movement of people's guards into being. Detachments of people's guards are formed in enterprises and residential areas and operate under the direction of a city or district headquarters. Recruitment is said to be 'strictly voluntary' although, in fact, frequent cases of involuntary conscription have been reported.[22] Many of the *druzhinniki* are young men (the minimum age is 18) who perform their duties as part of their Komsomol assignments.[23] A 1966 decree provided for the encouragement of 'outstanding' *druzhinniki* by such rewards as additional paid leave, honorary certificates, cash bonuses and 'valuable gifts'.[24]

The main task of the people's guards is to aid the militia in maintaining public order and preventing a variety of antisocial acts of the kind dealt with by the comrades' courts. In practice this has meant that groups of people's guards, identified by armbands and badges, patrol streets, parks, places of amusement, etc., not only for the purpose of ensuring the safety of citizens, by apprehending drunkards, rowdies and other transgressors against public order and escorting them to the nearest police station, but also for the purpose of enforcing the official conventions of 'communist morality', by combating all manifestations of non-conformist behaviour – from unauthorized poetry readings to Western-style dancing. In the pursuit of their manifold, ill-defined duties people's guards have been known to invade private homes and residential hostels to check on the inhabitants and to seek out and harass 'parasites', 'speculators' and other deviants, occasionally resorting to 'summary justice'

---

21 In contrast to the comrades' courts, which are formally independent, party control of the people's guards is constantly stressed as an essential requisite of their work. (See, e.g. *Partiinaya zhizn'*, 1966, no. 17, p. 18; *Agitator*, 1969, no. 5, pp. 56–7.)

22 See, e.g. *Izvestiya*, 21 April 1966; *Pravda*, 27 April 1971.

23 The share of Komsomol members was put at one-third. (*Komsomol'skaya pravda*, 2 March 1969.)

24 *Pravda*, 27 July 1966.

of a kind aptly described by one Soviet source as 'hooliganism sanctified in the name of order'.[25]

When they were first introduced the comrades' courts and the people's guards were widely hailed as milestones on the road to the non-state communist society. As yet, however, they represent obvious and – from the standpoint of legal stability – extraordinarily arbitrary devices for the extension of public control over private lives.[26] Their true objective was expressed at the time by a secretary of the Leningrad Province Party Committee when he said: 'We want every person . . . to find himself within the range of vision of the collective, of the public.'[27] The theme of the 'withering-away' of the state has gone out of vogue since Khrushchev's fall; the para-judicial and para-police 'voluntary public organizations' have remained – over 200,000 comrades' courts and some 6.5 million people's guards are reported to be in existence.[28] Moreover, notwithstanding their relatively outspoken

[25] *Komsomol'skaya pravda*, 20 February 1968.
[26] A potentially more dangerous innovation of 'socialist legality' introduced under Khrushchev was the 'anti-parasite' legislation which, in the form finally adopted in 1961, empowered 'collectives of working people', alongside the regular people's courts, to sentence to exile of from two to five years a particular category of 'parasites', namely, those 'working only for the sake of appearances' and committing 'anti-social acts'. (Other 'parasites' who did not even work 'for the sake of appearances' were under the exclusive jurisdiction of the people's courts.) The legislation, which aroused considerable controversy in Soviet legal circles, was subsequently amended in 1965 and again in 1970. The 1965 amendments, among others, abolished the concurrent jurisdiction of the 'collectives of working people'. (For further details see M. Armstrong, 'The Campaign Against Parasites', in P. H. Juviler and H. W. Morton, eds., *Soviet Policy-Making*, New York, 1967, pp. 163–82; H. J. Berman, *Justice in Russia*, Cambridge, Mass., 1968, pp. 291ff; and L. Lipson, 'Hosts and Pests: The Fight against Parasites', *Problems of Communism*, 1965, no. 2, pp. 72ff; A. Bilinsky, 'Novellierung der Parasitengesetze in der UdSSR', *Jahrbuch fuer Ostrecht*, 1965, no. 2, pp. 201ff. A first-hand account of the persecution, trial before a people's court and exile of one 'parasite' is A. Amalrik, *Involuntary Journey to Siberia*, London, 1970.)
[27] *Pravda*, 14 September 1960. Comparing the position in 1964 to that in 1956, a Western authority concluded that 'the range of institutionally supervised conduct' had markedly increased as the result of the 'popularization' of Soviet justice. (L. Lipson, 'Law: The Function of Extra-Judicial Mechanisms', in D. W. Treadgold, ed., *Soviet and Chinese Communism: Similarities and Differences*, Seattle and London, 1967, p. 165.)
[28] *Izvestiya*, 1 August 1970; *Komsomol'skaya pravda*, 2 March 1969. These are substantially the same figures as those reported at the end of the Khrushchev era. (*Izvestiya*, 5 December 1964.)

criticisms of both institutions, Soviet sources have continued to call for the intensification of their activities and the strengthening of their powers.[29]

Transcending and supplementing the 'transmission' of the mass organizations, the party itself maintains direct contact with the masses through its own primary organizations. The CPSU organizes its members, in the main, according to their places of work. The primary organization of the party embraces all party members working in a particular enterprise, factory, educational institution, army unit, government department or collective farm.[30] This organizational form had proved its usefulness during the clandestine, pre-revolutionary activity of the party, for by facilitating regular contact among members it reduced one of the main hazards of conspiratorial action. At the same time it was not only in keeping with the purported class character of the party but also particularly suited to influence the process of economic construction after the party's accession to power.

The latest Party Statutes, adopted at the 22nd Congress in 1961, provide for the establishment of territorial primary organizations in residential areas. As a rule their members comprise housewives, pensioners, employees of housing administrations and, mainly in the villages, persons employed by institutions with no primary organization of their own.[31] As will be seen later, the formation of the territorial primary organizations coincided roughly with the extension of the party's 'mass-political work' to residential areas.

The total number of primary organizations stood at around 375,000 in 1972.[32] But the extent of the party's organizational

---

[29] See, e.g. *Izvestiya*, 11 September 1968; *Pravda*, 16 July 1971.

[30] Primary organizations may be formed with a minimum of three members.

[31] See *Programmy i ustavy KPSS*, pp. 362 and 388. In 1972 over 320,000 members were on the rolls of party organizations of housing administrations. (*Partiinaya zhizn'*, 1972, no. 21, p. 49.)

[32] *Partiinaya zhizn'*, 1972, no. 17, p. 4. For many years the number of primary organizations had been far below that, as can be seen from the following figures.

1922	32,281	1947	296,568
1927	38,978	1957	344,325
1937	102,475	1967	337,915

(*KPSS. Naglyadnoe posobe po partiinomu stroitel'stvu*, Moscow, 1969, p. 49; *Kommunist, Kalendar'-spravochnik 1968*, Moscow, 1967, p. 364.) The above figures do not reflect a decline of some 50,000 primary organizations in the latter half of the 1950s, largely due to the amalgamation of collective farms, so that by 1961 the number of primary organizations was once again down to the 1947 level of some 295,000,

network among the masses is only partially reflected in the number of its primary organizations. For many of these are subdivided into shop or sectional organizations and the latter – as well as the smaller party organizations – may once again be split into party groups, with their own secretaries or group organizers, and in the case of shop organizations with more than 15 members their own party bureaux, whose functions in respect of the masses are identical with those of the smaller primary organizations.[33] The general tendency is to form subdivisions of the primary organizations wherever possible in order to adapt the party's structure as closely as possible to the productive process and thus to enhance its capacity for control; party organizations are enjoined to avoid 'the artificial unification' of members working in different branches of the same enterprise.[34] The 20th Congress amended the Party Statutes by reducing the minimum number of party members required for the formation of shop organizations within each primary organization from 100 to 50,[35] and one of the consequences of this measure has been an immense increase in the number of the party's effective outposts among the masses: between 1956 and 1971 shop organizations rose from 76,000 to 353,000 and party groups from 122,000 to 443,000.[36]

There has never been any doubt as to the responsibility which the primary organizations and their subdivisions exercise in regard to Soviet citizens outside the party's ranks. It is a responsibility which springs from the need 'to bring about a clear and profound understanding on the part of every person of his role and place in the common struggle'.[37] This refers first of all to the 'struggle' for production and implies that 'a man at work must always be in sight'.[38] The striking growth over the past 15 years in the number of party units is purposefully directed to this end. In agriculture, the party committees 'utilizing the net of brigade party organizations and party groups, can now broaden their

(*Partiinoe stroitel'stvo. Naglyadnoe posobe*, Moscow, 1971, p. 23.) The true measure of the growth in the number of primary party organizations in the past decade is therefore 75,000 or 25%.

[33] *Programmy i ustavy KPSS*, pp. 388–9.
[34] *Voprosy partiinoi raboty*, Moscow, 1959, pp. 214–15.
[35] *XX S'ezd*, vol. II, p. 431.
[36] *Partiinoe stroitel'stvo. Naglyadnoe posobe*, p. 23.
[37] *Partiinaya zhizn'*, 1959, no. 7, p. 4; 1972, no. 2, p. 6. See also para. 59 of the Party Statutes. (*Programmy i ustavy KPSS*, pp. 390–1.)
[38] *Pravda*, 21 January 1969.

influence, embrace every person and exercise systematic control over economic activity'.[39] In industry, 'the party *aktiv* of the shop organization knows the moods and needs of every person and makes possible the fullest use of his capabilities. Not a single incident . . . remains unnoticed in the collective'.[40]

But the party's responsibility also extends outside the enterprise to the private lives of Soviet citizens. Soviet sources continuously emphasize that 'to work in the families is a primary obligation of the factory party organization. The interests of the construction of communism demand that we shall not remain disinterested witnesses to what takes place in the Soviet family.'[41] Particularly in recent years, it has been noted that one of the main advantages of the smaller party units is their ability to know every person thoroughly not only at work but also at home. Writing of the party groups – the lowest units in the party hierarchy – two local functionaries put their case as follows:

In the centre of the party group's attention is the individual. The communists of the party group, communicating daily with the people, thoroughly study everyone: how he works, what his spiritual world is like, the peculiarities of his character, how he studies, broadens his horizons and spends his leisure, what conditions are like in the family. Nothing remains outside the range of vision of the communists.[42]

Once again, this is probably an overstatement of the actual situation. But it is a true statement of the aims of totalitarian organization. At any rate, it is this kind of activity by lower party organizations which more than anything else gives substance to the claims of Soviet spokesmen that the 'party enters organically into all cells and pores of Soviet society'.[43]

In Nazi Germany the organization of the masses was constructed on very similar lines. The direct responsibility of the party's primary organizations for the conduct and bearing of the population as well as the interlocking of the entire occupational and social structure with the centralized political hierarchy, the party, was even more pronounced than in Soviet Russia. For it was conducted with the typically German predisposition for

[39] *Ibid.*, 13 March 1968.   [40] *Kommunist*, 1968, no. 16, p. 79.
[41] *Partiinaya zhizn'*, 1960, no. 8, p. 51; also *Pravda*, 21 May 1968.
[42] *Partiinaya zhizn'*, 1967, no. 14, p. 44; also 1968, no. 1, pp. 43–6; 1969, no. 16, pp. 46–9.
[43] V. Stepanov, 'Partiya i kommunizm', *Kommunist*, 1967, no. 8, p. 21.

explicit organizational links and without the Soviet pretence of democratic forms.

What Lenin had termed 'transmission belts' Hitler no less appropriately described as 'smelting furnaces'.[44] According to Ley (who in his dual role as head of the party's organization department and leader of the German Labour Front was responsible both for the organizational activities of the party and for the largest of the mass organizations) the Nazis realized,

> that the organizational measures of the party could only come to full fruition when supplemented by the organization of the people, that is to say, by the mobilization of the energies of the people and by their concentration and deployment... If the party... represents the concentration of the political leadership of the people, then the people constitute the following and must be organized and trained according to the same principle.[45]

In contrast to Soviet Russia where the party strictly embraces only members (and candidate members), the Nazis constructed a four-tier organizational edifice in which the so-called party formations (*Partei-Gliederungen*), affiliated associations (*Angeschlossene Verbaende*) and organizations in the care of the party (*Betreute Organisationen*) were organizationally linked to the party proper, the NSDAP. The following were the principal organizations thus included:[46]

(1) *Party Formations (Partei-Gliederungen)*
      SS (*Schutzstaffel*)
      Stormtroops (*Sturmabteilungen* – SA)

[44] 'The gigantic organizations of our movement, the political bodies as well as the organizations of the SA and SS, the construction of our Labour Front, just as much as the state organizations of our army, these are all national and social smelting furnaces in which gradually a new German man will be formed.' (*Voelkischer Beobachter*, 3 May 1934.)

[45] *Voelkischer Beobachter*, 14 September 1936.

[46] Sources: H. Volz, *Daten der Geschichte der NSDAP*, Berlin-Leipzig, 1943; *Organisationsbuch*; Ruthe, *Nationalsozialismus*; H. Fabrizius, 'Organisatorischer Aufbau der NSDAP' in Lammers and Pfundtner, eds., *Verwaltungsakademie*, vol. I sequence 6a (see also vol. IV, *Nachtraege*); O. Gauweiler, *Die Rechtseinrichtungen und Rechtsaufgaben der Bewegung*, Munich, 1939; *Rang und Organisationsliste der NSDAP*, Stuttgart, n.d. (1946?). The formations and affiliated organizations of the party in existence as of 29 March 1935 are listed in a government decree of that date. (*Reichsgesetzblatt* – hereafter abbreviated as RGBl – vol. I, p. 502.)

NS-Motor Corps (*NS-Kraftfahr Korps* – NSKK)

NS-Women's League (*NS-Frauenschaft*)

NS-League of German Students (*NS-Deutscher Studentenbund* – NSDStB)

NS-League of German University Teachers (*NS-Deutscher Dozentenbund*)

Hitler Youth (*Hitlerjugend* – HJ)

NS-Flying Corps (*NS-Flieger Korps* – NSKF)

Reich Labour Service (*Reichsarbeitsdienst* – RAD)

(2) *Affiliated Associations (Angeschlossene Verbaende)*

German Labour Front (*Deutsche Arbeitsfront* – DAF)

NS-People's Welfare (*NS-Volkswohlfahrt* – NSV)

NS-League of German Physicians (*NS-Aerztebund*)

NS-League of Jurists (*NS-Reichtswahrerbund* – NSRB)

NS-League of Teachers (*NS-Lehrerbund* – NSLB)

NS-League of German Technology (*NS-Bund Deutscher Technik* – NSBDT)

NS-War Victims' Care (*NS-Kriegsopferversorgung* – NSKOV)

Reich League of German Civil Servants (*Reichsbund Deutscher Beamten* – RDB)

(3) *Organizations in the Care of the Party (Betreute Organisationen)*

German Women's Union (*Deutsches Frauenwerk*)

German Students' Association (*Deutsche Studentenschaft*)

NS-Association of University Alumni (*NS-Altherrenbund der Deutschen Studenten*)

NS-Reich League for Physical Exercises (*NS-Reichsbund fuer Leibesuebungen* – NSRL)

German Communal Association (*Deutscher Gemeindetag*).

Reich Food Estate (*Reichsnaehrstand*)

Reich Air Defence League (*Reichsluftschutzbund* – RLB)

NS-Reich Warriors' League (*NS-Reichskriegerbund*)

German Home Guard (*Deutscher Volkssturm*)

With the exception of the SS all the above organizations were effectively controlled by the party apparatus.[47] Their leaders

[47] It is no accident that the business interests, comprising the only associational groups with effective access to the centres of decision-making, especially in the early years, were not affiliated to the party, although

were usually either members of the party's Reich Directorate, the *Reichsleitung*, or occupied positions as departmental heads in it. This system of personal union reached down to all levels of the party hierarchy at which local branches of the organizations existed. As a rule this was the district (*Kreis*). Thus, for instance, the leader of the NS-League of Teachers was head of the Main Department for Educators (*Hauptamt fuer Erzieher*) in the Reich Directorate, while the leaders of the League's territorial subdivisions who bore the title of *Gau-* or *Kreiswalter* headed corresponding departments of *Gau* (region) or district officers of the party, as *Gau-* or *Kreisamtsleiter*. Some organizations such as the NS-League of University Teachers or the NS-League for German Technology maintained representatives only at the regional level, while the local leaders of others, notably of the Labour Front, the People's Welfare and Women's League, were attached to party organizations at all levels, down to the primary organization, the block (*Block*).

The position of four of the party formations, the SS, SA, NSKK and HJ was somewhat different. Their territorial units were placed 'at the disposition' of the corresponding offices of the party but they did not come under the disciplinary authority of the party's *Hoheitstraeger* (literally: bearer of sovereignty – the term was applied to all leaders of territorial party organizations down to the block). The SS moreover, although it was formally a party formation – its full title was *Schutzstaffel der NSDAP* – with an official party status equal to that of the SA, NSKK and HJ, could in no sense be regarded as a subordinate party organization. It was an elite corps reserved for special duties assigned by the Fuehrer, and for all practical purposes it existed outside the party.[48]

The NS-Flying Corps (NSFK) and the Reich Labour Service (RAD) are here classified as party formations although they were not officially designated as such. The NSFK was a para-military organization which incorporated the various pre-Nazi aviation

they were, of course, incorporated in the institutions of 'self-government' under the Minister of Economics. The many-cornered fights – involving agencies of the party, the Labour Front, and the Government – for organizational autonomy for business groups are discussed in A. Schweitzer, *Big Business in the Third Reich*, Bloomington, 1964.

[48] See *The Trial of the Major War Criminals before the International Military Tribunal* (henceforth cited as IMT), 42 vols., Nuremberg, 1947–9, vol. XXVI, pp. 190ff. The SA and NSKK also came under the direct command of Hitler but their status and power in relation to the party in no way equalled that of the SS.

societies. It came under the authority of Goering in his capacity as Minister of Aviation, but it had 'to fulfil political tasks exactly like the storm-troopers of the party formations',[49] and it was listed as one of the 'party formations' which Hitler Youth members were required to join on reaching the ages of 18 or 21.[50] RAD was the successor organization of the NS–Labour Service, a party formation created in 1931 but dissolved when the Law of 26 June 1935 introduced labour conscription for all Germans between the ages of 18–25.[51] This did not, however, affect 'the inner cohesiveness' between RAD and the party.[52] The leader of RAD was a *Reichsleiter* with a status analogous to that of the HJ leader and from 1942 RAD leaders were employed as senior party functionaries.[53] The territorial units of both the NSFK and RAD were placed 'at the disposition' of the party's *Hoheitstraeger* in the same way as other party formations, the former to district level and the latter down to that of the local group (*Ortsgruppe*), the next lower party echelon.

In general, it should be noted that the classification of the party's organizations was by no means uniform. Thus some Nazi sources list the German Women's Union as an affiliated organization and the Reich Food Estate either as an organization in the 'indirect' care of the party (*mittelbar betreute Organisation*), or not at all.[54] In a diagram which the former Treasurer of the party, Franz Xaver Schwarz, certified for the Nuremberg trials, an additional category of 'Further Organizations' (*Weitere Organisationen*) appears in which the Reich Food Estate is also grouped.[55] Other organizations thus classified by Schwarz are the Reich Air Defence League and the Home Guard. The former was incorporated into the party as late as 25 July 1944 and the relevant Fuehrer decree explicitly defined its status as 'an organization in the care of the party'.[56] The formation of the Home Guard was decreed two months later on 25 September 1944.[57]

[49] *Organisationsbuch*, p. 470e.
[50] *Vertrauliche Informationen* (confidential bulletin published by the Party Chancellory, Munich), 5 March 1943.
[51] RGBl, 1935, I, pp. 769–77.
[52] *Organisationsbuch*, p. 465.
[53] *Verfuegungen, Anordnungen, Bekanntgaben* – hereafter abbreviated as VAB – Partei-Kanzlei der NSDAP, 6 vols., Munich 1943–4, vol. I, pp. 724–5.
[54] See *Organisationsbuch*, p. 141; Volz, *Daten*, p. 151.
[55] IMT, vol. XXXI, in pocket at end of volume.
[56] RGBl, 1944, I, p. 165.　　　　　　　[57] *Ibid.*, p. 253.

It was militarily subordinated to Himmler in his capacity as C.-in-C. Home Army but its 'political and organizational' directives came from the Party Chancellory, where a special staff was created under the direction of a senior official, Helmut Friedrichs, who acted as Bormann's deputy.[58] The local units of the Home Guard were placed under the exclusive command of the regional leaders, who were also responsible for the selection of officers with the necessary 'political elan'.[59] Although it was not officially designated as a party organization, the Home Guard was indeed, as Bormann emphasized in one of his directives, a 'party affair'.[60]

Finally, the NS-Reich Warriors' League was never officially designated under any of the above categories; it is classed here among the third group of organizations because its status was wholly similar to that of other organizations in that group in fact, if not in name. The League was an outgrowth of the former *Kyffhaeuser Bund* and constituted a federation of veteran organizations; presumably because of its association with the armed forces, the League, beyond changing its name, was not overtly linked to the party. Its effective 'co-ordination' was nevertheless accomplished by 1938.[61] In June 1943 the League was dissolved and its constituent organizations were subordinated to the party 'in leadership, political and organizational matters'.[62]

---

58 *Ibid.* See also the captured Nazi records available on microfilm at the National Archives, Washington, D.C. – hereafter abbreviated as NA – Microcopy T–81, Roll 1, Serial number 1/11243.

59 NA, T–81, 1/11230, 1/11224–5.

60 *Ibid.*, 1/11229. On the role of the party, and particularly of its regional leaders, in the formation of the Home Guard, see also P. Huettenberger, *Die Gauleiter. Studie zum Wandel des Machtgefueges in der NSDAP*, Stuttgart, 1969, pp. 192ff.

61 See the reports of the security services on the reaction of veteran organizations to their incorporation into the League in NA, T–81, 153/157518–21. The dissolution of the *Stahlhelm*, politically the most active of the veteran organizations, was virtually completed by the end of 1935. (The minutes of a discussion held on 12 August 1935 between Hitler and Seldte, the leader of the *Stahlhelm*, which throw interesting light on the attitudes of both men to the question of the future of independent veteran organizations, are available at the Library of the British Foreign Office – henceforth cited as FO – File 3648H, Serial nos. EO32938–46.) For prior attempts to incorporate both the *Stahlhelm* and the *Kyffhaeuser* Bund into the SA as SA-Reserve I and SA-Reserve II respectively, see *Gutachten des Instituts fuer Zeitgeschichte*, Munich, 1957, pp. 370ff; also V. R. Berghahn, *Der Stahlhelm: Bund der Frontsoldaten 1918–1935*, Duesseldorf, 1966, pp. 263ff.

62 VAB, vol. IV, pp. 362 and 365.

However, no matter what the precise designation of any one organization might have been, it is clear that, with the exception of the SS, all of them were firmly anchored to the party both at the centre and at subordinate levels. Nor does it seem important to know what specific considerations led to the classification of an organization under any one of the three groups. The terminology used would imply different degrees of proximity to the party. It should be noted, however, that if proximity signified anything in this context – apart from distinctions in the legal status of each group, one of the main practical effects of which lay in the extent of the party's financial responsibility[63] – it does so only in terms of the national socialist convictions of the membership of the organizations as reflected in the proportion of party members (or potential party members, as in the case of the Hitler Youth) contained in each. It certainly does not indicate the degree of political control by the party; indeed, as has been seen, the authority with which the party *Hoheitstraeger* were vested in respect of some of the party formations fell short of that which they exercised over organizations in the second and third category.

The legitimation for the party's organizational leadership lay in its monopoly of *Menschenfuehrung*. In the words of the party manual, the party was 'responsible for the spiritual – ideological – national socialist preparation of the German people. From reasons of this kind alone derives the justification to organize people for their own sake.'[64] It was a monopoly which the party guarded zealously even in respect of its own creations. Thus, when Ley nurtured ambitions to make the Labour Front organizationally independent of the party, Hess in February 1938 emphasized in a letter to Goering:

> If today the German Labour Front is active in the field of *Menschenfuehrung*, it does so solely by order of the party . . . It is no accident that the Fuehrer, by a decree of 24 July 1934, that is, immediately following 30 June 1934 [the Roehm purge] entrusted me with the task of uniformly representing *the entire party* in the legislation of the Reich.[65]

[63] A. Lingg, *Die Verwaltung der Nationalsozialistischen Deutschen Arbeiterpartei*, Munich, 1939, pp. 114ff.
[64] *Organisationsbuch*, p. 86.
[65] NA, T-81, 1/11021–2. (Emphasis in original.) See also Schweitzer, *Big Business in the Third Reich*, pp. 519–20. As is instanced above, the Nazis sometimes used the terms 'party' or 'movement' to mean the entire complex of party-affiliated organizations.

The network of Nazi organizations reached into every section of German society. 'The organization of the community', Hitler declared

> is a thing gigantic and unique. There is hardly a German at the present time who is not personally anchored and active in one or another of the formations of the national socialist community. It reaches into every house, every workshop and every factory, into every town and village.[66]

The 'solid core' of these organizations, as Hitler reaffirmed on the same occasion in terms similar to the most popular of Soviet formulations, was the party. Nor were the Nazis notably reticent about the basic objectives of the organizational effort. As Ley put it: 'The organization of the party with its affiliated organizations must be in a position to compel every German to take up an attitude towards our ideas [*zur Stellungnahme zu unseren Ideen zu zwingen*].'[67]

That these were no idle pretentions may be readily seen from a directive of the regional party office (*Gauleitung*) of Baden, dated 5 March 1942, concerning recruitment into the party and its organizations among the population of newly-annexed Alsace.[68] The directive instructed subordinate party offices to compile rolls on which all inhabitants above the age of 18 were to be classified according to their eligibility for membership in the party or in one of its organizations. One roll was to include all those eligible for immediate recruitment, another was to list those for whom a period of probation would be required, while a third ('control list') was to be made up of the remainder. Even in regard to those listed on the first roll, party offices were told to be 'generous' and to overlook 'occasional grumbling and criticism'.

> As it is the aim of the movement [the directive went on] to embrace all Germans somehow in a national socialist organization so as to make it possible to influence and lead them in the spirit of the movement, the objective will be . . . to include

---

[66] *Voelkischer Beobachter*, 14 September 1938; also *ibid.*, 15 September 1935. For a similar statement by Ley, characteristically rendered more explicit by such boasts as 'Nobody can escape us . . .' see *Der Angriff*, 30 January 1942.

[67] Quoted from speech to a conference of HJ leaders, in *Hoheitstraeger*, 1937, no. 1, pp. 22–3.

[68] IMT, vol. xxxviii, pp. 576ff (732-RF).

around 90% of the population on the rolls and to enter onto the control list only those who as racially inferior, asocial or anti-German elements are unworthy to join an organization that is led by or is in the care of the party.

Similar measures with similar purpose had earlier been taken in the old Reich.[69] They reveal both the crucial importance in Nazi eyes of the organizational buttress needed 'to influence and lead . . . in the spirit of the movement' and the thoroughness with which the party set out to organize the nation.

Just as the Bolsheviks did in Soviet Russia, so the Nazis in Germany also forged direct links between the leadership and the people by means of the party's basic units, with the difference that once again the Nazis were able to do so not only much faster but also much more methodically. The membership of the NSDAP was organized according to residence: the primary organization of the party was the residential block. The outstanding feature of Nazi organization was the fact that this primary unit upon which the entire party pyramid rested was formed on the basis not of party membership but of population. The party manual prescribed that a block should consist of 40–60 households but that 'if possible' the number of households should not exceed fifty.[70] The presence or absence of party members in the block was irrelevant to its territorial boundaries. All that was necessary was that one party member capable of fulfilling the duties of the block leader should be available. During the war years even this requirement was not always met, and in the absence of a suitable party member, other persons, usually from among those active in one of the party's formations or affiliated associations, were assigned to the post.[71] This organizational structure alone, adapted as it was not to the internal organizational requirements of the party but to the overriding purpose of mobilizing the masses, throws into relief one of the main functions of the party in Nazi Germany.

[69] See the 1938 data for 'non-organized' persons in 58 local groups of one district (Trier-Land-West) in F. J. Heyen, *Nationalsozialismus im Alltag*, Boppard-on-Rhine, 1967, pp. 328ff. ('Non-organized' is defined as referring to persons who did not belong to the party, its formations and affiliated associations, exclusive, that is, of members of organizations in the care of the party.)

[70] *Organisationsbuch*, p. 99.

[71] NA, T-81, 23/10928; see also K. Pokorny, *Kommentar zum Gesetz zur Befreiung von Nationalsozialismus und Militarismus*, Frankfurt, 1947, p. 319.

All *Hoheitstraeger* of the party were 'responsible for the orderly and good care of all members of the community within their areas of sovereignty'.[72] But the party's principal instrument in discharging this responsibility was the primary organization, the block. The block leader together with his assistants (*Blockhelfer*), who were placed in charge of individual houses or groups of houses,[73] and the block wardens (*Blockwalter*) of DAF, NSV and NS-Women's League, operating under the block leader's disciplinary authority, were in close and constant contact with the inhabitants of the block. Matters affecting the internal activities of the party were as a rule conducted by the next two higher party organizations, by the cell (*Zelle*) or, in smaller localities, by the local group. The internal party functions of the block leader were normally confined to the collection of party dues, his 'best opportunity for maintaining the necessary personal contact with party members'.[74] The primary responsibility of the block leader was to organize the masses. It was through him that the regime could hope to bring about a state of affairs in which 'not only every member of the community finds his or her way to the party in case of need, but the party, on its own initiative and in accordance with the will of the Fuehrer, reaches all members of the community and takes care of them'.[75] At the same time, it was the existence of the block leaders and their staffs which enabled men like Ley to claim that 'nothing escapes the party; the smallest movement, excitement, discontent or consent is noted by the party as by a never-failing seismograph'.[76]

In January 1943 there were altogether 581,347 blocks in an area containing a total population of 90.9 million out of which at least 4.5 million were officially regarded as non-Germans.[77] This would give an average of approximately one block to 150 inhabitants. The proportion of primary organizations to population in Soviet Russia is, of course, much lower – approximately 1:660. A comparison of the effective organizational coverage of

---

[72] *Organisationsbuch*, p. 98a; also p. 132/3/4.
[73] The party manual merely 'recommended' the appointment of such assistants – also known as house wardens (*Hauswarte*) – from among party members or other 'suitable' persons.
[74] *Organisationsbuch*, p. 102.
[75] *Ibid.*, p. 98a.
[76] *Der Angriff*, 9 April 1942.
[77] *Die Gaue und Kreise der NSDAP*, Der Reichsorganisationsleiter, Munich, 1943, sequence O1.

the two parties in these terms is not very meaningful, however, if only because the latter figure takes no account of the CPSU's shop organizations and party groups. All that can be said by way of comparison is that party outposts among the masses were more evenly distributed in Nazi Germany, where their deployment was directly related to the number of inhabitants in any given area, than in Soviet Russia where it is influenced by the irregular incidence of party membership.

Perhaps the last word on the effectiveness of the organizational leash which the Nazi party placed upon German society belongs to a report of the Main Security Office of the Reich (the *Reichs-sicherheitshauptamt* or RSHA) written at the end of March 1945:

> The German people are used to discipline. Since 1933 they have felt themselves watched and supervised from all sides right up to the door-step by the ramified apparatus of the party, its formations and affiliated associations. Traditional respect for the police does the rest . . .[78]

No more than the outlines of the organizational presence of the two parties have been sketched above. They may suffice, however, to indicate the main source of the party's strength in the mobilization of the masses – its ability to furnish the essential element of control. The party's organizational presence projected through its primary units – and indirectly through the mass organizations – embraced the people in a firm clasp within which their mobilization could proceed at the pace and in the direction dictated by the leadership. Hannah Arendt has rightly pointed out that it is organization rather than terror which should be seen as the reverse side of totalitarian propaganda.[79] At the same time, however, she has been one of the foremost exponents of the view that terror was the very hallmark of totalitarianism. This judgment and similar views of many others who wrote under the impact of the gas chambers and the 'corrective labour' camps, does not do justice to the immense potentialities for non-terroristic compulsion that inhere in totalitarian organization, a compulsion that is both quantitatively and qualitatively different from the kind of violence for which the SS in Germany and the NKVD in

---

[78] Quoted in M. G. Steinert, *Hitlers Krieg und die Deutschen*, Duesseldorf and Vienna, 1970, p. 576. The report is also interesting as an assessment by the RSHA of popular attitudes in the last weeks of the war.

[79] H. Arendt, *The Origins of Totalitarianism*, 2nd ed., New York, 1958, p. 364.

Stalinist Russia have become symbols. The use of massive terror, so long regarded as a distinctive feature of totalitarian government, may well become superfluous under 'perfect' totalitarian conditions, in which the mobilization of the masses is carried forward by a symbiosis of propaganda and organization along a new, uniquely totalitarian continuum, to which the conventional concepts of both consent and coercion are equally irrelevant.

4: POLITICAL AGITATION IN NAZI GERMANY

The Role of the Rank and File

The first feature to be noted about the propaganda contribution of the Nazi party is related to the existence of a mass party as such. The fact that millions of men and women protest their loyalty to the regime by joining the ranks of the party itself has a 'demonstration effect' on the population at large. In terms of the individual, the knowledge that one's friends and neighbours appear to be convinced Nazis may be fraught with propaganda significance more enduring and far-reaching than that which attaches to many of the formal and active propaganda measures. As Ernst Roehm, the leader of the SA, put it: 'Every brown troop marching under the swastika was a living call to the bystander: "Come along, comrade".'[1]

Long before coming to power the Nazis had claimed the status of an 'elite' for the party. These pretensions notwithstanding the NSDAP had grown into a mass party numbering over 1.1 million members on the day of the *Machtergreifung*.[2] A general restriction on party entry was imposed as of 1 May 1933 with the avowed objective of preventing the mass influx of opportunist

---

[1] 'Die braunen Bataillione der deutschen Revolution', *NS-Monatshefte*, 1934, no. 46, p. 8.

[2] The figure of 719,446 party members for 30 January 1933 given by W. Schaefer, *NSDAP, Entwicklung und Struktur der Staatspartei des Dritten Reiches*, Hanover and Frankfurt, 1956, p. 17, and D. Orlow, *The History of the Nazi Party: 1919–1933*, Pittsburgh, 1969, p. 239, n. 1, is based on a misreading of the 1935 party census data; the same is true of the figure of 850,000 members cited by D. Schoenbaum, *Hitler's Social Revolution: Class and Status in Nazi Germany 1933–1939*, London, 1967, pp. 38 and 71. Both figures relate to party members who joined before 30 January 1933 and were still in the party at the time of the 1935 census: 719,446 is the number of party members who joined between 15 September 1930 and 30 January 1933; 850,000 (more precisely – 849,009) is the total number of party members with pre-1933 seniority and is made up of the above 719,446 plus 129,563 earlier recruits. (*Partei-Statistik*, Der Reichsorganisationsleiter, 4 vols., n. p., n.d., vol. I, p. 16.)

elements into the party.[3] In fact, party growth continued at a rising rate throughout 1933 and 1934 and by the beginning of 1935 the party had more than doubled its size to some 2.5 million members. A further net expansion of close on 300,000 members occurred until mid-1937. On 1 May 1937 a 'relaxation' (*Lockerung*) of admissions was decreed and two years later (1 May 1939) restrictions on entry into the party were completely lifted. By this time party membership had doubled once again to 5.3 million. It continued to rise steadily to reach 7.1 million in February 1942, when entrance restrictions were reimposed for all except Hitler Youth graduates. But exceptions were made throughout the remaining war years not only for wounded war veterans but also for others whose membership was considered to serve the cause of the regime. Party growth continued unabated and in May 1943, the last date for which official figures are available, membership stood at 7.6 million.[4] An estimate of some 8 million party members at the end of the Third Reich cannot therefore be far off the mark.

In part, the continued expansion of the NSDAP no doubt derived from the enlistment of various elite groups: a high degree of fusion between social elite and ruling party is built into the totalitarian system. In Nazi Germany it resulted not only from the promotion of the party's 'old fighters' into the ranks of the Nazi

---

[3] In *Mein Kampf* (pp. 656–7), Hitler had already announced: 'The greatest danger that can threaten a movement is an abnormally rapid growth in membership as the result of too quick successes. For as carefully as all cowardly and selfish persons will shun a movement while it is engaged in bitter struggles, as quickly will they aspire to membership when events render a great success of the party probable . . . It is therefore very necessary that a movement should, out of sheer instinct for self-preservation, close admissions as soon as success is attained, and henceforward enlarge its organization only with the greatest care and after the most thorough examination. Only thus will it be able to maintain the nucleus of the movement fresh and healthy.'

[4] All figures, except that for the 1935 census, are from the records of the Party Treasurer's Office consulted at the Berlin Document Center. The Nazis, once in power, were extremely reticent about party membership data. As far as could be ascertained only two sets of figures covering the whole of the Reich were made public from official sources. The first related to the findings of the party census of 1935 and was published in the party training journal *Der Schulungsbrief*, 1938, no. 8–9. The second occasion when membership figures were released, this time to a wider public, was in 1943 when the *Voelkischer Beobachter* of 25–6 December, in an article designed to highlight the contribution of party members to the war effort, revealing that the party counted 6.5 million men in its ranks as of 1 May 1943. On 30 September 1944 the Party

elite, but also, to a more considerable extent, from the absorption of the pre-revolutionary elite into the ranks of the Nazi party. Yet this alone does not explain the enormous increase in membership which the NSDAP experienced during the 12 years of its existence as the ruling party of Nazi Germany. What explains it is the regime's need for a mass party to perform the manifold functions of mobilization.

The Nazis aimed at a party comprising 10% of the adult population.[5] Considerations about its social composition did not preoccupy the NSDAP in the immediate sense in which this has been true of the Soviet party. But the few central directives which concern themselves with the social profile of the party point to the aim of achieving a well-balanced membership that would be more or less representative of the socio-economic distribution of the population as a whole.[6] There are no data on the overall social composition of the party beyond the January 1935 party census. The 1935 data show that the circumstances of power did not transform the NSDAP into an exclusive organization of the socially privileged.[7] True, by and large elite groups were already

Treasurer ordered a general restriction on party recruitment 'until further notice' for all except soldiers wounded in combat. (NA, T-454, 7/914136.)

[5] Lingg, *Verwaltung*, p. 163. By 1940 this optimum level had been well exceeded: the number of adult Germans in May 1939 was 57 million. (*Statistisches Jahrbuch fuer das Deutsche Reich 1939–40*, p. 24.) During the war Hitler intimated to his associates that he would reduce membership to this proportion in the post-war years. (*Hitlers Tischgespraeche*, p. 491; see also below p. 95, n. 36.) Male party members already constituted 10.2% of male adults in the population in 1935. By 1943 this proportion had risen to 23% – 6.5 million male members out of a total male adult population of approx. 28.3 million. Thus well over every fifth German male was a member of the NSDAP. (The figure for male party members is from the special report of the party Statistical Office, published in part in *Voelkischer Beobachter*, 25–26 December 1943 as mentioned earlier. The figure for all adult German males is calculated from the data for May 1939 and the official projections for May 1945; see *Statistisches Jahrbuch fuer das Deutsche Reich 1941–2*, p. 25.) Women were always greatly under-represented in the party; in 1935 they numbered 136,197, or 5.5% of the party membership and 0.5% of all adult women in the population. (*Partei-Statistik*, vol. i, pp. 40, 43.)

[6] This is clearly evident in the proposal for future recruitment which the authors of the party census appended to their findings. (*Partei-Statistik*, vol. i, pp. 44, 56, 65 and *passim*.)

[7] Workers alone constituted 30.3% of the party and many members of the lower middle class may be presumed among such categories as white collar employees (19.4%), craftsmen (8.3%), farmers (10.2%) and several others. (*Ibid.*, p. 70.)

over-represented in the party relative to their numerical strength in the population: they were more vulnerable to the ever-present pressures and temptations to join the ranks of the ruling party. In later years party penetration of these groups undoubtedly increased further. But a party which included every tenth adult German in its ranks was well able to absorb such groups without impairing its character as a mass party with broad representation in the lower reaches of German society.

The Nazis did not only succeed in building up a mass organization relatively quickly; they were also particularly inventive at enhancing the party's 'demonstration effect' still further through the use of visual symbols. The existence of the manifold party formations and affiliated organizations, with a membership several times that of the party, and with uniforms and insignia which to the uninitiated were indistinguishable from those of the party itself, created an overwhelming impression of the party's omnipresence.[8] The technique that appealed to the intrinsic desire of the individual 'to belong', to be at one with the majority, which Hitler had so masterfully developed in the conduct of Nazi mass meetings in the early years, came to be applied on a nation-wide scale with evident deliberation and clear-headed purpose.

In the Third Reich it was not necessary to wait for the elections or sporadic plebiscites to find proof of support of 99.59% of the population for the regime. That support was demonstrated daily by the men and women who wore the party badge in their lapels on their way to and from work and the party uniforms on their way to and from public meetings and demonstrations. The purpose of the party emblem was 'to give expression to the strength and power of the movement ... to recall this strength and unity constantly to the consciousness of the people'.[9] An article in the party's propaganda organ declared:

The Fuehrer has not given the Political Leader his service dress so that he may cut a 'good figure' at social events. By wearing his uniform on every party duty and by having his

---

[8] The wearing of national socialist insignia at all times was obligatory for members of the party, its formations and affiliated organizations, except during working hours for those party members who were employed in Jewish enterprises. (*Organisationsbuch*, p. 8.) In 1944 the Party Chancellory reminded members that this applied also during visits abroad, with the single exceptions of Switzerland and Sweden. (VAB, vol. vi, pp. 7–9.)

[9] VAB, vol. i, p. 174.

badges *always visibly* pinned to his civilian dress, the Political Leader demonstrates that he . . . manifestly subordinates himself to the will of the Fuehrer. . . We must constantly . . . show that we exist. Those who opposed us yesterday and those who today view us with disfavour must day by day gain the impression that the Political Leaders stand guard over the achievements of the national socialist revolution. . .[10]

The propaganda effect of Nazi symbols was mainly projected through members of the party and its organizations; but in the course of time the ritual of the Third Reich transformed every German citizen into a permanent bearer of Nazi propaganda. One need not dwell on the consequences that could ensue for an unemployed person who failed to respond to the '*Heil Hitler!*' salute of a labour exchange official;[11] it required a person of considerable strength of character to resist for long this kind of 'voluntary compulsion' when it was exercised every day all around him. A person may have remained politically indifferent or even hostile to the regime, yet by raising his arm to the Fuehrer, he made a clearly visible gesture in support of the regime, and thereby turned himself into an agent of the 'demonstration effect' radiated by the party.[12]

---

[10] *Unser Wille und Weg*, 1935, no. 12, pp. 424–5. (Emphasis in original.) See also Schwarz von Berk, *Die sozialistische Auslese*, Breslau, 1934, pp. 25ff. The term 'Political Leader' (*Politischer Leiter*) applied to all party functionaries, i.e. it included the *Hoheitstraeger* as well as the members of their staffs, whether paid or unpaid.

During the war the wearing of party uniforms apparently also had some counterproductive aspects. A memorandum submitted to Rosenberg by a member of his staff in September 1944 refers to the fact that the brown uniforms have 'already created resentment' on the part of the people who asked themselves why their wearers had not been drafted into the armed forces. The memorandum which is extremely critical of the party's role during the war, and in particular of the bureaucratization engendered by Bormann's Chancellory is among the Rosenberg records in Archives du Centre de Documentation Juive Contemporaine – hereafter abbreviated to ACDJC – Paris, Document CXL-32. It bears the initials U/Sz and was presumably authored by either Gerhard Utikal or Gotthard Urban, but more probably by the former. (See also below p. 213.) Already for some time prior to this the party authorities had been troubled by rumours that party members were not being drafted to the same extent as others. (*Vertrauliche Informationen*, 6 and 25 June 1942.)

[11] F. M. Marx, 'State Propaganda in Nazi Germany', in H. L. Childs, ed., *Propaganda and Dictatorship*, Princeton, 1936, p. 17.

[12] Bruno Bettelheim stresses the disintegrative effect of the Hitler salute on the personality of the dissenter and its potency as an instrument of

The 'demonstration effect' of the Nazi party was further augmented by the deployment of massed formations at parades and public rallies. No propaganda meeting was complete without its contingent of uniformed party members who lined the stage and gangways and provided the indispensable 'extras' for Nazi pageantry. Few party orators would address a public meeting unless their entrances and exits were suitably accompanied by a party choir or band.[13] And the presence of large numbers of party members among the audience assured the speaker of a minimum guaranteed audience and a suitably enthusiastic 'resonance'.[14] The 'deliberately deployed applause'[15] was an essential component of the Nazi propaganda meeting, as were the inevitable chants of 'Sieg Heil!' which often drowned the speaker's more impassioned pronouncements. Thus, during a march-past, at a public rally, or at any one of the various national socialist propaganda events the party rank and file on the stage and among the audience improved both the quality of the propaganda performance and the enthusiasm of its reception.

The Nazis were not content with the largely passive 'demonstration effect' of the party masses. They demanded of the individual party member that he should be an active fighter on behalf of the cause. The propaganda relevance of such activism was twofold: every party member was required to be, first, a permanent mouthpiece of the regime, i.e. to spread the word of the party far and wide and instantly to counter rumours, defeatism and hostile views; and, secondly, to be in his conduct and actions a living example of national socialist 'bearing' (*Haltung*) upon which the rest of the population could model itself.

The NSDAP expected its members 'always and everywhere to

self-persuasion: 'To Hitler's followers, giving the salute was an expression of self-assertion, of power ... For an opponent of the regime it worked exactly the opposite. Every time he had to greet somebody in public he had an experience that shook and weakened his integration. More specifically, if the situation forced him to salute, he immediately felt a traitor to his deepest convictions. So he had to pretend to himself that it did not count. Or to put it another way: he could not change his action – he *had* to give the Hitler salute. Since one's integration rests on acting in accord with one's beliefs, the only way to retain his integration was to change his beliefs.' (*The Informed Heart*, New York, 1960, pp. 290–1.)

[13] *Die Propaganda Richtlinien fuer die Propagandisten der NSDAP*, Baden, 1942, p. 11.

[14] *Unser Wille und Weg*, 1936, no. 10, p. 326.

[15] *Ibid.*, 1939, no. 7, p. 166.

regard themselves as carriers of the Fuehrer's word'.[16] It was the duty of

> every party member ... if necessary relying only upon himself, to intervene and raise his voice wherever he encounters subversive rumours, thoughtless or malicious talk ... or views unworthy of a German ... Party members who maintain a tactless [*sic!*] and cowardly silence in the face of such things harm the prestige of the party and are not worthy to be its members.[17]

In the mass membership of the party the regime disposed over millions of informal propagandists who, moreover, dispensed a type of propaganda which none of the other media could match. It was a personal and therefore flexible propaganda, which was adjusted to the individual recipient (or number of recipients) and could take account of the specific circumstances of each case. Given a sufficiently large party membership and its optimal distribution among the population, the party's individual oral propaganda could operate automatically wherever the need arose. It did not have to wait for a signal from above but could react instantaneously wherever enthusiasm waned or discontent began to manifest itself. And finally, it was propaganda from below, from among the people, lacking the often distrusted imprint of official pronouncements. In the words of a propaganda directive issued by the Duesseldorf regional party office: 'The slogans have effect only when they are carried among the people, so to speak, privately and unobtrusively, i.e. unofficially', without 'any hint' that they derive 'from above'.[18]

The regime endeavoured to maintain the party masses at a high pitch of propaganda activism and constantly sought to impress the rank and file with the importance of what the Nazis

---

[16] *Hoheitstraeger*, 1937, no. 8, p. 23.

[17] Party Chancellory circular of 20 March 1943, in NA, T-81, 1/12144; also 1/10853–5 and 1/11628.

[18] NA, T-81, 32/28599. Especially in the last years of World War II the Nazis often sought 'neutral' media for their propaganda messages. In May 1943 regional propaganda offices were instructed to avoid issuing propaganda materials over the imprint of the party; instead brochures and posters were to bear the imprint 'Universum Publishing House' and the name of the regional capital in which the material was published. When one region published a propaganda brochure which was otherwise 'excellent' over the official party imprint, a central directive noted that the 'imprint necessarily reduces the effectiveness of the brochure as the party-official publication is at once recognizable'. (*Ibid.*, 24/21882.)

called word-of-mouth propaganda (*Mundpropaganda*). 'It is necessary', stated an article in the party's propaganda journal,

> to show the party member that he too can and must be a propagandist for the movement. Many believe that propaganda is a specialized activity which can only be carried on by the Reich Propaganda Office [*Reichspropagandaleitung*] and its subordinate agencies... Mass demonstrations, the use of the radio, films, the press, posters, etc., these are all tasks at which the individual may at most lend a helping hand. But one form of propaganda – and by no means the least important – will always have to be carried on by the individual party member: *propaganda from mouth to mouth, from person to person*; it is propaganda of the most advanced frontline.[19]

The Reich Propaganda Office of the party issued weekly slogans which were to guide the party's word-of-mouth propaganda throughout Germany during that week. Usually these were generalized affirmations such as 'Our strength lies in discipline' or 'In Germany no one thinks today of rotten compromise, the entire people think only of total war.'[20] In addition, the Reich Propaganda Office from time to time instructed party organizations on specific matters which in its opinion warranted informal propaganda intervention including, in some cases, the deliberate spreading of rumours. Thus one propaganda directive explained that the fact that so many Russians knew German was not indicative of a high cultural level but merely proof of the Soviet Union's longstanding subversive designs.[21] Another called on the party's word-of-mouth propaganda to combat rumours that the bombing of Berlin received more consideration by the authorities than that of other towns.[22]

Similar instructions were also issued by the regional and district propaganda offices of the party. Frequently these pertained to local developments, but sometimes they also dealt with

---

19 *Unser Wille und Weg*, 1939, no. 5, p. 116. (Emphasis in original.)
20 NA, T-81, 24/21901 and 117/137484.
21 *Ibid.*, 168/307579. That the confrontation of German civilians with Russians among the forced labourers (*Ostarbeiter*) and prisoners of war undermined the propaganda-fostered stereotype of Slavic 'bolshevized subhumanity' is repeatedly noted in the reports of the security services. (Bundesarchiv Koblenz – henceforth abbreviated as BA – File R 58/182; H. Boberach, ed., *Meldungen aus dem Reich. Auswahl aus den geheimen Lageberichten des Sicherheitsdientes der SS 1939–1944*, Berlin, 1965, pp. 287, 481ff; Steinert, *Hitler's Krieg*, pp. 309, 378ff.)
22 NA, T-81, 24/21923; see also *Goebbels Diaries*, pp. 335 and 421.

national themes. Thus, for instance, a directive of one district propaganda office instructed its local groups both in the current rumours and the replies to be given to them in the following manner: rumour – the Americans are 'quite decent fellows' because they had given prisoners of the Hitler Youth Division sweets and chocolates before sending them home on the ground that they did not fight women and children; reply – (a) America's war against women and children is confirmed by aerial strafing of civilians, (b) the Americans paved the way for Soviet domination and the spread of hunger and misery, (c) even if the individual enemy soldiers were decent men, this would not influence the Roosevelt–Churchill policies aimed at destroying the German nation.[23] A propaganda directive of another district office, referring to the plot of 20 July 1944, listed the points to be stressed in word-of-mouth propaganda as follows: Hitler's escape was not accidental but due to providence; it is wholly inappropriate to speak of 'treacherous officer cliques' – these 'few criminals' must not be allowed to besmirch the 'honourable name of the German officer and soldier', crises had always proved to be a source of strength to national socialism; and finally, it was to be especially emphasized that 'in the entire Reich not one hand was raised in support of the criminals'.[24]

In the latter case, word-of-mouth propaganda was merely used to amplify the official propaganda theme. Its real strength, as is already evident from the previously quoted examples, lay in the fact that it could tackle themes which official propaganda could not even afford to acknowledge. When in June 1940 some sections of the German public seemed to receive the news of Italy's belated entry into the war with a notable lack of enthusiasm and even with some suspicion and cynicism – recalling the behaviour of Italy in World War I and expressing disparaging views about the fighting qualities of the Italian soldier – Goebbels directed that

> a wrong conception of the Italian conduct of the war must be prevented from striking root; this would offend and depress the Italians. Through the skilful creation of rumours – since one can neither speak nor write of such matters – the realization must be anchored in the people that Italy did not yet attack simply because an attack at this moment was not desired, and

[23] NA, T-81, 65–74255; also BA, R 55/602, fol. 149.
[24] NA, T-81, 167/306442.

the conviction must be fostered that Italy would certainly attack when conditions were ripe . . .[25]

Another example, also concerned with the delicate subject of intra-Axis relations was the 'Yellow Peril' issue about which Goebbels wrote in his diary on 11 March 1942:

> This theme cannot be discussed at all today either positively or negatively. The excellent reasons which we can give for our present attitudes are unsuitable for public discussion because they would undoubtedly offend the Japanese . . . We must therefore try to carry the real reasons to the people by word-of-mouth propaganda but refrain from discussing the problem openly.[26]

In the latter half of World War II word-of-mouth propaganda was notably intensified in proportion as the morale of the nation declined and the regime's formal propaganda media became increasingly suspect in the eyes of the people. In February 1943 the party's 'call evenings' (*Sprechabende* – not to be confused with the *Volksprechtage* mentioned below) which had been customary in the years of the struggle for power were re-introduced.[27] These were closed party gatherings (held approximately once a month at the level of the party cell or the smaller local group) whose principal object was to mobilize the party membership for propaganda duties, and specifically 'to arm party members for all questions arising in public discussion'.[28] One month later the 'Propaganda Rings' which since their creation in 1935 had served to co-ordinate propaganda activities down to the district level and consisted predominantly of representatives of the party formations and organizations, were extended downwards to the local group for the declared purpose of augmenting the volume of word-of-mouth propaganda.[29] Not only members of the party and its organizations but school children of the higher grades and such persons as postmen, tram conductors, hairdressers, doctors and midwives, and gas and electricity meter

---

[25] W. A. Boelcke, ed., *Kriegspropaganda 1939–41: Geheime Minister-konferenzen im Reichspropagandaministerium*, Stuttgart, 1966, p. 392. One week later Goebbels found it necessary to return to the subject. (*Ibid.*, p. 402.)

[26] *Goebbels Diaries*, p. 79; see also VAB, vol. I, p. 174.

[27] VAB, vol. VI, pp. 24–7.

[28] NA, T-81, 117/137463–4.

[29] *Ibid.*, 63/70165–6.

readers were systematically deployed in the struggle against rapidly spreading defeatism.[30]

The following extract from a district propaganda directive dated 14 September 1944 conveys something of the near-hysteria which characterized the party's efforts to restore popular morale in the closing stages of the war:

> In recent days more and more complaints are heard that men and women when shopping in retail stores ... conduct in a wholly irresponsible manner defeatist conversations tending to destroy the morale of the people. Unfortunately it must be affirmed that a large number of shop owners, even when they are party members, not only tolerate such enemy propaganda, but in many cases partake in the disintegration of popular morale. The district leader will take the *strictest measures* against these members of the community and of the party. All Political Leaders and party members as well as all members of the NS-Women's League are to be *immediately* directed to oppose these despicable rumour-mongers and defeatists *with all means*. Shop owners who continue to tolerate such defeatist and destructive talk in their shops are to be reported to the district office at once ... Political Leaders, party members and members of the NS-Women's League who witness such occurrences in shops and do not immediately intervene with the necessary strictness become guilty of assisting the enemy and will be immediately brought to account.[31]

The third category of rank-and-file propaganda to be discussed is propaganda by emulation. To be a party member meant to be an example to others in deed as well as in word. In their daily conduct, their discipline, devotion, courage and industry, party members were to personify the virtues which the regime sought to instil in the population as a whole. It was through the party masses that the gradually emerging qualities of 'the new German man' would be demonstrated to the nation at every stage of the socialization process and in regard to such diverse matters as family morals, patriotism, artistic appreciation or the all-important, unquestioning obedience to the Fuehrer and his appointed officials. In the words of the director of party training: 'Every propaganda for a *Weltanschauung* is pointless if it is only carried

---

30 *Der Aktivist. Nationalsozialistische Propaganda im Gau Sued-Hannover–Braunschweig*, 1944, no. 4, p. 38; NA, T–81, 1/10817, 90/103632.
31 NA, T-81, 65/74256. (Emphasis in original.)

on by words ... If our movement is to live and be victorious for all times ... then every bearer of the movement and especially every leader must be a living model for this *Weltanschauung.*[32]

Apart from volunteering for active duty in the party and its ancilliary organizations, this meant generous contributions to the various welfare drives, regular attendance at public meetings and demonstrations, and the strict boycotting of Jewish shops and acquaintances. The party member was expected as a matter of course to lead an exemplary family life, to send his children to the Hitler Youth, to sever active connections with the Church and to bring his family to the various national socialist ceremonies aimed, among others, at undermining religious allegiance by replacing its ritual. The conduct of the party member's family was as important for the propaganda needs of the party as that of the party member himself. 'We must make it clear to every one', wrote one party official,

> that there can be no good national socialist whose wife has not learned to think and act as he himself. The unity of the family, not least in the ideological sphere, is an indispensable requirement. It cannot be a matter of indifference to the party if the wife of a party member grumbles in shops when for once there is a shortage of butter.[33]

Party members were urged to be polite and helpful to their fellow citizens at all times and encouraged to perform a daily average of three 'good deeds', such as helping elderly people across the street or vacating their seats in crowded tramcars. The idea was that boy-scout virtues of this type would pay propaganda dividends by endearing the party to the people. As one writer put it, a person witnessing such an incident,

> who sees your party emblem, although he may otherwise tend to complain and grumble, will at least be given cause for thought. If that happens to him often and he always sees our symbol on these occasions, be assured that he will gradually realize that butter and bacon contribute damned little to the unity of the people. If he only thinks, 'They are decent fellows after all', a great deal will already have been accomplished.[34]

[32] O. Gohdes, 'Der neue deutsche Mensch', *Schulungsbrief*, 1934, no. 7, p. 9.
[33] *Unser Wille und Weg*, 1939, no. 5, p. 116.
[34] *Ibid.*, 1936, no. 2, p. 58.

It was only with the outbreak of World War II that party membership came to involve both greater hazards and more strenuous duties. Party members were required to volunteer for active service and to excel at soldierly bearing in general. At home the party expected its members to be active in civil defence and to lead the rest of the population by helping to raise output in mine and factory and volunteering for such extra duties as bringing in the harvest, building fortifications and assisting in various welfare activities. As the tide of war began to turn and to impose its 'total' exigencies on Germany too, the exhortations of the leadership calling upon party members to place themselves at the vanguard of the national effort became ever more urgent. With every party member 'an activist, self-reliant fighter even more than hitherto', the party was to become 'the motor for the transformation of the home front'. What the 'relentless' nature of the struggle demanded of party members were no longer 'contributions but sacrifices'; the personal example of party members was 'indispensable in the present difficult times' and anyone found lacking was to be 'instantly' punished.[35]

In the nature of things the effect of rank-and-file propaganda is largely diffuse and therefore difficult to appraise except in the most general terms. The very size of the party, the existence of a multiplicity of ancilliary organizations and above all the massive display of symbols undoubtedly asserted the party's presence effectively throughout the society. There is, however, a point at which all propaganda begins to yield diminishing returns, and the 'demonstration effect' of the party is no exception. The perennial preoccupation of the Nazis with the opportunist *Konjunkturritter* testifies to the innate difficulty of a totalitarian ruling party in keeping its ranks free from elements who by their presence in the party invalidate much of its propaganda prestige among the masses.[36] The outward symbols so lavishly manipulated

---

[35] VAB, vol. i, pp. 5–8; NA, T-81, 1/10837.

[36] We have already noted that long before 1933 Hitler warned against the entry of opportunist elements into the party once victory was won. In the last years of the Third Reich he apparently saw his worst fears confirmed. Thus Bormann wrote to *Gauleiter* Sauckel on 27 May 1943: 'In former years the Fuehrer repeatedly emphasized that the NSDAP should not embrace more than 10% of adult Germans ... After the war we must carry out a very thorough purge of the party membership because in the meantime it has transpired that many persons were too hastily admitted into the party. There are very many persons who aspire to admission solely for their own benefit ... In the course of the war the Fuehrer often emphasized that the party should only be augmented

by the Nazis were also bound to lose much of their 'demonstration effect' in the course of time. In proportion as more and more people hung out their swastika flags, saluted each other by *'Heil Hitler!'* and even used the Nazi greeting to sign their letters,[37] the significance of these as affirmations of national socialist solidarity diminished, especially as it became known that failure to conform in such matters was carefully noted in the records kept by the party, and could have unpleasant if not serious repercussions.[38]

Reservations must also be applied to the personal oral propaganda conducted by the rank-and-file membership. That the aim to transform every party member into an active and vigilant propagandist of the regime was not always achieved in Nazi Germany is attested by such sources as the above-quoted directive of the district propaganda office. It is confirmed in a memorandum submitted to Bormann by a member of his staff in August 1943. The object of the memorandum was to call for a drastic intensification of the party's propaganda effort in order to overcome 'a great trough' in the morale of the people, caused by 'the strong air attacks, the events in Italy and the various military setbacks'. What is of interest here, however, is not the author's view of the low state of popular morale or of its causes but his appraisal of the effectiveness of the various propaganda instruments, including that of rank-and-file agitation. 'With the public and mechanical propaganda means', he writes, 'we shall not be able to dam up these most varied currents of morale. Press and radio are greatly discredited with the mass of the people, particularly as the result of the many false prophecies and numerous crass mistakes.' In the circumstances, the role of the party became crucial: 'Never before therefore has the steadfastness of the homeland depended so decisively on the firm bearing

from the ranks of youth ... and soldiers; other persons will no longer be admitted.' (BDC, File 16 A.)

    For the first onrush of post-*Machtergreifung* recruits – wrongly attributed to the period February–April 1933, because of the official restriction imposed in May – the 'old fighters' coined the contemptuous term *Maerzgefallene*. Other colloquialisms applied to opportunists were *Mitlaeufer* (also-rans) and *Karteigenossen* (card members).

[37] See the article in *Voelkischer Beobachter* of 25 April 1944 urging people to conclude their letters with *'Heil Hitler!'* instead of *'Mit deutschem Gruss!'* ('With German Greeting!'). 'German greeting' was in fact the designation of the *'Heil Hitler!'* salute.

[38] See below pp. 101ff.

and secure leadership of the party as today.' Yet, the party, too, had clearly failed its test:

> Unfortunately, a considerable number of our own party members in no way fulfilled their task ... Some of our party members are themselves swimming instead of leading. Already many of them no longer have sufficient boldness or the courage of their convictions to hurl themselves against the windbags and sneaking slackers.[39]

It is precisely during periods of crisis when popular morale is disturbed and deteriorating and word-of-mouth propaganda is needed more than ever that its inherent deficiency comes to the surface. For while all propaganda must, in order to be effective, take some account of popular feeling, the influence of the latter is nowhere felt as directly as in word-of-mouth propaganda. It may be unrealistic and therefore unwise of formal propaganda to ignore the sentiments and insult the intelligence of the people by continuing to issue themes which run directly counter to what the people feel and think. But in a totalitarian polity there is no technical reason which prevents the regime from doing so. The individual party member, however, faces his audience, is aware of its feelings, and often shares them. He will therefore sometimes prefer to remain silent rather than to make himself the spokesman for slogans which are either patently untrue or unpopular or both, and to ignore subversive views expressed in his presence rather than to incur the hostility of the people. And where he does feel compelled to speak up, because he fears the disciplinary consequences of failing to do so, his arguments will frequently reflect his own lack of conviction and remain correspondingly ineffectual. Indeed in the last years of the war party members did not only fail 'to hurl themselves' against demoralization with the requisite combativeness; more and more of them preferred to avoid any kind of outward identification with the regime, neglecting even the obligatory wearing of the party badge and the rendering of the Hitler salute. Reports of such

---

[39] BA, *Slg. Schumacher*/369. Seven months later, in March 1944, another official of the Party Chancellory, the earlier-mentioned Friedrichs, was to claim that the vigorous reactivation of the party had succeeded in restoring popular morale. (*Ibid.*, 368.) However, this statement was made in a speech to a conference of senior party leaders and itself had the ring of a morale-booster about it.

cases can be found as early as 1943 and the phenomenon increased considerably as the war neared its end.[40]

Perhaps the most difficult of achievement was the third form of propaganda practised by the party masses, propaganda by example. For this the mere willingness and ability to expouse the official cause in verbal 'combat' was no longer enough. Instead the party member was called upon to justify by his conduct the 'elitist' pretentions made by the party on his behalf. By no means all party members were able to do so. The records of the Third Reich, especially those of the party courts, throw much light on the various derelictions – not to mention the criminal offences punishable even under Nazi law – which tended to tarnish the official image of the model national socialist.[41] Yet most of the activist virtues demanded of the Nazis were of a political or behavioural character and well within the capacity of the average party member to perform. Moreover, anyone who consistently failed to live up to them could be subjected to the disciplinary pressures available to the party apparatus. A report by the block warden of the NSV that party member 'x' had not made a welfare contribution commensurate with his income, could and often did bring a party reprimand in its wake.[42] The same applied to party members who without valid reason refused to do 'voluntary' duty in the party or in one of its organizations or whose attendance at public demonstrations was irregular.[43] Similarly an order by the local party leader that all party members were to appear at 8 a.m. on Sunday morning for work on fortifications, the clearance of air-raid damage or welfare duties among refugees in the evacuation centres was usually sufficient to bring the party out in force.[44]

When party members were needed as recruits for the newly-constituted *Waffen-SS* in the beginning of 1940, the local party

[40] Boberach, *Meldungen*, pp. 419f, 430; Steinert, *Hitler's Krieg*, pp. 394, 539.
[41] A representative cross-section of such derelictions, ranging from 'political passivity' to participation in Church functions and the sale of 'one goat and two chickens to a Jew', will be found in Heyen, *Nationalsozialismus im Alltag*, pp. 154, 197, 272 and 322.
[42] NA, T-81, 153/0158504, 0158548–51, 0158565.
[43] See, e.g. the account of the expulsion of one party member who claimed he had no time for party duties but was found to 'indulge in hobbies', in IMT, vol. xlii, p. 325 (PL–8). For public meetings and national socialist ceremonies, the turn-out of party members was usually set by fixed contingents for each party organization. (NA, T-81, 65/74291.)
[44] NA, T-81, 127/149637.

organization would call a meeting of all party members eligible for military service, at which the 'wish of the Fuehrer' that party members should volunteer for the *Waffen-SS* was made known. The usual procedure was then for the local party leader to announce his intention to report that all those present had complied with the Fuehrer's wish and to call upon anyone refusing to do so to speak up and state his reasons. Some did speak up, usually to say that they were employed in essential war enterprises – this was, of course, the case with the majority of those who, although eligible for service, had not yet been called up by the regular armed forces (*Wehrmacht*) – and were therefore forbidden to leave their jobs without permission from their employers. But objections such as these were overruled on the spot, and at the end of the meeting all those present found that they had 'volunteered' for the *Waffen-SS*.[45]

It is not suggested that pressures such as these were wholly or even mainly responsible for the activism of the Nazi rank and file, only that their actual or potential use must have strengthened the average party member's resolve to respond to the demands of his leaders with the enthusiasm expected of him.

The Nazi Block Leader

A more systematic, institutionalized form of personal agitation was conducted by the party block leaders. The so-called 'speakers' (*Redner*) of the NSDAP were a relatively small band of professional or semi-professional propagandists – graded in a hierarchy reaching down from the *Reichsredner* to the *Kreis-redner* – who typically appeared before mass audiences.[46] Propaganda for industrial and agricultural productivity was largely in the hands of the Labour Front and the Reich Food Estate, and personal agitation played a very minor part in the activities of either of these two organizations. The block leader, however,

[45] The above account is taken from reports which reached the German army authorities who, incidentally, strongly objected to these recruitment methods. (See NA, T-81, 300/1128942 – 1129332.) See also G. H. Stein, *The Waffen SS*, Ithaca, N.Y., 1966, pp. 43ff. The author cites evidence that the 1940 drive to recruit party members into the *Waffen-SS* was not particularly successful.

[46] See R. Scanlan, 'The Nazi Rhetorician', *Quarterly Journal of Speech*, 1951, December, pp. 430–40; D. Sington and A. Weidenfeld, *The Goebbels Experiment*, London, 1942, pp. 41ff; Bramsted, *Goebbels and National Socialist Propaganda*, p. 73f. In May 1939 the number of officially authorized party speakers totalled 344. (See the list of names in BA, NS 25/470.)

was in close and perpetual contact with the inhabitants of his block. He was responsible not only for their political conduct but also for their private life. It was the block leader's task to serve as 'the pathfinder of the *Weltanschauung* for all members of the community', and while this did not, of course, disqualify him from applying the 'harder forms of education ... where the wrong conduct of an individual brings harm to himself and thereby to the entire community',[47] he was generally to be someone whom 'every member of the community regards as his friend and helpmate, to whom he can confidently turn in his need and of whom he knows that he will extend him counsel and help at all times'.[48] The model to which Nazi imagery aspired was that of a 'pastor' (*Seelsorger*), without, needless to add, 'the negative aspects' of the latter.[49]

The block leader did not hold group agitation meetings; his ideological 'pathfinder' duties consisted primarily of personal discussions with the inhabitants of the block. He was the party's principal bearer of word-of-mouth propaganda. In contrast to other party members who as national socialists had a general obligation to spread the word of the party far and wide, the block leader was charged with specific responsibility to acquaint all the inhabitants of his block with the slogans and demands of the regime. He was required to visit each household regularly and to use every available opportunity to influence the residents 'in the spirit of the movement'.[50] The houseboard with which every apartment house had to be equipped was in his charge. Here were displayed official notices, decrees, etc., as well as the 'Slogan of the Week' and similar propaganda posters.[51] In many instances special show-cases for propaganda materials – on the model of the notorious *Stuermer* cases which could be found on most street corners – were entrusted to the block leader. During the war, military maps showing the position at the various fronts

[47] Quoted in IMT, vol. xxx, p. 204, from a publication of the Reich Organization Office of the NSDAP, *Das Gesicht der Partei*, Munich, n.d., pp. 7–8.

[48] *Hoheitstraeger*, 1942, no. 4, p. 23.   [49] *Ibid.*, 1937, no. 1, p. 27.

[50] Other party members residing in the precincts of the block were to assist the block leader in his propaganda chores. They were to 'maintain close contact with other families ... pass on newspapers and periodicals that were oriented towards national socialism, and occasionally talk over ideological and political questions of the day with individual family members'. (*Ibid.*, 1938, no. 2, p. 28.)

[51] VAB, vol. i, p. 246; *Unser Wille und Weg*, 1941, no. 6, p. 81; NA, T-81, 24/21855, 21866 and 21989.

were often displayed in these cases. (In the closing years of the war when the frontline was retreating party organizations were instructed to remove the maps gradually and in 'a suitable manner'.)[52]

It was the block leader's duty to encourage people to ask him frank questions and to assure them that they would suffer no 'difficulties' in consequence, while at the same time warning them to refrain from 'loose talk' in conversations with their fellow-citizens.[53] He was to do all in his power in order to rectify the causes of just complaints of the people, but it was not his task 'to agree [merely in order] to show his solidarity'. Instead, he was to 'think positively' and to impress the people by his 'confident bearing'.[54] The main tangible objectives of his *Menschenfuehrung* were to prevail upon members of the households in his care to join one of the party formations or affiliated organizations, to turn out for national socialist demonstrations, to subscribe to the party press and to contribute to the various welfare drives. The success or failure with which he performed these tasks were the main criteria by which the work of the block leader as ideological 'pathfinder' was judged.[55]

More important was the block leader's role as political watchdog. Every local group office of the Nazi party maintained a detailed card index of all households (*Haushaltskartei*) in the locality. The principal source for the information recorded in the index of the local group was the block leader. The latter was required to keep 'household lists' in which he entered the facts subsequently to be recorded in the card index of the local group. The information in which the party was interested covered such details as whether the household subscribed to the party press, whether it owned a swastika flag, how much it contributed to the welfare collections and what type of radio set was in its possession. It included particulars regarding military service and membership of national socialist organizations, detailed information on the financial position of the household and on the past and present political attitude and conduct of each of its members. In short, the records were designed to give 'a clear picture' of every German citizen.[56] The relevant information, the block

---

[52] NA, T-81, 24/21942a.   [53] *Organisationsbuch*, p. 104.   [54] *Ibid.*

[55] W. Eitze, *Vom Wesen und den Formen der Schulung in der Ortsgruppe der NSDAP*, Hamburg, 1941, p. 46; also *Unser Wille und Weg*, 1939, no. 9, pp. 304–5 and *Schulungsbrief*, 1938, no. 8/9, p. 319.

[56] IMT, vol. xxxv, pp. 663–6.

leaders were told, was to be obtained through casual conversations and where possible checked against available records.[57] In all cases the block leader was responsible for the authenticity of the information entered into the household index.

It is easy to understand why Rudolf Hess found it necessary to warn the block leaders that their activities should on no account take the form of 'snooping or spying' for that would 'arouse not the trust but the distrust' of the population, but to see by what other name they could possibly be described is more difficult.[58] Certainly there could have been few Germans with any illusions about the nature of the block leader's functions.[59] The records of the Third Reich abound with cases in which a hastily-spoken phrase or undue slackness in the observance of national socialist canons led to denunciation by the block leader. From the impeachment of 'double earners' in the early period of the 'employment battle'[60] to the arraignment of 'defeatists' before the Special Courts in the war years,[61] the block leaders rarely flinched from applying 'the harder forms of education'.

Armed with the whip of the 'household list' the block leaders had little difficulty in mobilizing the people. Whether called upon to beflag their houses or to crowd into the streets to welcome a visiting party potentate, to make donations towards the Winter Help (WHW) or to lend a hand in the clearing of rubble after an air raid, the response of the population was rarely less than prompt. It was the existence of the block leaders which made it possible for their local group leader to make attendance at a public meeting 'the duty of every inhabitant above the age of 14 who is able to walk', and to know that he would be obeyed, or to send out invitations to a party-sponsored function in which the sentence, 'I am counting on your unconditional presence'

---

[57] A decree of the Minister of the Interior of 14 July 1939, enabled local-group leaders of the party to look into the records of local authorities in order to supplement their own household files with information about taxes and other confidential matters. (VAB, vol. I, p. 245.)

[58] IMT, vol. XLII, p. 327.

[59] Erich Kordt (*Wahn und Wirklichkeit*, Stuttgart, 1947, pp. 44–5) wrote that the block leaders had 'almost complete insight into the private life of the individual ... [and] by their daily, matter-of-fact and often unconscious supervision of the tenants contributed more to the strengthening of the regime than did the Gestapo ... It was considerably more difficult to keep a secret from one's often harmless block leader – who was however obliged to report all his observations – than to mislead the Gestapo.'

[60] NA, T-81, 168/307210.   [61] IMT, vol. V, p. 308.

could only be ignored at the recipient's peril.[62] The party official who concluded his 'invitation' to a propaganda meeting with the words, 'I hope therefore to have the opportunity of welcoming you and your family, since you do not wish to be hostile to the present state and the movement...'[63] was clearly expressing considerably more than a 'hope', and not least because the response of those 'invited' could be checked and recorded by their block leader.

Admittedly, the party leadership sought to discourage the more blatant use of coercive tactics. Lower organizations were frequently warned to desist from what the Nazis, with a characteristic fancy for euphemism, sometimes called 'propaganda with emphasis' (*Propaganda mit Nachdruck*), because it led only to 'resentment and discord' in the long run.[64] Indeed there was no need for much overt 'emphasis'. The organizational presence of the party enabled it to mobilize the people by less obtrusive means. The following incident which was cited in the party's propaganda journal as a model for the 'necessary tact' in party work will illustrate this: A block leader had the task of finding accommodation in his block for participants at a national convention. Among others he also called on a family who had been unco-operative in the past. Again both husband and wife refused to take anyone in. The block leader knew that there was a son in the family who was currently away on labour service and whose room was therefore free. 'But he must not demand, nor must he admonish...' Instead he asked how the son was and whether he would soon be home on leave. As was to be expected this transparent hint was enough to secure the required accommodation.[65] It was this kind of 'tact' which the leadership sought to develop among the lower party functionaries, at least in peace time. During the war this restraint was shed and party members were repeatedly called upon to combat defeatism and subversion by 'more massive means' of the kind 'that have stood us in such good stead' in the early period of the party's struggle for power.[66]

Next to the agents of the secret police the block leaders were probably the least popular representatives of the regime. Cer-

[62] NA, T-81, 181/331069 and 331119.
[63] *Unser Wille und Weg*, 1939, no. 1, p. 21.
[64] *Ibid.*, 1937, no. 3, pp. 92–3, no. 6, pp. 309–14; 1939, no. 6, p. 126.
[65] *Ibid.*, 1938, no. 2, p. 56.
[66] Bormann's circular letter of 18 December 1942, in NA, T-81, 1/10856.

tainly their perpetual snooping served to alienate them from the mass of the Germans, including many who unreservedly supported the general policies of the regime. The party realized

> how difficult it often is especially for the block leader to approach this or that member of the community, for not everyone extends the desired confidence towards him. We know that many members of the community conduct themselves differently towards their block leaders than they do towards the neighbour who is not a party member.[67]

Nor did the block leader's constant calls for subscriptions and donations help to endear him to the people, who, as one district leader put it, 'scent in the block leader only the money collector'.[68]

For party members the block leader's job entailed little prestige and a great deal of unrewarding work. In the course of time it came to be filled by the type of men who enjoyed the exercise of petty tyranny over their neighbours or who were incapable of serving in any other party capacity because of their physical or intellectual limitations. The activists who were physically fit tended to be absorbed in the party formations and looked upon the post of the block leader with the contempt which combat troops reserve for rear echelon units, while those whose education and intelligence permitted it rose to more responsible positions in the party hierarchy. In the words of another district leader writing in 1939, the corps of block leaders consisted 'to a large extent of aged, bodily handicapped and ... mentally inert and inactive persons'.[69]

Clearly, given this human element, the block leaders could not be expected to make a significant propaganda impact on a population that was educationally and culturally at least equal and more often than not superior to them and which, moreover, had effective access to the centrally directed communication media. The principal contribution of the block leaders to the mobilization of the masses lay in their organizational role, their proximity to the population and therefore their ability both to bring the people within the range of other, more effective propaganda media and to supervise the consummation of the rules of national socialist conduct in the daily life of every German.

[67] *Unser Wille und Weg*, 1936, no. 3, p. 90.
[68] NA, T-81, 119/138822.
[69] *Ibid.*, 119/139811–5.

5: POLITICAL AGITATION IN SOVIET RUSSIA

The Role of the Rank and File

The membership development of the CPSU, unlike that of the NSDAP, has been thoroughly studied, and need not occupy us except in brief outline. As already noted, the Soviet party was far smaller in 1917 than the Nazi party was in 1933. Moreover, starting out, as it did, from a much narrower numerical base, its growth interrupted by periodic purges, the Soviet party has taken considerably longer to reach membership figures comparable to those of the Nazis. It was only in 1927, or ten years after the revolution, that Soviet party membership attained the size of the Nazi party at the beginning of the Third Reich, and only in 1957, or after 40 years in power, that the CPSU approached the figure which the NSDAP had reached within ten years. If we look at the weight of the party in the population that of the CPSU is still today somewhat short of that achieved by the Nazi party less than seven years after its *Machtergreifung*.[1]

As in Nazi Germany, victory brought with it the inevitable influx of those seeking power and status in the new state: in the Soviet Union, too, the path to the top led through the ranks of the ruling party. Yet for the greater part of its post-revolutionary history the Soviet party has also been careful to foster a substantial representation among the manual classes. Exceptions were the latter 1930s until the outbreak of World War II, and the immediate post-war years until about 1954; but for the interruption of the war, which made it incumbent to strengthen 'the ties of the party with the working people' through mass recruitment among all social strata, Stalin was well on the way to turning the party into a narrow social elite. His successors, however, have

---

[1] In his report to the 24th Party Congress, Brezhnev noted that the party's current membership of 14,455,321 constituted 9% of the adult population. (*XXIV S'ezd*, vol. i, p. 117.) By mid-1973 party membership was reported at around 15m which is still slightly below 10% of all adults. (*Partiinaya zhizn'*, 1973, no. 11, p. 15.)

strikingly reversed this trend. The rapid membership expansion of the past decade-and-a-half – from around 7 million to around 15 million – has enabled the party to maintain and even to enlarge its penetration of different elite groups and at the same time to increase greatly the number of workers and collective farmers in its ranks.[2]

Admittedly, the Soviet party may be said to have an ideological commitment to include a sizeable working class component in its ranks in justification of its 'vanguard' role in society.[3] But this did not prevent Stalin from attempting to transform the party into an association of the privileged, and it is doubtful whether it would have sufficed to induce his successors to change Stalinist recruitment policies as radically and as consistently as they have done. If the partly successful 'proletarianization' of the party in the 1920s was still conducted in pursuance of this ideological commitment and also of the concurrent desire to promote socially reliable elements from among the 'formerly oppressed' into the new Soviet elite, post-Stalin recruitment was primarily orientated to create a party that was more firmly rooted in Soviet society as a whole. The aim was not so much to refurbish its image as a working class party – although this may have been a partial consideration – and still less to staff leading posts with persons of unsullied social origin – the rehabilitation of the new Soviet intelligentsia as a loyal 'stratum' of Soviet society alongside the two manual classes had already been accomplished by Stalin in the 1930s – but to provide the party with the cadres necessary for its mobilization functions. Only the 'foremost', 'best' or 'most advanced' representatives of the working class and the collective farm peasantry (as also of the intelligentsia) are considered worthy of party membership. In practice, 'foremost' etc., means those who excel at their occupations – the shock workers (*udarniki*), the 'pioneers of production', the

[2] Between 1957 and 1971 the number of workers in the party rose from 2.4 million to 5.8 million and that of collective farmers from 1.3 million to 2.2 million; while the relative share of workers increased in the same period from 32.0% to 40.1% that of collective farmers declined from 17.3% to 15.1%. Both these categories relate to 'social position' now defined as 'basic occupation at the time of joining the party'. They include former workers who have since advanced to supervisory positions as well as such 'white collar' farmers as kolkhoz administrative personnel, agronomists, zoo-technicians and others.

[3] The working class is still the 'leading class' of Soviet society, and the party, notwithstanding the fact that it is now 'a party of the whole people', considers itself duty-bound to strengthen its working class profile.

team and brigade leaders, etc., with marked preference being given to the more highly skilled trades in key branches of the economy (and even of individual enterprises). These are precisely the people on whom the party relies for support in its mobilization of the masses at large. In the conditions that have followed Stalin's death, the party required not only officers who could give orders and know that they would be obeyed because the NKVD (or its successors) stood poised in the wings, but also NCOs who lived and worked in close contact with the rank and file and could lead by constant exhortation and personal example. The 'foremost' workers and collective farmers are the pace-makers of the masses, deployed to stimulate the talents and efforts of their fellow workers without undue recourse to terroristic 'incentives' on the Stalinist model. The party as 'guide and teacher' of the masses is the better able to direct and control this process by absorbing its human media into its ranks.

There is no evidence that the present leaders of the Soviet Union have set themselves an optimal level for the size of the party, as the Nazis did, but it is highly improbable that they will continue to allow party expansion to exceed the rate of population growth for very much longer. There is clearly an upper limit beyond which further membership expansion would entail too costly a dilution of the party's status as a 'vanguard' force.[4]

Not only has the sheer numerical impact of the party membership been less significant in the Soviet Union than in Nazi Germany; there has also been no attempt to amplify it through any of the methods which the Nazis employed with such purpose and thoroughness. Thus, in the absence of outward means of identification by which Soviet party members can be distinguished from non-members, the 'demonstration effect' of party membership is necessarily confined to each member's personal friends and acquaintances. In other respects, however, the Soviet regime has shown itself equally aware of the potentialities inherent in the existence of a mass party and equally insistent on their exploitation in the service of its propaganda.

The Soviet party member, too, has always been required to conduct personal propaganda on behalf of the regime. The motto

[4] In recent years, and especially since 1971 when the 24th Congress resolved on the exchange of party cards currently under way, party growth did in fact decline substantially, not only in relative but also in absolute terms – from an average annual increase of approx. 600,000 to approx. 250,000.

'Every Bolshevik an agitator!' was coined in the earliest days of the revolution and has remained in force ever since. 'Every free day, every free hour of the conscious male and female worker must be employed for agitation', Lenin urged in 1919.[5] And 40 years later the party journal emphasized: 'Every Communist must be an agitator . . . it is important to approach every toiler with the word of the party – in the enterprise, in the brigade and at his place of residence.'[6] The favourite Soviet image of the party member, like that of the Nazis, is that of an 'active political fighter', and this means that he is obliged to 'explain the policy of the party to the masses', 'to unmask vigorously all manifestations of bourgeois ideology', 'to give a decisive rebuff to alien views', and 'to combat prejudices and vestiges of the past' wherever he comes up against them.[7] It also means that he must serve as an example to others at work as well as in his daily conduct, his family life, his political activism, etc. Patriotic, militant, politically 'conscious' and ideologically 'tempered', fearless and implacable to foes, selfless and considerate to friends, diligent in the performance of his duties, and above all else thoroughly disciplined – the catalogue of virtues which the ideal Soviet party member is expected to display in all spheres of life is altogether similar to that claimed for the model Nazi.[8]

[5] Lenin, *Pol. Sob. Soch.* vol. xxxviii, p. 319. Lenin coupled his demand with the promise that this 'effort is not necessary for long, for a few months, perhaps weeks, and will be the last and final for our victory is beyond doubt'. See also the resolution of the 13th Party Congress calling on all party members to become active agitators. (*Kommunisticheskaya Partiya Sovetskogo Soyuza v resolyutsiyakh i resheniyakh s'ezdov, konferentsii i plenumov Ts. K.*, 4 vols. 7th ed., Moscow, 1954–60, vol. i, p. 871.)

[6] *Partiinaya zhizn'*, 1959, no. 5, p. 4.

[7] Some of these duties are listed in para. 2 of the Statutes. (*Programmy i ustavy KPSS*, pp. 370–1.) Others are continually stressed in Soviet writings; see, e.g. *Pravda*, 15 August 1966; *Kommunist*, 1969, no. 14, pp. 9–11.

[8] See, e.g. *Pravda*, 2 June 1969 and 31 July 1971. On the crucial question of discipline Brezhnev himself deserves to be quoted: 'It is a profound mistake to think that Lenin's instructions on the need for iron discipline has meaning only in the period of direct revolutionary action and loses its urgency in the course of further social-economic and democratic transformations. Experience has incontrovertibly taught that the party is in need of firm, conscientious discipline both when it leads the masses to revolution and when, at the head of the masses, it fights for the creation of a socialist society, in the period of all-out construction of communism. Herein lies one of the most important sources of the party's strength, successes and victories.' (*Pravda*, 29 March 1968.) It may be instructive to compare this with a similar statement by Stalin in 1924. Stalin too, invoked Lenin's authority against any relaxation of discipline in the

If there is a difference between the two parties in this regard it is in the inordinate importance which the Soviet party attaches to the work performance of its members: 'The highest duty of the Communist is to be an example at work, actively to support and disseminate the standards of a conscious, creative attitude to work, to all production matters.'[9] To be sure, in the context of the party's contribution to propaganda by emulation the difference is not unimportant: the qualities that make for a high degree of occupational skill, at the work bench as in the research laboratory, are less susceptible to positive influence through the threats and exhortations of party functionaries than are such Nazi virtues as joining a storm troop or helping elderly ladies at a traffic crossing. Although party discipline and indoctrination may play some part in fostering a 'conscious, creative attitude to work', they cannot by themselves bring about that distinction in the production sphere which was and continues to be a major aim of Soviet propaganda and therefore always high among the demands which the party makes of its members. The implication is, of course, that if the party wants its members to excel at production it must recruit the 'foremost' workers into its ranks.

Have Soviet party members met the expectations of their leaders anymore than their counterparts did in Nazi Germany? Soviet leaders have certainly been no less conscious of the presence of 'careerists', 'time-servers' and 'self-seekers' in the party. Lenin noted in 1919 that the 'temptation' to join the ranks of the ruling party was 'gigantic',[10] and his successors – omitting the murderous paranoia of the 'period of the personality cult', when it seemed as if the party had been subverted at the highest levels by saboteurs and traitors and 'enemies of the people' of every description – have continued to be troubled by the problem ever since.[11] It is a reasonably certain, if paradoxical, aspect of

party – 'iron discipline' was indeed Lenin's prescription for many of the problems faced by the party both before and after its accession to power. But Stalin in 1924, unlike Brezhnev today, still found it necessary to declare that 'iron discipline does not preclude but presupposes criticism and conflict of opinion in the party'. (Stalin, *Problems of Leninism*, p. 105)

[9] *Pravda*, 13 February 1969. This point is stressed in virtually every statement on the party member's duties; for other examples, see *ibid.*, 29 August 1967 and 14 May 1971.

[10] Lenin, *Pol. Sob. Soch.*, vol. xlv, p. 19.

[11] At the 22nd Party Congress Khrushchev said: 'It must be admitted that there are still people who regard their entry into the ranks of the party as a means of improving their careers.' (*XXII S'ezd*, vol. i, p. 112.) Brezh-

totalitarian systems that their single parties, forever seeking 'monolithic unity' and demanding 'conscious' ideological militancy from their members, contain a higher share of politically disinterested persons, plain opportunists and even potential dissenters than do parties in democratic systems where the 'temptation' to join a particular party is generally less formidable.

Soviet experience also indicates that party members are not at all times ready to spring to the defence of official policies. And this not only in the early years of the regime and in periods of particular stress, such as the Kronstadt revolt or the forcible collectivization, when party members in their thousands were found sadly deficient in 'Bolshevik tempering', but even today when the personal agitation of party members undoubtedly operates within a much broader consensual framework. 'We have our "silent ones" too', runs one recent complaint.

> Probably every party organization has members, who though one would not call them passive are not . . . real fighters. Such Communists will carry out assignments accurately . . . But when conversations on controversial subjects arise spontaneously, such 'activists' keep quiet, as if their mouths were full of water.[12]

There are also party members whom one would, and does, call 'passive'. They forget that 'the work of the Communist among the masses is not a voluntary matter but an obligatory one'.[13] They do their best to shirk party assignments, they remain indifferent to shortcomings, do not participate in the life of the collective and ignore manifestations of 'anti-social' conduct on the part of their fellow citizens.[14] Sometimes the secretary of the party organisation succeeds in creating a 'social climate' which makes such dereliction of party duties 'simply impossible'.[15] Still, the problem is evidently sufficiently widespread to have led Brezhnev to take it up at the last party Congress:

> Unfortunately we still have party members who do not show themselves to be genuine political fighters. When they en-

nev in his reports to the 23rd and 24th Congress did not refer specifically to the problems of careerism, but he did on both occasions emphasize 'concern for the purity of the party's ranks'. (*XXIII S'ezd*, vol. i, p. 87; *XXIV S'ezd*, vol. i, p. 118.)

12 *Pravda*, 31 July 1968; see also 26 April 1973.
13 *Agitator*, 1966, no. 18, p. 3.
14 See, e.g. *Pravda*, 7 December 1967 and 31 July 1971.
15 *Ibid.*, 9 October 1968.

counter shortcomings or negative phenomena they pretend that they notice nothing, taking up a philistine position – 'this doesn't concern me, let others think about it'. There are also those whose activeness is only for show, designed for external effect. They talk more than others about the need to tackle this or that task [and] always lecture everybody else and exhort to something. But when it comes to get down to practical work, they contrive to stay somewhere on the sidelines, in the shadows.[16]

The conduct of party members in their private lives is similarly unsatisfactory. In the words of an editorial in the party journal: 'There are still not a few cases in which feudal-bey vestiges are preserved in the families of Communists and religious prejudices and private property ways manifest themselves.'[17]

Most serious of all, the production performance of some party members is such as to disqualify them utterly from serving as models for the rest of the population. The party press continuously reports cases of party members 'who do not justify the high and responsible calling of Communists and who by their remiss attitude to work . . . damage the authority of the party'.[18] In some rural party organizations more than half the members were said to 'idle about' – 'naturally because of such Communists the party lost all authority in the eyes of the collective farmers'.[19] In one collective farm in Uzbekistan, only ten out of 54 party members participated in the cotton harvest; what is more 'the non-party mechanics and truck drivers picked twice as much raw cotton as the party members. Just what sort of "personal example" can one speak of here?'[20]

Such criticisms indicate that Soviet party members still fall short of the regime's requirements. But while they may serve to put the more effusive official claims about the 'vanguard' qualities of the membership in proper perspective, they must not be taken as proof that these claims are wholly unfounded. There is much evidence in Soviet accounts that party members do indeed possess some of the virtues of the model Soviet citizen: they lead unexceptionable private lives, they are more active in taking on a variety of civic duties and they work harder and better than

16 *XXIV S'ezd*, vol. I, p. 121.
17 *Partiinaya zhizn'*, 1968, no. 1, p. 7.
18 *Ibid.*, 1960, no. 4, p. 71; 1971, no. 24, pp. 4–5.
19 *Ibid.*, 1957, no. 11, p. 45.
20 *Pravda*, 24 October 1967.

non-members. Nor is there any reason to write all this off as part of the party's image-building.[21] It would have been surprising if pre-selection by means of fairly rigorous screening of new recruits, constant inculcation of the 'moral traits of the Communist' and the creation of a suitable 'social climate' had not over the years produced a sample that was rather more closely moulded to the regime's design of the 'new man' than any random group of non-party members.

The Agitator

The precise number of Soviet agitators is one of the minor puzzles of the Soviet enigma. Such figures as are published by Soviet sources relate as a rule to individual regions or localities and are not very reliable. For many years now it has been all too clear that agitators frequently 'exist on paper only'.[22] They appear in the reports of local party organizations but 'they don't do anything', they are 'dead souls'.[23] While in some places inactive agitators continue to be carried on the rosters of local organizations more or less permanently (earning the epithet of 'life-time agitators'), the turnover in others remains excessively high.[24] It is presumably the resultant credibility gap, rather than a desire for secretiveness, which accounts for the conspicuous reluctance of central spokesmen to commit themselves to a figure for the total number of agitators in the country. While figures for propagandists, lecturers and other 'ideological workers' are frequently cited, references to the number of agitators are usually couched in vague terms, such as 'millions of agitators' or 'the numerous army of agitators'. A recent departure from this practice is the

[21] Increasingly, such evidence purports to rest on sociological surveys. Thus, for example, analysis of several party organizations in Moscow Province showed that party members were ahead of non-members in their rates of plan fulfilment and provided a higher than average share of the 'shock workers' and 'rationalizers'. (*Pravda*, 9 October 1968.) According to a survey of several thousand party members at the Ural Freight Car Construction Plant in Nizhny Tagil, 95% of them devoted 1–3 hours daily of their free time to public activity. (*Ibid.*, 22 October 1970.) See now also M. Matthews, *Class and Society in Soviet Russia*, London, 1972, pp. 243ff. For complaints that party members are overloaded with such assignments, see *Partiinaya zhizn'*, 1966, no. 20, p. 70; *Pravda*, 11 May 1969; 13 March 1973.)

[22] See, e.g. *Blocknot agitatora* (Moscow), 1956, no. 33. pp. 5 and 10; *Pravda*, 3 June 1967.

[23] *Agitator*, 1964, no. 7, p. 30; 1965, no. 14, p. 3.

[24] *Ibid.*, 1965, no. 21, p. 31; *Partiinaya zhizn'*, 1967, no. 9, p. 30.

disclosure, in an authoritative article by the newly-appointed head of the Section for Mass-Political Work (formerly the Agitation Section) in the Central Committee Propaganda Department, M. Rakhmankulov, that 'around 3.5 million' agitators were currently deployed in the country.[25] This, if correct, would yield an average of 44 adults for every agitator, and may well still fall short of what is officially regarded as the optimal ratio.[26]

The distribution of agitators in different parts of the Soviet Union shows wide variations. In general, the share of agitators appears to be higher among town dwellers than among the rural population. Thus, for example, the ratio of agitators to inhabitants is 1:100 in Vladimir Province and 1:59 in Vladimir city. Other towns, like Yaroslavl', or regions with a particularly large urban component, such as Voroshilovgrad Province, show a considerably higher concentration of agitators than the national average. But the correlation is by no means inevitable. Moreover, the published figures are subject to considerable fluctuations.[27]

The majority of agitators are drawn from the ranks of the party, with the remainder made up from the Komsomol and the so-called 'non-party *aktiv*'. One of the basic qualifications of the agitator is that he must be a 'politically literate' person. In the Soviet Union such literacy is officially monopolized by the party and the agitator's assignment is probably one of the most common ways in which it is harnessed to the service of the regime. But apart from being 'politically literate' the agitator is also required to be an 'authoritative' person who is 'well versed in production'. In order to meet these two additional requirements agitators are primarily selected from among the 'foremost' workers and collective farmers, who personify the industrial virtues which the regime seeks to foster among the mass of its citizens. As agitators they have two principal qualifications. One is their ability to persuade by example. That 'the best results are achieved by those agitators who know how to convince not only

25 *Agitator*, 1973, no. 9, p. 45.
26 One can occasionally come across statements that, for example, a total of 20 agitators in a collective farm with a work force of 800 is barely on the margins of adequacy and should be augmented. (*Agitator*, 1965, no. 15, p. 21.)
27 It is indicative of the mercurial quality of agitator statistics in recent years that the number of agitators in Moscow city apparently jumped from 120,000 in mid-1969 to 200,000 at the end of 1970. (The 1969 figure is in *Partiinaya zhizn'*, 1969, no. 11, p. 16; for the 1970 figure see *ibid.*, 1970, no. 23, p. 35 and also *Pravda*, 13 November 1970.)

by word but by personal example', is a basic axiom of Soviet mass-political work: 'If an agitator's word is divorced from the deed, people will not take notice of him, will not heed his voice and advice.' The other, related, qualification is their authority among fellow-workers based on their production achievements: they enjoy 'personal authority won through honest labour'. It is this which, together with their 'great experience of life', 'fully compensates' for any 'deficiency in general culture on the part of some of them'.[28]

The main field of the agitator's activity is the enterprise – factory, coal mine, collective farm, construction project, etc. The selection, training and deployment of agitators is in the charge of the primary party organization; where no primary organization exists agitators are directly subordinated to the district party committee. Agitators working in the same enterprise are grouped in agitation-collectives (*agitkollektivy*), headed either by the secretary of the party organization or by 'one of the most capable members of the party *aktiv*'.[29] In the larger industrial plants there may be over 1,000 agitators distributed among 60 or so agitation-collectives in the different shops and sections of the enterprise.[30]

Model themes for agitation work are published periodically in the central journals. They are then adapted by republic or province party organizations and provide the bases for detailed quarterly or monthly work plans drafted by each agitation-collective in conjunction with the relevant party organization.[31] The system is designed to ensure a degree of uniformity over relatively wide areas without losing sight of particular needs arising

---

[28] *Spravochnik sekretarya pervichnoi partiinoi organizatsii*, Moscow, 1964, p. 100. The 1967 edition of this handbook placed greater stress on the need for education. It defined the agitator as an 'authoritative, politically qualified and educated person', and also omitted the assertion that any cultural inadequacy on his part was made up by other qualities. But these, as well as other revisions, were probably dictated by a current controversy concerning the status of agitators. (See below pp. 147ff) Subsequent Soviet accounts of agitators leave no doubt that the views expressed in the 1964 edition continue to be valid. (See, e.g. *Agitator*, 1968, no. 12, p. 39; 1971, no. 9, p. 36.)

[29] *Spravochnik partiinogo rabotnika*, 1961, p. 456.

[30] *Partiinaya zhizn'*, 1966, no. 20, p. 50. The highest figure for agitators in a single enterprise that has come to my notice is 2,500. (*Agitator*, 1970, no. 3, p. 49.)

[31] *Voprosy partiinoi raboty*, Moscow, 1959, pp. 490–1. For some examples of the themes included in the work plans of agitation-collectives see *Agitator*, 1964, no. 7, p. 31; 1970, no. 5, p. 44.

from local conditions. Seminars and schools in which agitators are instructed in the methods and objectives of 'mass-political work' are run by the larger primary party organizations and by district committees.[32] Members of the agitation-collectives meet regularly to discuss their work and learn from mutual experience. Often such meetings are addressed by local party and state functionaries or by the director or chief engineer of the factory. In this way the agitators are kept abreast with the views of local leaders and the state of plan fulfilment in the enterprise or area.

From the standpoint of the regime the unique merit of the agitator lies in his close proximity to and thorough knowledge of his audience. 'The agitators are strong', it is said, 'by virtue of their intimate and permanent contact with the working mass. They are themselves workers, themselves the mass.'[33] The agitator's audience is composed of persons with whom he is in daily contact at the factory or collective farm. He knows – or is expected to know – each of his fellow-workers individually 'with his problems, errors and doubts'.[34] And he is required to stand ready at all times with both advice and practical help in solving the problems, correcting the errors and dispelling the doubts. Attention to work performance is primary but not sufficient. The task of 'helping everyone to develop the best qualities characteristic of our society, to rid oneself of shortcomings and the residues of the past', demands that the agitator should also take an interest in the 'mode of life' of the workers, i.e. what kind of books they read, if at all, how they treat their wives, whether they are concerned with the education of their children, whether they drink or gamble, whether, in short, they 'grow culturally'.[35] The true agitator is one who 'looks after his men', whom people 'approach as a friend' and with whom they 'share their joys and their sorrows'.[36] The following is the profile of an agitator of the kind that is constantly held up as a model in Soviet writings:

Personal example at work, in studies, in everyday life, in public activity, a sensitive approach to comrades, have earned him the respect of the working people of the whole plant. People turn to him for advice, go to him in joy and sorrow.

[32] See, e.g. *Partiinaya zhizn'*, 1957, no. 17, pp. 53–5; *Agitator*, 1971, no. 11, pp. 28–9.
[33] *Pravda*, 6 September 1968.
[34] *Partiinaya zhizn'*, 1957, no. 15, p. 71; *Agitator*, 1970, no. 15, p. 40.
[35] *Partiinaya zhizn'*, 1960, no. 7, p. 44; *Agitator*, 1970, no. 15, p. 40.
[36] *Partiinaya zhizn'*, 1956, no. 8, p. 49; *Agitator*, 1969, no. 6, p. 41.

He always responds, helps by word and by deed . . . [He] always knows with whom it is necessary to have a talk and on what subject, who needs to be told at greater length of the concrete tasks facing the shift, shop and plant.[37]

It is the agitator's 'intimate and permanent contact' with the broad mass of the people which ensures that his agitation will not bear that 'abstract, purely enlightening character' which is so antipathetic to Soviet propaganda doctrine, but will lead to the mobilization of the masses for the attainment of concrete goals. The agitator is not expected to expound on the significance of the communist apocalypse in sporadic bursts of oratorical fervour, but to conduct personal agitation 'day-in, day-out in inseparable contact with the life of the enterprise'.[38] *Krasnorechie*, or eloquence, is not a vital part of the equipment of the Soviet agitator. His characteristic quality is not rhetorical agility but occupational skill. What is expected of him above all is the ability to demonstrate the production process, to explain simply and clearly to every worker what his duties are – and to see to it that they are conscientiously fulfilled.

Although some stress has been laid in recent years on the development of oratorical skills the contemporary agitator is still essentially an 'agitator-organizer', far removed from the 'agitator-popularizer' of the 1920s. Everywhere his agitational activity is conducted 'in necessary conjunction with organizational work'.[39] Apart from acquainting his fellow-workers with the policies and demands of the regime, the agitator is responsible for such questions as work-discipline, labour productivity, the dissemination of new techniques, the elimination of shortcomings in production and other matters related to the contribution which the individual worker makes to the general task of economic construction:

The struggle for the fulfilment of jubilee undertakings is, of course, in the range of sight of the shop agitator. Questions of the quality of production, lowering of costs, utilization of reserves . . . cannot but concern the agitator and his role in the organization of socialist emulation is difficult to exaggerate.[40]

[37] *Voprosy ideologicheskoi raboty partii*, Moscow, 1966, p. 161.
[38] *Bloknot agitatora*, 1955, no. 13, p. 17; *Agitator*, 1967, no. 6, p. 29.
[39] *Agitator*, 1964, no. 24, p. 34; V. I. Brovikov and I. V. Popovich, *Sovremennye problemy politicheskoi informatsii i agitatsii*, Moscow, 1969, esp. pp. 88ff.
[40] *Agitator*, 1967, no. 6, p. 29.

No detail is too small for his attention: 'His art is characterized by the ability to keep in sight the most minute detail in the life of his shop, brigade, plant, collective farm.'[41] Where agitators perform their tasks properly 'not a single case of the manufacture of low-grade products goes unnoticed'.[42] The 'necessary conjunction' of agitation and organization is one of the most distinctive features of the agitator's role. The formulations of Soviet pronouncements on the subject may vary but the message is identical. 'The power of the word', the agitator is told, 'must be supplemented by the organization of the masses . . .'[43] He is 'not only the enlightener (*prosvetitel'*) of the masses but their organizer. His words must always be reinforced by the deed and the persuasive demonstration, by organization.'[44]

The meaning of 'organization' in this context is that the agitator must see to it that the job is done – by persuasion, if possible, by personal example, by demonstration, but if necessary also by compulsion. He is the regime's representative among the masses. He does not merely wield 'the power of the word', his words are backed by power: 'Certainly it is necessary to persuade. But in the struggle for the new, on the side of progress, must also be the support of authority, power, discipline.'[45] The presence of the agitator in the factory shop and the collective farm brigade is designed to ensure that the correct mixture of persuasion and coercion, of propaganda and organization, is applied at all times. True, the disciplinary instruments available to the agitator are relatively innocuous when compared to those exercised by other agents of the regime, but they are nonetheless effective for that. Because his role in the system of mass mobilization secures him access to higher authority – the party and trade union organizations, the managerial hierarchy at the enterprise, the agencies of enforcement (both state and 'social') – he has some say in the allocation of a wide range of rewards and sanctions. Soviet sources do not as a rule elaborate on this aspect of the agitator's activity. But they make no secret of the fact that one of the agitator's duties is to keep the appropriate party organization fully informed of the conduct and morale of his group, just as they frequently stress the rewards directly dispensed by the agitator,

41 *Ibid.*, 1969, no. 14, p. 4; 1972, no. 4, p. 25.
42 *Partiinaya zhizn'*, 1966, no. 20, p. 51.
43 *Blocknot agitatora*, 1955, no. 1, p. 43.
44 *Agitator*, 1964, no. 17, p. 6; 1971, no. 11, p. 26.
45 *Partiinaya zhizn'*, 1956, no. 4, p. 39; *Agitator*, 1972, no. 5, pp. 4–5.

as, for example, intercession with a local authority on behalf of a fellow-worker. When they do attempt to render allusions to 'authority, power, discipline' more explicit, it is usually with reference to the instruments of public opinion. It is his abilty to manipulate the opinion of the group, for approbation as well as for obloquy, which constitutes the principal, officially acknowledged source of the agitator's power over his group.

From time to time agitators have been warned not to neglect political questions. But by and large they are guided by the immediate need for practical measures in the realm of production, and this with the explicit sanction of the Soviet leadership. Plan fulfilment continues to be the dominant force in Soviet life and the main yardstick by which effort is assessed and rewarded. The constant pressures generated by the need to meet the economic goals set by the system are inevitably reflected in the work of the agitator. Such matters as the number of rationalizing proposals submitted by each shop or factory and the rate of 'socialist emulation' in the livestock brigade of a collective farm provide now as ever the chief criteria for the success or failure of the agitator. The following passage from an article by Morozov indicates the priorities which govern the agitator's preoccupations:

> Every agitator must learn to find his place in the solution of overall national tasks. It is known, for instance, that in the present time especially great importance attaches to the problem of raising the quality of production in all branches of the national economy. Can agitators disregard the fact that goods valued at 2.1 billion rubles which cannot find buyers have accumulated in the storehouses and trade network of the country?
>
> This is a major economic and political problem. Agitators are called upon to participate actively in its solution. It is also known that the majority of old stocks are supplied by clothing and footwear enterprises; their addresses are also known. Is it necessary to point out that for the agitators of the clothing and footwear industries the struggle for the quality of production is the first matter to which the full strength of the workers' collective must be directed! That is how it is everywhere: it is essential for the agitator to find the link between the policy of the party and the concrete concerns of the section in which he works.[46]

[46] *Agitator*, 1964, no. 24, p. 34.

The basic agitational frame at the enterprise is the group talk or *beseda*. At regular intervals, usually once weekly, the agitator assembles his fellow-workers for a short talk followed by discussion. *Besedy* last for approximately 15–20 minutes and until recently generally took place during lunch-hour breaks. Since the transition to the five-day week and the consequent reduction in the mid-day interval many agitation-collectives appear to prefer to hold their *besedy* at the beginning of the working shift.[47] The number of participants varies but the typical audience will not include more than 30 persons. Attendance is not formally compulsory and while there are many indications that it is often notably lacking in enthusiasm it would seem that the mechanisms of 'voluntary compulsion' generally suffice to ensure adequate turn-out. That one can occasionally read of the need to display 'tact' towards a worker who prefers to spend his rest period on other pursuits merely confirms this impression.[48] Certainly lack of attendance at *besedy* held in places of work is not regarded as a major problem by Soviet spokesmen, at least not when compared with the other shortcomings of oral agitation that are frequently mentioned in Soviet acounts.[49] Where it does occur it is mainly confined to individuals whose record is already marred by deviant behaviour. The majority of people evidently prefer to attend agitation sessions more or less regularly rather than draw attention to themselves by habitual evasion.

In his talk the agitator may explain the latest party decision on spring sowing or the growth of the chemical industry, he may comment on an event in the foreign policy of the USSR or deal with local questions affecting the district or town, such as the housing programme, public health, consumer supplies and related problems. Often he will read aloud from a newspaper or

---

[47] The 18th Party Conference in 1941 directed that meetings of any kind for the purpose of agitation must on no account be held during working hours. (*KPSS v rez.*, vol. III, pp. 434–5.) Occasionally the rule is broken, but when it is and the fact comes to the attention of superior authorities, a reprimand follows. (See, e.g. *Pravda*, 12 December 1965 and 9 January 1966; also the Central Committee decree of 27 December 1963 in *Spravochnik partiinogo rabotnika*, 1964, p. 300.)

[48] *Partiinaya zhizn'*, 1965, no. 1, p. 60.

[49] For a different view see J. Hough, *The Soviet Prefects*, Cambridge, Mass., 1969, pp. 133–4. Inkeles cited evidence from the first two decades of the Soviet regime showing that attendance at agitation sessions frequently did not exceed 50% and could even be as low as 10%. (*Public Opinion in Soviet Russia*, p. 122.) If this is still the case today I have found no evidence of it in contemporary Soviet sources.

assign a member of the group to do so and occasionally use the article as a basis for discussion. In the majority of cases, however, the topic of the *beseda* will pertain to the work of the plant or farm. Even when dealing with general issues such as the Five-Year Plan, the Model Charter for Collective Farms or industrial reform, the skilful agitator will seek to relate the broader theme to the production tasks of his enterprise. A common, officially approved, method is to contrast the production records of various members of the group, on the one hand, and the performance of the group as a whole with that of other comparable groups, on the other. This is how one kolkhoz agitator approached his task:

> Ivan Mikhailovich Balanescu sat in the Cabinet of Political Enlightenment. In front of him lay a notebook with the names of the milkmaids of the kolkhoz and the results of socialist emulation. The day before he had talked with the farm economist... and had obtained from her a detailed analysis of the work of every milkmaid on the farm... Some milkmaids had achieved high results... But their experiences had not yet been matched by everyone. For that the agitator also blamed himself. Apparently, he had not always succeeded in his *besedy* to arouse among the listeners the striving to work better, to compete with the pioneers.
>
> This time Ivan Mikhailovich prepared himself especially thoroughly for his *beseda*. He spoke of the people who worked well on neighbouring farms [and] on the kolkhoz, of their extensive knowledge, their sense of duty. When telling of the experience of advanced livestock farmers, he stressed that if everyone would work like Lidiya Buzhov, Anna Butsu and others, the farm would become one of the best in the district and the state would obtain much additional milk.[50]

But whatever the method adopted by the agitator, there is no question that the principal objective of the *beseda* is 'to lead the audience to a conclusion'. Nor is there any doubt as to the nature of that conclusion: 'Usually, at the end of the *beseda* the agitators formulate the concrete tasks confronting the collective or group of workers in the struggle for higher labour productivity [and] the successful fulfilment of socialist commitments.'[51]

Agitators are frequently reminded not only to speak of the successes but to give due attention to the failures. Such frank un-

[50] *Agitator,* 1971, no. 4, p. 30.
[51] *Ibid.,* 1970, no. 5, p. 45.

varnished treatment may seem to stand in sharp contrast to the overall propaganda line which never tires of proclaiming 'the giant strides of the Soviet people in fulfilling the majestic perspectives of communist construction'. The dualism between the tenor of local and central themes may be explained by the paramount urgency of mobilizing the masses for the fulfilment of the practical tasks set before them. Clearly, the fundamental purpose of mobilization would be defeated if the result of agitation were 'complacency' and not the 'will to overcome prevailing difficulties and obstacles [and] to uproot shortcomings'.[52] It is for this reason above all that the leadership prefers to run the calculated risk of conducting a propaganda whose central *motifs* are constantly pierced by discordant notes from below. Moreover, the party authorities are aware that 'the workers see not only the successes. They also know the shortcomings in production, the difficulties.'[53] For the agitator to ignore the failures in his daily work with the people would be to jeopardize the credibility of his agitation as a whole.

An essential attribute of the successful *beseda* is active audience participation. Agitators who do not make adequate allowance for discussion or whose talks fail to arouse their listeners to questions and comments are frequently reprimanded. The participation of the audience is, of course, regarded as a measure of its interest and attention. But beyond that it serves a threefold purpose. Firstly, it helps the agitator to get to know the individual members of his group and also provides the party organization with an important source of information on the popular mood. Secondly, it engenders a sense of involvement in the goals and objectives set by the regime. In a 'controlled environment' such as an agitation *beseda* the views expressed by the audience are not likely to diverge markedly from the propaganda message imparted by the agitator. Comment from a listener is therefore a sure way of eliciting commitment from him and reinforcing the impact of the propaganda message both on himself and on other members of the group. A properly conducted *beseda* ends in a chorus of approval for official policies and a pledge to fulfil the tasks placed before the collective.[54] And

---

[52] *Voprosy partiinoi raboty*, p. 484.

[53] *Agitator*, 1970, no. 15, p. 40.

[54] That group discussion is particularly effective in inducing opinion and action change – and that discussion plus goal-setting is superior to discussion alone – is suggested by experimental studies in group

thirdly, it provides a means by which questions can be asked, problems raised and grievances aired. Agitators are told not to evade 'trenchant' or 'difficult' questions but to endeavour to give clear and honest replies to the queries and complaints of their listeners – 'The party always tells the people the truth.'[55] But this does not mean that the agitator should necessarily agree with the substance of a particular complaint or show sympathy for the complainant. In general the advice to agitators is:

> If you start expressing sympathy...you are only making matters worse. You must strengthen the person's confidence, show that while difficulties exist, they do not spring from anyone's ill will but from such-and-such causes; the main thing is to show what is being done so that people may live better and better.[56]

This is not a recipe for all occasions. There are cases for which 'ill will' can be a more plausible explanation, provided always that the central authorities are exonerated and the resentment of the audience directed at local officials or – preferably still – turned inward at its own frailties. This, for example, is how one agitator dealt with a question concerning the shortage of bread in the shops:

> What should the agitator say? Should he...agree, sigh and commiserate...? Or should he try to say that things are not as bad as all that...? Both of these paths are incorrect. And Antsyfarov did not take either of them. He told why less bread had been produced during the current year and concentrated the main attention of the audience on the fact that the country was nevertheless assured of [a supply of] bread.
>
> How great is the might of our state – he said – if it can overcome such misfortune!
>
> At this point the agitator together with the others examined every case of interruption in supplies. It was found that bread

dynamics. (See K. Lewin, 'Group Decision and Social Change', in E. E. Maccoby, T. M. Newcomb and E. L. Hartley, eds., *Readings in Social Psychology*, 3rd ed., New York, 1958, pp. 197–211.) These studies have been challenged on a number of counts. In any case, the so-called 'participation hypothesis', even though it allows for a degree of 'pseudo participation', cannot be uncritically translated to the peculiar setting of the agitation *beseda*.

[55] *Voprosy partiinoi raboty*, p. 486; *Partiinaya zhizn'*, 1957, no. 2, p. 61; *Agitator*, 1965, no. 15, pp. 22–3.

[56] *Spravochnik sekretarya pervichnoi partiinoi organizatsii*, 1960, p. 521.

sales did not fall by comparison with last year. Why then the interruptions?

You must understand – he explained – that some people submitted to rumours and by excessive purchases 'for stock' created artificial difficulties.

And the people understood the agitator. . . . Replies could be heard:

– Such people should be exposed!

– They should be put to shame . . . that will have an effect![57]

Life in the Soviet Union naturally imposes its own fairly narrow limits on the type of 'difficult' questions that will be asked in public, but while few people would seek to challenge the general line of the party, complaints against specific aspects of its practical implementation at the local level are not infrequently voiced. It is then the duty of the agitator either to justify the measures of the local authority or, if necessary, to seek practical remedy. Thus, for instance, a foreman who had been particularly rude to one of his workers will be made to apologize in public, or the director of the plant, invited to hear criticisms of the quality of factory housing, will promise to initiate the necessary repairs. It is on matters of this kind that audiences are allowed to vent their grievances relatively freely. The aim is evidently to deflect popular dissatisfactions from the regime onto its local representatives and at the same time to combat local mismanagement and corruption: 'Let the bureaucrat or harsh administrator be afraid to behave wilfully. Let him know that the collective protects the affronted and the aggrieved and exacts amends from the offender.'[58] At the same time it also raises the standing of the agitator in the eyes of his audience:

If the listeners express critical remarks . . . and their advice is translated into action, then respect for the agitator will grow. His word will be heeded. Conversely, where attention has repeatedly been drawn to shortcomings and imperfections and yet everything remains as before, the listeners will become indifferent, the authority of the agitator [who is] powerless to do anything about it declines and in the end our agitation is harmed.[59]

That redress is not infrequently thwarted is attested by countless reports in the Soviet press. Many an agitator apparently finds

[57] *Agitator*, 1964, no. 1, pp. 35–6.
[58] *Ibid.*, 1965, no. 15, p. 23.   [59] *Ibid.*

it easier to 'administer' than to 'persuade', to suppress or ignore
the complaints of the workers than to undertake the troublesome
and possibly hazardous task of intervention on their behalf. The
Soviet press continuously reports instances of agitators and other
minor functionaries who in the course of such intervention in-
curred the displeasure of their superiors and suffered the consequences.[60] That these malpractices find their way into the
press – and it is a reasonable assumption that those publicized
comprise only a small share of the total – would seem to point
to the regime's genuine concern with the problem. On the other
hand it must also be recognized that, apart from furnishing a
supreme example of authoritarian methods of government by
its own conduct, the Soviet leadership encourages emulation by
reminding agitators that they must at all times distinguish between persons with just grievances and a genuine desire for
explanation and those who 'judge everything from the standpoint
of their personal interests' (*sudyat obo vsem so svoei kolokol'ni*),
the habitual grumblers and 'trouble-makers'.[61] The latter, as also
those posing 'demagogical questions' must be given a 'decisive
rebuff'. Any other response on the part of the agitator would
smack of 'tailism', would mean following in the wake of mass
sentiment rather than leading it, and that is still one of the least
forgivable sins to which a party activist may succumb.

Indeed, one of the principal functions of the *beseda* is to provide a forum for the public criticism of the workers themselves.
Thus a worker who has persistently failed to meet his work
norm or offended against factory discipline will be taken to task
by the agitator in front of his co-workers and appropriately reprimanded.[62] The same treatment is meted out to groups of workers
and to those responsible for the group's performance: ' "Your
brigade, comrade Zaitsev, has not been overly zealous" [said
one agitator at the conclusion of his *beseda*]. The reprimand was

---

[60] Perhaps the following comment from a rolling mill operator speaks for
itself: 'I very much like the article in the Statutes which states that
persons guilty of suppressing criticism or persecuting others for criticism
must be severely called to account... Yet I cannot remember that anyone
in our town has been expelled from the party or even severely punished
in recent years for suppressing criticism. Is it possible that there has not
been a single case of such suppression?' (*Pravda*, 7 December 1967.)

[61] *Voprosy partiioni raboty*, pp. 486–90; also *Spravochnik sekretarya pervichnoi partiinoi organizatsii*, 1960, pp. 522, 525; *Kommunist*, 1965,
no. 10, p. 47.

[62] See, e.g., *Partiinaya zhizn'*, 1956, no. 8, pp. 48–9; *Agitator*, 1973, no. 1,
p. 30.

just. The brigadier is aware of the reproachful looks of those present. "It will not happen again," – says Zaitsev.'[63] Such morality tales are perhaps a little too stylized to be taken at face value. One cannot help being somewhat sceptical about the 'reproachful looks' of the audience or about their instantaneous educative effect on the culprit. Lack of zeal in performing production tasks is not, one would think, the kind of 'deviation' that would automatically evoke social opprobrium from a typical audience of workers or collective farmers. Still, similar cases are constantly reported in the Soviet press reflecting the regime's faith in the agitator's ability to manipulate the pressure of group opinion, to subject the transgressor, as one editorial article put it, 'to the strict court of his collective'.[64]

The conscientious agitator is expected to extend his agitation beyond the forum of the group *beseda* and to conduct 'individual work with people' at every opportunity. 'The agitator cannot limit himself to official agitation, if one can call planned *besedy* thus . . . but must always be at his post.'[65] He agitates 'virtually day-by-day'.[66] It is the 'party's concern "to reach everyone"' and this cannot be done by group meetings alone, for 'people are different' and 'there cannot be a [single] mould for influencing their consciousness'.[67] What this means in practical terms – apart from the agitator's duty to keep a watchful eye on the collective at all times and to deal with any problems and queries as they come up – is that agitators must give individual attention to members of the group whose work performance or social conduct falls short of the required standards. Often young workers are placed under the wing of an agitator-mentor (*agitator-nastavnik*); religious believers, too, generally merit individual treatment by agitators.[68] As a rule it is those whom the party considers most in need of reform through agitation who do not appear regularly at the group *besedy* and, when they do, sit through them passively. It is the task of the agitator to single out such persons and by patient, day-to-day individual work bring them into the fold of the collective. The party press frequently reports cases of persons who have been thus 'rehabilitated' through the persistent efforts of the agitator.[69]

[63] *Partiinaya zhizn'*, 1962, no. 1, p. 35
[64] *Agitator*, 1972, no. 5, p. 4. [65] *Partiinaya zhizn'*, 1956, no. 8, p. 44.
[66] *Agitator*, 1968, no. 12, p. 39. [67] *Ibid.*, 1970, no. 15, p. 41.
[68] *Ibid.*, 1964, no. 14, p. 11; 1971, no. 15, pp. 26–7, no. 23, p. 29.
[69] See, e.g. *Partiinaya zhizn'*, 1957, no. 9, pp. 54–5; *Agitator*, 1972, no. 7, p. 35; 1973, no. 8, p. 31.

A large variety of visual and other technical aids, including posters, diagrams, wall newspapers, plant magazines, 'lightening bolts' (*molnii*), lantern slides, tape-recordings (of Lenin's speeches, for instance), films and closed-circuit television, increasingly supplement the work of the agitator. Apart from projecting the views and slogans of the regime into the factory and collective farm, these aids often contain technical information of direct relevance to specific production problems: the treatment of avitaminosis among pigs in a particular collective farm, for instance, might be the subject of a 'lightning bolt' issued by agitators. A common use of visual agitation is to inform the collective of the rate of plan fulfilment, to stimulate 'socialist emulation', and to highlight – by 'Rolls of Honour', 'Pennants of Fame' and similar displays – the outstanding production accomplishments of individual workers.[70] At the same time it also serves to reinforce the disciplinary function of the agitator. The skilful agitator will employ the various agitational means at his disposal in close conjunction. Thus a worker who is repeatedly late for work or a foreman with a penchant for playing dominoes during working hours may find himself the subject of a *beseda* one day and of a caricature in the wall newspaper on the next day. 'Satire Windows', 'Boards of Shame' or 'Conscience Books' (in which the workers confess their misdemeanours and promise to better their ways) round off the arsenal of agitational instruments.[71]

During elections to the soviets the agitation effort is greatly intensified. Elections, Soviet-style, are a grand roll-call of the nation. The objective is to evoke the unanimous acclaim of the masses for the Soviet leaders and their policies, and, more particularly, to generate a new burst of enthusiasm for the numerous tasks of 'socialist construction'. 'All agitation work in the election campaign' states an article on the 1971 elections, 'must be conducted under the sign of the mobilization of the Soviet people for the fulfilment of the decisions of the 24th Congress.'[72] The entire campaign, from nomination through to polling day, is not only a massive propaganda tournament but also a useful device for testing and retuning the machinery of control and manipulation. To the Soviet leadership the fact that over 99% of the people

[70] See, e.g. *Agitator*, 1970, no. 13, p. 4; 1971, no. 5, p. 30.
[71] *Pravda*, 29 June 1962; 8 April 1967; *Agitator*, 1964, no. 14, p. 12; 1971, no. 18, p. 32.
[72] *Agitator*, 1971, no. 8, p. 44.

have once again turned out to register their vote on behalf of the regime is proof that all systems continue to function smoothly.

The bases of electoral agitation are the agitation-points (*agit-punkty*), which were first established for the 1937 elections, and the electors' clubs, a more elaborate and as yet relatively rare innovation of recent years. *Agitpunkty* are set up in each polling district; electors' clubs, where they exist, cover larger areas. Lectures, meetings with candidates, question-and-answer evenings, cultural activities, exhibitions, etc., are arranged in these centres. As a rule they are run by the largest primary party organization in the locality, while the smaller organizations assume responsibility for different residential quarters, apartment houses, dormitories, etc. Care is taken to reach every single voter including 'shepherds in outlying pastures'.[73] Agitators are briefed that 'it is important to reach every person, know his mood, needs and requests and possibly help him in something'.[74] In the weeks preceding the elections they visit voters in their homes, listen to their problems, answer their questions, make sure they are duly registered and impress upon them the importance of voting; they also find out who is sick and unable to come to the poll and arrange for one of the mobile polling stations to collect the vote. It is the activity of the agitators above all which allows the Soviet authorities to boast that in contrast to 'bourgeois states' such as France, where it is possible for over 40% of the voters to abstain, the turnout at Soviet elections invariably exceeds the 99% mark;[75] it creates that 'environment of pressure'[76] which makes direct compulsion or the falsification of election returns quite unnecessary.

Similar efforts are launched in connection with the convocation of party congresses, the publication of Central Committee theses on such occasions as the 50th anniversary of the October revolution or the Lenin centenary, or other important events in the realm of party and state affairs. In rural areas, sowing and harvesting campaigns provide regular occasions for the periodic reinforcement of agitation. At such times motorized 'agit-brigades' and 'agit-trains' from the district centre or other larger towns visit the collective farmers and agricultural workers in the fields,

[73] *Partiinaya zhizn'*, 1957, no. 1, p. 59.
[74] *Pravda*, 17 February 1969.   [75] *Agitator*, 1965, no. 4, p. 6.
[76] The expression is from J. M. Gilison, 'Soviet Elections as a Measure of Dissent. The Missing One Percent', *Amer. Pol. Science Review*, 1968, no. 3, p. 816.

bringing with them groups of agitators, propagandists, lecturers, as well as an assortment of cultural and welfare facilities – amateur entertainment ensembles, mobile cinema, library, medical staff, canteen, barber, shoe-maker, etc.[77]

A major innovation of recent years has been the progressive extension of agitation to residential areas. Until the end of the 1950s agitators largely confined their activities to places of work. Party organization outside the enterprise was weak or non-existent and such oral agitation as was conducted in residential areas was for the most part desultory except during special mass campaigns and in the weeks preceding elections. In 1959 a Central Committee decree on mass-political work in Stalino Province (as it then was) called for the establishment of permanent *agitpunkty* in such places as clubs, hostels and large apartment blocks.[78] One year later the Central Committee decree 'On the Tasks of Party Propaganda in Contemporary Conditions', mentioned earlier, enjoined party organizations 'to strengthen idea-upbringing work among the working people in places of residence, widely practise individual forms of upbringing work and reach every Soviet person . . .'[79] At the same time the party press began to report on the attempts of local organizations to reach persons with whom 'contact had hitherto been weak', such as housewives, youths and old-age pensioners.[80] In 1962 a further Central Committee decree on mass-political work in Kuibyshev Province noted that 'considerable sections of the population, especially in places of residence, are outside the sphere of day-to-day political influence exerted by party organizations', and that there were 'not a few communities in which as many as half the residents are not covered by ideological work'.[81]

It soon became clear that what was required was not merely to bring wider sections of the non-working population into the ambit of regular mass-political work but to extend and intensify the agitational effort as a whole, including follow-up agitation for those already exposed to it at their places of work. As one agitator put it: 'Until recently people lived as if each one was for

[77] See, e.g. *Agitator*, 1968, no. 5, pp. 46–8; *Partiinaya zhizn'*, 1972, no. 22, pp. 60–5.
[78] *Spravochnik partiinogo rabotnika*, 1961, pp. 458–9.
[79] *Ibid.*, p. 496.
[80] *Partiinaya zhizn'*, 1959, no. 7, pp. 42–3, no. 9, pp. 38–40; 1960, no. 8, pp. 49–50
[81] *Spravochnik partiinogo rabotnika*, 1963, p. 441. See also the decree of the Central Committee plenum of June 1963, *ibid.*, 1964, pp. 14–15.

himself . . . by the private ownership precept – "My home is my castle. I can do in it as I please." [82] The party activist, too, apparently behaved as if his social and political duties did not extend beyond the factory gate. In the words of another functionary, it often happened that such an activist 'returned home, shut himself in his apartment and was neither seen nor heard'; neighbours might be committing a variety of anti-social acts while 'members of the party and the Komsomol, propagandists, agitators, people's guards . . . were detached onlookers or turned away diffidently pretending they had not noticed anything.' [83] By the mid 1960s the situation had evidently not yet improved to the satisfaction of the party authorities, for the 1966 edition of the *Handbook of the Propagandist and the Agitator* still complained that, in contrast to the enterprise there was 'in the majority of cases no permanent organized influence at places of residence. Instead, forces alien to us are at times active here: clergymen, sectarians and idlers not infrequently activate morally unstable people of all kinds and become the organizers of drinking bouts, card games, etc.' [84]

The introduction of the five-day working week in 1967 gave further impetus to the development of residential agitation. By prolonging the effective working day it limited the time available for agitation at the enterprise, and by creating two full non-working days in the week it enhanced both the need and the opportunity for party-sponsored leisure time activity, including oral agitation. Notwithstanding the growing pre-occupation with residential work, however, the main weight of the agitation effort is still directed at the production enterprise. And this, in the Soviet view, 'is as it should be [*zakonomerno*], because here the material-technical basis of communism is created, communist attitudes are formed, the process of labour upbringing is carried on and the views and convictions of people are taking shape'. [85]

The territorial primary party organizations which spread rapidly following the amendment of the Party Statutes in 1961 seemed originally to have been earmarked as the organizational buttress of residential mass-political work. In many cases it still is their membership which provides the nucleus for the agitation-

---

[82] *Agitator*, 1964, no. 17, p. 51; *Kommunist*, 1963, no. 3, p. 79.
[83] *Agitator*, 1963, no. 1, p. 35.
[84] *Spravochnik propagandista i agitatora*, Moscow, 1966, p. 109.
[85] V. A. Lapin, 'Osnovnye puti sochetaniya ideino-vospitatel'noi raboty na proizvodstve i v bytu', in Groshev *et al.*, eds., *Iz opyta ideologicheskoi raboty*, p. 249.

collectives and other groups of activists operating in places of residence. In others, however, reliance on territorial primary organizations was shown to be insufficient and the primary organizations of enterprises were urged to assume the 'patronage' (*shefstvo*) for agitation in the localities in which they are situated. There were too few residential territorial organizations, it was argued, and their members, consisting predominantly of old-age pensioners, were either unwilling or incapable of coping with the task.[86] More important, agitation at work and at home was a single process and responsibility for it should not be divided. By involving itself in residential work the enterprise primary organization would be able to extend its sights into the private lives of its workers and add a vital dimension to its 'upbringing' work at the enterprise. When a local conference of party officials resolved that residential agitation should be entrusted 'above all' to enterprise organizations, the reason given was:

> Because the Communists in a particular plant, factory, institution cannot be indifferent to how members of their collectives occupy themselves during their non-working time, what views and habits they form at home, how they extend their political and cultural horizon. The party organization is responsible for the conduct of 'its' workers and employees as much outside the enterprise as inside it.

The successful socialization of youth, too, required that the enterprise party organization should step in at an early stage:

> The adolescent who will enter the [production] collective tomorrow and will be in need of the attention of the Communists is today being brought up in the family, the school... The concept 'educating the educators'... must also include influence on the parents of the future workers, the school teachers – all those connected with the formation of the adolescent's character and personality. And this requires of the party organizations of production collectives day-to-day concern for the upbringing of the working people at places of residence.[87]

In practice, responsibility for agitation does of course frequently remain divided, not only between enterprise and territorial organizations but also between different enterprise party organi-

[86] *Agitator*, 1969, no. 8, p. 40; *Partiinaya zhizn'*, 1970, no. 20, p. 51.
[87] *Kommunist*, 1968, no. 18, pp. 49–50 and 52.

zations, since people do not necessarily reside in the vicinity of their work places, especially in the larger towns. This is recognized to be a more or less unavoidable impediment to the central purpose of the exercise, which is to perfect and supplement the party's 'day-to-day concern' by providing continuous, almost round-the-clock agitation coverage.

Another aspect of the organization of residential mass-political work which deserves to be briefly noted is the participation of the residents themselves in a hierarchy of communal councils and committees. The precise appellation and structure of these organs varies somewhat. But their formation, and, in some cases, their revival has been firmly pressed by local party organizations throughout the 1960s, and they now function in both towns and villages down to the level of individual apartment blocks or groups of houses and – in the larger apartment houses – even separate entrances. Their common aim is to enlist the residents in a variety of social and political activities, always, of course, under the indispensable guidance or 'patronage' of the appropriate party organizations. It is the combination of small territorial units, sometimes including no more than 10–20 households, together with the participation of the residents themselves, which is designed to break the 'private ownership precept' outside the production sphere and, in the words of the Moscow city agitprop chief, 'to create in every home, in every apartment, such conditions that not a single amoral act by anyone will remain unnoticed'.[88] Since comrades' courts and detachments of people's guards also function under the aegis of the residential councils, the latter dispose over their own agencies of enforcement, and are equipped not only to notice 'amoral acts' but also to discipline offenders.

The subject matter of residential agitation covers the entire spectrum of private and public conduct – from the struggle against 'religious prejudices' and other 'residues of the past' to family and community relations, 'cultural growth' and political activism in its manifold forms. Insofar as can be judged from the emphasis which Soviet sources place on them, by far the largest effort appears to be directed against the various categories of social deviants, particularly hooligans, drunkards and 'parasites'. In view of the high concentration of 'hard-core' believers among pensioners and housewives who cannot be reached at the

[88] *Po mestu zhitel'stva* . . ., Moscow, 1967, p. 15.

enterprise, atheist propaganda is now almost exclusively channelled to places of residence. Increasingly, too, social welfare work and cultural and recreational activities have moved into the orbit of residential agitation.[89] Economic themes, while not entirely neglected, occupy a relatively minor place. To quote Morozov:

> In the production enterprise political agitation is directed in the first place towards the attainment of work indices, towards the advance of the economy. In places of residence, first and foremost in mass work are questions pertaining to the observance of the rules of socialist society, communist morality, the upbringing of youth and children, the development of socialist principles in the daily lives of people.[90]

Everywhere the emphasis is on 'concrete' tasks. Residential agitation is said to achieve its purpose where it succeeds in reducing rowdyism, where church attendance declines, where family and community relations are congenial, where residents take an active interest in the affairs of their neighbourhood and the welfare of their neighbours, where newspaper subscriptions and library enrolment are on the increase and everyone joins wholeheartedly in the political and cultural activities provided for the community.

The forms of residential agitation also show considerable variety. There is the small group *beseda* conducted by the agitator in a specially designated room (usually in the home of the agitator or of the residents who may take it in turn to provide the facilities) known as *agitkvartir* or *komnata politicheskoi agitatsii*. And there are lectures, question-and-answer evenings, 'vocal newspapers', 'round-table' discussions, 'October readings' and similar events scheduled for larger audiences in clubs, Red Corners, Houses of Culture, permanent *agitpunkty* and – during the summer – in open-air agitation grounds (*agitploshchadki*) in parks, public squares and the courtyards of apartment blocks. Even the relatively numerous gatherings are frequently used to subject individual miscreants to the collective wrath of their fellow-residents. 'At these meetings', wrote a secretary of Novosibirsk Province, describing the work in a large *agitpunkt* seating 400 people,

---

[89] See below pp. 182ff and 216ff.
[90] Morozov, *Massovo-politicheskaya rabota partiinykh organizatsii*, pp. 29–30.

scapegraces, drunkards and those who fail to observe the rules of human society are sharply criticized. Of course, there are no such things as miracles and not all these individuals change there and then into exemplary persons, but it is perfectly clear that this approach towards violators of public order yields results.[91]

More important than any of the above is the agitators' 'individual work with people'; in the words of the party manual, it is 'the soul of agitation' in places of residence.[92] As a rule agitators are assigned on a more or less permanent basis to work with particular households. In most cases the criteria of assignment appear to be somewhat haphazard, depending in the main upon residential proximity. In others, a more discriminate approach is practised, enabling selected agitators to concentrate on the problem cases of Soviet society – religious believers, broken families, 'anti-social' elements and 'difficult' youths, as well as persons 'who are little interested in politics'.[93] But this does not mean that attention to ordinary, law-abiding, sober and well-adjusted citizens is allowed to wane. The overriding imperative, underlined in almost every Soviet account, is 'to enter every home', 'to reach literally every person'.[94] As a secretary of Odessa put it: 'We see our task in bringing the word of the party to every inhabitant of the city, whether worker, intellectual, housewife, pensioner or adolescent'; people to whom the word of the party is not thus brought, and there still are such people, 'at times fall under alien influence'.[95]

The main reasons for the prominence of individual agitation in residential mass-political work are three. Firstly, the natural target area of much residential agitation is the home of the Soviet citizen. It is not his production performance but his conduct in his private life which is to be assessed and influenced. To do so effectively is well-nigh impossible without seeking him out, without observing his home environment and his own 'mode of life' in that environment. Soviet spokesmen show themselves aware of the problem when they complain that agitators 'are still far from knowing enough about. . . the various aspects of the life

---

[91] *Izvestya*, 29 October 1964.
[92] *Spravochnik sekretarya pervichnoi partiinoi organizatsii*, 1967, p. 89.
[93] *Izvestiya*, 29 October 1964; *Partiinaya zhizn'*, 1966, no. 7, p. 52; 1967, no. 13, p. 48; 1971, no. 16, p. 55; *Agitator*, 1969, no. 8, p. 41.
[94] *Pravda*, 22 September 1969; *Agitator*, 1970, no. 8, p. 53, no. 22, p. 4.
[95] *Agitator*, 1969, no. 8, p. 42.

of Soviet people, especially the development of their world view and morality, their participation in social life and their daily life. This, it would seem, explains partly why agitation is weakest in the non-production sphere.'[96] Attaching agitators to individual families and ensuring that they visit them regularly for individual agitation is an obvious way of overcoming this deficiency. This, clearly, was the experience of the party organization of one Moldavian kolkhoz, comprising three villages with a total population of 4,625:

> In order to reach every family we divided the villages into 48 sections ... Every agitator has a notebook in which the inhabitants of the section are listed together with brief information about them: age, education, where they work, how they fulfil their socialist obligations, how they conduct themselves in daily life, [whether they are] believers or non-believers.[97]

If individual work is 'the soul of agitation' in places of residence then the agitator's thorough knowledge of his audience is the backbone of individual work. It is the absolute *sine qua non* of success; no other aspect of the agitator's responsibilities is more persistently emphasized in Soviet writings.

Secondly, the typical audience is considerably more heterogeneous than at the enterprise, combining as it often does people of different backgrounds, ages, occupations, interests and cultural standards. A differentiated approach, generally impressed upon agitators as desirable, is therefore deemed essential for residential work. Some party organizations conducted fairly extensive sociological surveys to study the composition of the local population and the consumption of alternative media before embarking on their programme of residential agitation.[98] Frequently, too, mass and group oral communication activities are scheduled for particular audiences. Manifestly, however, the need for a highly differentiated approach places a premium on the individual work of the agitator who, on the basis of his knowledge of his fellow-residents, is able to take account of the interests and predilections of each and thus help to ensure that the propaganda message reaches its target in the most palatable form. To quote the party manual once again:

[96] *Ibid.*, 1966, no. 1, p. 29.   [97] *Ibid.*, 1970, no. 8, p. 55.
[98] *Partiinaya zhizn'*, 1966, no. 7, p. 52; 1969, no. 7, p. 58; *Kommunist*, 1969, no. 18, p. 47; *Agitator*, 1969, no. 8, p. 41; 1971, no. 16, p. 27.

The true agitator has friendly relations with the residents, he is received in [their] homes as a welcome guest, people share their thoughts with him, [their] sorrows and joys. And this because he knows how to find the right approach to everyone, to speak to everyone of that which is nearest to him and most intelligible, which concerns him most.[99]

The third reason for the salience of individual work in residential areas derives from the problem of marshalling the audience for group or mass activities. People have to be induced to leave their homes and give up their free time. This not only requires that such activities should be more interesting and attractive than at the enterprise, it also poses 'organizational' problems not encountered at the enterprise where attendance, if not always attention, can be more easily controlled.[100] There are, it is freely admitted, still many cases of people evading participation in residential activities, and often these are precisely the people at whom these activities are aimed most of all. Understandably enough, atheist propaganda will not be particularly attractive to religious persons, just as 'parasites' will not flock to lectures expounding the redeeming virtues of socialist labour.[101]

This is not, of course, a problem peculiar to the Soviet Union. People everywhere tend to avoid persuasion that conflicts with their opinions and actions, particularly those rooted in basic attitudes. However, the Soviet regime possesses in the residential agitator an instrument capable of counteracting such selective exposure in two ways. Firstly, the agitator can carry 'the word of the party' to a reluctant audience; in particularly obstinate cases his individual work is virtually the only channel by which the regime can hope to penetrate the spontaneous defence mechanisms of the propaganda recipient, since the processes of selective exposure (as well as those of selective perception and retention)

[99] *Spravochnik sekretarya pervichnoi partiinoi organizatsii*, 1967, pp. 89–90.
[100] 'While at the factory or institute people occasionally come to some lectures or speeches which do not interest them much, out of a sense of duty, subordinating themselves to discipline, similar measures are altogether excluded at places of residence. Who will make a person give up his free time if he does not want to?' (*Kommunist*, 1963, no. 8, p. 70, see also *Agitator*, 1969, no. 8, p. 41, no. 12, p. 46.)
[101] See F. A. Lukinskii, 'Ob opyte partiinykh organizatsii po ateisticheskomu vospitaniyu mass v sovremennykh usloviyakh', in G. E. Glezerman, *et al*, eds., *Voprosy teorii i praktiki kommunisticheskogo vospitaniya*, Moscow, 1962, p. 347; also D. Powell, 'The Effectiveness of Soviet Anti-Religious Propaganda', *Public Opinion Quarterly*, 1967, no. 3, pp. 366–80.

operate equally in respect of other communication media. And secondly, the agitator can encourage maximum attendance, particularly of the target audience, at the various communication activities conducted in places of residence; he knows who among the residents would benefit most from a particular lecture and is able to ensure that a personal invitation is extended – and accepted.[102] The problem of selective exposure as it relates to religious believers is highlighted in the following passage from a speech by the former CC Secretary and head of the agitprop apparatus, L. F. Ilyichev, in 1963:

> A clergyman named Vvedensky, of Sverdlovsk Province, declared not long ago: 'Anti-religious propaganda does not bother us. The atheists work with the atheists in their clubs and we work with believers in church.' [Laughter in the hall.] 'The atheists do not come to us and the believers do not go to the clubs. We do not interfere with each other.' [Laughter in the hall.] Here is a testimonial to our anti-religious propaganda. One cannot but agree with it.[103]

Remaining still in the realm of atheist propaganda, the contribution of the individual work of agitators to the solution of the problem is reflected in another 'testimonial', this time from an official of the Kuibyshev Province Committee, in 1970:

> The experience of Maria Ivanona Ushakova and other agitator-atheists attests that individual work is the most effective form of anti-religious propaganda. It provides an opportunity to reach every believer, to clarify the cause and character of his religious beliefs, the range of his interest and needs, [and] to influence him in the formation of a materialist world view.[104]

If these are the features of individual agitation which account for its unique importance in residential mass-political work there are others which apply to places of residence no less than they do to places of work. In residential areas, too, the presence of the agitator helps to ensure the penetration of communication media

---

[102] For an example of how local activists devise and 'courteously' deliver personal invitations to religious believers in their community see *Nauka i religiya*, 1968, no. 4, p. 43; also *Agitator*, 1966, no. 23, p. 43 and *Partiinaya zhizn'*, 1968, no. 8, p. 60. For another claiming that as a result of such personal invitations 'not a single believer stays at home' when the local atheist club holds a lecture, see G. V. Vorontsov, 'Ateisticheskoe vospitanie–sostavnaya chast' ideologicheskoi raboty partii na sovremennom etape', in Smyshlyaev *et al.*, eds., *KPSS v period stroitel'stva kommunizma*, p. 125.

[103] *Pravda*, 19 June 1963.   [104] *Agitator*, 1970, no. 16, p. 39.

generally. The agitprop head of Belgorod Province, referring to agitation in rural areas, thus described this aspect of the agitator's work:

A specific number of houses is attached to each agitator. The agitator informs the collective farmers of what is new today on the stage of the House of Culture, on the television set, which new accessions of the library will bring pleasure in the coming days. Usually after this a relaxed, friendly conversation is started up. In its course the interests and requirements of the people come to light.[105]

Undoubtedly, what comes to light too is whether a particular collective farmer avails himself of the advice proffered by his agitator and benefits from it.

Above all, there is the ability of the agitator to supervise compliance. Whatever the particular demand made upon the individual or the collective, the agitator is near at hand to check on fulfilment and, where necessary, to set in motion appropriate disciplinary action. Perhaps the following case history will best illustrate the *modus operandi* of residential agitation; it was related by the secretary of a party organization in Moscow (in an article entitled 'Approach humanely...') and concerns one Kuznetsov, a housepainter:

He drank, behaved like a hooligan and terrorized his family. We talked to him a great deal. He listened and agreed but went home and resumed his old ways.

It became clear that our words did not reach him. It was decided to bring him before the comrades' court. However, this had no influence on Kuznetsov. Then, after his next noisy drinking bout, we passed the matter on to the people's court. it was necessary to isolate the hooligan from society, to save the family from mockery and let the neighbours have peace.

The court sitting took place in the assembly hall of the school. The day before, our activists posted announcements and visited the homes of residents and invited them to attend the court. Of course, attention was above all given to those who drink and behave like hooligans so that they might learn a useful lesson.

The hall was overcrowded. The public accuser from our organization was Colonel Nikolai Nilovich Kolosov (ret.), a

---

[105] *Ibid.*, no. 11, p. 32.

man of great culture and education, a former submariner and the holder of thirteen decorations and medals.

His speech to the court was gripping. The hall listened with bated attention. Even the prosecutor said afterwards that he had not heard such a powerful and well-argued speech in a long time.

Kuznetsov was sentenced to two-and-a-half years of strict regime [imprisonment]. He served his sentence and returned to us with a good reference. We acted on the principle 'Forgive and forget . . .' We helped him to find a job, had heart-to-heart talks with him, supported him, but to be frank, we did not take our eyes off him. And possibly all would have been well if he had not met his old drinking companions. Kuznetsov again broke loose. He began to insult his wife and children. We invited him [for further heart-to-heart talks] . . . Realizing that his outrageous behaviour would not be tolerated Kuznetsov left for Tula and took a job in a factory. We thought then that all our work had not brought the desired results, but we were mistaken. He had taken to heart not a little of our talks. Now he writes us that he understands and realizes much of what we had said to him . . .[106]

The case is typical for the way in which Soviet residential agitation attempts to deal with deviant behaviour: the close surveillance by the party organization and its activists, the 'heart-to-heart talks' with the malefactor, the deployment of the collective, the recourse to the penal process (first 'social' then state), with activists again playing a vital role before and during the trial and later in the process of rehabilitation. In other cases a somewhat different dosage of these ingredients may be prescribed; invariably, however, the treatment will rely on the close interaction of persuasion and organization which is so crucial to the mobilizing function of Soviet agitation everywhere.[107]

In some respects residential agitation differs from its counterpart at the enterprise: it is rather more varied in form and con-

---

[106] *Po mestu zhitel'stva . . .*, p. 41.

[107] Once in a while the press carries articles condemning 'excesses' of overzealous activists, as in the case of one residential council which 'instituted the title of "social parasite" and publicly bestowed it upon residents . . . who, though they worked hard at their jobs, did not eagerly accept the duties assigned to them by the house council'. (*Izvestiya*, 20 December 1964.) But it is difficult to see how this case differed from other procedures of organized public pressure enjoying full official encouragement.

tent and as yet less intensive and single-minded. But its essential features are very similar. It is primarily oriented towards 'concrete' problems – with political and social conformity instead of production performance as its central concerns. It serves both to transmit official demands and to enforce compliance: the audience is not only being informed of its tasks, it is being organized for their fulfilment. And finally, by invoking the ubiquitous 'influence of the collective', it manipulates the instruments of public opinion itself to overcome the resistance of individuals or groups.

In assessing the role of the Soviet agitator the comparison with 'opinion leaders' is near at hand. The key mediating function of such 'molecular' leaders has become part of the conventional wisdom of Western communications specialists, and it may be tempting to ascribe comparable potentialities to the Soviet agitator. The similarities are indeed obvious enough. The agitator, like the Western opinion leader, is a member of the primary group in which he conducts his communication activity. He shares its values and beliefs. If properly selected, he is an 'authoritative' member of the group; if properly briefed and trained, he knows more than other members of the group and has the necessary skills to communicate that knowledge. The 'ifs' are obviously crucial. But even on the assumption that the conditions necessary for the optimal functioning of the Soviet agitators are everywhere fulfilled – and they are not – important differences remain.

The agitator is not spontaneously 'nominated' by the group but appointed from above. However much he may share the norms of the group, he cannot shed his identification as an agent of the regime. It is implicit in his assignment and constantly thrust forward in the execution of his duties. To this extent, therefore, the effect of persuasion from below, from within the group, is necessarily impaired. Moreover, the agitator's functions require him to initiate persuasion. He does not merely respond to demands made by members of the group upon his superior knowledge and judgment; rather the demands of the regime compel him to impose its (his?) views on the group. And this further reduces the potential of his personal influence.[108]

Lastly, there is the question of his superior knowledge and

---

[108] This point is noted by Powell, 'Effectiveness of Anti-Religious Propaganda', who also cites supporting evidence derived from American experience.

judgment, of his authority. Studies of group-nominated opinion leaders in competitive communication systems have shown that opinion leadership is not a general characteristic of a person but always limited to specific issue areas: people turn to particular opinion leaders for advice on particular topics.[109] The Soviet agitator, by contrast, is conceived as a sort of universal guide to the perplexed, with wide-ranging authority embracing all possible problems arising within the group. This is manifestly an artificial construct which no amount of refinement in selection procedures can turn into reality. Soviet workers may possibly regard their agitators as natural opinion leaders in production matters: since it is competence in this sphere which is an essential qualification for the agitator's assignment at places of work, official and spontaneous selection may largely overlap. But it is exceedingly unlikely that they would credit their agitators with similar authority in other fields.[110]

In the context of the last point it may be of some interest to note that in the mid-1960s many local party organizations began to experiment with a system of specialized agitators. The pattern of specialization adopted was by no means uniform but it generally included such subject areas as economic or production matters, domestic and foreign policy, 'communist morality', atheism and problems of youth. The argument for specialization was that the general cultural level of the population had risen to a point where the traditional agitator-generalist (*agitator-universal*) had little, if anything, to add to what could be learned from other sources, notably the mass media. It was only by specializing in a particular field that the agitator could hope to make a positive contribution to the 'enlightenment' of the masses and thus justify his role in the communication process.[111]

While the attitude of the local functionaries reporting on the

---

[109] But see A. S. Marcus and R. A. Bauer. 'Yes: There Are Generalized Opinion Leaders', *Public Opinion Quarterly*, 1964, no. 4, pp. 628–32.

[110] When 250 participants in party studies in three cities were asked in the course of a sociological survey, to list the people whom they normally approached with questions on political problems, agitators received the lowest share of the 'nominations' – 6.4%, and (not surprisingly) friends and fellow-workers received the highest – 51.2%. (Efimov and Pozdnyakov, *Nauchnye osnovy*, pp. 99–100.) See also G. T. Zhuravlev and A. S. Seregin, 'Materialy konkretnogo sotsiologicheskogo issledovaniya ideino-vospitatel'noi raboty sredi naseleniya po mestu zhitel'stva', in P. K. Kurochkin *et al.*, eds., *Voprosy teorii i metodov ideologicheskoi raboty*, Vyp. 1, Moscow, 1972, p. 295.

[111] *Agitator*, 1965, no. 6, p. 30, no. 16, pp. 24–5; 1966, no. 5, p. 43.

work of their specialized agitators was wholly enthusiastic, the initial response of the central agitprop establishment could be described as one of guarded approval at best.[112] The latest accounts indicate that the experiment has since been quietly abandoned. In any event, although it might have raised the expertise of agitators in their areas of specialization, it clearly would not have met the objection concerning the comparability of the role of agitators to that of opinion leaders in a spontaneous communication environment. Existing cadres of agitators were simply assigned to different specializations according to either or both of two criteria: their own inclinations and the valuations of their superiors of their aptitudes. Neither of these necessarily coincides with the natural, unconstrained pattern of opinion formation within the group.

None of the above is to deny that Soviet agitators contribute significantly to the dissemination of official views and policies, but merely to warn against unguarded generalizations drawn from the experience of superficially similar face-to-face communication situations in very different political systems. While the institution of the agitator may be profitably viewed as an attempt by the regime to usurp the 'social relay points' of opinion leadership, it would be quite wrong to mistake the attempt for the accomplished fact. On the contrary, there is every reason to believe that a network of informal opinion leaders persists in the Soviet Union alongside the official agents of oral agitation.

The picture of the Soviet agitator would not be complete without some mention of the inherent dilemmas and chronic shortcomings which have continued to inhibit his activities – even within the limits sketched out above. One such dilemma is that of dual loyalty: to the group of which he is a member and to the regime of which he is a representative. The very proximity of the agitator to his audience – otherwise the main source of his strength – renders him highly susceptible to its views and reactions. Placed between the hammer of disciplinary pressure from above and the anvil of social resistance from below, not every agitator can find in himself sufficient 'Bolshevik tempering' to broach unpopular issues and incur the social stigma which too ardent identification with the more exacting demands of the regime may involve.[113] This is, of course, the problem already

---

[112] *Ibid.*, 1965, no. 10, pp. 19–21.
[113] These 'cross-pressures' are analyzed in Inkeles, *Public Opinion in Soviet Russia*, pp. 80ff.

encountered in connection with the word-of-mouth propaganda of the party rank and file. In the case of the agitator it will probably be more often resolved in favour of the regime, if only because the degree of the agitator's institutionalized responsibility for mass-political work is far greater than that of the ordinary party member. But among agitators, too, there are those who are found to be deficient in vigilance, hesitant in criticism of their fellow workers and half-hearted in the defence of official policies, men whose 'mistaken' notion of group solidarity is responsible for their reluctance 'to carry the dirt outside the room'.[114]

Whereas Soviet sources have occasionally acknowledged the existence of this dilemma, they have so far displayed little awareness and less understanding of another conflict inherent in the agitator's assignment: that between instrumental or task leader on the one hand and social-emotional leader on the other. The agitator's dual task as organizer and persuader involves him in both these roles and thus exposes him to their conflicting requirements. To be sure, the performance-oriented ethos of Soviet agitation makes it virtually certain that in practice the instrumental-adaptive functions associated with task leadership will take precedence over the integrative-expressive functions associated with social leadership; in other words, agitators will seek to accomplish the tasks set for the group rather than to keep its members happy and harmonious. And this may go a long way to explain why Soviet spokesmen have not been overly concerned with the problem, apart from occasional warnings to agitators to refrain from a 'commanding tone' in their dealings with fellow-workers.[115] Still, the fact remains that – ignoring for the moment all other limiting factors – the agitator's responsibilities as organizer of the collective cannot be expected to engender the 'sensitive approach to comrades' which the regime seems to require of him, nor, for that matter, can they be expected to encourage his comrades to turn to him 'in joy and in sorrow'.

For many years now, Soviet accounts of the work of agitators have revealed a series of endemic deficiencies. Some of these are embedded in the above role conflicts, others derive from a multiplicity of different causes. The existence of totally inactive agitators has already been mentioned. Of those agitators who are active some are prone to a variety of sins of omission and commission which in the Soviet idiom are subsumed under the

[114] *Bloknot agitatora*, 1955, no. 13, p. 14.
[115] See e.g. *Agitator*, 1963, no. 5, pp. 32–3; *Pravda*, 28 May 1969.

'declarative, superficial and formal character' of their agitation.[116] There are agitators who open the *beseda* with the question 'How are things?' and end it when the reply is 'Fine.'[117] Even at election time some agitators do not take their work very seriously and limit their persuasion to a few sentences, such as: 'I know that you are not voting for the first time and that there is no need to convince you. Come and vote. Good-bye.'[118] More frequent is the case of agitators whose *besedy* are dull and repetitive and consist of laboriously rendered readings from prepared notes.[119] Such agitation, it is said 'does not get to the people involved, does not reach their minds and hearts'.[120] At the other end of the scale there are 'not a few agitators who speak "prettily" but do not convince anyone' because of their addiction to 'memorized, high-flown phrases'.[121] Very often *besedy* consist exclusively of readings from newspaper articles; this is particularly objectionable when the agitator 'specializes' in fictional short stories or foreign news,[122] a choice which in most cases probably reflects the genuine preferences of the audience.

A frequent criticism is directed at the fact that the themes for *besedy* are too general and not sufficiently related to the 'concrete' tasks of the production unit. The incorrect selection of topics is said among others to be responsible for such inattentiveness on the part of the audience as is attested by the lack of questions and even talking and reading while the *beseda* is in progress.[123] One reason for the selection of themes that do not deal with problems 'troubling the people' is the fact that agitation plans are too often dictated by the district party committee without consultation with the primary organization. This practice has

---

[116] *Partiinaya zhizn'*, 1959, no. 6, p. 24; *Pravda*, 10 October 1966; *Agitator*, 1971, no. 3, p. 27.

[117] *Partiinaya zhizn'*, 1960, no. 2, p. 33; see also *Agitator*, 1965, no. 3, p. 32.

[118] *Agitator*, 1965, no. 14, p. 3; see also 1966, no. 7, p. 13.

[119] *Partiinaya zhizn'*, 1956, no. 6, pp. 6–7; *Pravda*, 10 October 1966; *Agitator*, 1968, no. 6, p. 21. Some of these critical accounts of agitation *besedy* remind one of nothing so much as of Marchenko's description of the political instruction sessions in Soviet labour camps. (A. Marchenko, *My Testimony*, London, 1969, pp. 255ff.)

[120] *Pravda*, 23 February 1966.

[121] *Partiinaya zhizn'*, 1956, no. 8, p. 42; see also *Agitator*, 1964, no. 18, p. 37.

[122] *Partiinaya zhizn'*, 1966, no. 24, p. 56; *Agitator*, 1967, no. 8, p. 32. It is worth recalling that as late as 1959 the Central Committee specifically recommended the reading aloud from newspapers as one of the forms of mass-political work. (*Spravochnik partiinogo rabotnika*, 1961, p. 457.)

[123] *Partiinaya zhizn'*, 1957, no. 15, p. 69; *Agitator*, 1970, no. 22, p. 4.

had the even more harmful effect of stifling the agitational initiative of the men on the spot who may neglect to acquaint the people with such important and impeccable materials as result from a Central Committee plenum on the ground that they had not yet received the appropriate guiding directives from the district party committee.[124]

Visual agitation, too, is often neglected. In some places posters and diagrams are kept 'under lock and key'. In others they are 'designed' over-night in response to an urgent signal from the district party committee announcing the imminent arrival of an inspection commission. (It later transpired that the signal was only a ruse aimed at 'bringing order into visual agitation'.)[125] The artistic quality of such materials has also been sharply criticized and even ridiculed in the Soviet press.[126]

Nor has the sustained insertion of agitation into places of residence everywhere had the desired results. Residential agitation is still said to be 'poorly organized', 'unsystematic' and lacking the necessary 'differentiated approach', especially in small and outlying districts.[127] According to one local party functionary,

> The basic trouble is that upbringing work and the organization of leisure in places of residence is conducted without . . . a clear understanding of the forms and methods that are most appropriate to one or another section of the population. Although fairly many different measures are carried out in places of residence, they are, as a rule, badly attended, because usually the people for whom these measures were designed are not invited.[128]

Characteristically, a more sharply worded criticism of the failure of mass-political work to curb hooliganism, especially among youth, was made by the USSR Deputy Minister of Internal Affairs, K. I. Nikitin:

> Today barely 15% of all hooligans found culpable are the subjects of discussions by the collectives to which they belong. Such discussions as are held are often of a formal nature . . . Simply no one seems to reach out to the hooligans. Ordinary

124 *Partiinaya zhizn'*, 1960, no. 8, p. 70.
125 *Agitator*, 1965, no. 14, p. 3.
126 See, e.g. *Novyi mir*, 1961, no. 7, p. 12; *Agitator*, 1966, no. 12, pp. 35–7.
127 *Pravda*, 9 March 1966; *Partiinaya zhizn'*, 1967, no. 16, pp. 52–3; 1972, no. 3, p. 60.
128 *Partiinaya zhizn'*, 1967, no. 17, p. 40.

agitational appeals will not remake them. They attend no lectures and read no newspapers. Every hooligan and rowdy should be personally known and given no peace.[129]

As is their wont in dealing with other shortcomings in the system, Soviet spokesmen have generally attributed the failings of agitators to secondary causes at the level of execution. Again, as in other spheres, cadre policy, in this case the incorrect selection and training of agitators and inadequate party supervision over their work, have had to bear the brunt of official criticism. Party secretaries intent upon 'statistical success' have recruited 'improperly prepared, incompetent and sometimes even politically immature people' into the ranks of the agitators.[130] Many agitators not only lack a 'firm grounding' in Marxism–Leninism, but their 'general education, too, is wholly inadequate'.[131] In fairness to party secretaries it should perhaps be pointed out that they are frequently faced with attempts at shirking agitational duties, particularly by members of the intelligentsia, who are presumably less tempted than manual workers by the rewards in prestige and other privileges that may accrue to the agitator's assignment and more resentful of the demands that it makes on their time. Economic managers, in particular, tend not only to avoid active involvement themselves but also to deprecate the importance of agitational activities for others because they regard such activities as 'irrelevant to the solution of concrete production tasks'.[132]

Even so, there is no overlooking the fact that many party officials take a singularly lackadaisical view of their responsibilities in regard to the selection of agitators, basing themselves on the residual 'principle': 'You have no other load (*nagruzka*), you'll become an agitator.'[133] In the words of the agitprop chief of Donetsk:

The whole question turns on who should be entrusted with agitational work. It is no secret that ... agitation was assigned

---

129 *Komsomol'skaya pravda*, 3 November 1969. More recently these sentiments were echoed by Minister Shchelokov himself. (*Pravda*, 17 March 1973.)
130 *Pravda*, 12 April 1959; *Agitator*, 1966, no. 18, p. 3; 1967, no. 18, p. 42; 1968, no. 19, p. 52.
131 *Agitator*, 1965, no. 18, pp. 3–6, 18; *Partiinaya zhizn'*, 1967, no. 15, p. 12.
132 *Agitator*, 1965, no. 3, p. 32.
133 *Ibid.*, no. 21, p. 31.

to people whose general–cultural and political development did not qualify them for it, or whose personal qualities did not enable them to exercise a positive influence on their fellow-workers. You ask some secretary of a party organization: 'Why was this person given the job of agitator?' And he replies: 'Others are occupied.'[134]

A similar attitude apparently prevails in the party's current guidance of the work of the agitators. Thus, for example, in a poll of over 1,000 agitators in Leningrad only around 40% affirmed that their party organization 'approached agitation work seriously', 60% replied that they were not provided with essential information and 90% admitted that reading aloud from newspapers was their main agitational activity.[135] Findings such as these confirm that the strictures, concerning the neglect of mass-political work by local party organizations, which find their way into Central Committee decrees with almost unfailing regularity, are more than ritualistic incantations.

What the mass of the Soviet people think of the agitators' activities it is naturally difficult to ascertain. One may assume that the great majority is none too pleased with the continued supervision and exhortations which form an integral part of the agitators' functions. A proportion of people may still welcome the informational aspects of Soviet agitation, although here too such reports as appear in the Soviet press from time to time about the inattentiveness of the audience and the dry, platitudinous style of many agitational activities, warrant the belief that popular response is often considerably short of enthusiastic.[136]

Moreover, as the cultural development of Soviet society has advanced, so dependence on oral agitation as a medium of information has declined. In recent years, particularly, the press has carried many reports indicating that the agitators no longer meet the information needs of an increasingly literate population with ready access to the mass media. According to the First Secretary of Krasnodarsk Territory, writing in 1967, a poll of the local population revealed that nearly three-quarters of the people regarded the information supplied by agitators as inadequate

---

[134] *Pravda*, 15 November 1966   [135] *Ibid.*, 10 October 1966.

[136] A recent survey among workers and employees of one industrial plant placed agitators and visual agitation at the bottom of a popularity scale for various forms of ideological work. (Reported in P. Kurochkin, 'Aktual'nye problemy nauchnogo issledovaniya ideologicheskoi raboty', *Kommunist Sov. Latvii*, 1972, no. 6, p. 37.)

and demanded a 'fundamental improvement of oral information'.[137] The following is an example of the kind of views
reported from different parts of the Soviet Union:

> ... he [the agitator] has the same information at his disposal
> that we have, no more. Someone asks a question ... The agita-
> tor is unable to say anything on the subject. Once more – out of
> politeness, perhaps – we listen to 'reading aloud'. I understand
> how necessary that was when a Communist agitator came to
> illiterate Donetsk miners with the only available copy of a
> newspaper. But now ...[138]

It was possibly under the influence of audience reactions such
as these that doubts concerning the continued need for oral
agitation spread in the mid-1960s to party officials, including –
according to one account at least – 'a considerable part of our
ideological workers'.[139] With the rise in mass media consumption,
it was argued, oral agitation had become altogether redundant,
or, at best, was needed for the 'backward strata' of the population only.[140] In the context of the hallowed traditions of Soviet
agitation such views were little short of heretical and the fact
that they were given any publicity at all indicates that they
had substantial backing in party circles. It must be stressed,
however, that when these arguments were first advanced they
were instantly and unequivocally refuted in the Soviet press.
One such refutation deserves particular notice because it comes
from the pen of the then chief editor of *Agitator*, M. S. Kuryanov,
and thus bears the hallmark of an authoritative statement from
the central agitprop apparatus. Writing in the party's chief
theoretical journal, *Kommunist*, in 1965, Kuryanov condemned
the views ('which can sometimes be heard') that oral agitation
had 'lost its former significance' and demanded instead greater
recognition for 'the noble and responsible work of the agitators'.
He went on to reaffirm the official case for the agitator as
opinion leader:

> It is true that the mass media of political agitation, in
> particular radio and television, have undergone broad develop-
> ment. But notwithstanding their importance and mass charac-
> ter, they cannot replace the living word of the agitator, [his]

---

[137] *Partiinaya zhizn'*, 1967, no. 15, p. 12.
[138] *Pravda*, 17 March 1967.
[139] *Agitator*, 1965, no. 21, p. 31.
[140] *Ibid.*, 1965, no. 16, p. 2; 1966, no. 6, p. 37–8.

direct interaction with the audience. A person listening to the radio, watching television, reading an article, wishes to talk matters over, to exchange views, to receive a reply to questions. Naturally, he turns to the agitator at his side. Besides, in everyday life there are not a few questions to which it is essential to give a reply without waiting for a radio broadcast or a newspaper.[141]

It was only towards the latter half of 1966 and particularly in October of that year, at a Conference-Seminar of ideological functionaries convened in Moscow, that the doubts about the agitator's continued usefulness were taken up by the agitprop leadership, not, however, to deny the need for oral agitation as such but to press for the replacement of the agitator by a more knowledgeable and sophisticated type of oral communicator who has since come to be known as the *politinformator*. The former head of the CC Propaganda Department, V. I. Stepakov, was prominently associated with this demand. The immediate causes that led to the Stepakov initiative are not clear, but it should be noted that it coincided with a period in which criticisms of agitators in the Soviet press had become particularly frequent and outspoken. This may, of course, have been the result of a deliberate strategy. The progress of the campaign against the agitators – it was conducted cautiously and deviously and it encountered growing and ultimately successful opposition – strongly suggested that the Stepakov forces in the party were not at all sure of their ground.[142] It would not have been difficult for the head of the CC Propaganda Department and his supporters to inspire the desired 'feedback' from the grassroots and ensure that it received adequate publicity in the press. A few judicious hints would probably have sufficed to elicit a fair amount of that exuberance with which Soviet functionaries customarily condemn the old at the same time as they acclaim the new. This, after all, is a very characteristic feature of the Soviet political style; it applies to methods and institutions no less than to individuals, and is part of the legitimation of change.

On the other hand, it is equally possible that the attempt to reform the system of oral agitation came as a response to accumulated dissatisfactions with the work of the agitators, reflected in

---

[141] *Kommunist*, 1965, no. 10, pp. 45–6, 52.

[142] I have dealt with this in some detail in an article 'Politinformator or Agitator: A Decision Blocked', *Problems of Communism*, 1970, no. 5, pp. 30–43

growing criticisms in the press (and probably also in internal party reports). Many of the allegations against the agitators were not new in substance. What was new was their concentration and candour. Besides, the argument that the traditional forms of oral agitation were no longer appropriate to contemporary Soviet society does sound plausible on its own merits – irrespective of the many defects which have persistently beset the implementation of agitation policies in daily practice. A further precipitating factor may have been the findings of 'concrete' sociological research. As already noted, only the mere glimpses of these have so far been published, but it is a reasonable inference that they have helped to dispel some of the long-cherished official notions about the agitator and his contribution to the communication process.

Whatever the immediate circumstances that prompted the abortive onslaught on the agitators, the fact that it was launched is significant, not only as a reflection of the current state of Soviet agitation but also as a possible portent for the future. It was the first attempt at a fundamental reassessment of the function of oral agitation in the Soviet Union in the light of changing cultural patterns and information needs, and it may well be followed by further such attempts in years to come. No less significant, and more immediately relevant, however, is the fact that it has failed. After considerable initial disarray, which in some cases led to the dissolution of the agitation-collectives and in others to more or less disguised resistance, criticisms of agitators of the kind that were quite common in the Soviet press several years ago have once again given way to glowing accounts of their work. There is thus no doubt, that the agitators have been given a new lease of life.[143] By its renewed confidence in the agitator the Soviet leadership may be said to have demonstrated more convincingly than ever that it regards him not merely as an additional spokesman transmitting official views and demands, but as an organizer leading and supervising their implementation in practice. However serious the failings of the agitator as communicator, his

---

[143] The final turning point came in July 1969 with the publication of an editorial in *Agitator* entitled 'The Agitator – An Active Fighter of the Party'. It was the first such editorial for several years and was unmistakably designed to mark the complete rehabilitation of the agitator. (*Agitator*, 1969, no. 14, pp. 3–6.) Since then, indeed, the official view seems to be that agitators will continue to be needed in the era of full communism, even though some of their functions may change. (Brovikov and Popovich, *Sovremenny problemy*, pp. 117–118.)

role as the organizer of his collective, in places of work as well as in places of residence, is apparently still judged essential to the functioning of the Soviet system.[144] The abolition of the agitators would have deprived the regime of an important instrument of social control and, by the same token, would have freed the mass of Soviet citizens from a form of petty tutelage which, especially after the decline of police terror, must be among the most obnoxious aspects of life in the Soviet Union. That it did not come to pass says much not only for the intentions of the present leadership but also for the basic resilience of the totalitarian features of the Soviet polity.

The Politinformator

The politinformators appeared on the Soviet scene in the beginning of 1967, unheralded by a formal public announcement or official decree of any kind. Some nine months earlier, in April 1966, the 23rd Party Congress had adopted a resolution calling for 'serious improvements in mass-political work', which would, among others, take account of 'the heightened cultural and educational level of the Soviet people', and also provide for 'regular reports to the working people by party, state, economic and public leaders'. The resolution included the sentence: 'All political agitation must be based on the broad and regular dissemination of information to the population on the political, economic and cultural life of the country and the international situation.'[145] It was this sentence which was subsequently to be cited as authority for the creation of the politinformators.

Neither at the Congress itself, however, nor in the months immediately following it was there any other indication that the Congress had sanctioned the introduction of a new type of oral

---

[144] Admittedly, the reasons for the retention of agitators were never made explicit, and one cannot rule out the possibility that they had little or nothing to do with official recognition of the agitator's continued usefulness as either communicator or organizer. But it may be noted that when Stepakov first formulated his proposals at the October 1966 Conference-Seminar one of the two other participants whose views on the subject were reported in the press pointed out, in apparent opposition to Stepakov's proposal, that the agitator's were 'not only informators but also organizers of competition', while the other emphasized that 'political agitation is not only information, although that is an important part of it; agitation is a form and method by which political ideas are actively carried to the masses'. (*Agitator*, 1966, no. 21, pp. 19–20.)

[145] *XXIII S'ezd*, vol. II, 316–17.

communicator. Only at the above-mentioned Conference-Seminar of ideological workers of October 1966 was the 23rd Congress resolution first interpreted in this way. In his opening address to the Conference-Seminar, Stepakov then 'posed for discussion' the question: 'Under contemporary conditions and in accord with the demands of the 23rd Congress of the CPSU, what persons and what institutions can best ensure broad and consistent oral information for the public?' His own reply was that none of the existing ideological cadres could cope with the task, either because they were already otherwise occupied or because, as in the case of the agitators, they were inherently incapable of it. Instead:

> We need qualified informators, people capable of conducting this section of work ... Let them be conditionally called propagandist-informator, propagandist-commentator. The matter is not in the name but in the essence. And the essence is that the training and general culture of this person must be considerably higher than those of the agitator.[146]

Following the October Conference-Seminar a central directive calling for the setting-up of politinformator groups must have been issued. The existence of such a directive, though mentioned in some reports is denied in others.[147] In any event, by March 1967, *Pravda*, summarizing a discussion on 'Political Agitation and Life' that had been conducted in its columns since the previous October, was able to report that 'life itself' had called forth 'a qualitatively new type of worker carrying on political agitation' known as the politinformator.[148]

One year later some 600,000 politinformators were reported to be operating in the USSR.[149] Since then their number has greatly increased. In the beginning of 1970 Kuryanov claimed that there were 15–20,000 politinformators in each of the provinces of the Soviet Union.[150] But this, if strictly interpreted, would put their total number at the time at around 2.5 million and is highly unlikely. Subsequent accounts mentioned the existence of over 1.5 million politinformators in 1972 and again in 1973 and there is no reason to assume that a substantial decline took place in the intervening years.[151] As in the case of the agitators the great majority of politinformators consists of party members.

---

[146] *Agitator*, 1966, no. 21, p. 19.   [147] *Pravda*, 25 December 1967.
[148] *Ibid.*, 17 March 1967.   [149] *Agitator*, 1968, no. 6, p. 21 and no. 8, p. 44.
[150] *Ibid.*, 1970, no. 3, p. 50.   [151] *Ibid.*, 1972, no. 15, p. 28; 1973, n. 9, p. 45.

The functions of the politinformator are very similar to those of the agitator, inasmuch as the former is also required to conduct oral propaganda on current topics before small groups at regular (usually weekly) intervals. Indeed, since the politinformator was originally conceived as a substitute for the agitator their functions overlap a great deal, and although Soviet commentators have been at pains to carve out separate roles for each it is still far from clear how they divide their work in practice. Fully three years after the introduction of the politinformators and over half a year after the controversy over the retention of agitators had been laid to rest local party functionaries were still exercised by the question: 'Wherein lies the difference between the agitation-collectives and the politinformator groups? Surely, there must be one. What is it, then? In the localities there is still great confusion.'[152]

The theory appears to be that agitators should concentrate on local questions while politinformators deal with national themes.[153] At the same time, however, the politinformators are constantly reminded that the ground-rules of agitation apply in equal measure to their own work, viz., that it must be 'operative', 'concrete', 'purposeful', 'close to life', etc., in short, that it is the politinformators' task to 'organize the masses' as well as to 'convince people'.[154] The practical result of this has necessarily been that they frequently encroach upon the local preserve of the agitator and, especially when dealing with economic themes, address themselves to the immediate problems of the work collective. This in fact is no more than is demanded of them when they are told that 'it is essential to give maximum attention to those problems the solution of which depends on the listeners, on which the collective of the shift, section and shop itself has direct influence. Only in this case will the *beseda* have practical value'.[155]

Far from being merely informative in character, as the name might imply, the politinformator's work, like that of the agitator is designed to mobilize people for action. If at first there were

---

[152] *Agitator*, 1970, no. 3, p. 50; see also *Partiinaya zhizn'*, 1971, no. 4, p. 49.
[153] See, e.g. M. Kuryanov, 'Organizatsionnye formy politicheskoi raboty v massakh', *Agitator*, 1968, no. 12, p. 40. The author was prominent among Soviet commentators in attempting to define the distinctions between the politinformators and the agitators.
[154] *Agitator*, 1968, no. 19, p. 53; 1969, no. 5, p. 47, no. 9, p. 44; 1970, no. 18, p. 34; *Pravda*, 6 April 1968; *Partiinaya zhizn'*, 1971, no. 4, p. 50.
[155] *Agitator*, 1970, no. 3, p. 45.

some who refused the politinformator's assignment in the belief that he was no more than 'a competent bookworm who regurgitates whatever he has been fed', they were instantly and authoritatively rebuked:

> Oral information is not an end in itself for the party but an effective means of public opinion formation, of political influence over people, of their mobilization for active and conscious participation in everything by which the state lives ... The view that the task of the politinformator is confined to coming to people, informing them, answering one or two questions and then going away unconcerned is not only profoundly wrong but, to put it frankly, harmful to the cause.[156]

The politinformator, it has repeatedly been emphasized 'is not a simple conveyer of information'; instead, 'every *beseda* conducted by a politinformator must be charged, so to speak, with effectiveness. It is important that as a result of the *beseda* the listeners should not only learn and "take cognisance" of something new, but should show activeness.'[157] It is presumably in line with the claim that by 'correctly forming public opinion, political information helps party organizations to mobilize the Soviet people better for the solution of economic, social [and] political tasks',[158] that a politinformator concluded his talk on the Model Kolkhoz Charter to members of a collective farm brigade with an affirmation of his conviction that the new Charter would 'help field workers to achieve even greater successes in agricultural production', while his listeners 'supported that conclusion and pledged themselves ... to obtain a rich harvest during the current year and fulfil all pledges which they had undertaken on account of the centenary of V. I. Lenin's birth'.[159] Similarly, the politinformators of the 'Zaporozhstroi' trust seek

> to activate the listeners and to create a situation in which everyone is imbued with a sense of his role in the common enterprise and strives to fulfil that role better and more effectively. The effectiveness of the politinformator's *besedy* is here assessed by the concrete contribution of every listener to the work of the brigade, section, administration and trust.[160]

[156] *Ibid.*, 1968, no. 19, pp. 50–1.
[157] *Ibid.*, no 15, pp. 51–2.   [158] *Ibid.*, 1969, no. 7, p. 3.
[159] *Ibid.*, no. 12, p. 37.   [160] *Ibid.*, 1970, no. 23, p. 42.

Even when dealing with international themes the task of the politinformator is not limited

> to information on events abroad and on the foreign policy of the USSR which corresponds to the interests of all progressive mankind and the cause of peace on earth. He must explain that the policy is conditioned by the very nature of the socialist system [and is] indissolubly linked with the internal political situation and the growth of the economic and defence might of the Soviet Union. And this in turn dictates the necessity of turning the attention of the listeners to that which is being done in that direction in the country, republic, territory, province, to that which they themselves are called upon to do concretely in order to strengthen our might and enable it to grow continually.[161]

Again, the intention appears to be to leave individual work exclusively in the hands of the agitators. But this is not interpreted to mean that politinformators should confine themselves to the setting of the group *beseda* (or *politinformatsia*, as the group sessions of the politinformators are sometimes called), or that the failings of individuals are too trivial to merit the attention of the politinformator. Writing of the work of the politinformators in the machine-tractor shop of a kolkhoz one local functionary affirmed:

> Now while conducting their political information sessions, Communists find room to talk of matters of the collective. They single out the pioneers and criticize the slackers and the transgressors of discipline. This, not in order to give them a 'dressing down'. But simply in the course of things, albeit very appropriately. That cuts to the quick, because it is said publicly in front of [other] people.[162]

In another account a politinformator describes how he dealt with a letter received from the militia concerning one, Yuri Kostyunin, who had been apprehended for rowdyism in a cinema:

> During the *beseda* when the talk came round to the undisciplined conduct of some workers I looked at Kostyunin and passed him the letter. 'Look what we have received,' I said. 'Perhaps you'll read it aloud, Yuri?' 'If it's necessary, why not? I'll read it,' he agreed readily. He took the paper, unfolded

---

[161] *Ibid.*, no. 9, p. 5.   [162] *Partiinaya zhizn'*, 1969, no. 22, p. 52.

it and – stopped short. He blushed. But immediately took hold of himself and read the letter aloud. Afterwards we continued our talk with the audience on discipline, on behaviour in public places, on the moral make-up of the Soviet worker. Yuri gave a correct, evaluation of his conduct and promised that it would not recur.[163]

These are, of course, precisely the kind of activities that have always been pre-eminently in the domain of the agitator.

Nor is there any difference between the politinformator and the agitator as to the kind of location in which each operates. The politinformators are probably less active in places of residence than the agitators, especially in the all-important realm of individual work, but accounts of political information sessions and even specially designated political information clubs in housing estates, hostels, etc., have been appearing in the press for some time. How their activities there differ from those of the agitators it is difficult to tell. In recent elections politinformators appeared alongside agitators;[164] and there have also been some reports of political information activities on board ships.[165]

Such differences as exist between the politinformators and the agitators boil down to three. Firstly, in contrast to the agitator who is generally expected to conduct talks on a wide variety of topics, the politinformator specializes in one of four broad subject areas: domestic policy, international affairs, economics and so-called 'cultural life'. Occasionally, these divisions are reduced or slightly altered. In some places politinformators specialize in only three fields, for example, technical-economic problems, domestic policy and international events; in others the four-fold division is varied somewhat to include such headings as communist upbringing and technical progress. Further sub-divisions are not unknown, as for example, when politinformators specializing in international affairs concentrate on particular geographical areas (the Middle East, Western Europe, etc.) or on specific issues (the workers' movement in capitalist countries, anti-colonialism, etc.).[166] Under the heading 'cultural life'

---

[163] *Agitator*, 1968, no. 24, p. 37.
[164] See, e.g. *Agitator*, 1970, no. 8, p. 45, no. 10, pp. 12–13; *Pravda*, 11 May 1971.
[165] *Partiinaya zhizn'*, 1967, no. 7, p. 59.
[166] M. Kuryanov, 'O spetsializatsii politinformatorov', *Agitator*, 1967, no. 24, pp. 25–30; also *Partiinaya zhizn'*, 1967, no. 3, p. 56, and *Pravda*, 3 June 1967.

the population is to be regularly informed of Soviet achievements in the arts and sciences, and this because the 'party requires that the spiritual world of a person should always be in the field of vision of every party organization'.[167] As interpreted in practice, such subjects as hooliganism, drunkenness, labour discipline, atheism and other aspects of 'communist morality' are usually subsumed under this heading. Political information sessions are generally held three or four times monthly; the duration of sessions is somewhat longer than that of the agitator's *besedy* and may last up to 40 minutes, but audiences are also small and the whole setting is similarly designed for 'intimate, relaxed talks' in which the audience participates through questions and discussion instead of listening passively to formal speeches.

The second difference is one of organization and deployment. Unlike the agitators whose agitation-collectives operate at the lowest level of the party hierarchy, down to the party group, the politinformators are organized in separate 'groups' under the direct guidance of either the committees of the larger primary party organizations (those with at least 300 members in industry and 50 members in agriculture) or the committees of the district party organizations. The implications of this are, apart from supposedly stricter criteria of selection and supervision, that while the agitators conduct their mass-political work exclusively within the section of the enterprise in which they work (or the residential area to which they have been assigned), the politinformators can and often do rotate among different sections of the same enterprise and, in the case of politinformators subordinate to district committees, among different enterprises in the same district.[168] It should, however, be added that some party organi-

---

[167] *Agitator*, 1967, no. 24, p. 28. Another writer referred to the politinformamator's tasks in the following terms: 'A fierce ideological struggle for the minds and hearts of people is going on in the world. It is going on uninterruptedly in all spheres of social life, including the cultural front. Unable to overcome our people in open battle, the enemy attempts to sow in the minds of Soviet people, especially youth, the poisonous seeds of nihilism and apathy ... It is essential that every word directed at people by the politinformator should strengthen in them the consciousness of high responsibility for the triumph of the ideals of communism, expose the true face of bourgeois culture, educate Soviet people towards a class approach in the assessment of books, films, concert programmes and radio broadcasts.' (*Agitator*, 1969, no. 4, p. 8.)

[168] These differences are explained in M. Kuryanov, 'Agitkollektiv i institut politinformatorov', *Agitator*, 1970, no. 3, p. 51; see also *Partiinaya zhizn'*, 1971, no. 4, p. 49.

zations, presumably those with numerous politinformators at their disposal, have found it preferable to attach them to individual shops and sections of enterprises, because

> a politinformator who appears permanently in one and the same shop, establishes close contact with the audience, is able to reply to listeners' questions more thoroughly using concrete materials of the given shop and, what is very important, has the possibility to control the effectiveness of explanatory work.[169]

The third and probably the most significant difference relates to social status and educational accomplishment. Whereas agitators are primarily recruited from the ranks of workers and peasants (albeit, the 'more advanced' among them), the great majority of the politinformators are party and state officials, economic managers, scientists, engineers, agronomists, etc. Virtually all accounts by local party leaders stress the extent to which 'leading workers' and specialists have been drawn into the work of political information and many provide figures to substantiate their claims.[170] Some have even gone so far as to suggest that a foreman, for example, although he might be a competent agitator, was unqualified to become a politinformator because 'a profound analysis . . . is still beyond him',[171] others have warned that it was 'wrong to assign all leaders in every shop to conduct political information sessions merely because they are leaders.'[172]

Whether these differences justify the deployment of the politinformators alongside the traditional agitators is a question that cannot be answered with any degree of certainty; perhaps it should not even be asked since the original plan did not envisage that the two would be run in harness. That the introduction of the politinformators brought some improvement into the quality of oral propaganda in the Soviet Union may be readily conceded. The average member of the politinformators' group is a more educated person than his counterpart in the agitation-collective and this, together with a sounder knowledge of his subject that comes from specialization, may be expected to render the political information session more interesting and instructive than the typical agitation *beseda*. However, while the activity of the politinformators may have gone some way in meeting audience objections of the kind listed earlier, it need not, for that reason,

169 *Agitator*, 1968, no. 7, p. 45; see also 1967, no. 11, p. 38.
170 See, e.g. *Ibid.*, 1967, no. 16, p. 43; *Partiinaya zhizn'*, 1969, no. 20. p. 61.
171 *Agitator*, 1968, no. 18, p. 32; see also no. 19, p. 52 and *Pravda*, 3 May 1973.   172 *Agitator*, 1968, no. 24, p. 36.

be any more effective in meeting the immediate, baldly action-oriented communication goals of the regime.

The politinformator does not, as a rule, have the same intimate knowledge as the agitator of his audience and its individual members. In most cases he descends to the group from a higher social milieu, his contact with the group limited to the fleeting moment of the *beseda*. He may be immune to some of the group pressures which inhibit the agitator when the demands and policies of the regime conflict with the preferences of his fellow-workers, but he is also more likely to be oblivious to the cross-currents of thought and sentiment within the group. His words may carry authority, but it is not the authority of the group; they come from outside the group in the same sense as the messages transmitted by press and radio. The activities of the politinformators, even more than those of the agitators, should therefore be seen as supplementing the flow of communications from other media quantitatively rather than reinforcing it qualitatively. There can be no pretence here, as there is in the case of the agitators, of an attempt to anchor communication in its social moorings via opinion leaders.

This is not to discount the propaganda benefits of political information altogether, of course. The impressive gross indices of media consumption in the Soviet Union conceal wide and – to the propaganda authorities – disconcerting gaps. Soviet citizens, like those of other lands, exercise the sovereign right of selection. Even when they subscribe to several newspapers and journals and own a radio and television set, what they choose to read, to listen to or to view accords, to some degree at least, with their own preferences rather than those of the communicators. Monopolization of the media is one answer to this problem, but it is not the whole answer: an official, propaganda-saturated communications network, while greatly limiting individual choice, does not abolish it altogether. In this regard, too, recent communication research in the Soviet Union has probably had some sobering effect, if only because it has produced the cold figures showing that Soviet citizens often prefer fiction, sport reports, light entertainment, etc., to leading articles, CC plenum resolutions and the speeches of party leaders.[173] A campaign to supplement the mass media by intensified face-to-face communication

[173] Referring to the preliminary results of a survey of *Izvestiya* readers, which showed among others that only 30% of subscribers read editorial articles regularly, the paper's chief editor, L. Tolkunov, described them

of the kind now provided by the politinformators, would be a characteristic, almost a predictable, Soviet response to such findings. For the regime it is a way of reimposing its own priorities. The reader who skims through the latest Brezhnev speech reproduced in *Pravda*, or the listener who turns his radio off when the target figures of the Five-Year Plan are to be 'discussed', will now find themselves exposed to these topics at one of the next political information sessions. In the past such supplementation was part of the agitator's task; it has now, with the continuing cultural transformation of Soviet society, passed into the hands of the more sophisticated politinformator.[174]

Soviet claims for the politinformators go further than this. The politinformators do not merely carry the regime's message to those who opt out of the mass media network, wholly or selectively; they are also said to provide much-needed additional information and guidance for all others. In the words of the deputy head of the CC Propaganda Department, A. Dmitryuk, the task of the politinformator includes 'the skilful explanation of events and facts, the disclosure of their interconnection, causality and internal logic'.[175] And to a Secretary of Chelyabinsk Province Committee it is the 'politinformator's duty not only to tell of an event that has occurred but also to explain its causes and consequences and to define our attitude to that event'.[176] The

as 'grave and alarming'. (*Izvestiya*, 14 March 1967.) There are few signs that the contents, presentation or style of the Soviet press have so far been appreciably affected by the findings of survey research into readership preferences but it does seem that propaganda officials at all levels are now more aware of (or more ready to recognize in public) the hurdles of selective exposure which are so frustrating to communicators everywhere. Soviet media research is reported in G. Durham Hollander, *Soviet Political Indoctrination: Developments in Mass Media and Propaganda since Stalin*, New York, 1972.

174 According to a survey conducted by Brovikov and Popovich in Taganrog and Mukachevo in early 1968, the percentage of respondents who cited *besedy* and *politinformatsii* among their sources of political information was nearly as high as that of respondents who cited radio and television and considerably in excess of those who cited *Pravda* and *Izvestiya*. (*Sovremennye problemy*, p. 16.) But compare this with the rather different findings of what appears to be a later survey of Taganrog reported in P. K. Kurochkin, 'Sredstva massovoi informatsii i propagandy i ikh rol' v formirovanii novogo cheloveka', in M .T. Iovchuk et al.. eds., *Problemy sovremennoi ideologicheskoi borby, razvitiya sotsialisticheskoi ideologii i kul'tury*, Moscow, 1972, p. 57. See also V. I. Bekesh and M. V. Balimasova, *Sotsiologiya i propaganda*, Leningrad, 1971, p. 63.

175 *Agitator*, 1968, no. 6, p. 21.   176 *Ibid.*, 1969, no. 12, p. 41.

politinformator is expected to do this by virtue of his superior knowledge and persuasive skill and by taking advantage of the opportunity of his face-to-face contact with his listeners.

Soviet accounts constantly emphasize that the political information session must not only be 'theoretically correct', 'politically sound', 'purposeful', etc., but also 'well-argued and convincing'.[177] It is not enough for the politinformator to master his subject; he must have 'the gift of the word' and know 'how to convince, how to arouse to active deeds'.[178] At numerous 'methodological conferences' of politinformators the call went out to transform 'every *beseda* into a creative work',[179] to make it 'vivid' so that it may 'reach the heart and mind' of the listener.[180] Greater access to the mass media does not reduce the need for oral information. According to the First Secretary of the Krasnodarsk Territory Committee, G. Zolotukhin,

> the absolute majority of working people [in Krasnodarsk] receives information from the newspapers, radio and television. But can one in that case consider the problem of informing the population as solved? Of course, one cannot. Not every person is capable of properly taking in the flow of information reaching him through these channels . . .[181]

Identical views have been expressed by party officials up and down the country. It is true that every home has a radio, wrote the Secretary of Gorlovsk, in the Ukraine, but 'if something is not clear you can't ask a question of a radio receiver'.[182] And the agitprop chief of Moscow emphasized that 'under conditions of a rapidly growing flow of information [from the mass media] there arises the need to concentrate attention on the most important [events] in the life of the country'.[183] Indeed it was precisely the spread of the mass media which rendered the provision of oral information even more urgent: 'The more media of mass communication there are', wrote Kuryanov, 'the more strongly is the

---

177   *Pravda*, 28 May 1969; *Partiinaya zhizn'*, 1971, no. 4, p. 48.
178   *Agitator*, 1969, no. 9, p. 44; 1970, no. 19, p. 38.
179   *Ibid.*, 1969, no. 2, p. 51.
180   *Ibid.*, no. 9, p. 42.
181   *Partiinaya zhizn'*, 1967, no. 15, p. 12. The suggestion that the politinformators might be superfluous in such places as scientific institutions because their staffs were already well informed, was dismissed out of hand by the First Secretary of Minsk Province Committee. (*Kommunist*, 1969, no. 15, pp. 56–7.)
182   *Agitator*, 1967, no. 1, p. 33.   183   *Ibid.*, no. 3, p. 35.

need felt for oral information, for living interaction, for an exchange of views.'[184] Besides, as he noted on another occasion, in 'life it quite often happens that events develop swiftly . . . And not everyone is capable of orientating himself, of correctly approaching this or that situation, of drawing the right conclusions . . .'[185]

It may be doubted whether the politinformators meet these expectations. As far as can be judged from the accounts of their talks that have been published in the press, those not dealing with purely local matters are wholly devoid of originality in either style or content. Far from trying to be 'vivid', not to say 'creative', most politinformators tend to follow the example of other Soviet media in striving above all to be 'politically sound'. The result is that their talks are for the most part typical specimen of the kind of bureaucratic prose familiar from *Pravda* editorials and other official pronouncements: lifeless, replete with all the soporific platitudes and utterly predictable.[186]

That this is not an unduly harsh judgment is partly confirmed by the fact that after a brief initial period immediately following the introduction of the politinformators, when their appearance had been universally acclaimed as meeting the long-felt need of the population for oral information, Soviet sources have themselves begun to criticize the politinformators. And this in terms

---

[184] *Agitator*, 1968, no. 12, p. 38; see also 1969, no. 17, p. 33.

[185] *Ibid.*, 1967, no. 17, p. 28: see also 1969, no. 10, p. 39.

[186] This is how one politinformator opened his *beseda* on the subject of 'Thrift – a Communist Characteristic': 'I will begin by reminding you of the resolution of the CC of the CPSU, the Council of Ministers of the USSR and the Central Council of Trade Unions of 24 November 1967 "On the Initiative of Collectives of Industrial and Transport Enterprises, Construction Organizations and Collective and State Farms for the Pre-Schedule Fulfilment of the 5-Year Plan for the Development of the National Economy". That resolution recommended in particular to dedicate socialist emulation to the struggle for an all-round increase in the economic effectiveness of production, the maximum utilization of reserves and the improvement of the quality of production. To succeed in that emulation means not only to work creatively, devoting the entire strength, knowledge and experience to the cause, but also to be thrifty at all times, to maintain an economic approach to wealth, to guard it always and to eradicate decisively still existing manifestations of the plunder of socialist property.' (*Agitator*, 1968, no. 17, p. 45.)

Presumably this and similar talks reproduced in the party press are regarded as models of their kind. For the (admittedly, culture-bound) Western reader they raise the question of what the Soviet propaganda authorities have in mind when they ask for 'vivid' or 'creative' political information.

altogether reminiscent of those applied earlier to the agitators.
In respect of the politinformators, too, it now transpires, selection
has all too often suffered from a 'formal approach', opening their
ranks to people with 'low political and general cultural prepared-
ness'.[187] In part, this was due to the fact that local party leaders
had solved the problem of appointing politinformators, which 'life
itself' had suddenly thrust upon them, by simply changing their
agitators into politinformators 'with the stroke of the pen'.[188]
Thus 'yesterday there was an agitation-collective – today it is
already called politinformator group';[189] in truth, as one functionary observed, 'there are neither agitators nor politinformators'.[190]
This 'changing of the signboards', as it came to be called, was
clearly a widespread practice especially in the early days when it
appeared that the fate of the agitators had been sealed.

The reading aloud from newspapers, so often condemned when
practised by the agitators, is also regarded by some politinformators as an easy way of discharging their responsibilities. Take the
case of one director who

> took one of the central newspapers and without lifting his eyes
> from the newspaper page, read off part of a report by N. L.
> Baibakov at the Session of the Supreme Soviet and then part
> of a report by the First Secretary of the Sterlitamak District
> Committee . . . and – the political information session was
> carried out.

The official reporting the case asks why an audience is available
for this sort of thing and goes on to record his answer: 'It appears,
it is simple: an administrator reads the paper and his subordinates
have to listen because they have been invited to a *beseda* by
their leader.'[191] Common complaints against the politinformators,
too, are that their work is 'superficial and formal' and not sufficiently 'operative', 'concrete' or 'militant', that it bears a 'narrow,
purely-enlightening character' and lacks 'fighting spirit and

---

[187] *Agitator*, 1969, no. 9, p. 44; 1970, no. 14, p. 41. Audience scepticism of
the kind familiar from the work of the agitators ('What can you tell
us, we've read it all already . . .'), which was originally said to have been
quickly overcome by politinformators (*Agitator*, 1968, no. 11, p. 47, no.
13, p. 53.) is once again being vented in the press. (*Pravda*, 26 March
1973; *Partiinaya zhizn'*, 1973, no. 8, p. 74.)

[188] *Agitator*, 1969, no. 6, p. 42.

[189] *Pravda*, 17 March 1967; *Agitator*, 1968, no. 3, p. 5, no. 14, p. 47.

[190] *Agitator*, 1969, no. 9, p. 43.

[191] *Ibid.*, no. 7, pp. 51–2.

mobilizing character', and is altogether too 'objectivist';[192] that politinformators present 'accidental, untypical matters'[193] or, conversely, avoid 'sharp corners'.[194] Some politinformators, failing to appreciate the distinction between 'simplicity and simplification', are prone to 'vulgarization'; this was the particular fault of one politinformator who tried to elucidate the term 'convergence' as 'a kind of trick [*eto takaya shtuka*]', instead of explaining 'simply and clearly that convergence is a bourgeois "theory" of the drawing together of capitalism and socialism designed to deceive the masses'.[195]

An obvious and oft-repeated requirement of political information is that it should be up-to-date. Yet there are still politinformators who adhere rigidly to their assigned themes and ignore more recent events, although the latter may be of greater importance and more immediate interest to the audience. As the First Secretary of Sverdlovsk Province, K. Nikolaev, put it: 'The event has taken place, it is being discussed and sometimes incorrectly interpreted, but the politinformators are silent. They are waiting for "instructions".' The fault, as Nikolaev admits, does not lie entirely with the politinformators, but also with the responsible party organization as well as the local and central press which do not always provide them with the necessary materials.[196]

But these strictures reveal the consequences rather than the causes of the difficulty of running truly up-to-date 'current affairs programmes' in a highly centralized communication system, such as that of the Soviet Union: the sluggishness that springs from caution and is built into the system over and above bureaucratic inertia. It is a rule of self-preservation in a totalitarian system that political opinions are not voiced, especially from official platforms, without prior, indisputable guidance from above. That it should be known also to most politinformators and that they should therefore prefer to 'await instructions' rather than rush into commitment is only to be expected. And if there were some politinformators who did not yet know it, they would undoubtedly have become aware of it when told that 'the politinformator

---

192 *Agitator*, 1969, no. 11, p. 45, no. 20, p. 38; 1970, no. 2, p. 48, no. 18, p. 33; *Partiinaya zhizn'*, 1969, no. 17, p. 64.
193 *Pravda*, 5 March 1969.
194 *Agitator*, 1968, no. 24, p. 36.
195 *Ibid.*, 1969, no. 5, p. 48.
196 *Pravda*, 14 December 1967; see also *Agitator*, 1969, no. 2, p. 46; *Partiinaya zhizn'*, 1970, no. 22, p. 46.

is obliged to keep in step with events, but he has no right to speak of them before their political aspect has been defined, if he does not wish to lead his listeners into error'.[197]

There is no evidence that the party leadership recognizes the inherent limitations of its political information network. Where it is critical of the politinformator's performance it looks for improvement to administrative measures of one kind or another, to stricter selection procedures and better training, including the study of psychology and pedagogy (and the speeches of Lenin). It is only rarely that one catches glimpses of a comparatively sober, unblinkered appraisal, as when the secretary of a shop party organization, writing of cases 'when people do not attend political information sessions gladly, and when they do attend, because they are disciplined, they do not listen', hints at the underlying reasons, as follows:

> The explanation, in my view, is this. In our times a person receives daily a large volume of information – from the radio and television, from the newspapers, from the politinformators. And often one and the same [information] in one and the same form. Yet the human psyche is so formed that it does not suffer unending repetition of one and the same thing.[198]

The official argument does not, of course, admit the possibility that the politinformators may be merely contributing to the process of 'unending repetition'. The formulations justifying the politinformator's role have tended to vary somewhat, mainly as the result of the ongoing rivalry with the agitators, but in so far as they have been made explicit they have invariably adhered to the proposition that the politinformator has a vital, independent function – informative, explanatory and mobilizing – in the Soviet communication system.

Finally, mention must be made of one further aspect of the functions of the politinformators which may well be more-far-reaching in its propaganda implications than those mentioned hitherto; namely, the effect of their persuasive activities on the politinformators themselves, as distinct from that on their audiences. Without wishing to go too far in drawing upon the findings of social psychology in respect of self-persuasion and dissonance-reduction one may assume that the principle 'saying is believing' is not invalidated by the particular circumstances of

[197] *Agitator*, 1969, no. 6, p. 62.   [198] *Partiinaya zhizn'*, 1969, no. 1, p. 43.

forced compliance in which the Soviet politinformator finds himself. Whether or not his private opinions accord with those he is expected to defend in public, his role as an active exponent of official views and doctrines is likely to render him more susceptible to their persuasive potential. By enrolling considerable sections of the bureaucratic, managerial and technical-scientific intelligentsia into mass-political work the regime elicits from them a regular, continuous commitment on its behalf, which whatever its effectiveness in the dissemination of propaganda to the public at large, may be expected to strengthen their own allegiance to the system. And this clearly is no mean propaganda achievement in its own right. In the past, the demand for the participation of leading personnel in agitprop activities of one kind or another had largely been framed in the form of general exhortations. It was part of the conventions of virtuous leadership to appear before the masses, to maintain close contact with them, to remain attuned to their needs, etc., and like many other such conventions it was frequently ignored in practice. With the establishment of the politinformator groups an institutional framework has been created, with its own discipline and dynamics, which should make the shirking of this particular public duty much more difficult.[199]

This 'persuasion of the persuaders' may not have been a principal or even a conscious objective of the policy decision which led to the setting-up of the politinformator groups. Yet while it has at no time been explicitly formulated as such, various Soviet spokesmen have from the very beginning alluded to it as an important by-product of that decision. Thus, for example, the First Secretary of Omsk wrote:

[199] That it is not impossible even now is attested by numerous complaints in the press. Indeed a Central Committee decree of December 1971 voiced severe strictures on this score. (The text of the decree is in *Pravda*, 29 December 1971; see also the editorial comment, *ibid.*, 5 and 13 January 1972, and the inevitable self-criticism of the party organization concerned in *Partiinaya zhizn'*, 1972, no. 2, pp. 8–15.) Nevertheless, when the secretariat of a province party committee approves the quarterly plan for the work of politinformators 'listing names and topics' and the agitprop department of the province committee 'submits special information on how the plan was fulfilled' (with similar arrangements pertaining at the district and city levels), it is not surprising that it should be 'the unanimous opinion of party committees that the formation of this institution [of politinformators] has made it possible to attract new forces to active political work from among well-qualified people . . . party, soviet and economic leaders and engineering-technical personnel.' (*Partiinaya zhizn'*, 1969, no. 19, pp. 54–5.)

Political information sessions have important significance also for those conducting them. It is the unanimous view of our leaders that they enrich the information, oblige them to be abreast of events, to study revolutionary theory profoundly [and] allow them to draw experience from the people, strengthen living ties with people ... I often think how very naïve are the proposals of those comrades who yearn for a strict, meticulous control over those studying questions of Marxist–Leninist theory on their own. They suggest examinations, tests. But one would have thought that there is no better control over their studies than their appearances before the working people. If these are interesting appearances, gathering large audiences, if those appearing can convincingly reply to questions – is that not a better verification of knowledge, of the Marxist–Leninist tempering of a Communist?[200]

It may be appropriate to recall that it was in connection with the demand for 'regular reports to the working people' by leading cadres that the notion of information as the basis for all agitation first made its appearance in the resolution of the 23rd Party Congress. But whether or not the institution of the politinformators was originally conceived with an eye to the 'Marxist–Leninist tempering' of leading cadres it would seem that its potential in that regard has been duly recognized by the party leadership.

[200] *Pravda*, 27 October 1966.

6: INDIRECT PROPAGANDA: THE
USURPATION OF LEISURE AND RITUAL

The term 'indirect propaganda' as used here denotes the purposive dissemination of propaganda messages through channels which are not ostensibly or not primarily associated with the manipulation of political symbols. The distinction between indirect propaganda in this sense and all other, i.e. direct, propaganda is one of degree rather than of kind and in practice it will no doubt often be difficult to draw the line. Nevertheless, it is a distinction worth attempting wherever possible, particularly with reference to totalitarian systems where indirect propaganda occupies an extraordinarily large segment of the official communication spectrum – from arithmetic primers to treatises in advanced physics, from 'Nordic' sculpture to the literature of socialist realism.[1]

Indirect propaganda includes instances in which the propaganda message is surreptitiously woven into the general theme of the communication and where this is skilfully done the audience may well be unaware that it is confronting an attempt at political persuasion.[2] But it also includes many instances in

---

[1] In stressing this point I am not unmindful of the fact that in non-totalitarian systems, too, the products of culture and especially of mass culture often tend to reinforce the values and beliefs dominant in the society. The much-maligned Hollywood film advertising 'the American way of life' springs to mind at once, but many other less obvious examples of what Jacques Ellul calls 'sociological propaganda' could be cited. (J. Ellul, *Propaganda*, New York, 1966, pp. 62ff.) I have no doubt that a Soviet commentator would not find it difficult to regard Western arithmetic primers, with their stress on such concepts as profit, interest, dividends, etc., as propaganda vehicles for capitalism. (J. A. C. Brown, *Techniques of Persuasion: From Propaganda to Brainwashing*, London, 1963, p. 22.) Indeed, it is probably true that 'in one context or another all nations indulge in some form of political indoctrination through textbooks and classroom materials'. (R. E. Dawson and K. Prewitt, *Political Socialization*, Boston, 1969, p. 154.)

[2] Whether a particular piece of propaganda may be considered as concealed propaganda depends, of course, not only on the intentions and skill of the propagandist but also on the discernment of the propagandee:

which both the political orientations and the persuasive intent are explicitly asserted by the propagandist and implicitly accepted by the propagandee; indeed often it is only when these elements are clearly and unmistakably present that the necessary ideological legitimacy can be invoked to sanction the communication act. It is the pervasiveness of propaganda throughout the system, the deliberate and often manifest incursion of political persuasion into all spheres of social communication, including those which are elsewhere regarded as outside the arena in which political discourse customarily takes place, that is characteristic of the totalitarian polity, rather than the different techniques of dissimulation and concealment which to some extent at least are inseparable from propaganda as such and can probably be found wherever men seek to persuade each other for political ends.

It cannot be our purpose here to explore the manifold means and methods of indirect propaganda employed in Nazi Germany and Soviet Russia. Instead, as in the case of direct propaganda discussed earlier, we shall once again confine ourselves to activities in which the two parties were directly involved. These activities, which may be said to constitute the specific contribution of the party to the multi-faceted indirect propaganda effort of totalitarian systems, can best be traced against the background of each regime's concern with leisure and ritual.

The phenomenon of mass leisure and the problems that have come in its wake may be found in all industrial societies, with their clear-cut differentiation between working and non-working time and the continuing growth of the latter, the erosion of traditional values and beliefs, the technological development of amenities and the rise of popular culture. All such societies have increasingly become aware of the need to provide guidance on the use of leisure so that it may contribute both to the personal fulfilment of the individual and to the well-being of the society as a whole. For totalitarian regimes, however, leisure presents a unique challenge. If by leisure we mean time spent on cultural and/or recreational pursuits (including passive relaxation) which are solely determined by the free choice of the individual concerned and also genuinely disinterested in that they are not intended to serve utilitarian ends of any kind, then it is clear that the very concept of leisure is antithetical to mobilization. A fully mobilized society would enjoy no leisure at

what is concealed propaganda to one audience may well be revealed propaganda to another.

all. It would have free time, i.e. time free from work and its attendant chores, from domestic responsibilities and physiological needs (sleeping, eating, etc.), but such free time would be wholly taken up by functional activities determined by the political leadership. Some of these – e.g. playing football, watching television, reading professional literature – might well accord with the preferences of particular individuals, but they would be permitted only to the extent that they corresponded to the functional ends laid down by the regime. It would be the regime which would decide that office workers should do ten hours of calisthenics per month or that miners should spend Sundays on excursions to the countryside and every second evening watching television rather than gather over a pint of beer or round a bottle of vodka.

Neither Nazi Germany nor Soviet Russia can be regarded as fully mobilized societies in this sense; in both the individual has enjoyed not only free time but also leisure. Yet for the regime the challenge of leisure remained, both as a threat and an opportunity; as a threat, primarily because leisure is a time when the individual is able to withdraw from the constraints of daily life and to make a variety of private choices that are relatively far removed from the reach of organized society, including choices which may expose him to the pernicious effects of 'alien influence'; as an opportunity, primarily because leisure represents an untapped reserve of time which can be harnessed to the purpose of society as conceived by the political leadership. Both regimes have therefore fought leisure in two ways. One – it could perhaps be described as the overt way – has been to reduce the amount of leisure available to the population; not, it should be stressed, by reducing the amount of free time – on the contrary, in the Soviet Union, the attack on leisure only began with the expansion of free time in recent years and as a direct consequence of it – but by seeking to usurp as large a share of free time as possible for utilitarian ends: participating in communal projects, attending political meetings, reading *Mein Kampf* or the *History of the CPSU*, or – in the Soviet Union particularly – studying for a higher professional qualification. In these and similar ways the two regimes may be said to have taken a growing share of free time out of the realm of private choice and placed it in the realm of public purpose. The result has been to curtail the amount of free time – at least in relative terms – available for genuine leisure.

The second, covert, way by which both regimes have sought to attack leisure has been to subvert it from within, so to speak, for the purpose of indirect propaganda. In other words, such leisure as has remained for the individual to dispose of more or less in accordance with his unfettered inclinations has been utilized as a channel through which each regime has sought to insinuate its propaganda messages. This is generally recognized to apply to novels, plays, films, art exhibitions, etc.; the individual may have been free to turn to any of these for disinterested enlightenment or enjoyment but, wherever he turned, he was likely to encounter a more or less skilful, more or less strident, attempt at persuasion. It applies equally to a variety of other cultural and recreational activities with which the party was directly concerned, including in particular the many rituals and ceremonies, private and public, solemn and joyous, which form part of the culture of every society.[3]

For the Nazis there was never any doubt that the organization of cultural and recreational activities belonged properly to the domain of *Menschenfuehrung*. 'Cultural work', wrote Bormann, 'is political work . . . not a deviation from political work towards aesthetic pretensions but the fulfilment of the task of political leadership in that sphere which speaks most directly and profoundly to the people.'[4] And the authors of an official handbook on community activities emphasized:

> Especially when we are enjoying ourselves we must show that for us the national socialist *Weltanschauung* is not only intended for the duration of duty . . . but also for our private and personal life. Just as our *Weltanschauung* does not demand

[3] It may perhaps be objected that rituals and ceremonies should not properly be regarded as leisure activities. This is an objection which cannot and need not be faced in the limited context in which these concepts are used here. It is enough for our purpose to assume that for some people some rituals and ceremonies are sufficiently permissive to be subsumed under leisure. Clearly there are others, notably those associated with religious observance, which are more peremptory in their prescriptions and cannot therefore be easily accommodated under a strict interpretation of leisure as truly discretionary time use. But then, no realm of human behaviour is wholly exempt from normative constraints; and many of modern man's typical play-time pursuits have taken on distinct features of ritual.

[4] M. Bormann, 'Klopft an das deutsche Herz', *Die neue Gemeinschaft*, 1943, no. 1, p. 10; see also O. Schmidt, *Volkstumarbeit als politische Aufgabe*, Hamburg, 1943, p. 25.

that we pass our time in a prudish and straight-laced fashion, so it does not allow us to regard cheerful, relaxing enjoyment as standing outside the idea.[5]

The mass functions of the Labour Front's 'Strength through Joy' movement, with its excursion boats and holiday camps, provided the more spectacular and better known features of this kind of indirect propaganda. Equally, if not more important, were the everyday activities carried on up and down the country under the leadership of the party. All the various forms of communal recreation from folk dancing, amateur drama groups and sport competitions, to collective theatre, cinema and concert outgoings were fostered and controlled by the local leader of the party in the drive to draw the people away from 'non-committing private amusement' and into 'the festive community'.[6]

One of the earliest Nazi endeavours was directed towards the perversion of traditional holidays and festivities.[7] Thus International Labour Day on 1 May became the 'Festival of National Brotherhood' on which ancient German customs were skilfully blended with Nazi symbols in an attempt to impose the concept of national solidarity upon the traditional holiday of the working class.[8] It was intended as the nation's principal holiday, not 'merely one of the many festivities to be arranged by the movement in the course of the year ... On this day everything is to be marshalled which the movement and the state have to offer in splendour, power and beauty.'[9] A similar fate befell Remembrance Day in memory of the fallen of the First World War

[5] G. H. Dohlhoff and W. Schneefuss, *Handbuch der Gemeinschaftspflege*, Munich, 1939, p. 11.

[6] W. Scholz, 'Der Tanz in der Dorfarbeit', *Schulungsbrief*, 1938, no. 7, p. 256; see also VAB, vol. I, pp. 187–9. For Nazi attempts to render 'the *Weltanschauung* graphic, comprehensive and tangible' through communal recreation, see *Das Volksspiel im nationalsozialistichen Gemeinschaftsleben*, Munich, n.d., p. 41 and *passim*: also *Die Betreuung des Dorfes*, Berlin, n.d., *passim*. In the smaller localities amateur puppet shows were thought particularly suitable as 'powerful instruments for the formation of public opinion', for they enabled the party 'to pillory' those individuals who 'could not find their way into the community of the people'. (C. Bauer, 'Das Puppentheater als Instrument politischer Fuehrung', *Unser Wille und Weg*, 1938, no. 11, pp. 347–8.)

[7] See Schmeer, *Regie*, pp. 68ff.

[8] One writer described it as a 'national and popular festival whose motives are rooted in the Germanic soul'. (K. Zergiebel, 'Der Propagandaleiter und der 1. Mai', *Unser Wille und Weg*, 1939, no. 3, p. 68.)

[9] L. Gutterer, 'Der 1. Mai in der Reichshauptstadt und im Reich', *ibid.*, 1936, no. 4, p. 117.

which under the Nazis became 'Heroes' Remembrance Day' (*Heldengedenktag*); it was closely associated with the rebirth of the German army,[10] and dedicated to the glory and nobility of military service. The ceremonies arranged by the party in co-operation with the armed forces, it was said, 'should not be characterized by mourning but should be an expression of strength, of the untamed will to life and victory' and 'therefore testify less to the death of our fallen, but rather to the greatness of their achievements, their struggles and their sacrifices'.[11]

Traditional folk festivals were revived and placed under party direction, as in the case of the Harvest Festival which in 1934 became an official holiday and was celebrated on 1 October in the towns and villages as 'the day of honour of the German peasantry'. The tone of the harvest festivities was set by the grandiose demonstrations at the Bueckeberg in Westphalia where hundreds of thousands of farmers gathered in a huge natural arena to hear Hitler and Darré expound the principles of 'blood and soil'.[12] But miniature replicas of the Bueckeberg ritual were performed under the watchful guidance of the party throughout the land.[13] Explaining the success of the Harvest Festival in South and East Germany as contrasted with other areas, the party periodical reported:

> In these regions the direction and execution of celebrations was left largely to the peasants themselves, so that they had the feeling of organizing 'their celebration' by themselves. The party stood, of course, behind the entire arrangement but appeared outwardly in an organizational capacity only insofar as it was necessary for the purpose of giving a national socialist direction to the celebration. In particular, all still existing cultural organizations such as choirs, bands, ... etc., were included and this by itself ensured the strongest participation of the majority of the villagers.[14]

The same tendency to exploit customs and traditions was evident in regard to religious holidays and ceremonies, although here it was clearly impossible for the party to conceal its 'organi-

---

[10] The re-introduction of conscription was announced on 16 March 1935, one day prior to Heroes' Remembrance Day.

[11] *Die neue Gemeinschaft*, 1944, no. 1, p. 21.

[12] See, e.g. *Voelkischer Beobachter*, 2 October 1934.

[13] See H. Riess, 'Stadt und Land feiern gemeinsamen Erntedank', *Unser Wille und Weg*, 1937, no. 2, pp. 44–6.

[14] *Die neue Gemeinschaft*, 1944, no. 6–7, p. 261.

zational capacity' since the institutions of the Church – even those of the ill-fated 'German Christians' – could not be relied upon to co-operate in replacing the religious content of the ceremonies by the neo-pagan rites of national socialism. If Christmas celebrations were to become 'an expression of the national socialist *Weltanschauung*'[15] and if Easter was to be stripped of its 'confessional cover' and revived as the 'spring festival passed on to us through millenia or primeval Germanic history',[16] the functionaries of the party, as the priesthood of the new faith, would have to perform the ceremonies. In 1937 the party's central propaganda office drew up a series of proposals for the holding of communal Christmas celebrations. They included detailed instructions on the decoration of the hall with Nazi emblems and Germanic runes and on the sequence and content of the repertoire, in which songs, classical music, poetry recitals and pageants led up to the sermon of the party leader. Invariably the proceedings were to end with a hymn to the Fuehrer.[17]

As many of the religious holidays, and particularly Christmas, were traditionally celebrated in the family circle, the party also published instruction books designed to assist the 'patriarch' (*Sippenaelteste*) in the national socialist conduct of the celebrations.[18] In all cases it was essential to impress upon the celebrants that they were not performing a private ritual but participating in an experience formed and shared by the community as a whole, 'that every "private" celebration ... is in the last analysis related to the *Volk*, i.e. is a political celebration'.[19]

Another inroad into the sphere of religious tradition was the party's usurpation of the mourning ritual. In the month of November both Protestants and Catholics annually held commemoration services in honour of their dead, while 9 November, the anniversary of the Nazi Putsch of 1923, was since 1926 the 'Reich Day of Mourning of the NSDAP'.[20] This coincidence in dates was gradually utilized by the Nazis in order to fuse the

15 *Ibid.*, 1937, no. 11, pp. 10001a–9.
16 *Ibid.*, 1944, no. 2, p. 91; Schmeer, *Regie*, p. 93.
17 *Ibid.*, 1937, no. 11, pp. 10001a–9. See also H. J. Gamm, *Der braune Kult*, Hamburg, 1962, pp. 182–6. For instruction in the holding of wartime Christmas see NA, T-81, 117/137537–9.
18 *Das Deutsche Hausbuch*, Berlin, 1943 and *Deutsche Kriegsweihnachten*, Berlin, 1943, both published by the Main Cultural Department of the Reich Propaganda Office. See also H. Schnitzler and A. Boss, eds., *Das Feierbuch der deutschen Sippe*, Berlin, 1941.
19 H. Roth, *Die Feier. Sinn und Gestaltung*, Leipzig, 1939, p. 13.
20 Volz, *Daten*, p. 23.

ceremonies held for the fallen of the movement with those hitherto conducted by the Churches. In 1942 party organizations were instructed that it was to become their 'custom' not merely to decorate the graves of their dead comrades but to do the same for 'all the graves of the locality'.[21] And by 1944, 9 November had officially become the 'Memorial Day for the Dead of the People' (*Totengedenktag*). Party functionaries were directed to conduct a commemoration service in each locality, to visit the bereaved and to hand them a booklet prepared for the occasion by the Main Cultural Department of the Reich Propaganda Office. Again there was to be 'no sorrow' but emphasis on the theme that 'the dead live eternally amid the people'.[22]

More important than the party's drive to impose its influence over annual events was the attempt to introduce the national socialist 'morning celebration' (*Morgenfeier*) as a substitute for the Sunday services of the Churches. The party knew that if its 'idea was to be anchored in the soul of every member of the community' it would be necessary 'to look beyond the form of the meeting and the roll-call for access to the German soul'.[23] The morning celebration was ideally suited as 'a regular, obligatory appeal to the soul of every single member of the party and the community'. Its purpose was

> to awake and kindle for ever anew the forces of instinct, of emotion and of the soul which are vital for the struggle for existence and the bearing of our people and our race for all times: the affirmation of life, determination in struggle, honour, loyalty, love of freedom, awareness of duty, diligence, obedience, self-discipline, courage, valour, readiness in sacrifice.[24]

The morning celebrations were originally conceived as part of the party's internal training programme and as such came under the supervision of Rosenberg, whose department issued general directives on matters of ideological indoctrination for the party

[21] *Die neue Gemeinschaft*, 1942, no. 9, p. 492; Schmeer, *Regie*, p. 104.
[22] NA, T-81, 23/20865 and 117/137443–6.
[23] E. Hilbig, 'Sind Feierstunden notwendig?' *Unser Wille und Weg*, 1939, no. 7, p. 164; see also Schmeer, *Regie*, pp. 57ff.
[24] K. Studentkovsky, 'Warum nationalsoziolistiche Morgenfeiern?' *ibid.*, no. 12, p. 262. It has been rightly noted that the German word 'Appell', here translated as 'appeal' also has the additional connotation of 'roll-call'. (R. Grunberger, *A Social History of the Third Reich*, London, 1971, p. 77.)

and its organizations. However, it had always been the party's intention that 'the celebrations of the NSDAP must not be closed to outsiders, but that the entire population of a locality must be assembled in celebrating congregation'.[25] In 1942 an agreement was signed between Rosenberg and Goebbels for the purpose of clarifying conflicting jurisdictions. Under the agreement morning celebrations became the responsibility of Goebbels' Reich Propaganda Office and thus an integral part of the party's propaganda activities.[26] The new direction did not, however, alter the basic character of the morning celebrations. Decor and programme were purposely restrained to evoke an atmosphere of pathos and solemnity. Against a background of selected music by classical or contemporary 'accepted' German composers a Hitler Youth choir declaimed an ode to the glory of the 'Thousand Year Reich', extracts were read from the speeches and writings of the Fuehrer and other Nazi luminaries and the ranking party leader gave a brief but impassioned address.[27] All in all the morning celebration was a supreme example of the 'appeal to the elevated emotions',[28] and its practitioners took unconcealed pride in citing such examples of their impact on the popular mind as the following – from a German worker: 'I often go to church but such solemn calm and reverence as with you this morning one still rarely finds there.'[29]

In its attempt to oust the influence of the Churches by plagiarizing time-proven rituals the regime was most concerned lest

[25] *Die neue Gemeinschaft*, 1942, no. 10, p. 574. A decree of 21 April 1941 ordered the gradual transformation of school prayers into national socialist morning celebrations. (See R. Eilers, *Die nationalsozialistische Schulpolitik*, Cologne and Opladen, 1963, p. 25, n. 153.)

[26] NA, T-81, 1/11850–2.

[27] See the instructions in *Die neue Gemeinschaft*, 1942, no. 11, pp. 598–612; also Gamm, *Der braune Kult*, p. 211, n. 30.

[28] W. Hagemann, *Publizistik im Dritten Reich*, Hamburg, 1948, p. 127f.

[29] *Hoheitstraeger*, 1939, no. 3, p. 29. 'Under Goebbels' skilful manipulations', wrote an American clergyman who had spent several years in Germany, 'political festivals are turning into solemn festivals and the solemn festivals to quasi-religious services. The final goal is a full-dress substitute for Christianity.' (S. W. Herman, *It's Your Souls We Want*, London, 1943, p. 19.) For the author's eye-witness account of a Heroes' Remembrance Day rite with the service looking 'suspiciously like a Christian liturgy with its hymns, psalms and scripture readings from the law and the prophets', see *ibid.*, pp. 24–5. The former German diplomatist Weizaecker reports a German priest in Rome to the effect that the Catholic Church feared the impact of Nazi rituals more than that of its *Weltanschauung*. (E. v. Weizaecker, *Erinnerungen*, Munich, 1950, p. 208.)

the party's own 'counter-ceremonies'[30] should assume the character of religious services to the detriment of their political content. Referring to the morning celebrations, the Party Chancellory emphasized that they must not 'serve religious soul-searching and edification but the formation of the political will'; their fundamental purpose was 'to bring the national socialist *Weltanschauung* close to every member of the party and the community and to spur them on to the highest strength and achievement for the community'.[31] Although national socialism was manifestly establishing a cult of its own it denied doing so. At the 1938 Party Congress Hitler declared that 'cult activities' (*kultische Handlungen*) fell within the competency of the Churches and not of the Nazi movement.[32] In the attempt to live up to the Fuehrer's injunctions subsequent Nazi pronouncements sought refuge in a curious 'Newspeak' and instead of using the term *Kult* the Nazis spoke of *Brauchtumspflege* (the cultivation of customs). Whereas *Kult* was limited to mean 'the form of expression of religion', *Brauchtum* was defined as 'the expression of a *Weltanschauung* and a racially determined belief in destiny'.[33]

A direct onslaught on the last preserves of privacy was represented by the so-called 'life celebration' (*Lebensfeier*). This was an attempt to associate the party directly with the most important and intimate events in the life of the individual and the family – birth, marriage and death. In the pompous prose of Nazi officialdom, the life celebrations were

> a decisive, essential part ... of the ideological struggle, of the great spiritual controversy ... They are the last decisive touchstone for the implementation and realization of the total political-ideological leadership of the movement. Thus we recognize today in the life celebrations a new ideological leadership task of the movement which alone can bring about the final decision in our great struggle, the total exclusive leadership of the German people by the NSDAP.[34]

---

[30] Gamm, *Der braune Kult*, p. 182.
[31] VAB, vol. I, p. 106; also p. 186.
[32] *Voelkischer Beobachter*, 8 September 1938.
[33] See O. Soehngen, *Saekulasierter Kultus*, Guetersloh, 1950, p. 11. Earlier Rosenberg, for one, had no such inhibitions. 'We know', he wrote in 1934 '... that a geninue *Weltanschauung* cannot express itself creatively in theoretical principles only, nor in spiritual creeds, but that it *must take on the form of a cult.*' (*Schulungsbrief*, 1934, no. 7, p. 15 – emphasis in original.)
[34] *Lebensfeiern*, p. 5.

Again the ritual closely followed traditional usage and care was taken to impart an atmosphere of solemnity to the occasion. The exchange of wedding rings and the institution of god-parents were retained and special commemoration sheets with an appropriate saying of the Fuehrer, engraved in golden lettering and elaborately framed by clusters of leaves and Germanic symbols, were handed to the celebrants. The place of the clergyman was taken by the party *Hoheitstraeger*. It was he who in a brief speech reminded the newly-weds of their obligation to multiply the race, and who in due course consecrated the new-born in the name of *Volk* and Fuehrer.[35]

The somewhat incongruously named 'death celebration' (*Totenfeier*), concluded the cycle of life celebrations. During the war the number of those who fell in battle or died as the result of air attacks often provided more occasions for indirect propaganda at the graveside than the party could cope with. But party organizations were instructed to encourage the national socialist funeral rites as widely as possible as long as their frequency did not threaten to upset local morale; 'on no account' was it to be left to the Churches to conduct memorial services 'on a large scale'.[36] Above all, it was important that the party ceremony should 'always bear a public character, i.e. the entire population . . . be invited to the celebration'.[37] For the death celebration for a fallen soldier (*Heldenehrungsfeier* or simply *Gefallenenfeier*) it was the party which, in the words of Goebbels, 'as guardian of all vital needs of the German people had to take in hand the task of the dignified commemoration of our dead soldiers';[38] the

---

35 *Die neue Gemeinschaft*, 1938, no. 9, pp. 10002a–c and 1943, no. 5–6, p. 316; VAB, vol. I, pp. 197–8; see also Soehngen, *Saekularisierter Kultus*, pp. 26–8; Gamm, *Der braune Kult*, p. 177f; W. Niemoeller, *Kampf und Zeugnis der Bekennenden Kirche*, Bielefeld, 1948, p. 279f. The party leader's speech at a national socialist name-giving ceremony was to contain 'three thoughts': (1) the 'obligation' of parents and god-parents to raise the child to be an 'upright German and loyal national socialist'; (2) 'gratitude to the German mother who has again bestowed a child to the German people and thus contributed to the maintenance of the *Volk*'; (3) the 'congratulations of the party'. By adding the signature of the party leader to that of the parents and god-parents on documents and affixing the official stamp of the local party organization 'the leadership claim of the NSDAP will here too be unequivocally manifested and implemented'. (*Lebensfeiern*, pp. 31–2, also pp. 79ff.)
36 VAB, vol. I, pp. 178–9; *Die neue Gemeinschaft*, 1942, no. 9, p. 503; see also Boelcke, *Kriegspropaganda*, p. 441; *Lebensfeiern*, p. 143.
37 *Die neue Gemeinschaft*, 1942, no. 10, p. 574.
38 *Ibid.*, no. 9, p. 503; see also Schmeer, *Regie*, p. 64.

function of the army was confined to 'expressing the close unity of party and army through the dispatch of representatives'.[39] Party organizations were told to avoid 'church forms' in arranging death celebrations; the decoration of the hall with an abundance of black drapes was particularly frowned upon and party functionaries were warned not to emulate in their speeches the tone of a priest's funeral oration ('*Grabesstimme*').[40] A properly conducted death celebration employed, according to Bormann, 'all means of expression compatible with our mission' and was 'at the same time both consolation for the bereaved and confession of loyalty for the survivors'.[41] There can be little doubt that it was the latter which was regarded as the more important of the two objectives.

In the fifth year of the war the Nazis introduced 'a further instrument of *Menschenfuehrung*' in the form of the 'national socialist family evening'.[42] According to a directive of the Party Chancellory of 3 April 1944, family evenings with the participation of parents and children – 'without constraint or importunity' – were to be held at intervals of four to six weeks. Their avowed purpose was to maintain the 'internal spiritual and moral accord of the family' which in the view of the regime was being jeopardized by the prolonged duration of the war; in particular, the estrangement among members of the family resulting from physical separation unavoidable in time of war could have 'unfavourable political' repercussions. It was therefore incumbent upon 'the political leadership to do everything in order to include family life more than hitherto in its political work'. All the offices and organizations of the party were instructed to assist the local party leader in arranging family evenings that are 'lively [and] colourful', preceded by music and songs and followed by a 'brief political speech'. It is doubtful whether in view of the rapidly growing dislocation of the last war year the scheme for family evenings could be brought to full fruition. But the fact that it was launched at a time when the resources of the party were already greatly strained as a result of war-time conditions

---

[39] Letter of the Supreme Command of the Armed Forces (OKW) of 31 December 1942, in NA, T–81, 1/11721.
[40] VAB, vol. I, p. 179. For the content and setting of these ceremonies see the pamphlet issued by the Main Cultural Department of the Reich Propaganda Office, *Die Heldenehrungsfeier der NSDAP*, Berlin, 1942.
[41] *Die neue Gemeinschaft*, 1943, no. 1, p. 7.
[42] All quotations in this paragraph are from VAB. vol. VI, pp. 25–8.

attests to the faith which the leadership reposed in the instruments of indirect propaganda.

Indeed, many of the activities described above were either inaugurated or considerably intensified in the last years of the Third Reich. The hardships of the war placed popular morale under additional strains – a development which the regime sought to counter by the intensification of its propaganda effort in all spheres, but particularly in the cultural sphere. In 1940 the NS–Cultural Project (*NS–Kulturwerk*) was called into being – in 1942 its scope was extended under the name of NS–People's Cultural Project (NS–*Volkskulturwerk*) – with a view to harnessing the main amateur artistic associations to the indirect propaganda of the party.[43] The leadership of the NS–*Volkskulturwerk* was entrusted to the Cultural Department of the Reich Propaganda Office which was at the same time promoted to the status of a Main Deparment (*Hauptamt*). Throughout the war the directives of the Party Chancellory sought to impress regional organizations with the importance of fostering and supervising cultural activities of all kinds. 'It must be pointed out with full emphasis', reads one such directive of December 1942, 'that especially during the further course of the war cultural work must become one of our most important and most meaningful instruments'.[44]

The conduct of Nazi propaganda suffered from over-organization and a lack of clearly delimited competencies. Rosenberg's ideologists, Goebbels' propagandists and Ley's specialists in organized joy competed with one another in this sphere as in several others, and above them all stood Bormann's Party Chancellory, with its own very definite ideas, especially in regard to matters affecting the struggle against the Churches. It is clear from published Nazi sources as well as from reports of local party organizations and security agencies that the popularity of the party's 'counter-ceremonies' varied greatly in different localities and often fell considerably short of the party's aims.

Next to the social and religious background of the local population and what in Nazi terminology was frequently described as the 'pastoral propaganda' (*Seelsorgepropaganda*) of the

---

43 See the agreement between Goebbels and Ley whose 'Strength through Joy' organization had formerly sought to concentrate the cultural activities of amateur associations in its own hands, in VAB, vol. i, pp. 509–10, and NA, T–81, 1/11852. Under the agreement the head of the Department 'After Work' (*Feierabend*) of the 'Strength through Joy' became deputy head of the NS-*Volkskulturwerk* in the Main Cultural Department.

44 VAB, vol. i, p. 189.

Churches, failure was often attributed to the lack of a 'fixed and uniform' national socialist ritual able to compete with the old-established traditions of Christianity, the shortage of suitable halls comparable to 'the artistic and architectonic effectiveness of a church', and the fact that, due to inadequate publicity, many people believed the new ceremonies to be internal party affairs designed for party members only.[45] A frequent complaint concerned the unwillingness and/or inability of local party functionaries to cultivate the new *Brauchtum*. Some were unduly occupied with other responsibilities and failed to recognize the importance of the subject, others found it difficult to break away from the style of straightforward propaganda meetings.[46] A tendency to triteness or *Kitsch* in party-sponsored ceremonies was another constant source of irritation of the central planners, who found it necessary to instruct local leaders in the most elementary rules of good taste.[47]

According to the reports of the security services, the *Hoheitstraeger* were often unable to find the 'correct tone' appropriate to a life celebration. They 'confront such questions as God, fate, immortality, etc., utterly helplessly and uncomprehendingly' and they 'shy away from a personal note because they do not want "to preach like a pastor"'.[48] Yet it was precisely 'on the wedding day or at the grave of a person [that] people are particularly accessible to a *weltanschaulich*-religious mode of thought...'[49] Several reports emphasized that the reluctance of party leaders to refer to religion placed them at a disadvantage vis-à-vis the clergy. There was a need 'to stimulate religious emotion in the participants' and it was 'a mistake to shrink back from mention of the word "God"'. ('After all the Fuehrer also speaks time and again of God the Almighty and of Providence.')[50] Another disadvantage, 'purely psychological', which apparently applied in particular to the death celebrations for soldiers, was that the clergyman could treat the 'negative aspect' of the death of a soldier ('pain, grief and mourning') and console the bereaved with

---

[45] H. Boberach, ed., *Berichte des SD und der Gestapo ueber Kirchen und Kirchenvolk in Deutschland 1934–1944*, Mainz, 1971, pp. 468, 488, 844ff, 874ff.

[46] *Ibid.*, pp. 737 and 846; NA, T-81, 23/117420–3; see also *Unser Wille und Weg*, 1939, no. 12, p. 262f.

[47] H. Kremer, 'Schluss mit dem Pappendeckelzauber', *Unser Wille und Weg*, 1939, no. 2, pp. 40–4; also W. M. Mundt, 'Die Ortsgruppe feiert', *ibid.*, 1936, no. 7, p. 234.   [48] Boberbach, *Berichte ueber Kirchen*, p. 846.

[49] *Ibid.*, p. 875.   [50] *Ibid.*, pp. 484, 875.

references to reunion in the after-world, whereas 'the political leader has to appeal to the inner bearing of the relatives and to emphasize above all else that the soldier fell at the front for the cause of the Reich and that his relatives should be proud of him'.[51]

Claims of growing popular appreciation for the party rites which are to be found in some of the confidential reports, as well as in the published sources, are contradicted by other reports which continue to complain of widespread participation at religious ceremonies. In areas in which the population preserved strong religious allegiances there were even cases in which Church ceremonies were extended as a direct reaction to party competition 'with numbers of participants such as had not been observed in past years'.[52] In Baden, party organizations went so far as to claim that the Catholic Church had deliberately set out to imitate the party's own ceremonies. That party members continued to participate in religious ceremonies was a recurrent complaint from this and several other regions.[53] Even in predominantly Protestant areas there were indications that the party was losing out in the rivalry of rituals. Noting in December 1942 that the influence of the clergy had grown since the beginning of the war, one district leader in Schleswig-Holstein thought this was 'in large part' due to the mourning ritual of the Protestant Church: 'There are still very many persons who in their mourning submit rather to the influence of the Church than to that of the party.'[54]

In respect of celebrations that were not specifically antireligious in aim and character, success was also not easily assured. Thus party functionaries responsible for working class districts found that 'with processions and folk dances nothing much can be achieved here'.[55] And of cultural work in the villages Bormann wrote to the regional leaders in 1942 (after the replacement of Darré) that 'we undoubtedly have a great deal of ground to make up'.[56]

[51] *Ibid.*, p. 738.
[52] B. Vollmer, *Volksopposition im Polizeistaat: Gestapo und Regierungsberichte 1934–6*, Stuttgart, 1957, p. 279f; also Boberach, *Berichte ueber Kirchen*, pp. 468, 844, 874; H. Witetschek, ed., *Die Kirchliche Lage in Bayern nach den Regierungspraesidentenberichten 1933–1943*, 2 vols., 1966, 1967, vol. I, p. 349f.
[53] J. S. Steward, *Sieg des Glaubens*, Zurich, 1946, pp. 36–7, 44, 47, 62–3, 93.
[54] NA, T-81, 163/300987.
[55] *Unser Wille und Weg*, 1939, no. 3, p. 68.
[56] NA, T-81, 1/11777.

It is probably true to say that many of the new rites did not succeed in making significant inroads into German life, particularly where, as in the case of the life celebrations and anti-religious holidays, the party came into direct confrontation with the Churches. However, the party impresarios were undeterred. There can be no doubt of their conviction that they had found an effective means of 'access to the German soul', or of their determination to explore it as fully as conditions permitted.

The Soviet party, too, has always regarded cultural and recreational activities as falling within the purview of its mass-political work. But it was only in the years following Stalin's death that the propaganda potentialities of such activities began to be fully recognized. Recognition has come as part of the general process by which the post-Stalin leadership has attempted to adapt its policies in general and its communication policy in particular to the needs of a modern industrial society. The attempt, already noted, to enliven the style and contents of the mass media was one result of this process; the emphasis on cultural and recreational centres as 'the supporting bases of party organizations in mass-political work'[57] was another.

In particular, it was at this time that the problem of leisure came to the fore as a problem in its own right, adding a new urgency and a new dimension to the party's concern with culture and recreation. For the first time in Soviet history the reduction of the work-week and – to a lesser extent – the improvement of amenities, provided broad strata of the urban working population with a surplus of free time that was not taken up by the needs of daily living. From the mid-1950s onward the question of the use to which this incremental time was to be put came increasingly under scrutiny by both social scientists and agitprop specialists. It was given an ideological reference point in the 1961 Programme of the CPSU which suddenly moved the onset of the Communist era forward from the distant future into the life-span of the present generation. Accordingly, most Soviet writings on the subject are overlaid with the obligatory obeisances to the Marxist vision of the good society in which the conventional distinctions between labour and leisure are obliterated in proportion as labour (no longer alienated) is transformed from a 'means of life' into 'life's primary want'. But leisure has very

[57] *Partiinaya zhizn'*, 1957, no. 10, p. 23.

real and immediate implications for contemporary Soviet society, irrespective of the pace with which it may be advancing along the Marxist road of historical evolution, and it is with these that Soviet writings are primarily concerned.

Two distinct vantage points may be discerned in recent Soviet statements on the subject: the social, which – Marxist futurology apart – Soviet writers share with writers in other countries where leisure has become a mass phenomenon, and the political, which reflects the particular problems of the totalitarian polity. Since the latter will also be the focus of our own interest in the following pages it is only fair to emphasize that it does not represent the full spectrum of Soviet thinking on leisure. There is another 'school' which appears to be genuinely concerned with leisure as a means of personal fulfilment. Some of its members clearly regard leisure as an end in itself, even as they pay tribute to the puritanical strain of 'Communist morality' by stressing the value of political education and of participation in civic projects as leisure time pursuits.[58] Others have openly pleaded for free time that is 'simply free'.[59]

The perspective of the party functionaries is rather different. It is perhaps best reflected in the warning by a borough secretary of Perm that it was precisely during leisure time that 'party organizations are frequently losing their influence'.[60] There are of course other problems connected with the growth of leisure which may well give cause for concern to a party which regards itself as primarily responsible for the 'moral make-up of Soviet man'. But in the party's view the solution of these is predicated first and foremost on the party maintaining its influence. This is the iron rule, almost the conditioned reflex, of the party approach to all phenomena of Soviet life, old and new, simple and complex. The phenomenon of leisure, so closely associated with the party's responsibility for 'work with people', is no exception. That the party seeks to legitimize its involvement with reference to the

[58] See, e.g. the works of N. Klimov, *Rabochi den' v obshchestve stroyashchem kommunizma*, Moscow, 1961 and B. Grushin. *Svobodnoe vremya*, Moscow, 1967.

[59] I. Zhukovitsky in *Literaturnaya gazeta*, 4 January 1967, p. 7. See also an article by I. Prus in which the author complains that the various organized cultural activities are driving people 'to the point of collapse', and calls instead for the formation of 'personal interest clubs' which people would attend voluntarily and not as happens in the case of 'the usual drama circle [where] they haul the audience in against its will'. (*Ibid.*, 6 September 1967.)

[60] *Pravda*, 13 June 1967.

broader social purposes of leisure, including the much-vaunted 'all-round development of the personality', merely obscures the central thrust of the exercise. It is in order to ensure that party organizations do *not* lose their influence when the individual steps outside the reach of the work collective that the party has extended its political agitation to places of residence. And it is in order to ensure that party organizations do *not* lose their influence when the individual seeks to utilize the newly available leisure that the party has involved itself more intensively than hitherto in cultural and recreational activities.

In the terms outlined at the opening of this chapter the extension of agitation to residential areas may be seen as an attempt to attack leisure overtly, from without, while the party's heightened concern with cultural and recreational activities may be seen as an attempt to attack leisure covertly, from within. To emphasize what from the party's point of view is the negative aspect of leisure, i.e. the threat to party influence, is not to ignore its positive aspect: the opportunity for increased propaganda, both direct and indirect, presented by the increments of time freed from work and other essential chores. The threat of leisure, after all, arises only to the extent that the opportunity is not met. It is with this in mind that the party launched its two-pronged attack on leisure more or less simultaneously in the latter half of the 1950s.

The campaign for the intensification of indirect propaganda through cultural and recreational pursuits was inaugurated under the motto: 'The worker rests but the party committee must see to it that he receives healthy spiritual nourishment also during his leisure time.'[61] Neither the ingredients of this spiritual nourishment nor its propagandistic flavouring differ in essence from those provided by the Nazi party twenty or so years earlier. Where the Nazis sought 'access to the soul', Soviet party organizations are enjoined 'to search persistently for the keys to the heart and the mind'.[62] As in Nazi Germany, the search has encompassed the entire gamut of cultural and recreational activities, some of them, indeed, bearing remarkably similar names. From 'family

[61] *Partiinaya zhizn'*, 1956, no. 8, p. 52.
[62] *Pravda*, 14 October 1960; also *Partiinaya zhizn'*, 1961, no. 4, pp. 22ff. Soviet pronouncements emphasize that 'the communist upbringing of the working people is directed not only at the development of political consciousness and at broadening the social and political horizons of Soviet people. Along with this . . . it also presupposes the correct inculcation of social emotions and feelings.' (*Pravda*, 19 September 1969.)

evenings' in the collective farms of Tadjikistan to 'Sunday readings' in the Palaces of Culture of Moscow, including excursions, folk dancing, amateur drama, collective theatre outings, etc., the party is now actively engaged in promoting

> effective new forms and methods of propaganda and agitation ... [which] have made it possible to exercise political influence on broader strata of the population, to employ a diversified approach to various groups ... to introduce more personal warmth into mass-political work and to bring it closer to the individual, to his place of work and residence.[63]

Many of these activities, designed, in Soviet parlance, 'to impart an organized character to relaxation',[64] are administered by other agencies and social organizations (notably the trade unions and the Komsomol) but there is no question that it is the party which guides and co-ordinates them at all levels. In the words of an instructor of the CC Propaganda Department:

> The formation of the spiritual culture of people is certainly not a simple matter. It requires time, attention and the efforts of many organizations ... Naturally, the party committee must direct their activity ... [and] actively insert itself into the ongoing processes.[65]

If it is thus taken for granted that the party must involve itself actively it is because the party alone can ensure that such 'processes' are properly integrated into the agitational effort as a whole. Not only are they often combined with straightforward propaganda measures, as when an evening's entertainment at the local club is preceded by a lecture or a political information session,[66] but the cultural or recreational event itself serves as a medium for indirect propaganda. This applies to excursions, walking tours, etc., which 'with proper organization ... become important components of ideological activity' capable of utilizing the 'possibilities for Communist upbringing in the richest

---

63 *Partiinaya zhizn'*, 1960, no. 10, pp. 57–9.
64 *Ibid.*, 1970, no. 20, p. 54.
65 *Ibid.*, 1967, no. 24, p. 51.
66 See, e.g. E. Belkin, *Lektsionnaya propaganda v klube*, Moscow, 1953, p. 62; *Pravda*, 18 March 1968. See also Durham Hollander, *Soviet Political Indoctrination*, p. 163. The author was present at one such joint programme in Kiev where the doors were locked to ensure that members of the audience would not limit their attendance to the lighter side of the evening's fare.

revolutionary, military and labour traditions',[67] no less than it does to amateur artistic groups who are called upon to give expression to 'historic-revolutionary, heroic-patriotic themes', 'the achievements of Lenin and the party', 'the friendship of the peoples of the USSR', etc.[68] Insofar as the functionaries of the party are concerned 'each centre of culture must be a true centre of political work'.[69] While this does not mean that the various clubs, Red Corners, Houses and Palaces of Culture, etc., must be wholly devoted to 'political enlightenment', it does mean at the very least that they must provide opportunities for indirect propaganda, whether it is in the form of collective television viewing[70] or of amateur activities ostensibly designed solely to foster artistic 'self-expression'. That some clubs are almost entirely given over to dances and Western film shows is a measure of their failure to serve as 'true centres of political work', and cause for frequent criticism on the grounds of 'insufficient political direction'.[71]

Understandably enough, Soviet youth is the principal target of the new 'cultural' offensive, particularly in the countryside where leisure problems are more acute and said to bear a major responsibility for such undesirable social and economic consequences as the flight of young people from the land.[72] But even in its application to youth, cultural work is not regarded otherwise than in the context of ideological work in general. The former First Secretary of the Komsomol, S. Pavlov, echoed the words of Bormann when he dismissed 'the scarecrow of *kul'turnichestvo*' (i.e. cultural work devoid of political significance), apparently raised by 'some people' to justify their neglect of cultural activity, and affirmed instead:

We must not merely see a narrow 'cultural' side to the organiza-

[67] *Partiinaya zhizn'*, 1968, no. 3, p. 53 and 1969, no. 19, p. 60.
[68] *Pravda*, 28 July 1968.
[69] *Ibid.*, 12 January 1968.
[70] Several observers have noted that Soviet students of leisure do not as a rule share the misgivings of their counterparts in the West in regard to the effects of television viewing. See, e.g. M. Yanowitch, 'Soviet Patterns of Time Use and Concepts of Leisure', *Soviet Studies*, 1963, no. 1, pp. 34–5.
[71] *Sovetskaya kul'tura*, 16 January 1968; *Spravochnik partiinogo rabotnika*, 1968, p. 236.
[72] For a fairly typical complaint see *Komsomol'skaya pravda*, 24 May 1970: 'There is nothing to do after work. The clubs are empty . . . Little wonder, therefore, that everyone who has the opportunity leaves and seeks his fortune elsewhere.'

tion of universities of culture, clubs of all kinds and amateur art groups, and forget that all this furthers the ideological, moral and physical development of youth. The Young Communist League must be able, in every sphere of its activity, to create the ideological temperature that tempers the character, moulds the convictions and develops the talents of young people.[73]

The emphasis on controlled and collective leisure as distinct from spontaneous and private leisure is as pronounced in the Soviet Union as it was in Nazi Germany. When Soviet spokesmen refer to the 'organization of leisure' (or of 'cultured leisure'), as they almost invariably do when commenting on the subject, they mean to be taken literally. This is perhaps nowhere more strikingly evident than in the recommendation by two social scientists that 'instead of spontaneously formed (so-called "informal") groups, which can take on an anti-social or other undesirable orientation, we can form groups with a given set of goals and with a predetermined orientation'. Such groups ('of desirable composition') would then be provided with 'all kinds of mutual, collective recreation'. The authors acknowledge the possibility that 'even organized bodies of this kind may break up into informal groups ... However, they are more easily controlled and influenced.'[74] If the party needs justification for intervening in the 'organization of leisure' it is ready at hand: leisure is an achievement of socialist construction, it is part of the nation's wealth and must be used wisely and constructively and not frittered away. 'The Soviet state makes great efforts for the expansion of free time', wrote a party secretary of Krasnoyarsk, 'thus, leisure is not a personal matter.'[75]

[73] *Pravda*, 29 August 1965.
[74] *Ekonomika Radyans'koyi Ukrainy*, 1968, no. 3, pp. 58–64 (quoted from translated excerpt in *Digest of the Soviet Ukrainian Press*, 1968, no. 6, p. 4.) The authors proposed a supplementary approach designed to control informal groups: 'This could be done through an individual in whom we would instil a resistance to the influence of informal groups with anti-social orientation.'
[75] *Pravda*, 13 February 1968. The secretary, Baikova, was co-author of a book entitled *Free Time and the All-Round Development of the Personality* (V. G. Baikova, A. S. Duchal and A. A. Zemtsov, *Svobodnoe vremya i vsestoronnee razvitie lichnosti*, Moscow, 1965.) See also A. V. Netsenko, *Svobodnoe vremya i ego vospol'zovanie*, Leningrad, 1964, p. 55. A recent *Pravda* editorial noted disapprovingly that some people were 'still inclined' to regard leisure as something 'purely personal'. (4 June 1971.) See also the article by Prof. Yu. Zhdanov, the son of A. A.

The ways in which Soviet citizens actually spend their leisure show that as yet many of them do regard leisure as a 'personal matter'. Card or domino games and drinking bouts continue to be among the more common, socially disapproved, ways of spending private leisure. Meeting friends and relatives in an intimate private environment is another favourite leisure time activity which the authorities, however, can hardly disapprove of, except by claiming that such meetings frequently lead to anti-social acts. It was such a claim, substantiated by figures showing among others that friends and neighbours comprised a relatively high share of the victims of hooliganism whereas only a small proportion of acts of violence were committed in such public places as cafes and restaurants, which led the head of the Leningrad Militia Administration to demand 'that people should spend more time in public places, where, remaining with their own group, they will at the same time fall under the moral and legal control of society'.[76]

But it is in its utilization of religious rituals and folk customs that Soviet indirect propaganda has of late come to reveal its most remarkable similarity to Nazi practices. Attempts to introduce new Soviet ceremonies and celebrations date from the early 1920s. It was then that young couples among the more enthusiastic atheists in the party and especially in the Komsomol celebrated the so-called 'red weddings', to compensate themselves for the emotional uplift of the church ceremony, while the new-born of the Soviet era were submitted to the Communist 'baptism' of the *oktyabrina* – derived from the Russian for October, the month of the revolution, and *krestiny* (christening) – and given all manner of eccentric, 'revolutionary' names such as Komintern, Elektrifikatsiya or Iskra.[77] Anti-religious Christmas and Easter

---

Zhdanov and Stalin's former son-in-law, who did however warn of the need for 'maximum care in steering the ship of our leisure between the Scylla of spontaneity and the Charybdis of over-organization'. (*Komsomol'skaya pravda*, 20 January 1968.) Brezhnev himself left little doubt as to his own position: 'Free time', he told delegates to the 15th Trade Union Congress, 'is not time free from responsibility to society.' (*Pravda*, 21 March 1972.)

[76] *Izvestiya*, 27 May 1967. On the other hand, a study of leisure among youth in East Kazakhstan found that 'there still exists an unfortunate tradition of invariably getting drunk when gathered at a restaurant table, with the likely result of a scandal or brawl of some sort'. (*Komsomol'skaya pravda*, 27 December 1963.)

[77] 'Now [1964] this raises smiles.' (*Komsomol'skaya zhizn'*, 1964, no. 24, p. 7.)

carnivals were organized by the Komsomol and the new Harvest
Day, first held in 1923, was also at least partly anti-religious in
character inasmuch as it was designed 'to emphasize that good
harvests come from scientific methods of agriculture and not
from the observance of the saints' days of the church calendar'.[78]

On the whole these new private and public rites received little
support from the party authorities, and they quickly fell into
oblivion. Quite apart from the political considerations which
governed the regime's varying tactics in its struggle with the
Churches, there was a general reluctance to fight religion on the
battleground of ceremony. Where the authorities did not resort
to administrative and punitive measures, they placed their faith
in the efficacy of 'scientific' propaganda and agitation. There
was little understanding of the place of ritual and ceremony in
the lives of the people, but rather an indiscriminate contempt for
cultural traits and conventions inherited from the past. Clearly,
to take a particularly obvious example, the 'glass of water theory'
of sexual morality did not provide a propitious climate for the
cultivation of family rituals. The men who set out to build the
proletarian order were not going to imitate what they regarded
as the ageless guiles of the clerics: the New Soviet Man was cast
in the image of a 'rational' being, unmoved by emotional mum-
mery and ceremonial trappings.

A number of public holidays, not specifically designed to compete with religious celebrations, were also introduced in the
early post-revolutionary period, notably, of course, International
Labour Day and the Anniversary of the October Revolution, but
also several others, such as the anniversary of 'Bloody Sunday' in
1905 which later merged with the anniversary of Lenin's death
(21 January) and Paris Commune Day (18 March). Their number
and composition has varied somewhat over the years[79] For the
most part they have come to be marked by a leaden, stereotyped
pattern of processions, slogans and speeches. Whatever solemnity
or festive enthusiasm they might have aroused originally, the
majority of the people soon came to see their main significance
in the fact that they afforded time off from work. In the words of

[78] S. N. Harper, *Civic Training in Soviet Russia*, Chicago, 1929, p. 228.
[79] The main all-Union public holidays which are also official rest days are
now New Year, International Women's Day, International Labour Day,
Victory Day (World War II), the Anniversary of the Revolution and Constitution Day (5 December). In addition there are some 35 other non-rest
commemoration days in the year (Cosmonaut Day, Radio Day, Militia
Day, Light Industry Day, Machinebuilders' Day, etc., etc.).

a contemporary Soviet source, they were 'replaced by tedium, conventionalism and official pomposity and after a while one ceased paying attention to them altogether'.[80]

It was only in the late 1950s that attention once again began to focus on the creation of secular rituals and celebrations. The first 'experiments' to establish 'a harmonious system of new non-religious ceremonies' were made in 1957 and 1958 in the two (predominantly Lutheran) Baltic Republics of Latvia and Estonia.[81] From early 1958 onwards the Komsomol took the initiative in calling for similar ceremonies in other parts of the USSR. The response was quick and generally favourable and appropriate action soon followed.[82] Indeed the speed with which the Komsomol initiative was translated into action leaves little doubt that it was undertaken at the instigation of higher party authorities.

Official justification for what quickly came to be labelled 'new traditions' was mainly stated in terms of the struggle against religion.[83] Church rituals, it was argued, were the last bastions of 'religious prejudice' in Soviet society. Not only did they have a powerful influence in reinforcing religious belief, but even convinced atheists still submitted to their emotional attraction. Thus, for both devout believers and for those whose only links with religion were ceremonial and aesthetic, the creation of new Communist rites, no less festive and memorable than those of the Churches, was a most effective means of breaking the remaining hold of religion.[84]

But underlying the belief in the efficacy of secular rites as weapons in the campaign against religion there was explicit recognition of the fact that man – even Soviet man – had an innate need for ceremonial and festivity. As one participant in a

---

[80] *Nauka i religiya*, 1964, no. 8, p. 86.
[81] *Literaturnaya gazeta*, 28 January 1965, p. 2. The two Republics have continued to be held up as models ever since.
[82] As far as I have been able to trace it the first Komsomol call was published in *Komsomol'skaya pravda* of 2 February 1958; see below p. 192.
[83] The onset of a general anti-religious campaign in 1959 coincided roughly with the introduction of the secular rites.
[84] The above is a brief summary of the anti-religious argument for 'new traditions' which runs like a refrain through all Soviet writings. It will be encountered again in some of the passages quoted in the text below. For other examples see Yu. V. Krianev and P. S. Popov, 'Emotsional'noe vozdeistviya religioznoi obryadnosti i ego preodolenie', *Voprosy filosofii*, 1963, no. 9, pp. 70–7; R. M. Madzhidov, 'Puti preodoleniya religioznoi obryadnosti', *ibid.*, 1967, no. 7, pp. 109–16; Yu. V. Gagarin, 'Izzhivanie religioznykh traditsii i formirovanie novykh prazdnichnykh obychaev v Komi ASSR', *Sovetskaya etnografiya*, 1965, no. 4, pp. 148–59.

discussion on the importance of the new rites put it: 'Life has fooled the nihilists. Customs and certain ceremonials, certain conventions in man's spiritual existence, in his way of life, in his habits and behaviour have proved to be necessary in the new socialist society, too.'[85] This was something which the Churches, unlike the unnamed 'nihilists', had always understood. Many of the most popular ceremonies and celebrations had their origins deep in the history and folklore of the different nationalities of the Soviet Union. The Churches had merely taken them over and invested them with religious significance. What was needed now was to strip them of their 'religious cover' and adapt them to the needs of Soviet socialist secular society.[86] Once it was thus accepted that private ceremony and public pageantry were essential elements in the life of every society, it was inevitable that the attempt should be made to develop 'new traditions' as channels of indirect propaganda – not only to overcome the 'last residues' of religious belief and practice, but to diffuse officially prescribed attitudes in general.

In part, at least, the search for new ceremonies and celebrations may well have come in response to genuine popular demand. By the end of the 1950s Soviet society had begun to recover from the tumult and furor of the Stalinist era. It was a society in the process of settling down and it was looking for symbolic ways to assert its cultural identity. The dizzy heights of socialism, so

[85] A. Laptev in *Literaturnaya gazeta*, 21 January 1965, p. 2.
[86] *Agitator*, 1964, no. 22, pp. 47–8; *Nauka i religiya*, 1964, no. 8, p. 87. The following particularly enthusiastic advocate of the new ritual deserves to be quoted at some length: 'The specific internal atmosphere – the monumental decoration, the ritual splendour, the solemn singing, the inspirational sermon, the theatrical gestures of the ministers – all this duly affects the believer's mind ... in the field of new civic forms of commemorating special occasions, the primary requirement is co-ordination, the firm uniformity of new ceremonies ... And co-ordination requires in turn a ritual centre, a distinctive base. And this base, in my view, could be some kind of new ritual replacing the church liturgy. In devising such a ritual we shall by no means be creating a "new religion", we shall simply be daring to create an intellectual–emotional holiday – an apotheosis of human genius and a counter-weight to church worship ... A holiday of man! As in Gorky. '(*Komsomol'skaya pravda*, 15 August 1965.) Readers of Solzhenitsyn's *The First Circle* may be reminded of the Communist Rubin's draft 'Proposal for the Establishment of Civic Temples'. See also an article by a Soviet architect calling for the design of 'aesthetically appropriate' buildings to house the new ceremonies and reminding his readers that 'throughout the ages the greatest artists consecrated their work to the Church'. (*Sovetskaya kul'tura*, 22 July 1972.)

resplendent from afar, had been climbed but the landscape that presented itself was still uniformly grey and cheerless. The ardour, the excitement with which the climb had begun, had long been spent; the daily fear continuously rekindled by Stalin's very own mountaineering style had subsided; there was a modicum of material affluence and more free time to spend on non-productive cultural and recreational pursuits. It was altogether natural that the lack of colour and festivity in Soviet life should make itself felt with particular acuteness at this time.

Yet while in this sense there is some truth in the statement that the new ceremonies 'arose out of social necessity, by the will of the people'[87] it would be naïve to assume that 'the will of the people' could have been expressed, let alone lead to responsive action by the regime, if it had not also coincided with the policy objectives of the regime itself. However potent and widespread popular longing may have been, if the Soviet leadership saw fit to satisfy it, it was above all because its propagandists were looking for new opportunities to provide the Soviet citizen with 'healthy spiritual nourishment' as part of the drive for the subversion of leisure.[88]

Both the popular striving for colourful rituals in private and public life and the manner in which the regime proposed to utilize it for the purpose of indirect propaganda are reflected in the first 'pathbreaking' article on the subject in *Komsomol'skaya pravda* of 2 February 1958. 'What should a betrothal, a wedding be like?' asked the author, one A. Nuikin from Novosibirsk. 'How to mark the birth of a baby, the coming-of-age and other festive events in life? These questions have long agitated our youth . . . It is time to answer these questions.' The resemblance of his own answers to those of the Nazis is too striking to require special emphasis. Proceeding from the assumption that 'without celebrations human life is inconceivable', the author criticized the uninspiring style of many Soviet festivities with their invariable round of speeches and citations to which 'not many listen attentively' and which communicate but 'little solemnity and festive

---

[87] *Literaturnaya gazeta*, 10 December 1964, p. 3.
[88] Some ten years later the link between the new leisure and the new ritual was explicitly acknowledged when a conference on the subject of the secular rites noted that 'the socialist ceremonial is one of the most effective forms of the sensible and captivating organization of leisure and the filling of free time' and that 'the need of working people to mark personal and public events grew noticeably' after the transition of the five-day working week. (*Nauka i religiya*, 1968, no. 8, pp. 19–20.)

spirit' to an audience that is never moved beyond the role of detached onlooker. Like the Nazis before him, the Komsomol author looks towards celebrations that enter 'the home, the family, the soul of the people', and like them he finds the tradi‐tional festivities as ideal avenues of approach to the soul of the people. Whitsun, Christmas, Easter-week and carnival night – these had long been occasions for exhilarating and joyful cele‐bration. 'What is their strength? Certainly not their religious con‐tent.' The Church, recognizing 'the immense strength of celebra‐tions', had attempted 'to impress its own brand on each of them, to impregnate them with religious spirit'. It was now the task of the Soviet regime to 'rehabilitate the old folk customs and ceremonies ... [and] to enrich our celebrations with new ones ... [that] will be popular in content, in appeal, in form, and do not change from year to year but become tradition ...' The same tendency to link up with traditional ceremonial should also be followed in regard to the celebration of family events. Although terminological changes are 'of course' necessary, 'is it a bad custom to have two of your best friends become god-parents to your baby? There was a need for 'festive weddings without clerics, for baptism without the Church, for coming-of-age con‐firmation without priests'.

Other articles with similar recommendations followed in quick succession[89] and the movement for 'new traditions' soon took on some of the typical features of a Soviet-style mass campaign. Local and national conferences were convened; commissions, councils and bureaux were established bearing such titles as Communist Customs Council and Bureau for Civil Ceremonies and employing full-time officials known as Chief Organizer of Festivals (*glavnyi ustroitel' prazdnikov*); sociologists and ethno‐graphers set out to analyze the role of traditions, old and 'new'; artists were urged to apply their talents to the creation of

[89] *Komsomol'skaya pravda*, 23 and 24 March 1958, 25 January 1959, 26 March 1959, 13 June 1959, 24 October 1959. In February 1960 a plenum of the Komsomol Central Committee adopted a resolution calling on 'youth collectives to mark memorable events in the life of young people, such as their coming-of-age; the start of their working life ... marriage, the birth of a child, etc. Every such celebration and holiday should be accompanied by colourful and memorable ceremonies that make creative use of the best customs and rituals of the people and of national tradi‐tions.' (*Ibid.*, 5 February 1960.) See also *Izvestiya*, 4 November 1959 and 17 March 1960; and A. Kharchev, 'Sem'ya i kommunizm', *Kommunist*, 1960, no. 7, esp. p. 62 and I. Kryvelev. 'Vazhnaya storona byta', *ibid.*, no. 8, esp. p. 71–2.

ceremonial costumes, songs and scenarios; and books and brochures with such titles as 'Solemn, beautiful, memorable!' and
'Traditions – A Means for the Upbringing of the New Man'
began to come off the printing presses.[90]

The result of all this flurry of activity has been a veritable
mushrooming of new ceremonies and celebrations. The opening
at the end of 1959 of the first Palace of Marriage in Leningrad,
where a bust of Lenin looks on benignly from a niche as a
Deputy from the City Soviet presides over a wedding ceremony
complete with an exchange of vows and wedding rings to the
accompaniment of 'solemn strains' of music by Massenet, Beethoven and Chopin, followed by a 'stately march' by Tchaikovsky,
was a significant milestone on the road towards 'simple, beautiful
and meaningful ceremonies'.[91] Similar centres, also known as
Palaces of Happiness or, more modestly, Houses of Civil Ritual,
now exist in most other cities; in the smaller localities specially
decorated rooms have been set aside in clubs, Houses of Culture,
etc. Here other rites of passage are also celebrated. The birth of a
baby is no longer simply registered by the state, 'as if it were a
table or a chair to be entered in the inventory book',[92] but
solemnized in a ceremony appropriate to the occasion: representatives of social organizations come bearing gifts and congratula-
tory messages, a 'beautifully designed certificate' is handed to the
parents, Young Pioneers recite verses and a sapling is planted in
the Park of the Newborn.[93]

[90] V. I. Murasheva and I. N. Romanov, eds., *Torzhestvenno, krasivo, pamyatno!*, Moscow, 1966; P. P. Mozhayev, *Traditsii – sredstvo vospitaniya
novogo cheloveka*, Leningrad, 1968.

[91] *Kommunist*, 1960, no. 7, p. 62; *Komsomol'skaya pravda*, 24 October
1959 and 5 February 1960. Persons marrying for the second or subsequent time are not permitted to marry at the Palace of Marriage. For
an account by a Western observer of the wedding ceremony at the
Palace of Marriage in Moscow see, C. Curtiss, 'The Way People Live',
in H. E. Salisbury, ed., *Anatomy of the Soviet Union*, London, 1967, pp.
54ff.

[92] *Agitator*, 1964, no. 24, p. 24.

[93] The children of Leningrad receive an engraved medal 'Born in Leningrad' as part of the festive registration ceremony. The anticipated educational effect was described as follows: 'Years pass. The little one, sitting
on his father's knees, takes the blue disc in his hands. "This was given
to you because you were born in Leningrad", says his father. "You are
a Leningrader, born in the city in which Soviet power was born. Look,
here is Il'ich in an armoured car." These words are not wasted. Possibly
through them the notion of October, of the revolution, enters the consciousness of the little one...' (*Komsomol'skaya pravda*, 5 February
1964.)

Other festive events include the day on which youngsters reaching the age of 16 receive their (internal) passport (and vow 'to bear the title of Soviet citizen with honour');[94] the coming-of-age day at 18 (when the young adults swear an 'oath of loyalty' at the graves of revolutionary fighters);[95] and the day of enlistment into the army (which among others provides an opportunity for the conscripts to kiss their 'very own [*rodnoe*] Komsomol flag').[96] Several celebrations are frequently mentioned in Soviet sources but rarely described in any detail; among these are the first pay-day, retirement from work and silver and golden wedding anniversaries.[97] For Soviet dignitaries there have always been fairly elaborate secular funeral ceremonies, complete with music, flower wreaths, procession, guard of honour and funeral oration. There are some indications that similar, if more modest, solemnities are now to be extended to ordinary members of Soviet society. As yet, however, the last rite is conspicuously missing from the new ceremonial cycle, – with the exception of Latvia and Estonia where 'something has been done in the past ten years'.[98]

In many of these ceremonies traditional elements are retained or adapted, particularly in the countryside: 'bread and salt', the fake abduction of the bride, the exchange of wedding rings, the institution of 'honorary parents', the wearing of white at 'civil confirmation', etc. At the same time a conscious effort is made to place all celebrations in the public realm. The view, 'not infrequently found', that they are 'purely private events' is sharply

---

94 *Izvestiya*, 23 June 1962; *Pravda*, 4 December 1970.
95 *Pravda*, 3 June 1966 and 18 April 1968; *Agitator*, 1970, no. 12, p. 50.
96 *Agitator*, 1964, no. 12, p. 39; *Partiinaya zhizn'*, 1968, no. 6, p. 64.
97 See, e.g. *Partiinaya zhizn'*, 1967, no. 11, p. 55; *Izvestiya*, 16 December 1970. In the town of Zyryanovsk (Kazakhstan) which won an award for its ceremonies, a 'Golden Wedding' medal was instituted. (*Nauka i religiya*, 1970, no. 3, p. 49.) Earlier a similar proposal had been ridiculed in the literary weekly: 'But won't "levelling" enter into the picture? After all, a couple can live together for 25 or 50 years in different ways. Perhaps medals of different rank should be issued? Let us say that a first-degree gold medal is issued "For a Blameless Family Life', a second-degree silver medal "For an Almost Blameless Family Life".' (*Literaturnaya gazeta*, 10 December 1964, p. 3.)
98 *Nauka i religiya*, 1968, no. 12, p. 77. See this source also for some examples of the funeral rites introduced in these two Republics as well as for some of the procedural problems encountered, e.g. whether or not to ring bells ('Under no circumstances will we imitate the priests.'), or whether to throw flowers into the grave instead of the traditional handful of gravel.

condemned in the Soviet press.[99] Instead, the community as a whole is to be drawn into the festivities, as at the 'Family Chronicles' in Odessa where residents 'share their joys' in an 'unconstrained atmosphere',[100] or at the enterprises of Sumgait in Azerbaidjan where a wedding is 'an event for the entire collective'.[101] In the words of a recent *Pravda* editorial: 'It is important that a marriage or the birth of a child be not only the occasion for a private celebration but also a festive occasion for others.'[102] Sometimes this implies fairly active involvement by outsiders. Thus, when a wedding takes place, fellow-workers help 'in making the wedding dress, preparing the food, buying the rings' and also 'choose a best man and a matron of honour in the old tradition'. When a child is born the members of the mother's 'entire Communist Labour Brigade are named honorary parents' at a 'solemn ceremony' which includes 'a pledge by the collective to help in bringing up the child'.[103] The avowed objective is to raise the 'social significance' of the event and at the same time to create a feeling of togetherness on the part of all participants. The kind of popular comment which Soviet sources are particularly fond of quoting, in this as in other contexts of mass-political work, is: 'People used to lead secluded lives, everyone by himself and for himself, but now we live as a friendly, consolidated family.'[104]

Alongside these rites designed to mark events in the life of the individual and the family there now exists a wide variety of public festivals: Spring and Winter Festivals, Festival of the First Furrow, Harvest Festival, Corngrowers' Festival, Birch Tree Festival, Hammer and Sickle Festival (to celebrate the friendship between town and country), Street Festivals (in honour of the person after whom the street is named, or of a historical event – revolutionary battle, demonstration, etc. – associated with the street), Festival of Labour Glory (to celebrate production achievements), Heroes' Commemoration Day – these

[99] *Sovetskaya Rossiya*, 19 November 1966; *Nauka i religiya*, 1969, no. 2, p. 37.
[100] *Agitator*, 1969, no. 8, p. 42.
[101] *Pravda*, 25 March 1968.
[102] *Ibid.*, 18 August 1971.
[103] *Sovetskaya etnografiya*, 1962, no. 1, p. 80.
[104] *Pravda*, 3 July 1966. In the earlier-mentioned Zyryanovsk the public character of the celebration is underlined in their designations as 'Public Registration of the Newborn', 'Public Registration of Marriage', etc. For a comprehensive inventory of new celebrations in Kazakhstan, see *Nauka i religiya*, 1971, no. 5, pp. 16–18.

are but some of the more common festivities introduced in different parts of the Soviet Union over the past ten years.

Again, as their names indicate many of these 'new traditions' are being built on the foundations of old folk customs and religious observances. The Harvest Festival celebrated in Turkmenistan, for example, is an up-dated, Soviet version of the traditional *Kharman-toi*. In the words of Ya. Khudaiberdyev, then Secretary of the Turkmenistan Central Committee, the decision, taken 'at one time', to abolish this ancient festival, reflected 'a mechanical, unthinking approach', for 'certain old traditions and civil ceremonials can be widely utilized and filled with new content'. In 1965 the Harvest Festival coincided with a Ten-Day Festival of Russian Culture and turned into 'a demonstration of the friendship of nations'.[105] Similarly, the Spring Festival first celebrated in Baku in 1967 is closely modelled on the ancient Azerbaidjani folk festival *Novruz-bairam*, which was never 'organically linked with religion' and despite the attempts of Islam 'to take it in hand and utilize it for its own purposes' retained its 'popular, life-affirming character' to the present day. Where Islam had allegedly failed Soviet communism is determined to succeed. According to the Secretary of the Baku party committee the main difference between the ancient and the modern festival is in the 'collective, organized, contemporary' character of the latter.[106] The Birch Tree Festival was conceived to rival Whitsun. As celebrated in Moscow, it included such elements as a 'Festival Hostess' (*khozyaika prazdnika*) – 'beautiful and slender as the birch tree itself' – songs, dances, torch parades and fireworks. 'There were no speeches [or] reports.' Instead, 'famous heroes of labour' spoke of spring and 'the beauty of human labour'. The success of the festival was complete: 'The people carried away joy in their hearts and gratitude towards those who had organized such a festival. Only the faces of the clergymen were gloomy . . .'[107]

Commemoration ceremonies, too, it is affirmed, are rooted in ancient folk tradition: 'Christianity succeeded in giving commemoration ceremonies cult character, but in the consciousness of the people . . . [they] always had broader significance.'[108] In Georgia, the religious commemoration rituals traditionally held

[105] *Pravda*, 15 September 1966.
[106] *Nauka i religiya*, 1969, no. 4, p. 74.
[107] *Ibid.*, 1964, no. 8, p. 86.
[108] *Ibid.*, 1969, no. 2, p. 32.

in early May are now replaced by a Day of Remembrance for the fallen of World War II.[109] In the Latvian settlement of Palsmane, which seems to serve as something of a model for the country as a whole in this field, the attempt 'to dislodge the clerics from their last stronghold' took the form of 'cemetery festivals' (*kladbishchie prazdniki*) in which 'brief appearances by the best local speakers alternate with music, choir and solo performances and the reading of verses', and loudspeakers carry the proceedings to all inhabitants assembled at the cemetery.[110] On Commemoration Day in Tallin, music by Chopin, Beethoven, Schubert and Handel, and speeches stressing themes such as the 'struggle for the liberation of mankind', 'the friendship of nations' and 'loyalty to the principles of Leninism' help to create a 'solemn-majestic ceremonial, free from religion, life-affirming, imbued with respect for man the creator, man the toiler'. This and similar ceremonies conducted also in the villages of Estonia are said to enjoy 'enormous popularity'. What is more, their 'educational importance is great' because those who attend, and they are said to include the majority of believers, are 'not detached onlookers but active participants in a ceremony which in its essence is profoundly atheistic'.[111]

Soviet sources claim that the 'new traditions' have fully justified the expectations placed in them. Figures are adduced, in some cases supported by social surveys, to show that attendance at religious ceremonies has dropped dramatically and even ceased altogether in certain areas.[112] The validity of these claims is open to doubt. Apart from the need to discount the statistical exuberance of local reports, one must make some allowance for the inherent limitations of Soviet social research when tackling a delicate and politically sensitive issue. Still, Soviet official spokesmen, no less than their predecessors in Nazi Germany, appear convinced that their 'new traditions' are a key 'to the heart and mind' of the Soviet citizen. And, while they generally tend to support their conviction with such 'concrete' indicators as the fall in attendance at religious observances, they do not conceal that broader purposes are involved. The following

[109] *Izvestiya*, 3 August 1968.   [110] *Agitator*, 1966, no. 24, p. 25.

[111] *Nauka i religiya*, 1969, no. 2, pp. 32–5.

[112] See, e.g. D. M. Aptekman, 'Prichiny zhivuchesti religioznogo obryada kreshcheniya v sovremennykh usloviyakh', *Vopsosy filosofii*, 1965, no. 3, pp. 83–9; G. I. Popov, 'Konkretnye sotsial'nye issledovaniya v praktike ideologicheskoi raboty', *Sotsiologiya v SSSR*, 2 vols., Moscow, 1965, vol. i, pp. 83–4; also *Partiinaya zhizn'*, 1972, no. 2, p. 37.

is the kind of vindication of the new rituals that can be frequently encountered in the Soviet press:

> When in the second half of the 1950s the suggestion was put forward to organize a 'secular' civil confirmation [in Latvia] it seemed to many an inadmissable competition with the Church while others regarded it as the adoption of a religious tradition. But in 1957 the festival ... began its victory march. Somehow from the very beginning everything in it proved successful. In the first place the name – 'Coming-of-Age Festival.' And most important – the ritual itself, emotional, colourful, up-to-date, which is needed not only in order to oust religious confirmation ... In fact it has already ousted the Lutheran confirmation. Last year around 15,000 participated in the coming-of-age festival in the Republic, that is the overwhelming majority of the 18-year-olds. And only several dozens of young people were confirmed in church. Fifteen years ago the proportions were the reverse. However, the significance of the new ceremony lies not only in its ousting of religious relics: it educates young men and girls to devotion to Leninist ideals, to Soviet patriotism, internationalism (youths of different nationalities participate in the festival), readiness to work honourably for the good of society and take up the banner of revolutionary and labour traditions from the older generation.[113]

Occasionally, to be sure, this generally bright scene is overcast by scattered clouds of doubt and criticism. The opposition to the new rituals which, as the above passage indicates, attended the introduction of the confirmation ceremony in Latvia, seems to have persisted in other parts of the country: 'Sometimes people ask: the 20th Century – and yet ceremonies? This indeed is the trouble – the ceremonies are regarded as relics.'[114] As in Nazi Germany there are local leaders who have 'not yet developed a taste' for the secular rituals and lack understanding of their 'political and moral significance'.[115] just as there are party and Komsomol members who 'do not consider it shameful to participate in ceremonies and rituals bearing openly religious character'.[116] While some organizations have been slow to introduce

---

[113] *Agitator*, 1970, no. 12, p. 50; see also *Izvestiya*, 28 October 1971.
[114] *Nauka i religiya*, 1968, no. 2, p. 24.
[115] *Pravda*, 22 March 1967.
[116] *Ibid.*, 25 March 1968: 'How, one asks, can people have faith in the purity of the atheist convictions of these Communists?'

the new ceremonies, others have been quick to abandon them after one or two cursory attempts. Even among the Komsomol much of the initial enthusiasm seems to have waned fairly quickly, and already in 1964 the head of the Civil Registry Office (ZAGS) in Leningrad was moved to exclaim plaintively: 'What do we expect from Komsomol members? Attention! Elementary attention.'[117] In 1971 readers' letters to the press still indicated that 'Soviet rituals are being neglected, with the result that religious rituals fill the vacuum.'[118] The long-established revolutionary holidays are still 'not infrequently' attended by 'banality and formalism',[119] while the 'new traditions' are already 'dull and monotonous', marred by 'bureaucratization' and devoid of 'feeling and expressiveness'.[120] The inevitable abuses have also set in. In Khabarovsk Territory a Festival of Labour Heroes was celebrated for 'no other reason' than that the 'agricultural administration allocated the funds'; what is more, there was even 'no proper merriment – only an inept call for it'.[121] In the Transbaikal – 'as a result of the position of non-interference in the "private" lives of collective farmers and workers that is taken by some public organizations' – weddings have turned into extended eating and drinking carousals, causing great economic damage and 'moral losses [which] defy calculation', and the 'saddest thing is that people justify such noisy and drunken assemblages as a re-birth of national customs and traditions'.[122] Other examples attesting to the deficiencies and deformities of the secular ceremonies could be culled from the Soviet press; it will suffice to quote the verdict of the Director of the Institute of Scientific Atheism, A. Okulov:

> This work still lacks centralization and stability and the necessary attention to the form and to the emotional and aesthetic content of the new holidays and ceremonies. Every

---

[117] *Komsomol'skaya pravda*, 13 August 1964.
[118] *Ibid.*, 6 January 1971.
[119] *Nauka i religiya*, 1967, no. 1, p. 8. 'Almost every step of the column is regulated and appropriately directed in advance, long meetings with stereotyped speeches in which every speaker repeats the self-same commonplaces – this unfortunately is what the essence of the festivity has been reduced to. The evenings devoted to our holidays are also schematic: presidium, report, concert.' (*Ibid.*)
[120] *Sovetskaya Rossiya*, 21 March 1969; *Nauka i religiya*, 1968, no. 2, p. 24; 1970, no. 3, pp. 28, 30; 1972, no. 5, pp. 26–8.
[121] *Komsomol'skaya pravda*, 5 February 1961.
[122] *Pravda*, 13 January 1969.

province conducts this work in its own way and often un-
systematically and primitively. This is particularly regrettable
because it undermines the faith in the idea itself.[123]

It is difficult, if not impossible, to make a meaningful comparison between the quality of the 'counter-ceremonies' in Soviet
Russia and Nazi Germany. Some of the new Soviet rites do
indeed strike one as 'primitive' to a degree that makes the crude
plagiarisms of Nazi *Brauchtum* stand out as models of sophistication. But then they are intended for a very different cultural
environment. Although they may be unable – at least as presently
constituted – to take the place of time-honoured folk customs and
religious observances, it is not inconceivable that they help to fill
a significant emotional void in the lives of the mass of the
Soviet people. The new family rites may well seem a welcome
change from the matter-of-fact, bureaucratic 'inventory' style in
which these events were previously marked. And the same is
probably true of the effect of the new or revived public celebrations on people who have no life-experience of genuine, popular
festivity, only of sterile slogans, flag-waving and interminable
speeches.

But whatever the difference in the artistic quality of Soviet
ceremonies as compared to those of the Nazis, their political purpose is identical. There is no doubt in the minds of the protagonists of Soviet 'new traditions', just as there was none in the
minds of the exponents of Nazi *Brauchtum*, that 'traditions must
also actively work for our common cause',[124] that, in fact, 'every
festival must be utilized as a means of ideological upbringing'.[125]
Street celebrations, for instance, are 'not only relaxation but also
a means of organizing people, a means of political influence',[126]
and even silver and golden wedding anniversaries have 'great
upbringing importance'.[127] 'The new ceremonies do not only
carry into life beauty, festivity and variety', wrote a secretary of
the East Kazakhstan Province Committee of the party, 'they also
have important social-ideological significance: they form the
materialist world-view, enrich the spiritual world of man, link the
individual to the collective and strengthen the family.'[128] This is
a common formula. The First Secretary of the Belorussian
Republic, P. Masherov, went even further when he claimed that

---

[123] *Nauka i religiya*, 1967, no. 8, p. 17.
[125] *Ibid.*, 22 March 1967.
[127] *Nauka i religiya*, 1964, no. 7, p. 86.

[124] *Pravda*, 4 August 1968.
[126] *Ibid.*, 6 March 1969.
[128] *Ibid.*, 1970, no. 3, p. 45.

it was precisely their political content which helped to account for the success of the public festivals:

> What makes these mass holidays attractive? First of all, the wide range of the means for influencing the masses politically – rallies, ceremonial processions, speeches by old Communists, advanced workers and labour innovators; the great strength of emotional influence – concerts ... brilliant national costumes and elements of folk rituals with up-to-date content; and finally, the entertainment element – folk games and sport contests. The popular mass holidays successfully combine political upbringing, the propaganda of advanced experience, collective recreation and moral incentives for the best toilers.[129]

The necessary corollary to this view of the role of the 'new traditions' is, of course, that they cannot be allowed to evolve otherwise than under close party supervision. If there were some voices which seemed to plead for an unconstrained, eclectic growth of customs and celebrations,[130] they were promptly dismissed as an 'apologia for spontaneity' and a 'philistine position'.[131] For the functionaries of the party any other reaction would indeed be quite unthinkable. Since the new ceremonies are instruments of 'ideological upbringing', as in the conditions

---

[129] *Pravda*, 26 March 1966.
[130] A. Petukhov, 'Bumazhnye tsvety', *Novyi mir*, 1969, no. 6, pp. 272–7. This is a review article discussing several of the new books on secular ceremonies. The author's approach, reflected in the article's title ('Paper Flowers'), is refreshingly sceptical: 'Yes, festivals can be created and organized. It is possible to devise and implement a ceremonial for some rite or other. But an organized festival is not a popular festival in the true sense of the word. A devised "rite" is ... only a staged show (*instsenirovka*), a performance, which may be interesting and even beautiful, but no more than that.' The author is also rare, if not alone, among Soviet commentators in noting that 'new traditions' is a contradiction in terms: '... if "tradition" – it means that it is not all that "new", and if "new" ... time alone will show whether it will become a real tradition.'
[131] *Nauka i religiya*, 1970, no. 3, p. 28. A clinching argument was adduced from the example of Christian ceremonial: 'It is a fact that it triumphed not at all spontaneously but thanks to the energetic – and at times outright forcible – actions of the Church in the course of tens and hundreds of years.' (*Ibid.*) That the process of 'creating a new ceremonial cannot proceed spontaneously' was a 'main conclusion' of a recent conference held in the Ukraine. (*Nauka i religiya*, 1970, no. 5, p. 19.) See also *Pravda*, 22 March 1967: 'Of course they [the new ceremonies] cannot be allowed to drift. Of course, they need proper organization.'

of the Soviet Union they must be, it is self-evident that the party alone is qualified to wield them. As a propaganda official of the Latvian Central Committee put it: 'Our Soviet ceremonial has a beneficial influence on the work and the social-political activity of a person. That is why the improvement of Soviet every-day ceremonies is an important section of ideological work and is properly considered a purely party affair'.[132] In short, ceremony is influential, therefore ceremony is part of ideological work, and ideological work belongs to the party. The logic of the *apparatchik* in such matters is implacable.

[132] *Nauka i religiya*, 1969, no. 2, p. 36.

7: PROPAGANDA OF THE DEED: WELFARE

Party-sponsored assistance by word and deed constitutes an excellent springboard for the mobilization of the masses, not only because the confidence and gratitude engendered assure the propaganda message of a sympathetic reception, but also because the mechanics of welfare administration project party influence into the home and family and thus provide an additional channel of party control. The insight into the intimate affairs of the individual and the family that was ordinarily denied to the party functionary was available to the social worker, and by assuming in part the role of the latter, he greatly enhanced his opportunities for both control and propaganda. The Nazis often used the term *Betreuung* – which is only imperfectly translated as 'care' – in reference to their activities vis-à-vis the people. But they made no secret of the fact that for them *Betreuung* included the two concepts of 'education and supervision': in entrusting the care of the people to the national socialist movement the Fuehrer had charged it with the tasks of 'continued education and lasting supervision of our people'.[1] A directive of the Party Chancellory expressly stated that 'care must of course be extended independently of a person's previous attitude towards the party and national socialism'. But it went on to declare in the very next sentence:

> Applicants in whom an understanding for the aims and concepts of the party and national socialism has only been awakened by the manner in which their requests are treated and the ideological explanation which accompanies it, must be given on request the opportunity for closer education within the activities of the local party group.[2]

The Soviet attitude was once expressed in similar terms by Kalinin when he stated:

[1] *Unser Wille und Weg*, 1938, no. 2, p. 58.
[2] VAB, vol. I, p. 61.

If a person asks for assistance he should be helped, but at the same time he should be told: 'Look here, the Party or Trade Union organization is assisting you, helping you on. But we want you, when the time comes, not to stand aloof, but to join with the rest in advancing the common cause.' This line should be adhered to in all our work among the masses.[3]

For the Nazis, social welfare was pre-eminently an expression of that 'socialism of the deed' which loomed so large in national socialist imagery. In the conditions of economic depression and widespread unemployment of the early 1930s it was probably inevitable that the party should be quick to recognize the propaganda dividends to be earned from a massive welfare effort that was unmistakably associated with the new order and its principal harbinger, the national socialist movement; and this all the more so as the leaders of the Third Reich were unlikely to sanction a more radical redistribution of wealth and income. Indeed the party lost no time in turning itself into a welfare agency in its own right, dispensing material and non-material benefits on an increasing scale through its own organizations. Chief among these was the NS–People's Welfare, or NSV.[4] Created in April 1932 as an internal welfare agency for party members, the NSV soon after the Nazi accession to power began to co-ordinate and absorb existing voluntary welfare institutions, and eventually came to dominate the entire field of welfare work in Nazi Germany.[5] In the words of Hilgenfeld, the leader of the NSV: 'Out of the totalitarian claim of our idea we determine and demand today the leadership of all spheres of people's welfare and

---

[3] M. I. Kalinin, *On Communist Education*, Moscow, 1949, p. 225.
[4] Other party organizations – the Hitler Youth, the Labour Front, the NS-Women's League, the NS-War Victims' Care, to name several – also performed welfare functions of one kind or another. But it was the NSV which was primarily responsible for the administration of the party's national welfare effort.
[5] Ruthe, *Nationalsozialismus*, p. 49. Membership of the NSV jumped from 112,000 in December 1933 to 3.7 million one year later. (H. Althaus, *Nationalsozialistische Volkswohlfahrt*, Berlin, 1935, p. 42.) By 1939 it numbered 10.7 million members and by 1943, the last year for which figures are available, 15.3 million members were recorded. The latter figure represented over 60% of all households; distribution varied widely, with 105% of households as the highest density (Moselland) and 30% as the lowest (Hamburg). (NA, T-81, 85/96844–5, 96756.) As a rule, NSV membership implied no more than the regular payment of contributions and was a relatively unburdensome form of demonstrating the necessary Nazi sentiments (*nationalsozialistische Gesinnung*).

relief.'[6] In regard to the welfare functions of the state, a student of NSV activities in one district found that the NSV evolved 'of itself into a position of something like a control organ which makes sure that the assistance prescribed by the law does indeed benefit the person in need'.[7] One of the NSV's major projects was the famous Winter Help (*Winterhilfswerk* – WHW) which from its annual collection campaigns placed considerable sums of money and large quantities of foodstuffs, clothing and other consumer articles at the disposal of party welfare distribution.[8] Another important NSV enterprise was the 'Mother and Child' project with its far-flung network of medical clinics and welfare centres. During the war the NSV expanded its activities greatly; it cared for the Germans returning to the Reich from occupied and other eastern territories, it played an increasing part in the care of soldiers and their families, it organized transports of wounded soldiers and finally it was placed in charge of refugee relief in bombed-out areas.[9]

This is not the place to enter into a detailed description of the many undoubtedly beneficial functions in which the NSV was engaged.[10] One feature, however, was common to them all:

[6] E. Hilgenfeld, *Aufgaben der nationalsozialistischen Wohlfahrtspflege*, Munich, 1937, p. 16.

[7] K. Mennecke, *Ein westdeutscher NSV-Kreis* (Diss.), Cologne, 1936, p. 33.

[8] In 1933–4 the number of WHW beneficiaries exceeded 16.6 million persons: every fourth German received some measure of WHW assistance. By 1939–40, and in proportion as the economic crisis and its accompanying unemployment receded, the number of WHW beneficiaries had dropped by nearly two thirds to some six million persons, or 7.5% of the population. Direct WHW relief to individuals was on principle given in kind only, mainly in the form of food, coal and clothing; 'assistance in cash is not granted so as to prevent misuse of any kind'. (E. Wulff, *Das Winterhilfswerk des Deutschen Volkes*, Berlin, 1940, pp. 13, 67, 97–8; *Statistisches Jahrbuch fuer das Deutsche Reich 1941–1942*, pp. 630–1.)

By law of 1 December 1936 the WHW became formally an institution of the state. (RGBI, 1936, i, p. 995.) But its administration remained in the hands of the NSV and for all practical purposes it was 'in fact the exclusive affair of the NSV and therefore of the party'. (H. Stoermer, *Das rechtliche Verhaeltnis der NS-Volkswohlfahrt und des Winterhilfswerkes zu den Betreuten im Vergleich zur oeffentlichen Wohlfahrtspflege*, Berlin, 1940, p. 53.)

[9] See H. Bernsee, *Aufgaben der NS-Volkswohlfahrt im Kriege*, Berlin, 1941, pp. 9–11, 22–37.

[10] Welfare beneficiaries were by no means unanimous in their enthusiasm for the administration of the various services. For a particularly outspoken criticism of red tape ('we are being chased from pillar to post . . .') and a strongly implied allegation of 'jurisdictional wrangles [*Kompetenzhaendelei*]' between party and state, see the security service report for

until the growing exigencies of the war made genuine, politically indiscriminate welfare a task of vital urgency for the survival of the nation, all the activities of the NSV were principally oriented towards propaganda goals. As one Nazi writer put it, 'national socialist welfare is essentially educational welfare'; beyond extending material assistance it strove 'to influence the inner spiritual attitude' of the person cared for and 'by employing national socialist motives . . . to turn him into a useful, work-willing member of the community. NS–People's Welfare is therefore the cultivation of a mental attitude.'[11] To Hilgenfeld, the NS–Sister who ministered to the health of the German mother and her child was the 'female soldier of the Fuehrer' and the 'bearer of the national socialist *Weltanschauung*'.[12] Whatever formulation they chose in making their point, practically all writers on the NSV emphasized that 'next to its social achievement stands the still more valuable political one'.[13]

Not only was the dispensation of welfare itself conceived as part of the regime's total propaganda effort, but the ability to extend or withhold welfare support provided the party with an important lever of social control. Whether or not the party leadership was sincere when it declared that assistance would be accorded irrespective of a person's past attitude towards the regime, there can be little doubt that the beneficiaries of NSV welfare who were less than enthusiastic in their current protestations of national socialist loyalty were few and far between. Some may have found their way to national socialism through genuine gratitude, others may have made a deliberate effort at outward conformity in the knowledge that failure to do so would deprive them of the welfare benefits; but many must have hovered permanently in the vast but vaguely delimited no-man's-land of 'voluntary compulsion', unwilling or unable to account even to themselves for the motives that prompted their political behaviour. For their part, local party functionaries had little compunction about using welfare levers in order to enforce

November 1943 in Boberach, *Meldungen aus dem Reich*, pp, 450–1.

11 Althaus, *Volkswohlfahrt*, pp. 13–14. In contrast to religious welfare institutions which were motivated by consideration of mercy and dispensed assistance in proportion to the wretchedness of applicants, the NSV 'on principle' served solely progenitive persons; there was 'no pointless welfare, wasteful of national resources, for the hereditary ill'. (*Ibid.*, pp. 17, 25–7.)

12 Hilgenfeld, *Aufgaben*, p. 12.

13 Ruthe, *Nationalsozialismus*, p. 51.

political demands. Thus, persons refusing to subscribe to the party paper would find that their child benefits had been cut off,[14] while others who had got themselves into the bad books of their block leader – allegedly for 'unsocial conduct' – found that their names had been struck from the lists of WHW beneficiaries.[15]

The distribution of welfare was one instrument of *Menschenfuehrung*. No less important were the collection drives which provided the necessary resources for the party's welfare activities. Regular NSV members, it will be recalled included over 60% of all households in 1943. In addition to the contributions derived from the organized NSV membership, however, there were the collection campaigns addressed to the nation as a whole. The Winter Help, organized by Goebbels for the first time in 1933 and thereafter conducted every winter, was designed to impress the concept of national solidarity upon the people by eliciting a contribution from every citizen. 'The people must... believe in something', Hitler declared when he opened the 1934–1935 WHW campaign on 9 October 1934. 'If you take from it the faith in international solidarity then you must give it faith in national solidarity instead.'[16] The intensive publicity campaigns in the course of which over a million voluntary helpers, drawn mainly from the party and its organizations, distributed badges in the streets and visited homes and farms throughout Germany, the demonstrations and speeches connected with each drive and the profusion of symbols that seemed to descend upon the whole of the country, were admirable propaganda instruments to that end. The purpose of the WHW, as Goebbels stated on the same occasion, was 'to produce national socialist conviction'. Goebbels knew, perhaps better than anyone else before or since, that few people would wish or dare to disassociate themselves from the affirmation of political loyalty that was extracted by way of a welfare appeal. 'We have a right to expect', he declared, 'that the entire community will pay us allegiance when we come to the aid of the poorest of the poor and prove to them by deed that the concept of the people's community is not an empty phrase.'[17] Whether or not it was true that the WHW was 'the

[14] VAB, vol. I, p. 450.
[15] NA, T-81, 23/157928.
[16] *Voelkischer Beobachter*, 10 October 1934.
[17] *Ibid.* On the propaganda preparations see Bramsted, *Goebbels and National Socialist Propaganda*, pp. 102–4.

greatest social project of all time',[18] it clearly was an excellent vehicle by which to carry the message of national socialism to millions of Germans week after week each winter. That it was the Minister of Propaganda and Public Enlightenment who was responsible for the WHW underlines its propagandistic intent.

What was true of the WHW was also true of the other collection campaigns organized by the party, and especially during the war years these recurred with increasing frequency. Money for the Red Cross, books for soldiers' rest homes, winter clothing for the army on the Russian front and for the families rendered homeless by air attack, scrap iron for the munitions industries – the various collection drives followed each other in quick succession.[19] The basic attitude of the party leadership to the collections can be read from a circular letter of the Party Chancellory of 22 May 1943.[20] The main purpose of the letter was to persuade local party organizations of the 'extraordinary political significance' of the collections and the consequent need for their 'superior and farsighted direction'. The letter goes on to declare: 'Collections of money and articles indicate to every person the great tasks of the community in a propagandistically effective and thorough manner.' In some cases, the funds collected could easily have been made available from other sources through the state budget. Yet despite the demands on scarce manpower made by the collections, the Fuehrer had purposely retained them for their 'irreplaceable educational function'.[21] In addition, the collections provided 'one of the most precise and reliable means by which the leadership can ascertain the real attitude of the people to its measures and plans'.

Time and again the central offices of the party and the Propaganda Ministry condemned the 'ever-increasing gross infractions of collection procedures'.[22] As the above circular of the Party Chancellory makes clear, it was because it viewed the collection

[18] Hitler at the inauguration of the 1937 campaign, *Voelkischer Beobachter*, 6 October 1937.
[19] For a survey of these drives and other welfare activities conducted by one regional party organization during the early years of the war, see the report 'Uebersicht zum Kriegseinsatz der NSDAP, ihrer Gliederungen und Verbaende im Gau Sued-Hannover–Braunschweig fuer die Zeit v. 1. ix. 39–31. xii. 42', in BA, NS 26/141.
[20] VAB, vol. IV, pp. 207–10. The facts and quotations in this and the following paragraph are taken from this source, unless otherwise indicated.
[21] This point had earlier been repeatedly made by Hitler in connection with the WHW. (See Wulff, *Winterhilfswerk*, p. 62.)
[22] NA, T-81, 24/21782; VAB, vol. IV, p. 210.

campaigns primarily as instruments for the mobilization of the masses that the party leadership was so unusually sensitive about some of the methods used by local party officials who, failing to grasp the 'educational' function of collections, resorted to various pressure tactics in order to boost the returns for the areas for which they were responsible. Even such relatively mild forms of persuasion as 'the public announcement of individual paltry contributions on the notice boards of the local party group, in the press or at meetings, the exercise of moral pressure through personal letters or visits of leading party members to individual members of the community or to economic enterprises', were declared to be harmful to the underlying purpose of the campaigns. 'Such measures may serve to create the outward impression... of an especially enthusiastic participation of the populace at political events... in reality, however, the general morale of the community will be most heavily damaged.' Moreover, the value of welfare collections as instruments for the gauging of public opinion was greatly impaired if the principle of voluntary contributions was ignored: by employing pressure the local party leader 'builds a Potemkin village for his superiors and ultimately for the Fuehrer himself'. On the other hand, since it was the party leader who was primarily responsible for the state of popular morale in his territorial domain, the results of collections reflected on the quality of his *Menschenfuehrung* in general and thus influenced his standing in the estimation of his superiors in the party hierarchy. It was therefore precisely the 'knowledge that the collection results are a kind of barometer for the weather conditions of popular morale that has led many a *Hoheitstraeger* to enforce a high result by all kinds of measures'. In order to reduce this built-in distortion in the 'barometer' of collection campaigns, the Party Chancellory was even prepared to curtail such competitive incentives as were derived from the publication of returns for individual areas. That the party leadership should be content to forego the increase in returns which competitive practices undoubtedly fostered, for fear that competition would lead to excesses and thereby to distortions of the character of the campaigns as public opinion polls, is perhaps better proof of the importance which the regime attached to its welfare campaigns as propaganda instruments than any number of verbal admonitions about the need to refrain from compulsion. At the same time it demonstrates once again how close to the surface of Nazi *Menschenfuehrung* the use of force was, and how difficult the leadership found it to uphold those few expressions of voluntary action which it deemed essential for the sake of the broader objectives of its mobilization of the masses. In illustration of this point the following passage from a not untypical letter of the head of an NSV district office in Mainfranken speaks volumes:

> As a matter of principle it must be stressed that all collections for the WHW are voluntary contributions for those of our people who are in need of help; and as is well known, no one can be freed from a voluntary contribution ... We request that all civil servants who refuse to make money donations ... be reported by name so that we can inform the Office for Civil Servants [of the party] accordingly ...[23]

23 NA, T-81, 153/0158576. See also the letter of a district leader listing the names of farmers who had not 'filled their quota' in recent NSV collections and requesting that 'these gentlemen be excluded from all state benefits' and have their tax arrears 'ruthlessly collected'. (Heyen, *Nationalsozialismus im Alltag*, p. 289.)

Of considerable interest, too, is the correspondence concerning Count Franz von Galen, a brother of the Bishop of Muenster who became one of the more outspoken opponents of the regime in the Catholic hierarchy, in ACDJC, Document CXLIII – 371. The correspondence dating from November–December 1939, includes a letter from the local NSV official to the party district office noting that Galen was not a member of the NSV and listing the precise amounts which he had contributed to WHW collections (50 pfennig, 25 pfennig, 10 pfennig etc.). The district leader, in a subsequent letter to Galen, writes that he does not assume that the latter's conduct was due to 'ill will, particularly as you owe your pension [as a former officer of the Imperial Army] to the national socialist state', and reminds him of the Fuehrer's words that 'today more than ever a sacrifice is nothing else but the fulfilment of one's duty'. (An application form for NSV membership was enclosed with the letter.) In his reply (signed '*Heil Hitler!*') Galen hints that the district leader's letter supported the allegations of 'the foreign press hostile to Germany' that welfare collections were 'a camouflaged tax', and firmly rejects the insinuation that he owed his pension to the Nazis. ('I have never [in the past] ... had the feeling as if I owed the pension "after all only to the Weimar Republic" although there were at that time enough influential people who expected and even demanded such an attitude from us, the royal Prussian officers'.) Galen further explained that he could not join the NSV 'for reasons of principle', that he was a member of the Catholic welfare organization 'Caritas' and that his economic circumstances did not enable him to take on the responsibility of dual membership. Presumably because of Galen's family connections to the Bishop of Muenster the correspondence was passed on to the highest authorities of the party – including Hilgenfeld, Rosenberg and Bormann and possibly even Hitler himself. (A recommendation to bring Galen's 'impossible' attitude to Hitler's attention is contained in a letter from *Gauleiter* Alfred Meyer to Hilgenfeld.)

The records of the Third Reich reflect the thoroughness with which the organizations of the party managed to intrude into the administration of spiritual and material welfare. The slogan 'Member of the Community! If you need advice and help apply to the local party group!' which appeared over the doors of party offices and on the houseboards of the block leaders and was displayed on huge posters at party rallies, was meant to be taken seriously. Special party advisory bureaux (*NS–Beratungsstellen*) operated in some, if not all, regions and dealt with a variety of problems and grievances – from employment matters to family quarrels, including the complaint of a girl who had been asked 'unprintable questions' in confessional.[24] Party leaders from the rank of local group leader upward were urged to hold special 'people's call days' (*Volkssprechtage*) on which the citizen could come with his troubles to the party. The time expended on the *Volkssprechtage* was considered 'well worth-while' because they served among others to strengthen 'the confidence of the people in their *Hoheitstraeger*'.[25] A person in trouble was on no account to be refused an interview even if it meant receiving him at home outside office hours. Even in matters in which the party leader was not qualified to help, e.g. in inheritance disputes, he was told to let the caller pour his heart out, (a) because it relieves him to speak to someone about his troubles, and (b) because in this way the party leader 'gets to know the citizens of his locality, which is also of great importance'.[26] The many requests for help that were addressed to Hitler personally – or to other Nazi leaders – were usually forwarded to the party office in the locality in which the applicant resided for its opinion.[27] In some districts, at least, there was a standing order to municipalities and lower party organizations to bring all accidents or misfortunes immediately – by phone or special messenger – to the attention of the district leader so that he might decide on the appropriate relief measures.[28]

[24] *Hoheitstraeger*, 1938, no. 1, p. 36.
[25] NA, T-81, 127/149662–3; also VAB, vol. I, pp. 62–4. At the Nuremberg trials an affidavit by von Schirach's secretary was presented on his behalf in which she stated that in his capacity as regional leader of Vienna, von Schirach had usually conducted *Volkssprechtage* once a week, for an entire day: 'I heard time and again that the people of Vienna gratefully appreciated these *Volkssprechtage* and that they were very enthusiastic about this institution.' (IMT, vol. XLI, p. 315.)
[26] *Unser Wille und Weg*, 1936, no. 5, p. 177.
[27] NA, T-81, 1/10849 and 11630.
[28] *Ibid.*, 153/0158497. According to one local leader his district leader

During the war the large field of welfare work in respect of soldiers' families progressively devolved upon the party. It was the party *Hoheitstraeger* who 'in accordance with the wish of the Fuehrer'[29] brought notice of a soldier's death to his family and who thereafter assumed responsibility for the spiritual and material care of his widow and children. To be sure, from the standpoint of the party's propaganda objectives this close association with the main source of national woe was not always an unmixed blessing. As Bormann pointed out, the party uniform all too often identified its bearer as a 'messenger of death' and the wearing of uniforms on errands of mercy was therefore not always advisable.[30] A report of the secret police for the Linz area dated 25 January 1943, related how the party's unsolicited condolences gave rise to outbursts of anti-Nazi feeling. In one village the mother of a fallen soldier slapped one of the two party functionaries who visited the family while the father and sister shouted curses at them. The news quickly spread in the village and the affair ended with the arrest of the father and that of the local innkeeper who had publicly taken his side. In another village a farmer tore down the picture of Hitler from the wall of his living room and threw it at the party official who had come to bring him the party's condolences. (The report states that in this case no police action was taken because the incident had not leaked out to the public.)[31]

Despite these negative aspects, however, the party continued to regard its care of the families of fallen soldiers as 'one of the most beautiful and important leadership tasks'.[32] Regional and district party leaders were urged to dispatch 'personal' letters to the bereaved families and subordinate functionaries were instructed to visit them on birthdays and wedding anniversaries. 'On these days,' states the directive of the Party Chancellory, 'the families should not be left to themselves or perhaps even to other

demanded 'to be informed of everything, but everything, that goes on in the village, even, for example, when a birth is in preparation [sic!].' (Heyen, *Nationalsozialismus im Alltag*, p. 321.

29 Quoted from Keitel's directive to the commands of the armed forces of 3 June 1942. (BDC, File 16A.) For relevant directives of the Party Chancellory see NA, T-81, 1/11754–5.

30 *Hoheitstraeger*, 1942, no. 11, p. 23. The earlier-mentioned memorandum to Rosenberg (see above p. 87, n. 10), which refers critically to the party's preoccupation with welfare in general, quotes a popular saying: 'The party collects money and brings death.'

31 NA, T-81, 6/13248.

32 VAB, vol. I, p. 64.

undesirable influences.'[33] For the continued and regular care of the families special party officials were appointed in the lower party organizations. It was their duty to visit the families at regular intervals, to see that they were well provided for, to intervene on their behalf with government agencies and to secure for them rest cures where necessary. The children were to be given presents on Christmas and birthdays and the widow was to be invited to the party's cultural celebrations. By these and other means the party endeavoured to give the families of fallen soldiers 'the strong feeling and firm conviction that they have not been deserted, but that the party offers them firm aid and protection'.[34]

In all this protean welfare work the party was most concerned to thrust its role well forward into the consciousness of the people. This applied even to the welfare carried on by the party's own organizations. Thus the block leaders were told that while the routine tasks of welfare were to be left to their assistants from the affiliated associations it was the block leader's exclusive responsibility 'to supervise and organize all welfare' in the block. Under no circumstances was the impression to gain ground that the party and its affiliated associations were separate organizations; instead it was necessary 'for every member of the community to realize that the party ... in this case in the person of the block leader, is the bearer of the entire welfare of the people and that the individual associations are merely executive organs of the party'.[35]

Under the impact of rapidly growing distress, the ramification of party welfare had by the end of the war reached into nearly every German household. From the consolation of the families of fallen soldiers to the allocation of foreign women deportees as domestic servants,[36] the party missed no opportunity in order to insinuate itself into every crevice of private life that was opened by individual or national adversity. 'Like a stream fertilizing all life in nature,' reads the somewhat lyrical opening of an article in the *Voelkischer Beobachter* of 9–10 April 1944,

[33] *Ibid.*, p. 65.
[34] *Ibid.*, vol. iv, p. 31.
[35] *Hoheitstraeger*, 1938, no. 2, p. 28.
[36] Families that could prove a high degree of need (illness, a large number of dependents, etc.,) were allotted foreign workers as domestic help on recommendation by the *NS-Women's League* (which also supervised the conditions of employment) and on approval by the district leader. (NA, T-81, 1/11686.)

runs the work of the party through our people . . . After the
air attacks it is the party which intervenes helpfully and pro-
tectively . . . In the plants it is the party which looks after the
provision of food and medical care and resolves countless difficulties. It aids mothers, arranges rest cures, protects the lives
of their children and provides medical clinics . . . In all possible
ways the party enlightens the community, focusses its sights
onto what is decisive, contributes new courage and new
strength, acts soothingly and wants to be nothing else than
the good comrade of every decent man and every decent
woman.

While this passage should, of course, be read primarily as a
reflection of the image which the party sought to present to the
people, its picture of the scope of the party's welfare involvement
is not exaggerated. Nor is it without significance that all this
welfare activity found its 'organizational centre of gravity in the
different regional propaganda offices which derive their name not
from the antiquated conception of verbal propaganda but which
fight and propagate for the idea, the party and the state through
their practical work'.[37] Clearly no one was more qualified than
the party's professional propagandists to direct this new instrument of *Menschenfuehrung*.

The opportunities for surveillance and control in the party's
varied welfare activities are obvious enough: both sides of the
welfare operation, the collection of contributions no less than the
dispensation of relief, provided local functionaries with regular
avenues of access to the people, and thus with valuable means
for both investigating and enforcing the observance of national
socialist behaviour norms. Their value as channels of persuasive
communications is perhaps more open to doubt. As the collections multiplied there must have been not a few people whose
appreciation of their 'educational' properties was dampened by
resentment of the growing financial burden, if not of the recurrent
importunities of the party collectors. Certainly such information
on the misappropriation of welfare funds as reached the ears of
the public did little to raise the efficacy of party collections as
propaganda instruments.[38] In regard to the dispensation of

[37] G. Haegermann, *Die Arbeit der Partei fuer den deutschen Menschen*,
Berlin, 1940, p. 9.
[38] See Vollmer, *Volksopposition*, p. 115; Heyen, *Nationalsozialismus im
Alltag*, p. 287; Steinert, *Hitlers Krieg*, p. 281.

welfare, too, there were factors tending to vitiate some of its propaganda advantages. A system distributing material benefits according to vaguely defined criteria of political loyalty carries the seeds of corruption within itself, and no such system can hope to retain the good will even of its beneficiaries for long. Human nature being what it is, the spark of genuine gratitude that might have been kindled by the gift of a sack of potatoes from the WHW will be quickly extinguished, and may even inflame resentment, if a neighbour in similar circumstances receives two, merely because he was – or the NSV warden said he was – a better national socialist.[39] On balance, however, it must be admitted that, even if all its negative features are discounted, a solid residue of party-sponsored welfare remained.[40] And much of it served the cause of Nazi *Menschenfuehrung* well; certainly the Nazis themselves, who were perhaps the best judges, acted to the last in that belief.

In contrast to the far-flung, systematic welfare effort operated by the Nazis from the very beginning of the Third Reich, the Soviet party has until recently been content to leave the field to other state and social agencies, notably the trade unions. The image of a party 'near and dear' to the people has rested above all on its general policy which purports to regard the spiritual and material well-being of the masses as its overriding concern. In keeping with this image, party functionaries have been urged to be available at all times to hear the problems and complaints of the people and to act upon them promptly and conscientiously whenever necessary. The local party secretary as benevolent patron dealing efficiently and impartially with the requests and grievances of his petitioners, obtaining a badly needed rest cure for one and intervening with a local authority on behalf of another, is a stereotype of Soviet literature, idealized no doubt, but sufficiently rooted in fact to bear some semblance to reality. Local party leaders hold special weekly 'surgeries' for their

[39] Some awareness of this may perhaps be discerned in the words of one local NSV official who berated 'the grumblers' because instead of appreciating 'the greatness of the achievement as a whole' they were constantly searching 'for some minor flaw in the great work, where perhaps fifty pfennig might have been misappropriated . . . or one person might have received one pound more than another'. (R. Friedrich, *Zwei Jahre Tatsozialismus im Gau Duesseldorf*, n. p., n.d., p. 33.)

[40] See C. W. Guillebaud, *The Social Policy of Nazi Germany*, Cambridge, 1941, pp. 95ff and 129ff.

'constituents', and the people, the saying goes, 'bring to the party building their thoughts and concerns, their joys and sorrows';[41] they 'know that in the city party committee they receive needed help and counsel, that their suggestions and complaints will be attended to'.[42] The agitators, too, it will be recalled, are required to extend help and advice in regard to the personal problems of their fellow-workers and it may be assumed that the close contact thus established and the good will generated have stood them in good stead in the discharge of their agitational chores.

Citizens' letters are a major channel through which complaints and requests reach the party authorities. The regime has always endeavoured to keep this channel open and fully functioning, for it has several other uses: it helps to keep the leadership informed of the popular mood, it provides a safety valve through which grievances can find an outlet before they harden into irrepressible antagonism, it exposes bureaucratic inefficiency and other shortcomings and generally reinforces the regime's ability to control its subordinate agencies. But it also serves to bring to the attention of the party cases of persons who are in need of help and thus enables it to garner their gratitude if and when such help is given. That Soviet citizens make considerable use of this channel is beyond doubt; and this in itself may be taken as evidence of its efficacy. At the same time, repeated official reprimands indicate that the extent of the party's responsiveness does not yet meet the regime's requirements.[43]

In the past ten years or so, with the extension of mass-political work to places of residence, the party has intensified its involvement in welfare activities, both directly and through the various communal committees. Residential agitators and other activists now look after such matters as sanitation, greenery and repairs, organize 'model home' campaigns (in the course of which they check 'cleanliness and order, what family relations are like, how children are brought up') supervise recreation, and in various other ways give aid and comfort to people in need.[44] In some

---

[41] *Pravda*, 9 March 1968; also 10 January 1969, 24 November 1973.

[42] *Partiinaya zhizn'*, 1971, no. 21, p. 52; see also no. 12, p. 70.

[43] See the Central Committee decrees of 2 August 1958 and 29 August 1967 in *Spravochnik partiinogo rabotnika*, 1959, pp. 550ff and *ibid.*, 1968, pp. 298ff; also *Pravda*, 9 August 1967 and 22 February 1973; *Partiinaya zhizn'*, 1967, no. 18, pp. 8–10.

[44] *Kommunist*, 1963, no. 8, p. 75; *Partiinaya zhizn'*, 1967, no. 11, p. 55; 1969, no. 18, pp. 42–4; *Po mestu zhitel'stva . . .*, p. 44.

localities facilities for legal advice, medical aid and educational guidance are provided in residential clubs; in others, meetings between residents and officials of local authorities – education, social insurance, militia, etc. – have become a regular feature of the party's mass-political work.[45]

Many of these activities, as also some of the new ceremonies and celebrations, are aimed at fostering a community spirit. By getting people to take a greater interest in the preservation and enhancement of their physical environment as well as in the well-being of their neighbours it is hoped to forge them into a 'true collective' and thereby to overcome some of the strains of modern life, particularly in the large new housing estates. Where people hardly knew each other, 'did not greet each other', residential activists now 'send you a post-card for your birthday, congratulate you on important family events, talk over with you your children's work at school and look after residents in case of sickness'.[46] The extent to which the residential agitator has come to act the role of social worker may be gleaned from the diary of a political organizer in an Uzbekistan kolkhoz:

> Family evening at Talipova's. There were guests from all 'my' households . . . at Talipova's and in several other homes they have not yet installed gas stoves. Check with *raigaz* . . . Yesterday visited all families, made list of children who did badly at school. Talked with parents, we agreed what should be done and how. The school will organize supplementary tuition . . .[47]

It is not suggested that these activities are particularly effective in welfare terms – although they may well be – but that the party has begun to incorporate a variety of welfare functions into its mass-political work and that as a result the ambit of its influence over the lives of Soviet citizens has been correspondingly enlarged.

Where party welfare still falls short of its objectives is in its failure to provide adequate spiritual comfort in cases of personal distress and adversity. This at least is a view that is gaining ground in the Soviet Union where, just as in Nazi Germany three decades earlier, the need for such relief as well as the crucial role of the Churches in meeting it is now being increasingly recognized. Again, as in the case of the secular ceremonies and rituals,

---

[45] *Pravda*, 30 January 1968 and *Partiinaya zhizn'*, 1969, no. 18, pp. 42–3.
[46] *Agitator*, 1966, no. 17, pp. 34–5.
[47] *Pravda*, 13 December 1966; see also *Agitator*, 1972, no. 21, p. 40.

some of the most 'advanced' thinking on the subject has come from the Komsomol. An article by an *aspirant* at Voronezh University is indicative of this thinking and deserves to be quoted at some length:[48]

> We know many examples of grief thrusting a person into the embraces of the clerics ... two thousand years of Christianity feed upon sorrow. Today religion has finally moved over to the sombre sides of life. Only here does it now on the whole find its flock. It is the more successful in this the more we emphasize our reluctance not to speak about 'all these things'.

The Churches had always understood not only that grief was among the 'unavoidable conditions of the human soul' but also that it was 'probably in suffering that it [the soul] is more accessible to the world and its calls'. As one Baptist preacher was reported to have put it: 'And when the tears start running the soul is already like wax.' It was not enough to decry the methods of organized religion. 'One must know how to compete with it, one must know how to approach a person and talk to him in confidence, because by no means all intimate matters can be decided in public, in the collective.' That Soviet society adequately provided for the material wants of its members was true but not enough. The author cites the case of a widow who was perfectly satisfied with her social security benefits and yet, although she was a non-believer, she still went to church: 'I go to church in order to cry. In order to talk to Father Dimitri, a very sympathetic person.' In the social security office everyone was very courteous and efficient, but 'they look through you as if you were made of glass'. There was a need, in the author's view, to have 'our Soviet preacher and "comforter", our healer of the soul's wounds'. Soviet propaganda and Soviet life had registered 'enormous' successes in compelling religion to withdraw from the joyous aspects of life but 'we are not very keen to follow it into the shadows of unavoidable human grief'. Thus, while only 2% of all weddings in Voronezh Province took place in church, 60% of all funerals were still conducted by clergymen. 'Why don't they come to us?' the author asks in conclusion, 'They should come to us!'

The picture of the party or Komsomol *apparatchik* as 'healer of the soul's wounds' must seem rather far-fetched, though it is

---

[48] *Komsomol'skaya pravda*, 6 June 1968.

as well to remember that it is no more far-fetched than that of the
Nazi *Hoheitstraeger* in the role of 'pastor'. The day on which
such healers are appointed to the staffs of local committees alongside the 'Chief Organizers of Festivals' may not be near and may
indeed never come. As yet there is no more than the beginning of
an awareness that the 'sombre sides of life' are an important and
long-neglected domain of mass-political work. But if similar
soundings which emanated from the Komsomol ten years earlier
in respect of the 'new traditions' are any guide it may not be
long before the necessary 'organizational measures' are set in
motion.

8: REPORTING PUBLIC OPINION

Modern totalitarian rulers find it at once more necessary and more difficult than autocrats of earlier vintage to secure reliable and comprehensive information on the state of public opinion in their domains.[1] On the one hand, the need for public opinion information may be said to increase in proportion as a regime seeks to harness not only the energies but also the thoughts and feelings of the population to officially designated political and economic action. Clearly, mass mobilization can be conducted a great deal more efficiently if the leadership knows what the masses think and feel about its aims and policies. On the other hand, it may be assumed that the readiness with which people volunteer information on their true beliefs and sentiments decreases in inverse ratio to the scope of official dogma and the rigour with which deviations from it are persecuted. In short, the more 'captive' the people the less likely they are to speak their minds, with the result that it becomes correspondingly more difficult for their government to know what they are thinking. Although totalitarian rulers seek to develop to the utmost such channels of communication as twentieth-century technology and totalitarian political organization place at their disposal, these cannot – even when supplemented by the public opinion polls which have lately come into use in the Soviet Union – take the place of the continuous flow of messages from the public to the government provided by a modern competitive communication system in a free society. The records of the Third Reich strikingly reveal the regime's preoccupation with the supply of public opinion information from all possible sources. Almost every

[1] The term 'public opinion' is used here simply and loosely as a convenient synonym for current beliefs, attitudes, views, etc., that are popular in the sense of being held by significant numbers of people. The various stricter definitions that are to be found in the modern literature on the subject usually posit freedom of expression and a degree of efficacy for public opinion or, more precisely, the opinions of publics, not applicable to totalitarian systems.

official agency included such information in its periodical activity reports and nearly everyone who was in some way or other connected with the hierarchy of party or government felt obliged not only to report actual events bearing on popular morale, but also, in the absence of such information, to give his own impressions and opinions of the prevailing state of popular feeling. Perusing the private and semi-official correspondence included among the Nazi documents one cannot help being struck by the number and variety of amateur public opinion 'experts' which the Third Reich produced. It is almost as if everyone sensed the urgent need of the regime to obtain insight into the minds of the people and hoped, by the free gift of this scarce and therefore highly valued commodity to improve his standing with those in authority.

In both Nazi Germany and Soviet Russia the party has constituted one of the principal sources of information on the state of popular feeling. Through their constant 'work with people' the functionaries of the party are able to observe and report such expressions of the mood and aspirations of the masses as the conditions of totalitarian government permit. The range of officially 'permitted opinion' is, of course, extremely circumscribed. Above all, it does not include views that are critical of the leaders of party and government or of their major policy decisions. In this respect totalitarian rulers experience the reverse side of the process that compels their subjects 'to read between the lines' for much of their news. Just as the people cannot in general rely on the controlled press and radio to publicize such news as reflect discredit upon official policies, so the regime has to be largely content with indirect expressions of public opinion wherever that opinion is opposed to basic policy measures. While the totalitarian regime has undoubtedly gained considerable experience at interpreting these indirect manifestations of the public mind – in the same way as its people have become skilful at reading between the lines of official pronouncements – the essential limitations of this kind of 'coded communication' are obvious.

The archives of the Nazi party offer a unique inside view of its reporting procedures.[2] The reports differ from each other in form and quality, depending on the intelligence and conscientiousness

---

[2] The following discussion is based mainly on the reports of party organizations in the three regions of Baden, Hessen-Nassau and Schleswig-Holstein for the period 1939–44; several reports of party organizations in other regions have also been used.

of the reporting functionary, on the problems of the area and on the period of time to which they apply. Nevertheless, they reveal sufficient common characteristics to allow for several general observations that may throw some light on the limitations and potentialities of the totalitarian party's function as a public opinion agency.

The leaders of Nazi party organizations from the level of the local group upward were required to submit regular 'Political Situation Reports' (*Politische Lageberichte*).[3] The reports covered a variety of subjects, but their principal concern was with developments in the sphere of public opinion; indeed, internal party communications often referred to them simply as 'Morale Reports' (*Stimmungsberichte*). A detailed classification scheme, evolved in 1938, divided the contents of situation reports under 30 subject headings – and 82 sub-headings – ranging from Morale Survey of the General Political Situations, Propaganda, State Enemies and Justice, to Commerce and Crafts, Social Questions and Armed Forces.[4] This elaborate scheme was adhered to for some time, but with the outbreak of war it increasingly fell into disuse. A directive of the Baden regional party office of 19 November 1942 merely acknowledged the existing position when it stated that the classification had become 'obsolete'.[5] As a rule the situation reports within each region were made out at monthly intervals. News of particular interest was transmitted either immediately or in special 'mid-week reports'. The regional offices, however, reported regularly every week to the Party Chancellory, usually by teleprinter. The regional report incorporated material from the reports of the districts, the immediately subordinate party level, as well as from the copies of reports prepared by the various departments of the regional office (the Propaganda Department, the Department for Peasants, the *Gauwalter* of the Labour Front, etc.) and by various state agencies (the labour exchanges, the provincial governments, the armament commissions, etc.) for their superiors at the national level. At least one region (Oberdonau) also received weekly reports from the local agency of the SS Security Service, the

---

[3] In the case of the local-group leaders written reports were not obligatory, but many district leaders apparently demanded them.

[4] VAB, vol. I, p. 91. An earlier classification, issued in 1934, for what were then known as 'Activity and Morale Reports' (*Taetigkeits- und Stimmungsberichte*) is reproduced in P. Diehl-Thiele, *Partei und Staat im Dritten Reich*, Munich, 1969, pp. 230–1.

[5] NA, T-81, 127/149718.

Sicherheitsdienst or SD, and passed them on to the Party Chancellory together with its own weekly situation reports. The SD
reports that reached the regional party office (and through it
the Party Chancellory) were not, however, copies of the reports
which the SD branch submitted to its own superiors at the Main
Security Office of the Reich (RSHA), but were especially prepared for the regional party leadership and omitted information
which for one reason or another was intended exclusively for
the ears of the RSHA. If, as seems likely, the party offices of
other regions also received reports from SD agencies, it may be
assumed that the same procedure applied. For its part, the RSHA
submitted its own reports to the supreme agencies of the Reich,
including the Party Chancellory.[6]

The importance which the central leadership attached to the
party's reporting system is amply documented. Time and again
subordinate party organizations were reminded of the vital need
for exhaustive and regular reporting. 'The reports of the regional
leaders', stated a central party directive of 11 November 1938,
'which consist of the experience and observations of the lowest
cell of the leadership of the people, have enabled the Head of
the Party Chancellory to form a picture of the worries and needs
of the people and to eliminate arising defects and shortcomings.'[7]
A circular letter of the Baden regional office declared on 19
November 1942:

> The regular dispatch of situation reports serves ... the con-
> tinuous information of the Fuehrer and his leading agencies
> in regard to the political morale and the changing situation
> in all spheres of life. Thus the reporting system of the party
> is elevated to an instrument of party leadership which must not
> be underestimated and which particularly in war time can
> under no circumstances be dispensed with ... Experience has
> shown that many a report of incidences which had at first
> seemed unimportant ... often resulted in far-reaching measures
> by the party or, on the party's initiative, by the state authorities
> on the national level.[8]

---

[6] For a selection of these reports see the two volumes edited by Boberach;
the introduction to each volume contains a lucid description of SD reporting procedures.

[7] VAB, vol. I, p. 89. Presumably the directive in its original version referred
to the Fuehrer's Deputy. The VAB volumes were published after Hess's
flight to England.

[8] NA, T-81, 127/149716–7; see also 127/149627 and 65/74429.

In a speech to army officers in the spring of 1943 the regional leader of Munich, Adolf Wagner, stated that 'through [the party's] reporting system the leadership is informed of all positive or negative manifestations among the people',[9] and the NSDAP organizational manual claimed that 'the path from the lowest organs of the party upwards reveals ... the smallest fluctuations and changes in the morale of the people'.[10] In fact, as will be seen below, these statements greatly exaggerated the party's ability to provide the leaders of the Third Reich with an accurate and comprehensive picture of the popular mood.

A principal concern of the party's situation reports was the reaction of the people to various government measures. Thus, for instance, the report of one district leader dealt at length with the structure of agricultural prices and their effect on popular morale in his area.[11] Another criticized the discrepancy between the levels of agricultural and industrial wages, stressing that 'one must be clear about the fact that not words will help, but deeds'.[12] Yet another district leader, commenting on a regulation concerning rabbit breeding, stated in his report: 'The people apparently regard the regulation as just, for the lively discussions have receded. More worry is caused by the supply of potatoes and vegetables. In regard to this one frequently hears the opinion that quantities of potatoes are still stored in the cellars of evacuees.'[13] The supply of consumer goods and its repercussions on morale was a constantly recurring topic in party reports. One district leader, noting that the shortage of goods before Christmas 'was giving rise to grumbling' and that 'goods in short supply were being sold under the counter', went on to add: 'The distribution of scarce goods is particularly closely observed by the population. A stop must therefore be put to this at once, so that the soldiers at the front are not alarmed by the home country.'[14] Another district leader reported 'several unpleasant fluctuations in the morale of the people' and attributed their cause to three factors, the first two of which were (a) the lowering of the meat ration and (b) the shortage of potatoes. (The third factor listed in the report, which was dated 30 June 1941, i.e. one week after the attack on Soviet Russia, was 'the long intervals [sic!] in military activities.')[15]

9 FO, 5475/E 381766–806.   10 *Organisationsbuch*, pp. 148–9.
11 NA, T-81, 163/301160.   12 *Ibid.*, 119/139801.
13 *Ibid.*, 119/139595–6.   14 *Ibid.*, 163/300930; see also 300879.
15 *Ibid.*, 163/301608.

The situation reports also sought to expose various deficiencies and malpractices by official organs, with the contention, not always explicit, that they jeopardized popular morale. Almost every report included some such criticism, whether it was over a regulation of the Ministry of Interior concerning the robes to be worn by officials of registry offices, which in the opinion of the reporting district leader resembled too closely the robes of clergymen and therefore constituted 'a dilution of the national socialist *Weltanschauung*';[16] or over the dispatch, on the instruction of the Propaganda Ministry, of thousands of copies of a propaganda leaflet to a factory employing 180 workers;[17] or over the fact that old films starring Pola Negri, the 'German-hater', were still being shown in cinemas.[18] One local-group leader reported the following as popular comment on a German–Russian dictionary issued to the troops on the Eastern front: 'Why should they be able to ask in Russian for fried eggs, kidneys, liver, cutlets, fat, butter, and roast, when our propaganda always maintains that these things are altogether unobtainable in Russia?'[19] And a district leader complained that too many civil servants who were not politically active were being promoted by the state authorities, adding: 'It should be a matter of course that in the first instance only such civil servants should be recommended for promotion as have proved themselves both professionally and politically. And the latter qualification must be the decisive one.'[20]

Inquiries and intervention often followed upon the receipt of such complaints from subordinate party organizations, even where relatively trivial incidents were involved. In some cases the Party Chancellory itself followed up information contained in the weekly situation reports of the regions either with requests for further details or with corrective action where such was deemed appropriate. Usually the regional office would have to refer the matter back to the district which had originally reported it, and a protracted correspondence between district and region, and region and Party Chancellory ensued. One such case concerned the requisition without compensation by the army authorities of plots of land from three farmers in Schleswig-Holstein. In its weekly report to the Party Chancellory of 7 November 1941, the Schleswig-Holstein regional office first reported the incident. Five weeks later, on 15 December, the Party Chancellory wrote

---

[16] *Ibid.*, 119/139943.
[18] *Ibid.*, 163/301145.
[20] *Ibid.*, 119/139953.

[17] *Ibid.*, 24/21745.
[19] *Ibid.*, 119/139574.

back asking for further information, as it intended to take the matter up with the OKW. On 7 January 1942, the regional office wrote to the district leader of Echernfoerde for the necessary details. Three weeks later, on 28 January, the regional office was able to pass these on to the Party Chancellory, which had in the meantime already pressed for a reply to its original letter. On receipt of the regional office's reply the Party Chancellory wrote again on 13 February, and asked for confirmation that compensation had in fact not been paid. The regional office referred back to the district on 25 February, and on 6 March, the district office wrote that one farmer had been compensated and that negotiations with the other two were in progress. On 9 February, the regional office informed the Party Chancellory accordingly and the matter was closed.[21] Cases such as this may reflect upon the cumbersomeness of party reporting as well as on the party's all too obvious eagerness to denounce the misdeeds of other authorities. At the same time, however, they also illustrate the concern of the central leadership to uncover, and where possible to remedy, all manifestations of public life that threatened to impair popular morale.

The 'Activity of the Confessions' was another major preoccupation of the party's reporting system. The availability of information regarding the Churches and the importance which the party leadership attached to such information are evident from the frequency and detail with which it was reported by party organizations at all levels. When the Catholic Bishop of Mainz visited the township of Nieder-Oelm in June 1939, the local group leader reported the number of men (36) and women (50) who assembled in front of the church to greet him, as well as the number of families (5) which had decorated their houses for the occasion. His report noted with satisfaction that the majority of those present were elderly people, that 'the reception had never before been so miserable' and that the Bishop had 'certainly been disappointed' by it.[22] One particularly 'subversive' sermon delivered by a local Protestant clergyman on the occasion of Heroes' Memorial Day was summarized in detail in the weekly report of the Schleswig-Holstein regional office, taking up almost half of its total space.[23] (The files also contain a letter from the regional office to the *Gestapo* requesting the arrest of the clergyman.)[24]

[21] *Ibid.*, 163/301169–75.   [22] *Ibid.*, 119/139907–8.   [23] *Ibid.*, 163/300960.
[24] *Ibid.*, 163/301005; see also IMT, vol. xxxv, pp. 658–63.

Other recurrent topics of the party's situation reports were acts of sabotage, the behaviour of foreign workers and of 'hostile' elements such as Jews and ex-communists, and the effects of air-raids. Rumours too, in so far as they came to the notice of party functionaries, were regularly reported upward, whether they concerned the implications of tax vouchers for the Government's financial stability[25] or the anticipated progress of the North African campaign.[26]

The last fairly regular feature of the reports consisted of appraisals of various propaganda measures. These were made up, first, of reports on the success of the local organization's own propaganda activities; and, secondly of 'reviews' of films, broadcasts and newspaper articles, etc., with special emphasis on their propaganda effectiveness. As might be expected, in the vast majority of cases the reports presented the organization's own activities in a favourable light. When shortcomings were admitted, extenuating circumstances were usually cited, as, for example, in the case of the district leader who sought to explain low attendance at party meetings by the fact that Polish POW's working in the locality had been transferred to civilian status and were free to roam the streets.[27] In regard to films, broadcasts, newspaper articles, etc., the reports were more often critical. The local party functionaries evidently regarded it as their task not merely to report popular reaction, but also to pass on their own opinions and judgments, although they often phrased their comments in such a way as to imply that they reflected the views of the public. Thus for instance, one district leader complained that a film depicting life in the army did not stress the role of the HJ and SA in the preparation of recruits for military service.[28] Another criticized 'the unfortunate effect' of a scene in a comedy film in the course of which one actress speaks the line: 'Don't get cheeky! . . . I have a cousin in the party and that could become very unpleasant for you.'[29] (Other party leaders 'reviewing' the same film apparently did not find this scene objectionable.) The recurrence of jazz music on the radio was the subject of another district leader's criticism, because it 'let in through the back door a kind of culture or "art" which had been "officially" dismissed and branded by the party as Americanism'.[30] Newspaper articles, including those in the local party press, were

[25] NA, T-81, 65/74375.   [26] *Ibid.*, 65/74128.
[27] *Ibid.*, 163/301160.   [28] *Ibid.*, 119/139883.
[29] *Ibid.*, 163/300953.   [30] *Ibid.*, 119/139548.

sometimes criticized for inconsistencies with the general propaganda line and other shortcomings. Thus an article describing the leisure time activities of civilians in war-time Germany came in for sharp condemnation on the ground that people working on 12-hour shifts had no time for any of the activities mentioned, and that the article therefore served to exacerbate the 'already strong resentment of the working population towards those who have constantly evaded their responsibilities to people and fatherland'.[31] In another report it was said that the local party press 'had not found its way to the people', mainly because it placed too much emphasis on 'political information' and failed to satisfy 'the needs of the people for light, relaxing articles'.[32]

For the rest, the party's situation reports included odd items of information which had come to the notice of the local party leader and which he considered to be of interest to his superiors. Some party leaders occasionally related information on conditions at the front obtained from soldiers on leave, others attached copies of letters from friends or former colleagues serving in combat areas.[33] One district leader found (in his report for June 1939) that persons belonging to low-income groups increasingly purchased high quality radio sets and adduced that this was 'in many cases due to the desire to listen to foreign stations'.[34] Another, writing in March 1944, listed 'with pride' the recent procreative achievements of the married members of his staff.[35]

The above examples may serve to convey something of the flavour of party reporting as well as of its range. Undoubtedly the party's situation reports, covering regularly every locality of the Reich, made an important contribution to Nazi *Menschenfuehrung*. At the same time, however, it is clear, as much from the kind of information included in the reports as from that not included, that the party rarely overcame the fundamental handicap inherent in the fact that people living under a totalitarian regime do not as a rule air their doubts and criticisms of that regime in the presence of its representatives. On occasion a party leader would show himself regretfully aware of the limitations which this placed on the quality and scope of his information. 'The alarmists are very cautious', wrote one district leader in his report for October 1944, 'and reveal their pitiable wisdom only to persons of similar convictions, so that one can rarely get a

31 *Ibid.*, 119/145028.   32 *Ibid.*, 163/301223
33 *Ibid.*, 119/139545 and 139559.
34 *Ibid.*, 119/139880.   35 *Ibid.*, 119/139530.

grip on them.' (This did not, however, prevent him from adding that the 'decent population has no doubt but that this crisis too will be overcome and that victory awaits at the end'.)[36] Another district leader also admitted in his report for March 1944 that 'in general, people are very cautious about what they say, so that the direct determination of derogatory remarks is rather difficult, and yet, the activity of the *Gestapo* has surely become considerably more frequent'. The same functionary, while stressing that he did not want to appear a pessimist, could not help noting 'purely intuitively' the 'sullen looks which many soldiers assumed at the sight of the party uniform'; women, too, threw 'hateful glances' that seemed to say 'You are one of those who have caused the war.'[37] Such sensitivity was, however, rare; if it existed it was not mirrored in the situation reports. With one exception, all other party leaders reporting for the same period and in the same region (Hessen-Nassau) exuded the highest confidence in the state of popular morale, and none had any reservations as regards the reliability of his information. 'Hardness and confidence' were the 'characteristics of the general attitude' according to the district leader of Darmstadt, while a local-group leader of Frankfurt reported that 'especially those hit hardest [by a recent air attack] ... have become even more fanatical national socialists and ... know only the one faith that is called Adolf Hitler'.[38]

Indeed, this was the dominant tenor of the vast majority of public opinion 'appraisals', irrespective of the events to which they purported to relate. Reading the party's situation reports one could be led to believe that the feelings of the people for their leadership remained utterly unchanged in victory and defeat. If a comparison of reports dating from the early years of the war with those from 1944 does reveal traces of declining enthusiasm on the part of the population, it does so not directly, but by the increasing substitution of such phrases as 'unshaken faith' for 'calm confidence' or 'morale is not negative' for 'morale is positive'. Important military and political setbacks find no echo in the reports, or else are submerged amid fatuous generalities. Thus the district leader of Aachen-Land managed to write two reports for December 1942 and January 1943 without so much as mentioning the word 'Stalingrad'.[39] The district leader of

36 *Ibid.*, 163/302199.   37 *Ibid.*, 119/139536–7.
38 *Ibid.*, 119/139515 and 139589.   39 *Ibid.*, 163/301545–51.

Heidelberg, writing in October 1944, ventured the observation that 'it is constantly being established anew that the morale and attitude of the population are very strongly influenced by military events'.[40] And the district leader of Norder-Dithmarschen in Schleswig-Holstein took it upon himself to declare on 23 October 1941: 'The general opinion is that the entrance of America into the war will not influence the situation in any way. At the worst the war may thereby be prolonged.'[41]

When the district leader of Freiburg, in a letter of November 1942, admonished his local-group leaders that their reports were 'mostly vacuous, superficial and wordy' he stated no more than the bare truth.[42] But criticisms such as this were made rarely and, what is more, they were made in vain. For the local leaders of the party had little knowledge of the negative aspects of popular opinion other than that which they acquired 'purely intuitively'. The party operated in the open. Its members and functionaries were known or recognizable and the views expressed to them or in their presence were rarely of a kind that was likely to cast doubt on the fundamental national socialist loyalty of the person expressing them.[43] The odd denunciation by a neighbour or a fellow-worker might be brought to the notice of the local party leader and the subversive views or actions alleged would then be reported to higher party bodies. (As a rule the investigation of such denunciations was left to the secret police, the *Gestapo*.) But the local party organizations maintained no regular system of secret informers, and their access to the 'underground' levels of public opinion was therefore necessarily limited.

That the party's information system did no more than skim the surface of the popular mood is also readily apparent from a comparison of the party's reports with those of the security services. Where the party reports generally present a harmony of unflinching faith in the Fuehrer and his policies, only here and there marred by the sound of an individual discordant note, the reports of the security services mirror the ups and

---

[40] *Ibid.*, 163/302115.   [41] *Ibid.*, 163/301245.

[42] *Ibid.*, 65/74429.

[43] When the sun of the Third Reich visibly began to set and some party members sought to disassociate themselves from the regime by neglecting to wear their badges, the pretext was that 'only then can they hear the true opinions of the people'. But this was regarded by their superiors as 'an excuse that won't wash'. (*Der Aktivist. Nationalsozialistische Propaganda im Gau Sued-Hannover–Braunschweig*, 1944, no. 4, p. 37.)

downs of popular feeling closely, and on the whole, plausibly. Such revealing reflections of public opinion as current jokes about leading Nazi personalities were regularly reported by the SD but only rarely found their way into the situation reports of the party.[44] Whereas party organizations reported in generalities such as 'the mood is good' or 'confident' or 'steadfast', the security agencies sought to substantiate their statements with what purported to be direct quotations from a large number of individual opinions. The practice of quoting from the comment of the people was carried over into SD reports presented at the highest level. Thus, for example, in illustrating popular reaction to the military situation on the Eastern front, a report sent by Kaltenbrunner to Bormann on 28 July 1944 quotes people in the Eastern border areas as saying: 'Why work oneself to the bone over the harvest if it will have to be destroyed anyway so that the Bolsheviks don't get it?' In connection with an official communiqué regarding an air attack on Munich the report cites this revealing comment: 'How terrible it must be there if even the armed forces communiqué stresses the brave conduct of the population!'[45] In a letter sent by Himmler to Bormann on 7 March 1943 concerning Ley, the following reactions to the latter's broadcast on the occasion of the 10th anniversary of the Labour Front are cited: 'Valuable production has come to a standstill . . . and for what?' 'Once again he has spoilt our lunch hour.' 'As it was audible that he found speaking difficult one could not resist the suspicion that he was drunk or tipsy.' 'One can always abuse the Jews when there is nothing else to say.' 'I am often overcome by quiet fear of how matters are to go on if such people continue to remain in leading positions in the party.'[46] These illustrations of Ley's unpopularity sound authentic, but there is, of course, no means of verifying whether they had not been 'manufactured' by Himmler in pursuance of some private intrigue. The point is, however, that the functionaries of the party were seldom in a position to produce such a mass of 'original' adverse public opinion information, whether true or false, for the simple reason that their access to critical and therefore privately held opinion was limited, and known to be so.

But perhaps an even greater shortcoming of the Nazi party's

[44] NA, T-81, 6/13072; see also Boberach, *Meldungen*, p. 430 and *passim*.
[45] NA, T-81, 6/13534 and 13536.
[46] FO, 5474 H/E 381732–9; other examples will be found in Boberach, *Meldungen*, 427–8, 443–4 and *passim*.

reporting system stemmed from the fact that it was the party itself which was primarily responsible for the state of popular morale. In reporting on the state of public opinion in his area, each party leader knew that he was at the same time reporting on the success with which he was discharging one of his principal duties. Some party leaders were not beyond underlining this point rather obviously. Thus one district leader in Schleswig-Holstein wrote in October 1941: 'If in regard to morale, too, there are no particular difficulties to report, it is not least due to the constant work of the party and its organizations.'[47] Another district leader – in Hessen-Nassau – reported for February 1944: 'The basic attitude is positive. The activism of the party in my district radiates outward into the minutest events and keeps the people in motion.'[48] The central party leadership was aware that the temptation to present an unduly favourable picture of popular morale was built into the system. This is evident from the reference to 'Potemkin villages' cited previously in connection wth the welfare drives.[49] It is confirmed by the repeated stress that Party Chancellory instructions laid on the need for absolute truthfulness in reporting. A central directive of 11 November 1938 called for 'unsparing frankness' in the reports and emphasized that 'the task of *Menschenfuehrung* by the party requires an irreproachable, unadorned picture of the people's confidence in their leadership and of the effects of the work and decisions of their Government'.[50] In a letter to the regional leaders of December 1941, Bormann stated that 'the conditions of unconditional truthfulness and conscientiousness' which the Fuehrer demanded of the reports of his military commanders applied in equal measure to those of his political leaders.[51] And, in a directive of 1 February 1945, he emphasized:

> Dispatches and reports should give a sober, truthful picture of the situation. Every embellishment and every concealment of important facts is just as basically wrong as the frivolous passing on of negative rumours which for the most part do not relate to the true state of affairs, but are the products of the fantasies of anxious minds.[52]

From the date of the last of these injunctions one may assume that they had generally proved of little avail. Indeed, anything

47 NA, T-81, 163/301158.
48 *Ibid.*, 119/139527.
49 See above, p. 210.
50 VAB, vol. I, p. 90.
51 NA, T-81, 2/12223–4.
52 *Ibid.*, 1/10835–6.

else could hardly be expected. Often enough had the Party Chancellory reminded its subordinate organizations that 'the attitude of the members of the community will reveal whether the local leaders of the party possess the confidence of the people to the necessary extent and whether party members are really exemplary in their effort and combat readiness'.[53] It was Hitler himself who had warned party leaders: 'Let no one come and report to me that morale in his region, his district, his group or his cell could ever be bad. You are the bearers, the responsible bearers of morale.'[54] Nor could the party leaders be altogether blamed if, upon reading the Party Chancellory's circular letter of 18 December 1942, they felt encouraged to conceal even those few disquieting aspects of public opinion which did come to their notice. The letter deserves to be quoted at length:

> In recent times the Party Chancellory has received an increasing number of reports from regional leaders in which negative utterances of persons or more or less insignificant incidents pointing to a certain war-weariness are cited as proof of the allegedly bad morale of the population. Closer investigation revealed in most instances that these were individual cases which could in no way be regarded as symptomatic. Local ill-feeling, understandable nervous strain, utterances of incorrigible pessimists, expressions of fear and cowardice of bourgeois Philistines, were designated as barometers of morale and their insignificance within the general setting was misjudged.

The letter goes on to lay down the following 'guide lines obligatory for the party':

> (1) We live in the fourth year of a war that makes the highest demands upon the physical and moral resources of our people. Certain undesirable consequences of this fact are unavoidable and must be borne. (2) Among our people, too, there are – especially in bourgeois circles – next to the broad mass of well-meaning and willing elements, a small number of people who either still oppose us for political reasons or whose general attitude inclines towards pessimism and cowardice . . . (3) There is no doubt that the bearing of our people – and thus the essential element in judging its will to resist – is, in contrast to 1917–18, wholly unobjectionable.[55]

[53] VAB, vol. I, p. 6.
[54] Quoted in *Unser Wille und Weg*, 1939, no. 10, p. 223.
[55] VAB, vol· I, pp. 395–6.

Once the official thesis concerning the state of morale had been made known, not in a propaganda article but in an internal party communication, there was little left for the individual party leader but to confirm its validity in his situation reports. Indeed, one may well wonder whether, rather than a true picture of public opinion, it was not precisely such a confirmation of its propaganda thesis that the leadership expected from the situation reports.[56]

The reluctance to include such evidence of public opinion as might reflect negatively upon the leadership qualifications of the local functionary applied to party leaders at all levels, but it grew progressively in direct ratio to his rank and competency. Thus the local-group leader would have little or no hesitation in reporting that the regional party press was not having the desired appeal to the people of his locality, since he was in no way responsible for its deficiencies. The district leader for the same reason might include the information in his own report to the regional party office, but he might also be reluctant to identify himself too closely with what is, at least by implication, a criticism of his immediate superiors and either tone it down or partly disassociate himself from it by prefacing it with the words 'The local-group leaders report ...' The regional party leader, however, did exercise responsibility over the regional party press and its inadequacies could be chalked up on the debit side of the ledger which recorded his standing with his superiors, not to mention the inconvenience that could ensue if the Party Chancellory decided to press for an investigation, as it most probably would. More often than not, therefore, the weekly report of the regional party office carefully omitted to apprise the Party Chancellory of such negative developments in the sphere of public opinion as could be ascribed to its own activity or lack of activity. Such omissions occurred too often to allow for a more charitable interpretation. Self-incrimination is rare among bureaucrats anywhere, and there is no reason to expect that it would be widely practised by the *Hoheitstraeger* of the Nazi party.

The deliberateness of the alterations or deletions is especially obvious in those cases in which the regional leader (or his

---

[56] The Propaganda Ministry similarly instructed its regional offices on 27 February 1943 that 'trivial incidents' did not provide a reliable basis for the assessment of popular morale: 'These by no means typical manifestations of morale should rather be eliminated with the means of the period of struggle in [your] own domain instead of being reported here ...' (Quoted in Steinert, *Hitlers Krieg*, p. 43.)

deputy) marked entire passages in the reports submitted to him, for inclusion in his own report to the Party Chancellory. The manner of his selection and the kind of alterations that he inserted clearly illustrate the process of distortion at work. For instance, when one district leader complained of 'resentment among the population' because collection campaigns of various organizations had followed too closely upon one another owing to faulty co-ordination by the regional office, the entire sentence was struck from the passage which the regional leader's deputy marked for inclusion in the report to the Party Chancellory.[57] The same fate befell the following sentence in the report of the district leader of Kitzingen (Mainfranken): 'This has given rise to a great deal of grumbling in the past few weeks, especially as many people believe that neighbouring regions managed to overcome these difficulties [in the food supply].'[58] The district leader of Strasbourg reported on 8 October 1944 'the belief that the Americans could come overnight'; the weekly report of the Baden regional office reproduced this as 'the belief of a few persons that the Americans could come overnight'.[59] When all the district leaders reported on the same subject the regional office chose to transmit to the Party Chancellory only such information as happened to suit its own purposes. This is illustrated in the case of a special report prepared by the Schleswig-Holstein regional office for the Party Chancellory on party entrance celebrations for recruits from the Hitler Youth. The reports of the majority of district leaders were critical of the arrangements that had been made, arguing among other things that insufficient time had been allowed for preparations. The regional office thereupon drew up its own report which softened the tones of the district leaders' criticisms, but on the whole left the impression that the celebrations had not been an unqualified success. Before it was sent off, however, the report of an additional district leader (Flensburg) arrived at the regional office. The Flensburg functionary did not echo the criticisms of his colleagues, but reported that the celebrations in his district had been highly successful. The original regional report, prepared on the basis of several district reports, was promptly scrapped and a new report incorporating the text of the Flensburg report was dispatched to the Party Chancellory, as representative of the entire region.[60]

[57] NA T-81, 163/301247.   [58] *Ibid*, 178/326233.
[59] *Ibid*., 163/302113 and 302126.   [60] *Ibid*., 163/301059–77.

The practice of lifting entire passages from the district reports and including them in the reports of the regional office, without indicating that they related to a single district only, was widespread and added its own elements of distortion to the deliberate alterations and the even more frequent omissions. In part, it was engendered by the fact that the district organizations and regional departments – with the exception of the propaganda department – forwarded their reports at monthly intervals, while the regional party leaders were required to submit weekly reports to the Party Chancellory. In order to secure a steady flow of 'copy' the regional leaders spread the reporting dates of the districts more or less evenly over each month, with the result that regional offices had at any one time only one quarter of their district reports from which to make up their own weekly report to the Party Chancellory. At best, therefore, each weekly report could represent no more than a partial picture of the situation in the region; at worst – and this was more usual – each topic of the regional report related to the experience of one district only. The regional reports, however, rarely indicated this. On the contrary, when for instance, the district leader of Stormarn reported that 'party events were well attended and the membership meetings carried out by us met with extraordinary approval', the deputy regional leader of Schleswig-Holstein simply altered this to read: 'Party events were on the average well attended. Membership meetings met with extraordinary success', and marked it for inclusion in the regional report.[61] Occasionally, too, the views of individuals or groups standing outside the party were in this way vested with the authority of the regional leader. The following example will illustrate this. On 30 October 1941, an official who was apparently in charge of the labour exchange in Kiel sent the deputy leader of Schleswig-Holstein a 'personal memorandum' which strongly criticized the voluntary recruitment of foreign workers – 'every humanity is misplaced' – and a report of the naval establishment at Kiel appraising the abilities and conduct of the various nationality groups among the foreign workers in its employ. Two days later the regional office dispatched its weekly situation report to the Party Chancellory. It included the main part of the naval establishment's report without any indication of its source, thus extending whatever validity it might have had to the region as a whole, and the full text

[61] *Ibid.*, 163/301030.

of the 'personal memorandum' prefaced only by the words, 'In regard to the employment of foreign workers, it is my personal belief that . . .'[62]

Practices such as these may in the majority of cases have been due to lack of material or sheer indolence or a desire to impress the Party Chancellory with the thoroughness of the regional leader's investigations, rather than to any deliberate attempt at misrepresentation. But they underline the haphazard character of party reporting and the essential unreliability of much of the information that reached the Reich leadership through this channel.

It should be noted, however, that the regional leaders did not have a monopoly of reporting, even within the party. The central departments of the party were also kept informed of public opinion trends through the reports of their subordinate agencies at the regional level. For example, the Reich Propaganda Office received weekly reports from the regional propaganda departments, the Reich Office for Peasants received monthly reports from its representatives at the regional level, etc. These latter agencies were of course under the disciplinary authority of the regional party leader who also received copies of their reports. It was therefore unlikely that a departmental head would deliberately include in his official report information that might embarrass his regional leader. Moreover, it may be assumed that the same motives which kept the latter from transmitting self-incriminating information operated also in the case of the departmental officials. There was, therefore, little scope for substantial divergencies among the various reports. Yet, while the regional leader could suppress (or amend) information contained in the reports of his district leaders by a simple stroke of the pen, to do the same in the case of the departmental reports was rather more difficult. Unless he was prepared to enter into collusion with his departmental chiefs, the regional leader would either have to control the flow of information reaching the departments or content himself with *post-factum* reprimands. In fact, regional leaders at different times attempted to resort to both methods. Thus, for instance, the regional leader of Baden, Robert Wagner, instructed his district leaders in November 1942 to stop sending copies of their situation reports to the regional propaganda department – the most important of the regional leader's internal competitors in

[62] *Ibid.*, 163/301213 and 301230–2.

the field of public opinion reporting – and informed them that in future the regional staff office would forward 'the relevant information' to the propaganda department,[63] while the regional leader of Schleswig-Holstein, Hinrich Lohse, reminded the head of his Office for Peasants that 'it is not the purpose of the reporting system to describe individual, unimportant incidents especially as these can be settled locally, i.e. in the region itself'.[64]

A far more irritating and persistent source of embarrassment to the regional leaders, and indeed to the Party Chancellory, were the reports of the security services, and especially of the SD. These agencies relied on a network of 'confidence men' (*Vertrauensmaenner*, or more commonly, *V-Maenner*) who operated under cover. Even so, they suffered from the inevitable limitations of totalitarian reality. The *Gestapo* complained already in 1934 that 'it is difficult ... to obtain an objective picture of the true morale of the people, for there prevails in meetings and discussions, even in private conversations, widespread restraint in regard to the manner of thinking ... unless close acquaintances are involved'.[65] As the regime grew older and its security services more elaborate and more ruthless, the proportion of those who failed to exercise such restraints must have dwindled still further. As Goebbels noted in his diary on 12 November 1943, the imposition and publication of death sentences 'had a very sobering and deterrent effect on the defeatists'.[66] Nevertheless, the agents of the security services were in a far better position than the officials of the party to gain insight into negative manifestations of public opinion. Unlike party officials, too, they had no vested interest in concealing such manifestations. *Menschenfuehrung* was not the responsibility of the *Gestapo* or the SD. If anything, the efficiency and skill of any individual agent or head of a regional security branch were judged by the number of 'subversive statements' and 'hostile acts' that they managed to detect. And the prestige and power of the security services as a whole, and, therefore, of their leaders, depended to a large extent on how indispensable they could make themselves to the regime. Clearly, their own reports could eminently serve that end. Moreover, the security services were principally deployed for the surveillance of suspect sections of the community. The SD (more precisely, its Inland Service) in time undertook to provide general opinion research, but it had originally been set up to combat

[63] *Ibid.*, 127/149717.   [64] *Ibid.*, 163/302130.
[65] Vollmer, *Volksopposition*, p. 72.   [66] *Goebbels Diaries*, p. 415.

opposition elements and this bias undoubtedly continued to affect its operations and to colour its reports until the end.

Thus, where the reports of party organizations were heavily weighted in the direction of overestimating the calibre of popular morale, those of the security services were probably weighted in the opposite direction. This, in fact, was one of the party's main objections to the SD reports, as will be seen later. It is naturally difficult to assess the accuracy of individual items of information regarding public opinion – positive or negative – contained in SD reports, but the impression gained from the reports as a whole is that the SD allowed few inhibitions to stand in its way in presenting a picture of public opinion that was wholly unadorned and, for the Nazi leadership, often highly un-flattering.

Perhaps nothing illustrates the difference between the reports of the party and those of the SD so much as their different appraisals of the effectiveness of Nazi propaganda measures. By the time the reports of the party had passed through the various 'censorship' stages and reached the Party Chancellory, even the few technical criticisms made by lower party organizations had been deleted, thus leaving the central leadership with the impression that all was well in the realm of propaganda. The SD reports, by contrast, continuously and, it would seem, unhesi-tatingly laid bare the shortcomings of Nazi propaganda as they revealed themselves in popular reaction. An SD report for January 1943 noted 'the general prejudice against all propaganda' and ascribed it to its 'overbearing and boastful character'. Of the party press, the report says that even among party members it met with 'derogatory criticisms because of its predominantly propagandistic tendencies'.[67] A statement such as that 'the people feel over-tired and even often nauseated by the over-played instrument of the anti-Jewish campaign and other elaborate political essays' contained in an SD report for June 1943,[68] would have been inconceivable from the pen of a local party leader.

Indeed, it is worth noting that the lower party organizations

---

[67] NA, T-81, 6/13072. That the party press was boring and too obviously tendentious and that the people 'longed for real facts' was a constantly recurring complaint. (*Ibid.*, 7/14419.) For other criticisms of Nazi propa-ganda see Boberach, *Meldungen*, pp. 302, 344, 421ff and *passim*; also the *Gestapo* reports in Vollmer, *Volksopposition*, pp. 100, 113, 208, 265.

[68] *Ibid.*, 6/13189.

frequently served as dynamos, constantly recharging the regime's policies with new radicalism 'from below', especially in regard to the Jews and the Churches. Far from restraining the leadership in its pursuit of these policies, by reflecting such adverse effects as they had on public opinion, the situation reports of local party leaders seemed to vie with each other in proposing further and harsher measures. A much favoured method was to seek the cover of some alleged public opinion, as did, for instance, the district leader of Offenbach (Hessen-Nassau) who stated in his report for May–June 1939: 'The national socialist population does not understand that seven years after the seizure of power the Church is still in a position to conduct a propaganda action such as the latest Corpus Christi procession.'[69] The district leader of Rheingau-St Goarshausen, reporting for the same month to the same regional office recommended that religious pilgrimages be proscribed and added reassuringly: 'Such a prohibition will certainly be accepted in the same way as the proscription of religious instruction in schools by clergymen and the dissolution of monasteries etc.'[70] The reports of other district leaders of Hessen-Nassau for this month included *inter alia* suggestions for the dissolution of a protestant relief organization,[71] the abolition of the institution by which mayors became ex-officio members of church councils (in order to disembarrass them of the duty to greet visiting Church dignitaries) and the further 'reconstitution' of religious instruction in schools because it 'still plays . . . much too large a part',[72] the transfer of church record books to the care of the party,[73] and the intensified expulsion of Jewish families from their flats so as to make more accommodation available to others.[74] Nor was the radical tenor of the reports confined to the party's pet hates alone. The district leader of Suederdithmarschen (Schleswig-Holstein) declared in his report of 23 September 1941: 'One finds that people in war-time always have more understanding for well-intentioned and sometimes even harsh justice than for soft sentimentality.' (In the weekly report of the regional propaganda department of 6 October 1941 the district leader's 'findings' were reproduced literally prefaced only by the words: 'In general one finds . . .')[75] And the district leader of Odenwald (Hessen-Nassau) in his report of 9 February 1944,

[69] *Ibid.*, 119/139901.
[70] *Ibid.*, 119/139910.
[71] *Ibid.*, 119/139918.
[72] *Ibid.*, 119/139918, 139926, 139950.
[73] *Ibid.*, 119/139120.
[74] *Ibid.*, 119/139936.
[75] *Ibid.*, 163/301336–7.

called for a more vigorous prosecution of the total war effort at home in the following terms:

> The ordinary person rightly asks why matters of the war effort are not tackled more energetically. If this is not necessary – the leadership must know that – then the propaganda is untrue ... One cannot ... say that [our] fate is at stake if the ... Government does not take all measures that could be taken and does not tap all the material and human resources at our disposal in order to turn this fateful struggle to our advantage.[76]

In part, the radical temper of the party reports probably flowed from a desire of the local leaders to find favour with their superiors by the display of true 'national socialist fanaticism'; in part, it may have been due to a misreading of public opinion, made all the more probable for the one-sidedness of the information that normally reached the ears of the party functionary. The fact remains, however, that in its situation reports the party transmitted a picture of whole-hearted popular approval for official policies and of a general readiness for further sacrifices, which as the SD reports indicate often considerably exaggerated the extent to which the people were in fact prepared to follow the regime in the pursuit of its more radical measures.

It is easily seen that the existence of the SD information channel with its forthright and often quite gloomy appraisals of popular feelings, continuously casting doubts not only on the effectiveness of the party's *Menschenfuehrung* but also on the veracity of its situation reports, must have been a sizeable thorn in the flesh of the party. Equally, if not more, vexing to the party was the fact that the SD continued to report on the misdeeds and derelictions of party officials, not neglecting to underline their

---

[76] *Ibid.*, 119/139557. It may be noted that while the party reports were free with radical advice, when it came to the deed the regional leaders, at least, preferred a more cautious approach. According to Walter Rohland, a high official in Speer's Armament Ministry, the regional leaders at a meeting on 6 October 1943, opposed Speer's demands for the total mobilization of the German labour force on the grounds that 'the total war demanded by Speer would weaken the people's power of resistance'. (IMT, vol. XLI, p. 489.) Speer himself refers to this meeting in his memoirs but states that the regional leaders 'were less disturbed by the comprehensiveness of my programme' than by some references in his speech which they interpreted as a veiled threat that party leaders obstructing the proposed measures would be arrested. (*Inside the Third Reich*, p. 425f.)

harmful effect on popular morale. The same applied to the reports of the *Gestapo*, which was originally a state institution, and therefore lacked even such tenuous filial ties as still bound the SD to the party.[77] A report of the *Gestapo* in Koeln–Aachen of 4 September 1934 stated that the 'bad political morale among wide circles' was due in part to the fact that party positions were held by persons 'in whom the people have no confidence'.[78] Two months later the same source reported that 'the sentiments of the people towards the party are still strongly critical ... The many ... cases of convictions for embezzlement and misappropriation prove to them that the necessary caution in the selection of personnel is still not being exercised'.[79] The SD branch in Oberdonau region stressed in a report of 18 January 1941 that 'especially party functionaries' had increasingly been observed to make 'pessimistic remarks about the course of the war'.[80] When Goebbels in a radio broadcast following the events of 20 July 1944, and his own appointment as Commissioner for Total War, spoke of the increased responsibilities of the party in the intensification of the home effort, Kaltenbrunner stated in his report to the Party Chancellory of 28 July:

> Many people do not want to extend the confidence which is accorded to the person of the Minister to the entire party. That is why Dr. Goebbels' words that the party would become 'the main motor' [of the war effort at home] are not regarded entirely without apprehension. The fear is expressed that in any [increased] effort it would in the first instance be the turn of those 'who for one reason or another don't suit the responsible party leaders'.[81]

The word '*Giftzwerg*' (snake-in-the-grass; literally: poison-dwarf) pencilled in the margin of the above passage by someone clearly

---

[77] It was repeatedly asserted in the highest quarters that the SD was 'an internal party institution' whose task lay 'not in the surveillance of the party but in that of the party's enemies' (Fuehrer-decree of 14 December 1938, in VAB, vol. IV, p. 49; for similar statements by Heydrich in 1935 and Himmler in 1943, see Boberach, *Meldungen*, p. xviii.) In fact, of course, the internal affairs of the party did not remain immune from the reach of the SD and this provided fertile ground for resentment on the part of the NSDAP officialdom. See also Huettenberger, *Gauleiter*, pp. 175ff; H. Hoehne, *Der Orden unter dem Totenkopf*, Guetersloh, 1967, p. 391f; H. Krausnick, H. Buchheim, M. Broszat, H.-J. Jacobsen, *Anatomy of the SS-State*, London, 1968, p. 71.
[78] Vollmer, *Volksopposition*, p. 81. [79] *Ibid.*, p. 113.
[80] NA, T-81, 7/14474. [81] *Ibid.*, 6/13533.

high up in the Party Chancellory – the handwriting does not
appear to be that of Bormann – speaks volumes for the relations
that existed between the Party Chancellory and the RSHA at
that time. Several months later, on 31 October 1944, the head
of the SD Inland Service, Otto Ohlendorf, found it necessary to
share in a speech to senior SD officials his 'extraordinary concern'
lest the SD reports create the impression of the party as 'something negative or oppositional'.[82] But if this was an attempt to
protect the party from the damaging effect of SD criticism and
possibly to contain the enmity of the party apparatus towards his
own service, it came too late to achieve its purpose.

How embittered the party was by the SD reports may be seen
from the fact that on 4 April 1945, on what must have been one
of the last occasions on which he wrote to any agency of the
Reich, Bormann took time off from his duties in the Berlin
Fuehrerbunker in order to compose a personal letter to Kaltenbrunner refuting charges which the latest SD report had made
about the party. The letter begins as follows:

> The report which you have today handed over to me is a
> *typical* SD report: typical because it generalizes without any
> inhibitions from a few . . . incidents or situations. It does not
> say: individual party leaders swear at this or that army forma-
> tion . . . officers or staffs, but it generalizes by saying: *the* party
> swears at *the* armed forces and *the* armed forces swear at *the*
> party. Again generalizing it says: 'Only isolated persons are
> doing any work.' This impression is that of your reporter;
> from the many reports reaching me I have a different picture.

Bormann then goes on to justify the behaviour of party functionaries in evacuating their families from areas threatened by
the advance of Allied troops and attempts to explain the general
breakdown of evacuation and demolition procedures. The letter
ends on the following note:

> That parts of the population – the SD reporter writes simply
> only of *the* population – greeted the entry of Americans with
> joy is probably true. If one wishes to appraise this phenomenon
> justly, however, one must take into account the extraordinarily
> strong propaganda effect of enemy broadcasts and, on the other
> hand, the fact that meetings, call evenings [*Sprechabende*],
> etc., had been altogether impossible in the West for a consider-
> able time. All too gladly the people believe that which they

<hr>

[82] Quoted in Boberach, *Meldungen*, p. xviii.

hope for: namely, that the war is now at an end ... I am convinced that in a relatively short time – just as after 1918 – a very strong disillusionment will set in.[83]

For some time before the party had attempted to blunt the edge of the SD reports by bringing about a measure of 'consultation' between local party organizations and SD agencies. In August 1943 protracted negotiations between the Party Chancellory and the RSHA resulted in an agreement for 'an extensive exchange of reports and information between the Party Chancellory and the RSHA'. For its part the RSHA undertook to instruct its agencies 'to inform the responsible *Hoheitstraeger* continuously of matters of a political nature arising in his area of sovereignty', to meet his requests for reports in respect of subjects of 'particular interest for the purpose of political leadership', and also 'to get in touch' with him when reporting on 'especially important points in order to receive his opinion on the problem in question'.[84] The records do not reveal to what extent these undertakings were kept. In any case, the initiative for consultation was left at the discretion of the SD. If consultations did take place they certainly did not meet the party's grievances. In his letter to Kaltenbrunner, of 4 April 1945, Bormann again touched on the crux of the problem when he wrote: 'But that is precisely what I have against the SD: certain wholly irresponsible persons make allegations and reproaches while those responsible are not at all consulted.'

The reliability of SD reports is not the concern of this study. Their built-in bias has already been noted. Although the SD operated through a far-flung system of undercover informers, both the quality and the quantity of the population sample from which information on public opinion was collected clearly left much to be desired. It may also safely be assumed that Himmler and the men of the RSHA did not shrink from slanting their reports with a view to discrediting the party, and with it Bormann, in the prosecution of the intrigues and enmities that riddled the leadership of the Third Reich. The same process may well also have operated at lower levels. If evidence were required that the SD reports did not at all times uphold the highest standards of truthfulness, it could perhaps be adduced from a statement such as the following, included in Kaltenbrunner's

[83] NA, T-81, 5/13048–51. (Emphasis in the original.)
[84] VAB, vol. IV, pp. 47–8.

report of 28 July 1944: 'To the appointment of the *Reichs-fuehrer–SS* [Himmler] as C.-in-C. Home Army the people attach the hope that a "thorough clean-up" will now follow in all places where reactionary elements have crept in.'[85]

It it difficult to say which of the two channels of information had the greater influence on the policies of the Nazi leadership in general and on its public opinion policies in particular. On the face of it one would expect that the SD reports were regarded as the more reliable guide to popular morale, if not by the Party Chancellory then at least by the majority of other Reich agencies.[86] But the circle of Nazi leaders who were given access to the reports of the SD contracted progressively as the contents of the reports became more disturbing. Originally all Ministers and party *Reichsleiter* probably received the reports. From 1943 onwards, however, the combined efforts of Bormann and Goebbels seem to have succeeded in limiting the distribution of the reports considerably. For Bormann and the men of the party apparatus the SD had become a mouthpiece of defeatism.[87] Goebbels shared this view. 'The SD report is full of mischief', reads a diary entry for 17 April 1943.

It is entirely unpolitical and is sent to the various offices un-

[85] NA, T-81, 6/13532.
[86] As for Goebbels, there is no indication that he distinguished between SD and party in respect of the reliability of their information. Occasionally, indeed, he lumped the reports of SD, party and his own propaganda agencies together as equally unrepresentative of the true state of popular feeling which in his view was far more stable than appeared in the reports: '... one notes in the people themselves a firm conservatism which looks beyond the events of the day and loyally carries out [its] duties ...' (W. A. Belcke, ed., '*Wollt Ihr den totalen Krieg?*' *Die geheimen Goebbels-Konferenzen 1939–1943*, Stuttgart, 1967, p. 303.) His diary shows an altogether remarkable lack of discrimination in this regard. For instance, he was gullible enough – or expected his future readers to be gullible enough – to take letters that 'testify to the unqualified agreement of public opinion with my views', or that 'are full of praise for my work' at their face value. (*Goebbels Diaries*, pp. 293 and 320.) Another source of public opinion 'which to me always represents the voice of the people' was his mother: 'She knows the sentiments of the people better than most experts who judge from the ivory tower of scientific enquiry as in her case the voice of the people itself speaks.' (*Ibid.*, p. 22.) In the unpublished section of his diary Goebbels said of a 'statistical investigation ... in the manner of the Gallup Institute' conducted by the SD, that he did not value 'such investigations because they are always undertaken with a deliberate purpose in mind'. (L. W. Doob, 'Goebbels' Principles of Propaganda', *Public Opinion Quarterly*, 1950, no. 3, p. 422.)
[87] Boberach, *Meldungen*, p. xxvii.

sifted. That involves a certain danger, for most readers...
haven't enough political discernment to distinguish between
side issues and main issues... The leaders of the Reich certainly don't need to know whenever someone living in the back
of beyond unburdens his anguished heart.[88]

As the man who was primarily responsible for the direction of
Nazi propaganda – in his dual capacity as Minister for Propaganda and head of the Reich Propaganda Office of the party –
Goebbels' attitude towards the SD reports was probably
prompted in part by the same motives as that of Bormann.
Goebbels also resented the reflections on the success of his propaganda policies that were implied in the increasing manifestations
of popular discontent reported by the SD.[89] Like Bormann, too,
he felt that the SD material needed to be brought into line with
the 'political views' of the regional party leaders and propaganda
agencies, and in May 1943 he claimed to have succeeded in
persuading Himmler to stop sending the SD reports 'to every
sort of Minister as its effect is too defeatist'.[90] Nor, presumably,
did Goebbels have much difficulty in convincing Himmler, who
also thought the SD reports too pessimistic and would not for
that reason submit them to the Fuehrer.[91] Ohlendorf himself
confirmed that his reports did not as a rule reach Hitler personally.[92] He certainly felt that the Nazi leaders in general did
not properly appreciate the importance of the SD material, and
in a memorandum to the Doenitz Government in May 1945
mentioned in particular the Propaganda Ministry and the party

---

[88] *Goebbels Diaries*, pp. 258–9.
[89] It may be noted that in the majority of reports seen, regional SD
agencies reported favourable popular reaction to Goebbels' personal
speeches and writings. (See also Boberach, *Meldungen, passim.*) Occasionally, however, there were comments such as: 'The effects of his arguments suffered from the fact that people see in Dr. Goebbels too much
of the propagandist whose arguments, though skilfully constructed and
rhetorically flawless, nevertheless lack that inner warmth which emanates
from the words of the Fuehrer.' (NA, T–81, 7/14437; see also Steinert,
Hitlers Krieg, p. 372f.)
[90] *Goebbels Diaries*, p. 293.
[91] F. Kersten, *Totenkopf und Treue*, Hamburg, 1952, p. 260.
[92] One report which did reach Hitler evoked the marginal annotation: 'If
it mattered what people were always saying then everything would
have been lost long ago. The true bearing of the people lies more deeply
and is founded on a very firm inner bearing. If that were not the case
it would be impossible to explain all these achievements of the people.'
(Picker, *Hitlers Tischgespraeche*, p. 206.)

leadership among Nazi institutions that had 'tried to obstruct the work of the SD'.[93]

The danger of defeatism was not merely a pretext used by men like Bormann and Goebbels in order to cover up their all too understandable embarrassment at the information contained in the SD reports. Defeatism, on the part of the ruling circles no less than on the part of the broad masses, became a growing obsession of the totalitarian mentality as it unfolded itself in the setting of war-time Germany.[94] Perhaps its most tangible expression was the ban on listening to foreign broadcasts and the control over subscriptions to foreign newspapers, both of which were applied with increasing strictness even to Ministers of the Reich.[95] It was ultimately this fear which kept much unpalatable

---

[93] Boberach, *Meldungen*, pp. xxvii and 538. Boberach states that in the summer of 1944 Bormann and Ley forbade functionaries of the party and the Labour Front to work for the SD and that the regular twice-weekly SD reports – then known as *SD Berichte zu Inlandsfragen* – ceased altogether at this time. However, the evidence for both these assertions is indirect and inconclusive. It seems unlikely that Bormann, for one, would have gone so far as to proscribe co-operation with the SD, especially as such a measure could not in the nature of things be effectively enforced. Huettenberger cites a circular letter of the Party Chancellory dated 18 August 1944 instructing party organizations to place trusted party members at the disposal of the security police and assumes that the object was to enable the party to penetrate the SD. (*Gauleiter*, p. 177.) Even if the regular *Berichte zu Inlandsfragen* were discontinued in the summer of 1944 there can be no doubt that the SD network remained operational until the very end of the Third Reich.

[94] Indeed, Goebbels believed that the danger was even greater in the case of the leaders than in that of the people, because the former were exposed to defeatist propaganda without having been taught how to interpret it. (*Goebbels Diaries*, p. 17.)

[95] Already on 21 September 1939 Goebbels had circulated a letter to government departments which laid down the principle: 'No one has the right to listen [to foreign broadcasts] who does not have the duty to do so.' Senior officials only were to be allowed to listen to foreign broadcasts, and this on the personal recommendation of the responsible Minister. (FO, 4908 H/E 255313.) In October 1941 Hitler gave Goebbels authority to withdraw permission even from Ministers and Goebbels was not slow in applying it. (*Ibid.*, E255317.) On 30 January 1942 the dissemination of the bulletins of the Seehaus monitoring service was similarly restricted (*Ibid.*, E255399.) 'Everybody who counts', Goebbels noted in his diary on 26 January, 'now agrees with me that the dangerous manipulations of this service must be curbed to prevent a collapse of morale among the leaders of the state and the *Wehrmacht*.' And a day later he recorded Hitler's 'complete' agreement with this view; indeed, according to Goebbels, Hitler went 'even further. He believes the Seehaus Service should be distributed to only a few persons in the entire country.' (*Goebbels Diaries*, p. 16.) On 11 February 1942 Goebbels found

information on the state of German public opinion from all but a few members of the group that ruled Nazi Germany. For Goebbels, who was one of them, the negative effects of their information monopoly were easily outweighed by its allegedly positive effects on the morale of rulers and ruled alike. After a conversation with Ley, he noted in his diary on 19 September 1943:

> One can see that much of the information at my disposal is being withheld from him, otherwise he would judge the situation more realistically and not let his imagination roam. But it is a good thing that the men who frequently address the masses should be free from any knowledge of unpleasant news. This gives them much more self-assurance when they talk to the people.[96]

The Nazi party's reporting system fulfilled certain undoubtedly useful functions. It signalled upwards shortcomings in the implementation of official measures which might otherwise have remained unnoticed, and it was occasionally capable of conscientiously reporting popular feeling on a limited range of subjects. But as an instrument of public opinion polling which could enable the leadership to keep abreast with the true sentiments and aspirations of the mass of the people, it was superficial, irresponsible and fundamentally unreliable. Because it had easier access to critical opinion and no vested interest in its concealment, the SD network could have furnished a sobering and necessary contrast to the rose-coloured canvas of party reporting. But their obsessive preoccupation with defeatism caused the

it 'disgusting' that 'so many people in high office' were trying to convince him that they must listen to foreign stations, and nine days later he found it 'really amusing to see how all Ministers approach the Fuehrer asking his permission to listen to foreign broadcasts. The reason they assign is nothing short of grotesque.' (*Ibid.*, pp. 41 and 57.) Among the Nazi documents there are several letters sent by various ministers appealing against Goebbels' decision. The tone of some of them was indeed rather pitiful. Schacht alone sent a brief and indignant retort. (FO, 4908 H/E 255386–9. See the documentation in C. Latour, 'Goebbels' "Ausserordentliche Rundfunkmassnahmen" 1939–1942', *Vierteljahrshefte fuer Zeitgeschichte*, 1963, October, pp. 418–35; also H. Schacht, *My First Seventy-Six Years*, London, 1955, pp. 417–18.)

In December 1942 the names of organizations and individuals that were to be allowed to subscribe to Swiss newspapers were submitted by Himmler to the Fuehrer for his personal decision. (NA, T-81, 8/16755–6.)

[96] *Goebbels Diaries*, p. 369.

Nazis themselves to restrict the potentialities of this valuable channel of information. The majority of Nazi leaders had to fall back largely on the party reporting system, supplemented by the reports of their own departments and such informal sources as were at their disposal.

For its part, the information available to the party derived primarily from two sources. It came first from such freely observable manifestations of the popular mood as the size and enthusiasm of the audience at party-sponsored public meetings or, alternatively, at Church functions – the only 'competitive' form of assembly still sanctioned in the Third Reich. In view of the positive and negative incentives at work these were not very precise indicators of public opinion but, given conscientious reporting, broad trends could probably have been discerned. Second, the party's information came from such direct expressions of public opinion as were generally considered to be safe. This precluded any proper discussion of the merits of the regime, its leaders and its policies, but on the other hand it was by no means confined to the standard protestations of national socialist loyalty. Between the poles of silent negation and vociferous affirmation on politically sensitive topics there lay a range of neutral subjects, from the distribution of consumer goods to the quality of air-raid precautions which, within limits, were discussed freely and frequently. And what the people thought of these and related matters was clearly of some importance to the regime, if only because it could assist it in adapting its propaganda accordingly. However, while information from both these sources was relatively freely accessible to lower party organizations, it suffered significant distortions in its progress to the top of the party hierarchy. Some of these distortions were incidental and might have been eliminated with a more scrupulous approach to the task of reporting. Others were deliberate and endemic. The local party leaders could not be at one and the same time the manipulators of public opinion and its impartial observers. In the circumstances, it was only to be expected that their reported observations should tend to conform to the objectives of their manipulation.

Relatively little is known of the Soviet party's public opinion reporting system. The reports as such are, of course, confidential and one would not expect their contents to be widely discussed in published sources. The only materials of comparable provenance to the ones used above for the appraisal of Nazi practice are the so-called *Smolensk Archives* captured by the German army in the summer of 1941 and transferred to U.S. custody at the end of World War II. The *Archives*, which cover the period 1917–38, are, however, incomplete and contain relatively few materials that attest to the procedures and quality of party reporting. In particular, there is no coverage in depth comparable to that of the Nazi records. It is therefore impossible to trace the fate of reports in their passage upwards through the party network and the extent, if any, to which different party organs distorted or concealed information received from subordinate levels cannot be determined. Nevertheless, several comments can be made by way of comparison with Nazi practice.[97]

Firstly it must be said that, if the *Smolensk Archives* are at all representative, it would seem that the Soviet regime relied for the mainstay of its information concerning popular morale on the agencies of the secret police. The reports of the latter – and there are comparatively many in the *Archives* – provided detailed, comprehensive, frequent and, as far as can be judged, quite unadorned accounts of the changing trends of public opinion throughout the region.[98] By comparison, the 'information summary' (*informatsionnaya svodka*) of the party, both at the district and at the provincial level was essentially a progress report, covering all spheres of activity in the area and leaving comparatively little room for public opinion assessments. A typical two-weekly *svodka* of a district party committee included information under some twenty headings from 'Agriculture' to 'Transportation', from 'Militia' to 'Public Health' – all matters in which the party organization was directly involved and on which it reported in great detail, including figures of production plans, material stocks, manpower, etc.[99] Information on popular morale,

---

[97] A series of microfilms of the *Archives* were kindly made available by the Library of the British Foreign Office. Regrettably, the exposures did not contain serial numbers. The references given below correspond to the identification numbers of the original files, of which there are several to a microfilm reel.

[98] In 1930, for instance, the secret police forwarded a daily report to Moscow entitled 'On the political situation in the rural areas of the Western Province in connection with collectivization'. The reports were several pages long and contained detailed information, classified by district, on the state of popular morale during this exhaustive period. (WKP/260. See also M. Fainsod, *Smolensk under Soviet Rule*, London, 1959, pp. 43, 84, 156, 226, 248–51.)

[99] WKP/273.

unless, as in the early years, it was reported under such headings as 'Strikes', 'Counter-Revolutionary Occurrences' or 'Political Parties', was usually exhausted in a few sentences of the first section entitled 'General Political Situation'.

A significant contrast with Nazi practice was the fact that copies of secret police reports were regularly forwarded to party organs, not only at the provincial but also at the district level. It is most probable, indeed almost certain, that additional information was transmitted upwards within the police hierarchy, of which the party organizations in the region were left in ignorance, but the general impression left by the Smolensk materials is that police and party operated very much as two branches of one organization. In addition to its periodical reports the secret police sent the party notifications of individual acts of sabotage or of other state-hostile activities and not infrequently even passed on the minutes of its interrogations of various suspects.[100] In the late 1920s and early 1930s police agencies often acted as reconnaissance squads for the advancing front of collectivization, informing party organizations both of the villages ripe for assault and, while the assault was in progress, of the necessary 'measures towards cleansing obstructive elements'.[101]

While it is impossible to subject the Smolensk reports to the same scrutiny to which Nazi party reports can now be exposed, even a superficial comparison reveals the former as rather more truthful and realistic. For the most part, as has already been said, references to the popular mood in the Smolensk party reports are brief. Often one finds the same tendency towards stereotyped formulae which has already been noted as a feature of Nazi reports: 'the attitude of the workers to the party is good' or the 'attitude of the peasants towards the Soviet power is satisfactory' or even the rather more specific 'among teachers there is an inclination towards active participation in social work and co-operation with the party'.[102] There are appraisals which one cannot but suspect as being somewhat on the optimistic side such as – in 1924 – 'the influence of priests is notably declining' or 'the authority of SRs among workers and peasants has finally been lost', or – in 1928 – 'there is growing mass participation in carrying out the decisions of the Soviet power'.[103]

And yet, alongside banalities and half-truths, the reports were also capable of transmitting a more realistic picture of the

[100] WKP/187 and 261.
[101] WKP/166.
[102] WKP/273 and 278.
[103] WKP/278 and 296.

underlying temper of the masses. 'The mood of the peasants is ugly', reports one rural district committee in May 1929; 'The kulaks have completely turned the villagers against the Soviet power. Even the poor peasants are obstructive in some cases . . . Party officials hardly dare show themselves in the villages.'[104] Another district committee report of February 1931 noted in considerable detail the fears and resentments of the local peasants as well as the various malpractices in economic management which together enabled the kulaks to achieve the 'quiet but effective penetration of the collective farms'.[105] Other reports reflect with apparent lack of embellishment the grievances of the population in regard to working conditions, food supply and similar matters, occasionally even quoting such utterances as 'the party workers know how to look after themselves and their own, but the needs of the working people do not worry them'.[106] A special *svodka* of the province committee on popular reaction to the decisions of the Central Committee and Central Control Commission in connection with the 'Smolensk Scandal' of 1928 reports 'satisfaction that central organs have acted at last'. At the same time, however, the *svodka* lists such expressions of popular feeling as the demand for the restoration of other parties and a free press as well as for harsher punishment of the culprits – 'the big noises always get away leniently while the little man is punished'. Among the membership of the party, according to the report, 'reaction can be characterized as healthy'. Yet, in some party organizations the view was held that the 'Smolensk Scandal' was not an isolated affair, that similar occurrences were known in other areas and that the fault lay with the 'inadequate leadership' of the Central Committee and the Central Control Commission.[107]

The relative frankness of Smolensk party reports need not, of course, imply that the functionaries of the Soviet party were inherently more truthful than their counterparts in Nazi Germany. The 'dung heap' uncovered by the investigations into the 'Smolensk Scandal' was only the best-known of many cases reflecting equally, if less sensationally, on the moral integrity of party functionaries in the province. Nor does it mean that the natural temptation to avoid self-incrimination was miraculously absent from the Soviet system. The official of the Soviet party,

[104] WKP/297.   [105] WKP/159.   [106] WKP/297 and 166.
[107] WKP/296. The story of the 'Smolensk Scandal' is related in Fainsod, *Smolensk*, pp. 48–52.

too, was responsible for the state of public feeling in his domain and its negative manifestations could not but discredit the quality of his 'mass-political work'. If his *svodky* nevertheless presented a generally starker picture of the popular mood than one would obtain from reading the Nazi *Stimmungsberichte*, the reason must firstly be sought in the fact that the trend of popular feeling towards the regime was undoubtedly far less favourable in the Soviet Union during most of the years covered by the *Smolensk Archives* than was the case in Nazi Germany throughout the lifespan of the Third Reich. At the time of the collectivization, for instance, it would have been ludicrous for Soviet party officials to refer to the peasant mood in the glowing terms found in Nazi reports even in the last year of World War II. Clearly, no communist official could hope to get away with a statement such as 'the peasants know only one faith and that is Iosif Vissarionovich Stalin' in a confidential report to a superior party organ. What was probably a considerable exaggeration in Nazi Germany would have been an outrageous untruth in Soviet Russia. Thus while Soviet party reports were more sombre than those of the Nazis they need not, by the same token have been more truthful.

But there were also factors in the Soviet system which, to some extent at least, cancelled out any tendency to conceal unfavourable public reaction. Unlike the Nazi party whose primary sphere of activity was precisely the 'leadership of men', Soviet party organizations were also responsible for practical matters of administration and economic construction. The latter, especially, well-nigh monopolized the party's attention from the late 1920s onwards. As the pace of collectivization and industrialization increased so the burden of the party's responsibilities grew heavier and the pressure on party organizations at all levels to fulfil their plan quotas mounted. The materials of the *Smolensk Archives* reflect the atmosphere of permanent tension under which party organs worked while attempting to meet the seemingly insatiable demands of the centre for ever higher output. There was 'an implacable gauntlet that had constantly to be run, the race of production, in which, to borrow from Alice, one had always to run twice as fast in order to remain in the same place.'[108] In the circumstances, party organizations might well have been concerned at least as much with exaggerating difficulties as with minimizing popular dissatisfactions. If the workers or peasants in a particular area were especially unco-operative it

[108] Fainsod, *Smolensk*, p. 86.

reflected negatively on the responsible party secretary's agitational activities. On the other hand, if the latter succeeded in impressing upon his superiors the difficulties encountered in bringing about that co-operation, the effect might be both to explain past production failures and to reduce future quotas. If nothing else, it might induce higher authorities to alleviate some of the conditions which did in fact impede the execution of their demands. It was probably a consideration such as this which prompted one district deputy secretary in 1932 to describe the mood of the peasants as 'unhealthy' and to warn of 'a number of undesirable consequences' unless the provincial committee authorized the immediate dispatch of grain to the district.[109] In the final analysis, it was his success as production organizer rather than as agitator which determined the standing of a particular official in the party. So long as he met his targets he was relatively secure in his post, irrespective of the state of public opinion. The local party official knew that in the period of 'de-kulakization' and the first Five-Year Plans, his leaders would not be likely to be moved by the finer nuances of popular feeling. What counted above all was tangible success in production; if by presenting a frank or even an exaggerated version of popular dissatisfactions he could serve that end, it was a small price to pay.

The second factor that may well have made for a greater degree of truthfulness and realism in Smolensk party reports, was the access of party organizations to the secret police channel. Since the party secretary regularly received copies of the reports of the secret police organ in his area, this meant firstly that he was far better informed than the Nazi functionary who relied for his information largely on his own 'open' sources and therefore rarely penetrated below the surface of public opinion; and secondly, that he was compelled to harmonize his own *svodka* with that of the secret police organ. Occasionally he might have attempted to distort or suppress an item of information that had come to his knowledge through the police channel but which for one reason or another he did not wish to pass on to a higher party organ. To have done so consistenly, however, would have brought the practice to the attention of his superiors who, for their part, had access to the police channel at a higher level.

It is more than likely that the close co-operation of the party and police networks in the realm of public opinion reporting

[109] WKP/166.

continues to present; if anything, it has probably been strengthened as the result of the general reassertion of party control over
the secret police which has been a feature of the post-Stalin era.
In the long run, it is this interlocking of the two networks at all
levels which provides some guarantee that the information on the
state of popular morale contained in party reports does not
deviate too far from reality. To be sure, the opportunities for the
suppression or distortion of information are not thereby eliminated. The pressures of totalitarian government create their own
counter-pressures, not the least formidable of which are the
'family circles' or 'mutual protection societies' formed by officials
of different hierarchies in a given locality in order to conspire
against the central authority and to protect one another from the
consequences of their own misdeeds and shortcomings. Yet,
judging from the Smolensk materials, co-operation between party
and police does help to reduce that wide chasm of ignorance and
misinformation that is frequently apparent from the records of
the Nazi party.

In recent years questions of party reporting in general, including public opinion reporting, have come to be aired in the
party press. As a result some evidence, albeit fragmentary and
tentative, on the present scope, quality and organization of the
system has become available. What caused the unprecedented
emergence of the subject into the twilight of Soviet-style publicity
is a matter for conjecture, but it is clearly connected with an
attempt to imbue party cadres with a consciousness of the importance of a comprehensive, reliable and smoothly functioning
system of internal information. Virtually every contemporary
Soviet account on party reporting stresses the need for 'full and
truthful information', invoking in familiar fashion the authority of
Lenin to the affect that without such information 'we have
neither eyes, nor ears nor hands', that the party must be able 'to
determine unerringly the mood of the masses on any question, at
any moment'.[110]

As presently constituted the scope of party reporting is said
to embrace three main subject areas: 'In the first place, this is
information of a general political character, i.e. the mood of the
masses, their reactions to significant events in the life of the
country and abroad, to the most important decisions of the party
and the government . . .' Information about economic and cultural

110 See, e.g. *Agitator*, 1971, no. 6, pp. 42, 43; *Partiinaya zhin'*, 1971, no.
16, p. 4.

affairs and about internal party matters occupies second and third place respectively.[111] While the order in which the three subject areas are listed above need not perhaps reflect the weight given to each in actual reporting practice, it does seem that public attitudes and reactions now occupy a far more important place in party reports than was true throughout the period covered by the Smolensk materials.

With regard to the quality of information, there are many indications that Soviet party reports are not immune to the deficiencies and distortions which afflicted Nazi *Stimmungsberichte* in their time. Such epithets as 'formal', 'superficial' and 'declarative', with which Soviet sources frequently refer to the shortcomings of party officialdom in other spheres, are also applied to its reporting procedures. Party information, it has been authoritatively stated,

> must bear a generalizing, analytical character, provide food for thought, arouse to action. And here it must be emphasized: generalizing but not general. The fact is that in practice the one is often substituted for the other. Some party workers, guided by the laudable intention not to submerge in a multitude of concrete facts, go to the opposite extreme: they tend towards general theorizing unsupported by real facts.[112]

Similar criticisms recur with predictable regularity. The information contained in the reports of subordinate party organizations 'does not sufficiently base itself on an analysis of vital facts and phenomena',[113] it is 'too streamlined, without analysis, without suggestions',[114] 'poor in content and rather one-sided',[115] 'does not reflect important phenomena and profound processes in the life of the party organization, does not contain an analysis of the causes of failures and shortcomings, does not reveal positive

---

[111] A. Belyakov and I. Shvets, 'Partiinaya informatsiya', *Partiinaya zhizn'*, 1967, no. 8, p. 29. This article by the head and the deputy head of the Information Section in the Central Committee Department for Organizational–Party Work opened the subject for discussion in the press. See also the same authors' 'Informatsiya – deistvenny instrument partiinogo rukovodstva', *Kommunist*, 1969, no. 4, pp. 53–64, and I. A. Shvets, 'Vnutripartiinaya informatsiya kak instrument rukovodstva, sredstvo vospitanaya i kontrol'ya', in P. A. Rodionov *et al.*, eds., *Problemy partiinogo stroitel'stva*, Moscow, 1972, pp. 169–87, esp, pp. 176ff.

[112] *Partiinaya zhizn'*, 1967, no. 8, p. 31.

[113] *Ibid.*, 1969, no. 16, p. 37.

[114] *Ibid.*, no 19, p. 56.

[115] Shvets, 'Vnutripartiinaya informatsiya', p. 180.

experience thoroughly and in detail'.[116] All this, it is said, 'substantially lowers the effectiveness of such information, does not permit it to be utilized better for the correct appraisal of the situation and for timely intervention, the struggle against various rumours and fabrications [and] . . . the formation of a communist world view'.[117]

An even more serious failure of the reports is their lack of objectivity, their tendency to conceal or embellish facts likely to discredit the local functionary in the eyes of his superiors:

> The leaders of certain party committees and economic agencies do not spare glowing colours in painting every success achieved, but it is amazing how they lose their gift of eloquence when they are required to provide information on shortcomings, omissions and other unpleasant things.[118]

There are party functionaries who 'not wishing, as they say, to wash their dirty linen in public, sometimes do not inform superior organs objectively, do not report on failures and omissions',[119] and there are others who hold to the mistaken notion that 'once we know of the failures and take measures to correct them, there is no reason to inform superior organs; the main thing is to report that which has been done, which has been accomplished'.[120] The problem is familiar from our discussion of the Nazi party reports. Equally familiar – and apparently equally unavailing – are the recurrent exhortations designed to persuade local functionaries 'to show life as it is, without embellishments',[121] 'to convince them that to represent matters in a distorted light means to do harm'.[122]

Until recently internal party information was the exclusive responsibility of the professional functionaries of the party apparatus who reported on developments in their respective areas of competence to their superiors in the hierarchy. However, for some years past, approximately from 1967 onward, attempts have been made to draw so-called 'non-staff activists' into the network of party information. As far as can be made out from the scattered evidence available the participation of such activists

116 *Kommunist*, 1969, no. 4, p. 59; *Partiinaya zhizn'*, 1971, no. 16, pp. 4–7.
117 *Agitator*, 1969, no. 5, p. 3.
118 *Pravda*, 19 September 1969.
119 *Partiinaya zhizn'*, 1969, no. 7, p. 4; 1972, no. 16, pp. 79–80.
120 *Kommunist*, 1969, no. 4, pp. 59–60.
121 *Agitator*, 1969, no. 20, p. 38.
122 *Partiinaya zhizn'*, 1969, no. 19, p. 56; 1970, no. 6. p. 38.

is as yet far from general practice; nor are the procedures adopted as uniform or clear-cut as might have been expected. At the level of the primary party organization special party informators (*partinformatory*, not to be confused with the *politinformatory* discussed earlier) from among 'active party members with sufficient training and experience' were appointed in the larger organizations.[123] They operate under the direction of the regular functionaries of the party organization and 'they must not give some sort of official report to the district or city committees of the party, by-passing the secretary of the party organization'.[124] At higher levels, up to and including the province organization, 'information sections' (sometimes also called 'information groups') with a membership varying from 5 to 15 persons have been formed. Although they are usually referred to as 'non-staff' bodies they do in fact include personnel of the party apparatus together with such 'outside' functionaries as members of the Komsomol apparatus or of the People's Control Committee, and are invariably headed by a secretary, departmental head or full-time instructor of the appropriate party committee.[125] In some cases, indeed, they consist entirely of party officials or members of party committees or bureaux.[126]

In general, operating procedures appear to be remarkably varied and even casual. According to an editorial in the party journal 'many party committees have no reference-information service, and work on the collection, processing and systematization of information is inadequately organized'.[127] Party organizations, it

[123] *Ibid.*, 1968, no. 24, p. 61; 1970, no. 6, pp. 32–3; 1973, no. 2, pp. 50–2. Thus, e.g. the 3,000 party informators appointed in the primary party organizations of the Tatar ASSR include members of the party committees and bureaux, editors of plant and wall newspapers, economic specialists and propagandists. 'These comrades are always abreast with events, they know the moods and needs of people, which enables them to assist the party committee and bureau in informing superior party organs in a qualified and skilful manner.' (*Ibid.*, 1969, no. 19, p. 56.)

[124] *Ibid.*, 1967, no. 8, p. 34. In the smaller primary party organizations, the secretary fulfils the functions of *partinformator* (*Ibid.*, 1971, no. 14, p. 39, no. 21, p. 48.)

For earlier references to *partinformatory* as (undercover) informers within the party, see S. Harcave, *Structure and Functioning of the Lower Party Organizations in the Soviet Union*, Maxwell Air Force Base, Alabama, 1954, p. 23.

[125] *Partiinaya zhizn'*, 1969, no. 14, p. 37, no. 19, p. 57; 1971, no. 14, pp. 36–7; *Pravda*, 21 June 1969.

[126] *Partiinaya zhizn'*, 1969, no. 16, p. 37; 1970, no. 6, p. 40; 1972, no. 4, p. 45.

[127] *Ibid.*, 1969, no. 7, p. 4.

is admitted, adhere to 'different views' as regards the intervals of time at which information is to be submitted.[128] In the Kirov Borough of Riga, primary party organizations report 'on their own initiative' whenever a new development occurs.[129] In Rostov, primary organizations until recently 'informed borough committees about particular events or "when the bell rang", i.e. by request', and 'information procedures were no better at higher levels'. Now, however, borough committees forward a daily report on 'important measures carried out the day before in the borough, on the working people's responses to particular events and on the needs of the population in the realms of culture, home life, trade, public catering, medical services, etc.'. In addition, the city committee receives weekly reports 'summarizing observations of the past week and noting the measures and concrete proposals adopted by the borough committee and the primary organizations', as well as quarterly reports whose 'main concern is the organizational and political work of the borough committee and the primary party organizations, and interesting new forms and methods of this work'.[130]

In Omsk Province party information activity proceeds according to a quarterly work plan prepared by the non-staff information section of the province committee. For their part, the information sections of district (and borough) committees draw up 'lists' of questions on which the party organizations provide information... at various times'. The questions are designed to elicit information 'on the practice of preparing and holding meetings and sessions of party bureaux and committees and the critical comments made at these gatherings; on the fulfilment of party decisions; on the studies of the elected party, trade union and Komsomol *aktiv*; and on the working people's attitude to public and political events'. Some of them conduct 'questionnaire polls' (*anketnye oprosy*) of their own with a view to acquiring 'a more profound knowledge of the working people's needs and requirements'.[131] By contrast, the Urgut District Committee in Samarkand Province manages – 'unobtrusively' – to apply a system of 'continuous party "probing" of requirements, public opinion and the special features of situations evolving in the labour collectives, not through a rigid questionnaire set-up, but through a process of natural communication with people'.[132]

128 *Ibid.*, no. 19, p. 57.　　129 *Ibid.*, 1967, no. 8, p. 28.
130 *Pravda*, 21 June 1969.　　131 *Partiinaya zhizn'*, 1969, no. 14, p. 36.
132 *Pravda*, 17 September 1969.

According to the First Secretary of Novomoskovsk (Tula Province) his organization attaches 'special interest' to questions put at lectures and agitation *besedy;* monthly analysis of these by the local Propaganda and Agitation Department enables the party to study 'the mood and needs' of the people.[133] An instructor from Izhevsk (Udmurt ASSR) reports that 'on the second day' after the publication of the CC Theses on the Lenin Anniversary 'the party committee already had information from the *informatory* on how the reading of this document was progressing, what opinions there were and what questions were being asked by the workers'; this, she claims, is the case 'whenever party and government decrees are published and important campaigns are conducted'.[134]

While the current discussions in the party press provide no more than a perfunctory view of the party's reporting practices they do indicate that a major attempt to intensify and streamline the system is in progress. Two specific aims are discernible at this stage. One is to enhance the reliability of the information passing through the party channel by breaking the monopoly of the apparatus. To be sure, the latter still exercises a preponderant influence over access to information at all levels of the hierarchy. Nevertheless, the circle of those involved in the collection, analysis and transmission of information has been substantially widened, particularly at the grass roots. As a result, the information reaching the top echelons of the regime is probably more truthful now than was the case in the past when the party channel was under the exclusive control of bureaucrats with direct administrative responsibility for the state of affairs in their respective areas of competence – and consequently a vested interest in the concealment or embellishment of unfavourable phenomena.[135]

The second aim is to systematize and particularly to increase the flow of information from below. Perhaps the most interesting and potentially the most significant aspect of the current preoccupation with party reporting is the employment of modern information retrieval techniques. At the local and regional levels

[133] *Partiinaya zhizn'*, 1972, no. 4, p. 44.
[134] *Ibid.*, 1970, no. 13, p. 33.
[135] It is difficult to see what other considerations could have prompted the party leadership to expose intra-party information to the intrusion of 'outside' activists, however carefully selected. Indeed, that such a step was taken underlines the importance which the leadership attaches to raising the reliability of party reports.

these still consist of comparatively simple, manually operated punch-card systems.[136] But there are indications that a computerized system is already being employed at the centre, by the Information Section of the C Department for Organizational–Party Work, and that similar electronic devices are projected for the regional party organizations.[137] The optimal utilization of this sophisticated equipment requires the standardization of reporting procedures throughout the system, and the local and regional conferences, seminars and training courses for information officials, which have been reported from various parts of the Soviet Union over the past few years, are probably directed to this end.[138] More importantly, such devices expand the capacity of the system to process incoming information far beyond present limits. One need not be haunted by visions of '1984' to assume that the party's potential for political control will be greatly enhanced as the result of continued innovation in information technology.[139]

[136] *Partiinaya zhizn'*, 1967, no. 8, pp. 32–3; 1969, no. 7, p. 7, no. 14, p. 37; 1972, no. 4, pp. 41–5; 1973, no. 18, pp. 41–2.
[137] *Kommunist*, 1969, no. 4, p. 62.
[138] See, e.g. *Partiinaya zhizn'*, 1968, no. 24, p. 61 and 1971, no. 22, pp. 67–8.
[139] It may be noted that the 24th Party Congress called for the improvement of intra-party information 'as an instrument of leadership, a means of upbringing and control'. See Brezhnev's Central Committee Report and the Congress Resolutions in *XXIV S'ezd*, vol. I, p. 120 and vol. II, p. 238. To the best of my knowledge this is the first such reference to the subject at a congress of the Soviet party.

9: CONCLUDING REMARKS

Writers on totalitarianism often cite Tocqueville's famous forebodings about the future of democracy. Tocqueville perceived, perhaps more clearly than any other nineteenth-century thinker, not only the expansion and concentration of public power, which are here taken as the defining characteristics of 'totalitarianism' – he wrote of the 'two-fold growth of power' – but also the phenomenon that has since come to be known as 'mass society': he foresaw, it will be recalled, 'an innumerable multitude of men, alike and equal', strangers to each other and servants of an all-powerful government that provided for their needs at the same time as it sapped their individuality.[1] In our own time this theme has been taken up by a variety of writers, from Ortega y Gasset to Herbert Marcuse, and some of them have linked it to the rise of totalitarianism. We are not here concerned with the forces in modern life that threaten to transform contemporary democracies into mass societies and thereby render them vulnerable to totalitarianism, only with the fact that totalitarianism itself exemplifies the state of massdom. Whether or not mass society is a necessary condition for totalitarianism it would certainly seem to be the case that totalitarianism is a sufficient condition for mass society. If in regard to the Nazis it may perhaps be argued that developments in German society before 1933 prepared the ground which enabled a totalitarian movement to mobilize available masses in order to achieve power, the experience of the Bolsheviks leaves no doubt of the will and the ability of a totalitarian movement, once in power, to create masses, to destroy the associations and attachments that bind people into groups and groups into society, and to expose the individual, alone and unprotected by the intermediate relationships of the social framework, to the full reach of public power.

It has been widely noted that totalitarian regimes differ from earlier forms of tyranny in that they are based on mass support

[1] *Democracy in America*, 2 vols., New York, 1966, vol. II, pp. 887 and 898–9.

or even mass enthusiasm. These formulations are misleading if they suggest free volition that is incompatible with totalitarian practice. In both the cases examined in this book, mass support was mobilized from above with the aid of overt and covert coercion. Such words as 'support', 'enthusiasm', 'consent', 'loyalty', 'allegiance' etc. – which, in the absence of suitable alternatives, were also employed in these pages – must be reinterpreted to fit the peculiar pattern of 'voluntary compulsion' which in the conditions of totalitarianism is inextricably woven into the fabric of all social action. Yet, the efficacy of this kind of support must not be underestimated. Millions of Germans killed and were killed for the greater glory of the Thousand-Year Reich; the Nazi regime collapsed with units of high-school boys fighting the enemy off outside the *Fuehrerbunker*. And millions of Soviet people have now for over half a century willingly borne the burdens and fulfilled the duties which the regime imposed upon them. Charles Merriam wrote that the 'days work is in a sense, a perpetual plebiscite in which the votes are not formally cast but in which the signs and symbols of assent and dissent are clearly understood by skilful observers'.[2] Judged by this 'plebiscite' the assent of the Soviet people to their regime must be pronounced indisputable. Of course, in any society, no matter how repressive and unpopular its government, certain autonomous forces are at work which ensure a minimal degree of compliance on the part of a large section of the governed population. Political indifference and inertia, sheer habit of obedience and conformism, career motivation, the bonds and responsibilities of family, adherence to values that transcend those of the current political rulers – all of these and others may help to explain the absence of disaffection on a scale that would have seriously threatened the cohesion of the Nazi and Soviet systems. Yet, even if allowance is made for these diffuse forces, the ability of modern totalitarianism to enlist mass support remains a remarkable achievement, precisely because it is accomplished by a process fundamentally intolerant to every manifestation of true spontaneity and independence.

I have earlier referred to the mobilization of the masses as a system of 'positive' controls, 'positive', because not confined to checking or restraining but characterized instead by a kind of pre-emptive activism. To be sure, activism meets other systems

[2] *Systematic Politics*, Chicago, 1945, p. 103.

needs besides those of control. In a sense all modern governments seek to harness the energies and talents of their peoples to societal action and may thus be said to 'mobilize' the resources of the society. Constitutional democracies do so through the mediation of free institutions and processes. Totalitarian governments, in attempting to meet the same needs, resort to a substitute – the controlled manipulation of 'voluntary compulsion'.[3] But this is only one side of the coin. What distinguishes totalitarian mobilization from similar efforts by other governments is not only that it is subject to control at all stages, but that control is itself a primary objective. The individual inducted into the system of pre-emptive activism is at the same time enmeshed by the network of political control. The latter is as much a function of the mobilization of the masses as the former. There is no way in which the two can be distinguished. William Kornhauser has argued that the behaviour of people who have been torn from their social moorings is 'highly unpredictable and potentially explosive'.[4] If this view is correct, it follows that a totalitarian regime is committed to control as a first task of self-preservation. Without control – Kornhauser speaks of 'control-in-depth' – societies ruled by totalitarian regimes would fall apart at the seams.[5]

In Nazi Germany and Soviet Russia, the party has served as the principal instrument of mass mobilization or positive control. Both parties combined from the outset a narrowly elitist attitude toward the masses, fostered and legitimated in each case by the respective doctrine, with a high degree of pragmatic orientation on mass action, and both achieved in due course thoroughgoing membership and organizational penetration into all strata of society. It was this mass base, forged together and led from a single centre with the aid of a professional apparatus, which has enabled the party to provide the necessary mixture of propaganda and organization in a single uninterrupted process and in a manner which rendered the effect of one almost indistinguishable

---

[3] The question of comparable efficiency is one which, in view of the cost in human lives and values involved, must surely remain beyond the bounds of calculability.

[4] *The Politics of Mass Society*, New York, 1959, p. 62.

[5] It has been suggested that mass mobilization in the Soviet Union may be conceived as a kind of 'public relations' by which the decisions of the leaders are 'sold' to the masses. It is that, of course, but it is also much more. (T. H. Rigby, 'Traditional, Market and Organizational Societies', in F. L. Fleron, Jr, ed., *Communist Studies and the Social Sciences: Essays on Methodology and Empirical Theory*, Chicago, 1969, p. 183.)

from that of the other. Each regime early recognized this two-dimensional capacity of its party and each exploited it with deliberate and essentially similar design.

There were, to be sure, differences in tactics, reflecting the different conditions that faced the two parties and the different resources that were at their disposal. Thus, for example, the Soviet regime's preoccupation with the problems of industrialization and economic development in general have led the party to concentrate its main propaganda effort on fostering such virtues as labour productivity and labour discipline. The Nazis, by contrast, were able to link the party's propaganda to themes more closely related to political loyalty and activism. Again, the relative backwardness of the Soviet Union, especially in the early years, and the drive to modernize which was the direct consequence of that condition, directed Soviet propaganda into the channels of oral agitation. To this day, the agitator, recently reinforced by the politinformator, constitutes the backbone of the Soviet party's 'mass-political work'. In Germany, the greater accessibility of the population to centrally-directed and comparatively sophisticated mass media reduced both the need and the opportunity for systematic personal and group agitation. It was sufficient for the party's forces to herd the people within the range of the mass media, to disseminate the morale-boosting slogans that largely made up Nazi *Mundpropaganda*, to counter rumours and subversive views, and generally to exemplify the moral and political norms of national socialist 'bearing' in everyday life.

But these and other differences noted in the preceding chapters must not be allowed to obscure the fundamental similarities in the strategy of party deployment vis-à-vis the people in Nazi Germany and Soviet Russia. In each case it was the task of the party both to transmit the demands of the regime and to ensure their execution by the people. Directly through its own outposts among the masses, the primary organizations of the CPSU and the blocks of the NSDAP, and indirectly through the mass organizations – trade unions, youth movements, sport and cultural associations, etc. – the totalitarian party is in a position to control and influence literally every member of the society. It is through the party that ordinary men and women in Nazi Germany and Soviet Russia have felt the weight of totalitarian power in their daily lives.

The role of totalitarian parties in the mobilization of the masses has been compared to that of armies in contemporary military regimes and even to the 'mobilization' of Prussian society by the

Hohenzollern army.[6] It is difficult to see how any army can perform a comparable role. If nothing else, armies are by their professional functions set apart from, if not above, the every-day concerns of the broad mass of the people. That military regimes have in modern times tried to found parties in order to create a mass base and enlist popular activism may be taken as evidence that their armies alone are poor mobilizing agents. That they have not notably succeeded in these endeavours – post-revolutionary Egypt's three attempts at party formation are cases in point – may be taken as some indication that their armies do not easily run in harness with mass parties.

Be that as it may, in the two regimes here examined it was the party which operated the ramified, dual-purpose system of totalitarian mass mobilization. And it did so in ways that were altogether similar. Differences in national culture and temperament and in the levels of socio-economic development necessarily played a part. The characteristic features of the totalitarian structure, however, were common to both regimes. Insofar, at least, as the role of the party in relation to the broad mass of the people is concerned, they imposed their own imperatives and produced similar tools and techniques, irrespective of differences in the blueprint, in the landscape, in the quality of the designers and of the human building material.

The Nazi system has mercifully passed into history. Hitler's 12-year reign of apocalyptic evil has left deep scars on the body of humanity and it is to be hoped that no nation, if it should ever find itself in the deplorable conditions that marked the last years of the Weimar Republic, will again be tempted to resort to a similar 'panacea'. The Soviet regime, however, is still with us. It has many undoubted achievements to its credit; it has already been imitated in other lands and it continues to be a source of attraction to people in all parts of the world. If thinking men cannot but view Nazi Germany as a wholly disastrous example of man's folly and depravity, they may well look upon the Soviet Union as an at least partly successful example of man's ability to achieve the goals of social and economic transformation which loom so large in the aspirations of mankind. The continued viability of Soviet totalitarianism is therefore a question of more than scholarly interest.

In recent years some observers have begun to regard the Soviet

6 G. Ionescu, *The Politics of the European Communist States*, London, 1967, pp. 68ff.

Union as evolving away from totalitarianism towards a form of moderate authoritarianism. The usual argument is that economic development and its associated features – growing material affluence, rational modes of thinking, urbanization, buraucratization, specialization, etc. – have eroded the foundations of totalitarianism. There is, moreover, a strong implication that this process, usually depicted as a 'self-sustaining process', will eventually lead toward a pluralist society under effective constitutional rules akin to Western democracies. I cannot share this view and the expectations built upon it. The example of Nazi Germany remains a powerful reminder of the compatibility of industrial civilization with totalitarianism. We are in danger of missing the principal lesson of the Nazi phenomenon if we ignore the ease with which rational means can be linked to irrational ends and the consequences which may result when the means are those of an advanced industrial nation. It is one of the paradoxes of the discussion about the future of Soviet totalitarianism that at the same time as some students of Soviet politics pin their faith on the allegedly moderating and liberalizing forces of economic progress, critics of our own societies are pointing to these self-same forces as the causes of alleged 'totalitarian tendencies' in the West. The whole question of the correlation between levels of socio-economic development and forms of government remains to be explored far more thoroughly than it has been. If it is true that stable democracy cannot be sustained without a relatively high level of socio-economic development, it does not follow that a high level of socio-economic development cannot be sustained without democracy. All too often in our discussions of development or modernization we link economic development to 'political development' and mean by the latter the kind of process that has led to representative democracies in the West.

Of course, part of the debate on the survival of totalitarianism in the Soviet Union hinges on the meaning of 'totalitarianism'. If the term is taken to be roughly equivalent to Stalinism then Soviet totalitarianism by definition ended with the death of Stalin. Certainly, a good case can be made for the view that in his lifetime the late dictator was himself the most salient 'contour' of the regime he headed, and that his unlamented departure has irrevocably altered the nature of Soviet politics. There can be no question that the abolition of the mass terror – to take but one outstanding development most clearly associated with Stalin's death – has made an enormous difference to the lives of Soviet people. On the other hand, if 'totalitarianism' refers, as it does in this book, to the scope and distribution of public power, then it seems equally undeniable that Soviet totalitarianism has changed hardly at all over the past fifty years or so. Public power in the Soviet system is still concentrated in the hands of a small leadership group and is still radiated outward to all spheres of social existence.

To recognize this underlying continuity is not to accept the diagnosis of 'petrification – or – degeneration' which some analysts have counterpoised to that of 'pluralism'.[7] Essentially, the protagonists of both views extrapolate from 'subterranean' processes in the socio-economic base to arrive at opposing conclusions concerning the present state and future evolution of Soviet politics. The 'surface' features of the political scene provide scant support for either view. That the present leaders of the Soviet Union have made mistakes, that they have failed to solve certain fundamental problems and neglected to take new initiatives, that they come from different (so-called 'bureaucratic') career backgrounds, are older and enjoy longer tenures than their predecessors – all this falls considerably short of a case for 'petrification', just as the fact that they are more concerned for the welfare of the population, more accessible to the advice and needs of different groups and somewhat more tolerant to peripheral manifestations of dissent, is not necessarily proof of their retreat in the face of pluralist pressures from the society. It is perhaps altogether natural that we should constantly be on the look-out for 'cracks in the monolith'. Doubtless the cracks can be found if one knows where to look for them. But they are no more than cracks and they have not so far affected the fundamental stability of the totalitarian structure. Some cracks, indeed, were always there – even at the height of Stalinism. It was our own 'idealization' of totalitarianism – understandable enough in view of the novelty of the phenomenon, the numerous difficulties in the way of objective inquiry and the Soviet leaders' own extravagant claims – which prevented us from seeing them. If new cracks have appeared since Stalin's death, old ones have

7 See on this the essays first published in *Problems of Communism* and since reprinted in Z. K. Brzezinski, ed., *Dilemmas of Change in Soviet Politics*, New York, 1969, esp. Brzezinski's own opening contribution to the discussion; also an article by J. F. Hough, 'The Soviet System: Petrification or Pluralism?', *Problems of Communism*, 1972, no. 2, pp. 25–45, which critically examines the main views on the petrification–pluralism spectrum and argues the case for a model of 'institutional pluralism'.

disappeared. The survival of the regime for two decades, without the supreme Leader and without the terror, its capacity to absorb continuous change in the socio-economic environment and to cope with a series of domestic and international crises, including crises of succession and what must have been a formidable, if self-inflicted, crisis of confidence engendered by the de-Stalinization campaign, surely demonstrates that it rests on institutional buttresses of great strength and flexibility.

The evidence adduced in the foregoing chapters does not permit wide-ranging assessment of the present state of Soviet politics; still less does it support speculation on the future of Soviet totalitarianism. The point that arises from the subject area discussed in this book and needs to be unequivocally stated is that there has been no let-up whatsoever in the Soviet party's efforts at mobilizing the masses. It must be taken as a measure of the resilience of Soviet totalitarianism that after fifty years in power the regime relies on mass mobilization and its built-in controls no less than it did in the early years when it was consolidating its hold on the country and embarking on the great projects of social and economic transformation. Indeed, in some respects mass mobilization has been expanded and intensified in the post-Stalin period. The party's organizational presence has been greatly augmented and its 'mass-political work' now extends more effectively than in the past beyond the factory and collective farm to the home and the private life of the Soviet citizen. The 'voluntary compulsion' of the party is incomparably milder than the straightforward compulsion of Stalin's police agencies. But by keeping 'everyone in sight of the collective' it has almost single-handedly succeeded in ensuring the system needs of control and compliance. Whether it will continue to do so as memory of the terror fades, the future alone will tell. There is no precedent for totalitarian 'voluntary compulsion' on which to base credible prediction. What we must guard against, however, is misreading the signs of the present. Soviet experience in the years since Stalin does not warrant generalizations to the effect that 'mass participation declines sharply' and 'may also assume more spontaneous forms' as a revolutionary single-party regime matures,[8] or that ' "spontaneous" mass demonstrations and "voluntary" participation in political study groups disappear

[8] S. H. Huntington, 'Social and Institutional Dynamics of One-Party Systems', in S. H. Huntington and C. E. Moore, eds., *Authoritarian Politics in Modern Society*, New York and London, 1970, p. 38.

from everyday life and the sphere of privacy and autonomous leisure, in which the party and its mass organizations do not normally intrude, is correspondingly extended'.[9]

The opening paragraph of these remarks quoted from Tocqueville's classic study of American democracy. It may be fitting to conclude with a quotation from another famous Frenchman, the Marquis de Custine, who travelled eastward at about the same time as Tocqueville went to the west. 'Tyranny', he wrote, summarizing his impressions of the reign of Nicholas I, 'invents only the means of consolidating itself.'[10]

[9] R. Lowenthal, 'Development vs. Utopia in Communist Policy', in Ch. Johnson, ed., *Change in Communist Systems*, Stanford, Calif., 1970, p. 113.

[10] *Journey for our Time*, translated and edited by P. P. Kohler. London, 1953, p. 229.

LIST OF SOURCES

UNPUBLISHED SOURCES

Materials from the following archives were utilized:
ACDJC Archives du Centre de Documentation Juive Contemporaine, Paris.
BA Bundesarchiv, Koblenz.
BDC Berlin Document Center, Berlin.
FO Library of the British Foreign Office, London.
NA National Archives, Washington, D.C. and Alexandria, Va.
WKP 'Smolensk Archives' (made available on microfilm by the Library of the British Foreign Office).

PUBLISHED SOURCES

Only sources relating directly to Nazi Germany and/or Soviet Russia and referred to in the footnotes of this book are listed below.

Ahlberg, A. 'Theorie der oeffentlichen Meinung und empirische Meinungs-forschung in der UdSSR', *Osteuropa*, 1969, no. 3.
Allen, W. S. *The Nazi Seizure of Power: The Experience of a Single German Town*, London, 1966.
Althaus, H. *Nationalsozialistische Volkswohlfahrt*, Berlin, 1935.
Amalrik, A. *Involuntary Journey to Siberia*, London, 1970.
Aptekman, D. M. 'Prichiny zhivuchesti religioznogo obryada kreshcheniya v sovremennykh usloviyakh', *Voprosy filosofii*, 1965, no. 3.
Arendt, H. *The Origins of Totalitarianism*, 2nd ed., New York, 1958.
Armstrong, M. 'The Campaign Against Parasites', in Juviler and Morton, eds., *Soviet Policy-Making*.
Baikova, V. G., Duchal, A. S. and Zemtsov, A. A. *Svobodnoe vremya i vsestoronee razvitie lichnosti*, Moscow, 1965.
Barber, B. R. 'Conceptual Foundations of Totalitarianism', in Friedrich, Curtis and Barber, *Totalitarianism in Perspective*.
Bauer, C. 'Das Puppentheater als Instrument politischer Fuehrung', *Unser Wille und Weg*, 1938, no. 11.
Beaumont, M., *et al. The Third Reich*, London, 1955.
Bekesh, V. I. and Balimasova, M. V. *Sotsiologiya i propaganda*, Leningrad, 1971.
Belkin, E. *Lektsionnaya propaganda v klube*, Moscow, 1953.
Belyakov, A. and Shvets, I. 'Informatsiya – deistvenny instrument partii-nogo rukovodstva', *Kommunist*, 1969, no. 4.
'Partiinaya informatsiya', *Partiinaya zhizn'*, 1967, no. 8.

Benn, David Wedgewood. 'New Thinking in Soviet Propaganda', *Soviet Studies*, 1969, no. 1.

Berghahn, V. R. *Der Stahlhelm: Bund der Frontsoldaten 1918–1935*, Duesseldorf, 1966.

Berman, H. J. *Justice in Russia*, Cambridge, Mass., 1968.

Bernsee, H. *Aufgaben der NS-Volkswohlfahrt im Kriege*, Berlin, 1941. [*Die*] *Betreutung des Dorfes*, Berlin, n.d.

Bilinsky, A. 'Novellierung der Parasitengesetze in der UdSSR', *Jahrbuch fuer Ostrecht*, 1965, no. 2.

Boberach, H., ed. *Berichte des SD und der Gestapo ueber Kirchen und Kirchenvolk in Deutschland 1934–1944*, Mainz, 1971.

Meldungen aus dem Reich. Auswahl aus den geheimen Lageberichten des Sicherheitsdienstes der SS 1939–1944, Neuwied and Berlin, 1965.

Boelcke, W. A., ed. *Kriegspropaganda 1939–41: Geheime Ministerkonferenzen im Reichspropagandaministerium*, Stuttgart, 1966. *'Wollt Ihr den totalen Krieg?' Die geheimen Goebbels-Konferenzen 1939–1943*, Stuttgart, 1967.

Bormann, M. 'Klopft an das deutsche Herz', *Die neue Gemeinschaft*, 1943, no. 1.

Bracher, K. D. *Die Aufloesung der Weimarer Republik*, Stuttgart and Duesseldorf, 1955.

Bramsted, E. K. *Goebbels and National Socialist Propaganda 1925–1945*, East Lansing, 1965.

Brovikov, V. I. and Popovich, I. V. *Sovremennye problemy politicheskoi informatsii i agitatsii*, Moscow, 1969.

Brzezinski, Z., ed. *Dilemmas of Change in Soviet Politics*, New York, 1969.

Bugaev, E. I. and Leibzon, B. M. *Besedy ob ustave KPSS*, Moscow, 1964.

Bullock, A. *Hitler. A Study in Tyranny*, rev. ed., London, 1962.

Burden, H. T. *The Nuremberg Party Rallies: 1923–39*, London, 1967.

Chkhikvadze, V. M., et al., eds. *Politicheskaya organizatsiya sovetskogo obshchestva*, 1967.

Childs, H. L., ed. *Propaganda and Dictatorship*, Princeton, 1936.

Curtiss, C. 'The Way People Live', in Salisbury, ed. *Anatomy of the Soviet Union*.

Datsyuk, B. D., ed. *Voprosy teorii i praktiki massovykh sredstv propagandy*, Moscow, 1969.

Denitch, B. 'Sociology in Eastern Europe', *Slavic Review*, 1971, no. 2.

Denkler, W. *Wie halte ich eine Betriebsversammlung ab oder einen Betriebsappell*, Berlin, n.d.

[*Das*] *Deutsche Hausbuch*, Berlin, 1943.

Deutsche Kriegsweihnachten, Berlin, 1943.

Diehl-Thiele, P. *Partei und Staat im Dritten Reich*, Munich, 1969.

Dietrich, O. *Die philosophischen Grundlagen des National Sozialismus*, Breslau, 1936.

Dohlhoff, G. H. and Schneefuss, G. H. *Handbuch der Gemeinschaftspflege*, Munich, 1939.

Doob, L. W. 'Goebbels' Principles of Propaganda', *Public Opinion Quarterly*, 1950, no. 3.

Dovifat, E. *Rede und Redner*, Leipzig, 1937.

Durham Hollander, G. *Soviet Political Indoctrination. Developments in Mass Media and Propaganda since Stalin*, New York, 1972.

Efimov, A. G. and Pozdnyakov, P. V. *Nauchnye osnovy partiinoi propagandy*, Moscow, 1966.

Eilers, R. Die nationalsozialistische Schulpolitik, Cologne and Opladen, 1963.

Eitze, W. Vom Wesen und den Formen der Schulung in der Ortsgruppe der NSDAP, Hamburg, 1941.

Erhard, F. 'Propaganda und Agitation', Unser Wille und Weg, 1938, no. 1.

Fabrizius, H. 'Organisatorischer Aufbau der NSDAP', in Lammers and Pfundtner, eds., Verwaltungsakademie, vol. I.

Fainsod, M. How Russia is Ruled, 2nd ed., Cambridge, Mass., 1963.

Smolensk under Soviet Rule, London, 1959.

Fedoseev, P. 'Vozrastanie roli partii', Kommunist, 1971, no. 15.

Feifer, G. Justice in Moscow, London, 1964.

Fleron, F. L., Jr, ed. Communist Studies and the Social Sciences: Essays on Methodology and Empirical Theory, Chicago, 1969.

Friedrich, C. J. and Brzezinski, Z. K. Totalitarian Dictatorship and Autocracy, Cambridge, Mass., 1956 and 1965.

Friedrich, C. J., Curtis, M. and Barber, B. R. Totalitarianism in Perspective: Three Views, London, 1969.

Friedrich, R. Zwei Jahre Tatsozialismus im Gau Duesseldorf, n.p., n.d.

Friedrichs, A. ed. Die Nationalsozialistische Revolution, Berlin, 1935. (Volume I of P. Meier-Benneckenstein, ed. Dokumente der Deutschen Politik.)

Gagarin, Yu. V. 'Izzhivanie religioznykh traditsii i formirovanie novykh prazdnichnykh obychaev v Komi ASSR', Sovetskaya etnografiya, 1965, no. 4.

Gamm, H. J. Der braune Kult, Hamburg, 1962.

[Die] Gaue und Kreise der NSDAP, Munich, 1943.

Gauweiler, O. Die Rechtseinrichtungen und Rechtsaufgaben der Bewegung, Munich, 1939.

Gilison, J. M. 'Soviet Elections as a Measure of Dissent: The Missing One Percent', Amer. Pol. Science Review, 1968, no. 3.

Glezerman, G. E., et al., eds. Voprosy teorii i praktiki kommunisticheskogo vospitaniya, Moscow, 1962.

and Afanas'ev. V. G., eds. Opyt i metodika konkretnykh sotsiologicheskikh issledovanii, Moscow, 1965.

Goebbels, J. Der Kampf um Berlin, Munich, 1934.

Signale der neuen Zeit, Munich, 1934.

Vom Kaiserhof zur Reichskanzlei, Munich, 1934.

Wesen und Gestalt des Nationalsozialismus, Berlin, 1935.

[The] Goebbels Diaries, edited and translated by L. P. Lochner, London, 1948.

Gohdes, O. 'Der neue deutsche Mensch', Schulungsbrief, 1934, no. 7.

Griffith, F. 'A Tendency Analysis of Soviet Policy-Making', in Skilling and Griffith, eds., Interest Groups in Soviet Politics.

Groshev, I. I., et al., eds. Iz opyta ideologicheskoi raboty partiinykh organizatsii, Moscow, 1965.

Grunberger, R. A Social History of the Third Reich, London, 1971.

Grushin, B. A. 'K probleme kachestvennoi reprezentatsii v vyborochnom oprose', in Glezerman and Afanas'ev, eds., Opyt i metodika konkretnykh sotsiologicheskikh issledovanii.

Mnenya o mire i mir mnenii, Moscow, 1967.

Svobodnoe vremya, Moscow, 1967.

Guillebaud, C. W. The Social Policy of Nazi Germany, Cambridge, 1941.

Gutachten des Instituts fuer Zeitgeschichte, Munich, 1957.

Gutterer, L. 'Der 1. Mai in der Reichshauptstadt und im Reich', *Unser Wille und Weg*, 1936, no. 4.

Hadamovsky, E. *Propaganda und nationale Macht: Die Organisation der oeffentliechen Meinung.* Oldenburg, 1933.

Haegermann, G. *Die Arbeit der Partei fuer den deutschen Menschen,* Berlin, 1940.

Hagemann, W. *Publizistik im Dritten Reich,* Hamburg, 1948.

Harcave, S. *Structure and Functioning of the Lower Party Organizations in the Soviet Union,* Maxwell Air Force Base, Alabama, 1954.

Harper, S. N. *Civic Training in Soviet Russia,* Chicago, 1929.

[Die] *Heldenehrungsfeier der NSDAP,* Berlin, 1942.

Herman, S W. *It's Your Souls We Want,* London, 1943.

Heyen, F. J. *Nationalsozialismus im Alltag,* Boppard-on-Rhine, 1967.

Hilbig, E. 'Sind Feierstunden notwendig?' *Unser Wille und Weg,* 1939, no. 7.

Hilgenfeld, E. *Aufgaben der nationalsozialistischen Wohlfahrtspflege,* Munich, 1937.

Hippel, F. von. *Die nationalsozialistische Herrschaftsordnung als Warnung und Lehre,* Tuebingen, 1946.

Hitler, A. *Mein Kampf,* Munich, 1930.

Hoehne, H. *Der Orden unter dem Totenkopf,* Guetersloh, 1967.

Horn, W. *Fuehrerideologie und Parteiorganisation (1919–1933),* Duesseldorf, 1972.

Hough, J. F. *The Soviet Prefects,* Cambridge, Mass., 1969.
'The Soviet System: Petrification or Pluralism?', *Problems of Communism,* 1972, no. 2.

Huber, E. R. *Das Verfassungsrecht des Grossdeutschen Reichs,* Hamburg, 1939.

Huettenberger, P. *Die Gauleiter. Studie zum Wandel des Machtgefueges in der NSDAP,* Stuttgart, 1969.

Huntington, S. H. 'Social and Institutional Dynamics of One-Party Systems', in Huntington, S. H. and Moore, C. H., eds. *Authoritarian Politics in Modern Society,* New York and London, 1970.

Inkeles, A. *Public Opinion in Soviet Russia,* Cambridge, Mass., 1950 and 1967.

Ionescu, G. *The Politics of the European Communist States,* London, 1967.

Iovchuk, M. T. et al., eds. *Problemy sovremennoi ideologicheskoi borby, razvitiya sotsialisticheskoi ideologii i kul'tury,* Moscow, 1972.

Ipsen, H. P. 'Vom Begriff der Partei', *Zeitschrift fuer die gesamte Staatswissenschaft,* 1940, no. 4.

Irwahn, F. *Betriebsappelle und Kameradschaftsabende,* Hamburg, 1936.

Istoriya Kommunisticheskoi Partii Sovetskogo Soyuza, Moscow, 1962.

Johnson, Ch., ed. *Change in Communist Systems,* Stanford, Calif., 1970.

Juviler, P. H. and Morton, H. W., eds. *Soviet Policy-Making.* New York, 1967.

Kabanov, A. T. 'Leninskii printsip svyazi propagandy s zhiznyu', in Groshev et. al., eds., *Iz opyta ideologicheskoi raboty partiinykh organizatsii.*

Kalinin, M. I. *On Communist Education,* Moscow, 1949.
Rechi i Stati 1919–1935, Moscow, 1936.

Kersten, F. *Totenkopf und Treue,* Hamburg, 1952.

Kharchev, A. 'Sem'ya i kommunizm,' *Kommunist,* 1960, no. 7.

Klimov, N. *Rabochi den' v obshchestve stroyashchem kommunizma, Moscow,* 1961.

Klochko, V. F. *Partiya i massovye organizatsii trudyashchikhsya*, Moscow, 1967.

Kol'banovskii, V. N. and Sherkovin, Yu. A., comp. *Problemy sotsial'noi psikhologii i propaganda*, Moscow, 1971.

Kommunist. *Kalendar'-spravochnik 1968*, Moscow, 1967.

Kommunisticheskaya Partiya Sovetskogo Soyuza v rezolyutsiyakh i resheni-yakh s'ezdov, konferentsii i plenumov Ts. K., 7th ed., 4 vols., Moscow, 1954–60.

[*Der*] *Kongress zu Nuernberg vom 5 bis 10 September 1934. Offizieller Bericht ueber den Verlauf des Reichsparteitages mit saemtlichen Reden*, Munich, 1934.

Kordt, E. *Wahn und Wirklichkeit*, Stuttgart, 1947.

KPSS. Naglyodnoe posobie po partiinomu stroitel'stvu, Moscow, 1969.

Krausnick, H. Buchheim, H., Broszat, M. Jacobson, H.-J. *Anatomy of the SS State*, London, 1968.

Kremer, H. 'Schluss mit dem Pappendeckelzauber', *Unser Wille und Weg*, 1939, no. 22.

Krianev, Yu. V. and Popov, P. S. 'Emotsional'noe vozdeistviya religioznoi obryadnosti i ego preodolenie', *Voprosy filosofii*, 1963, no. 9.

Kryvelev, I. 'Vazhnaya storona byta', *Kommunist*, 1960, no. 8.

Kuliev, T. A. *Problema interesov v sotsialisticheskom obshchestve*, Moscow, 1967.

Kurochkin, P. 'Aktual'nye problemy nauchnogo issledovaniya ideologicheskoi raboty', *Kommunist Sov. Latvii*, 1972, no. 6.

'Sredstva massovoi informatsii i propagandy i ikh rol' v formirovanii novogo cheloveka', in Iovchuk *et al.*, eds., *Problemy sovremennoi ideologicheskoi borby*.

et al., eds. *Voprosy teorii i metodov ideologicheskoi raboty*, Vyp. 1, Moscow, 1972.

Kuryanov, M. 'Organizatsionny formy politicheskoi raboty v massakh', *Agitator*, 1968, no. 12.

'O spetsializatsii politinformatorov', *Agitator*, 1967, no. 24.

Lammers, H. H. and Pfundtner, H., eds. *Die Verwaltungsakademie. Ein Handbuch fuer Beamten im Deutschen Staat*, 4 vols., Berlin-Vienna, 1936–9.

Lapin, V. A. 'Osnovnye puti sochetaniya ideino-vospitatel'noi raboty na proizvodstve i v bytu', in Groshev et al., eds., *Iz opyta ideologicheskoi raboty partiinykh organizatsii*.

Latour, C. 'Goebbels' "Ausserordentliche Rundfunkmassnahmen" 1939–1942', *Vierteljahrshefte fuer Zeitgeschichte*, 1963, October.

Lenin, V. I. *Polnoe Sobranie Sochinenii*, 5th ed., 55 vols., Moscow, 1967–1970.

Leonhard, W. 'Adoption of the New Party Programme', in Schapiro, ed., *The USSR and the Future*.

Ley, R. *Der Weg zur Ordensburg*, Der Reichsorganisationsleiter, n.d., n.p.

Lingg, A. *Die Verwaltung der Nationalsozialistischen Deutschen Arbeiterpartei*, Munich, 1939.

Lipson, L. 'Hosts and Pests: The Fight against Parasites', *Problems of Communism*, 1965, no. 2.

'Law: The Function of Extra-Judicial Mechanisms', in Treadgold, ed., *Soviet and Chinese Communism*.

Lowenthal, R. 'Development vs. Utopia in Communist Policy', in Johnson, ed., *Change in Communist Systems*.

Lueddecke, Th. *Menschenfuehrung in den Betrieben*, Hamburg, 1934.
Lukinskii, F. A. 'Ob opyte partiinykh organizatsii po ateisticheskomu vospitaniyu mass v sovremennykh usloviyakh', in Glezerman, *et al.*, eds., *Voprosy teorii i praktiki kommunisticheskogo vospitaniya.*
Luxemburg, R. *Leninism or Marxism*, Glasgow, 1935.
Malyshev, I. V. 'Edinstvo partii i naroda – istochnik nesokrushimoi sily sovetskogo obshchestva', *Voprosy istorii KPSS*, 1972, no. 1.
Marchenko, A. *My Testimony*, London, 1969.
Marx, F. M. 'State Propaganda in Nazi Germany', in Childs, ed., *Propaganda and Dictatorship.*
Marx, K. *Enthuellungen ueber den Kommunisten Prozess zu Koeln*, introduced and annotated by F. Mehring, Berlin, 1914.
Marx, K. and Engels, F. *Letters to Americans*, New York, 1953.
   Selected Works, 2 vols., Moscow, 1951.
   Werke, 41 vols., Berlin, 1958–68.
Matthews, M. *Class and Society in Soviet Russia*, London, 1972.
Mazhidov, R. M. 'Puty preodoleniya religioznoi obryadnosti', *Voprosy filosofii*, 1967, no. 7.
Mehringer, H. *Die NSDAP als politische Ausleseorganisation*, Munich, 1938.
Meier-Benneckstein, P., ed. – later F. A. Six – *Dokumente der deutschen Politik*, 8 vols., Berlin, 1935–43.
Mennecke, K. *Ein westdeutscher NSV-Kreis* (Diss.), Cologne, 1936.
Meyer, A. G. *Leninism*, Cambridge, Mass., 1957.
Mickiewicz, E. Propper. 'The Modernization of Party Propaganda in the USSR', *Slavic Review*, 1971, no. 2.
   Soviet Political Schools, New Haven, Conn., 1967.
Morozov, M. A. *Massovo-politicheskaya rabota partiinykh organizatsii*, Moscow, 1967.
Mozhayev, P. P. *Traditsii – sredstvo vospitaniya novogo cheloveka*, Leningrad, 1968.
Mundt, W. M. 'Die Ortsgruppe feiert', *Unser Wille und Weg*, 1936, no. 7.
Murasheva, V. I. and Romanov, N. I., eds. *Torzhestvenno, krasivo, pamyatno!* Moscow, 1966.
Neesse, G. 'DieVerfassungsrechtliche Gestaltung der Ein-Partei', *Zeitschrift fuer die gesamte Staatswissenschaft*, 1938, no. 4.
Netsenko, A. V. *Svobodnoe vremya i ego vospol'zovanie*, Leningrad, 1964.
Niemoeller, W. *Kampf und Zeugnis der Bekennenden Kirche*, Bielefeld, 1948.
Organisationsbuch der NSDAP, Munich, 1943.
Orlow, D. *The History of the Nazi Party: 1919–1933*, Pittsburgh, 1969.
Pachter, H. M. 'National-Socialist and Fascist Propaganda in the Conquest of Power', in Beaumont *et al.*, *The Third Reich.*
Partei-Statistik, Der Reichsorganisationsleiter, 4 vols., n.d., n.p.
Partiinoe stroitel'stvo. Naglyadnoe posobe, Moscow, 1971.
Petukhov, A. 'Bumazhnye tsvety', *Novyi mir*, 1969, no. 6.
Picker, H. *Hitlers Tischgespraeche im Fuehrerhauptquartier 1941–42*, edited by P. E. Schram *et al.*, Stuttgart, 1963.
Plekhanov, G. V. *Sochineniya*, 8 vols., Moscow, 1923.
Plenum Tsentral'nogo Komiteta Kommunisticheskoi Partii Sovetskogo Soyuza, 15–19 dekabrya 1958 g. Stenograficheskii otchet, Moscow, 1958.
Po mestu zhitel'stva . . ., Moscow, 1967.
Pokorny, K. *Kommentar zum Gesetz zur Befreiung von Nationalsozialismus und Militarismus*, Frankfurt, 1947.

Popov, G. I. 'Konkretnye sotsial'nye issledovaniya v praktike ideologicheskoi raboty', in *Sotsiologiya v SSSR*.

Pospelov, P. N. *et al.*, eds. *Istoriya Kommunisticheskoi Partii Sovetskogo Soyuza*, 6 vols., Moscow, 1964–

Powell, D. 'The Effectiveness of Soviet Anti-Religious Propaganda', *Public Opinion Quarterly*, 1967, no. 3.

Prigozhin, A. I. 'Metodologicheskie problemy issledovania obshchestvennogo mnenya', *Voprosy filosofii*, 1969, no. 2.

Programmy i ustavy KPSS, Moscow, 1969.

Rang und Organisationsliste der NSDAP, Stuttgart, n.d. (1946?).

Rauschning, H. *Hitler Speaks*, London, 1939.

Riess, H. 'Stadt und Land feiern gemeinsamen Erntedank', *Unser Wille und Weg*, 1937, no. 2.

Rigby, T. H. 'Crypto Politics', *Survey*, 1964, January (no. 50).

 'Traditional, Market and Organizational Societies and the USSR', in Fleron, Jr, ed., *Communist Studies and the Social Sciences*.

Ritter, G. *The German Resistance*, London, 1958.

Rodionov, P. A. *et al.*, eds. *Problemy partiinogo stroitel'stva*, Moscow, 1972.

Roehm, E. 'Die braunen Bataillione der deutschen Revolution', *NS-Monatshefte*, 1934, no. 46.

Rosenberg, A. *Gestaltung der Idee. Reden und Aufsaetze von 1933–1935*. Munich, 1936.

 Der Mythus des XX Jahrhunderts, Munich, 1930.

Roth, H. *Die Feier. Sinn und Gestaltung*, Leipzig, 1939.

Ruthe, W. *Der Nationalsozialismus in seinen Programmpunkten, Organisationsformen und Aufbaumassnahmen*, Frankfurt, 1937.

Salisbury, H. E., ed. *Anatomy of the Soviet Union*, London, 1967.

Scanlan, R. 'The Nazi Rhetorician', *Quarterly Journal of Speech*, 1951, December.

Schacht, H. *My First Seventy-Six Years*, London, 1955.

Schaefer, W. *NSDAP. Entwicklung und Struktur der Staatspartei des Dritten Reiches*, Hanover and Frankfurt, 1956.

Schapiro, L., ed. *The USSR and the Future*, New York and London, 1963.

Schmeer, K. *Die Regie des oeffentlichen Lebens im Dritten Reich*, Munich, 1956.

Schmidt, O. *Volkstumarbeit als politische Aufgabe*, Hamburg, 1943.

Schnitzler, H. and Boss, A., eds. *Das Feierbuch der deutschen Sippe*, Berlin, 1941.

Schoenbaum, D. *Hitler's Social Revolution: Class and Status in Nazi Germany 1933–1939*, London, 1967.

Scholz, W. 'Der Tanz in der Dorfarbeit', *Schulungsbrief*, 1938, no. 7.

Schuette, M. *Politische Werbung und totalitaere Propaganda*, Duesseldorf, 1968.

Schwarz von Berk, *Die sozialistische Auslese*, Breslau, 1934.

Schweitzer, A. *Big Business in the Third Reich*, Bloomington, Indiana, 1964.

XX S'ezd Kommunisticheskoi Partii Sovetskogo Soyuza 14–25 fevralya 1956 goda. Stenograficheskii otchet, 2 vols., Moscow, 1956.

[*Vneocherednoi*] *XXI S'ezd Kommunisticheskoi Partii Sovetskogo Soyuza 27 yanvarya – 5 fevralya 1959 goda. Stenograficheskii otchet*, 2 vols., Moscow, 1959.

XXII S'ezd Kommunisticheskoi Partii Sovetskogo Soyuza 17–31 oktyabrya 1961 goda, Stenograficheskii otchet, 3 vols., Moscow, 1962.

XXIII S'ezd Kommunisticheskoi Partii Sovetskogo Soyuza 29 marta – 8 aprelya 1966 goda. Stenograficheskii otchet, 2 vols., Moscow, 1966.

Shikov, R. S. 'Partiya i narod v period stroitel'stva kommunizma', in Suvorov *et al.*, *Partiya i massy.*

Short History of the Communist Party of the Soviet Union (Bolsheviks), London, 1943.

Shtraks, G. M. *Sotsial'noe edinstvo i protivorechiya sotsialisticheskogo obshchestva*, Moscow, 1966.

Shvets I. A. 'Vnutripartiinaya informatsiya kak instrument rukovodstva, sredstvo vospitaniya i kontrol'ya, in Rodionov *et. al.*, eds., *Problemy partiinogo stroitel'stva.*

Sington, D. and Weidenfeld, A. *The Goebbels Experiment*, London, 1942.

Skilling, G. and Griffiths, F., eds. *Interest Groups in Soviet Politics*, Princeton, 1970.

Smyshlaev, V. A., *et al.*, eds. *KPSS v period stroitel'stva kommunizma*, Leningrad, 1967.

Soehngen, O. *Saekulasierter Kultus, Guetersloh*, 1950.

Sommer, W. 'Die NSDAP als Verfassungstraegerin', in Lammers and Pfundtner, eds., *Verwaltungsakademie.*

Sotsiologya v SSSR, Moscow, 1965.

Speer, A. *Inside the Third Reich*, London, 1971.

Spravochnik partiinogo rabotnika, Moscow, 1959–70.

Sprovochnik propagandista i agitatora, Moscow, 1966.

Spravochnik sekretarya pervichnoi partiinoi organizatsii, Moscow, 1960, 1964, 1967.

Stalin, J. *Problems of Leninism*, Moscow, 1954.

Statistisches Jahrbuch fuer des Deutsche Reich, Berlin, 1940, 1942.

Stein, G. H. *The Waffen SS*, Ithaca, N.Y., 1966.

Steinert, M. G. *Hitler's Krieg und die Deutschen*, Duesseldorf and Vienna, 1970.

Stepakov, V. I. *Partiinoi propagande – nauchnye osnovy*, Moscow, 1967.

Stepanov, V. 'Partiya i kommunizm', *Kommunist*, 1967, no. 8.

Steward, J. S. *Sieg des Glaubens*, Zurich, 1946.

Stoermer, H. *Das rechtliche Verhaeltnis der NS-Volkswohlfahrt und des Winterhilfswerkes zu den Betreuten im Vergleich zur oeffentlichen Wohlfahrtspflege*, Berlin, 1940.

Studentkovsky, K. 'Warum nationalsozialistische Morgenfeiern?' *Unser Wille und Weg*, 1939, no. 12.

Suvorov, K. I., *et al. Partiya i massy*, Moscow, 1966.

Tarasov, Yu. I. 'O edinstve ideologicheskoi i organizatorskoi raboty v kommunisticheskom vospitanii mass', in Smyshlyaev *et al.*, eds., *KPSS v period stroitel'stva kommunizma.*

Treadgold, D. W., ed. *Soviet and Chinese Communism: Similarities and Differences*, Seattle and London, 1967.

[The] *Trial of the Major War Criminals before the International Military Tribunal*, 42 vols., Nuremberg, 1947–49.

Trotsky, L., *The History of the Russian Revolution*, 3 vols., London, 1932–1933.

Uledov, A K. *Obshchestvennoe mnenie sovetskogo obshchestva*, Moscow, 1963.

Unger, A. L. 'Politinformator or Agitator: A Decision Blocked', *Problems of Communism*, 1970, no. 5.

Verfuegungen Anordnungen, Bekanntgaben, Partei-Kanzlei der NSDAP, 6 vols., Munich, 1943–4.

[*Das*] *Volksspiel im nationalsozialistischen Gemeinschaftsleben*, Munich, n.d.
Vollmer, B. *Volksopposition im Polizeistaat: Gestapo und Regierungsberichte 1934–36*, Stuttgart, 1957.
Volz, H. *Daten der Geschichte der NSDAP*, Berlin-Leipzig, 1943.
 ed. *Von der Grossmacht zur Weltmacht 1937*, Berlin, 1938. (Vol. III of P. Meier-Benneckenstein, ed., *Dokumente der deutschen Politik*.)
Voprosy ideologicheskoi raboty partii, Moscow, 1966.
Voprosy partiinoi raboty, Moscow, 1959.
Vorontsov, G. V. 'Ateisticheskoe vospitanie – sostavnaya chast' ideologicheskoi raboty partii na sovremennom estape', in Smyshlyaev *et. al.*, eds, *KPSS v period stroitel'stva kommunizma*.
Weizsaecker, E. von. *Erinnedungen*, Munich, 1950.
Witetschek, H., ed. *Die Kirchliche Lage in Bayern nach den Regierungspraesidentenberichten 1933–1943*, 2 vols., Mainz, 1966, 1967.
Wolfe, B. D. *Communist Totalitarianism*, 2nd rev. ed., Boston, 1961.
Wulff, E. *Das Winterhilfswerk des Deutschen Volkes*, Berlin, 1940.
Yanowitch, M. 'Soviet Patterns of Time Use and Concepts of Leisure', *Soviet Studies*, 1963, no. 1.
Zergiebel, K 'Der Propagandaleiter und der 1. Mai', *Unser Wille und Weg*, 1939, no. 3.
Zhuravlev, G. T. and Seregin, A. S. 'Materialy konkretnogo sotsiologicheskogo issledovaniya ideino-vospitatel'noi raboty', in Kurochkin *et al.*, eds., *Voprosy teorii i metodov ideologicheskoi raboty*.

INDEX

Aachen-Land, 230
Adzhubei, A., 54
agitation, 31; importance of, in Soviet Union, 50–2; Lenin on, 108; in Nazi terminology, 33n; Plekhanov on, 32–3. *See also* agitators, propaganda
agitators, 51–2, 151, 152, 266; and atheist propaganda, 125, 131–2, 136, 140; attempted replacement of 148–9; *besedy* of 119–25, 132, 143, 261; contact with masses, 115–16, 133–4; criticisms of 142–7; deployment, 113–14, 133; and elections, 126–7, 143; 'individual work' of, 125, 133–8, 154; and mass campaigns, 127–8; number of 112–13; and opinion leaders, 139–41; and oratorial skills, 54, 116; as organizers, 116–18, 149–50; and party organizations, 114, 143–4; and production tasks, 118, 120, 124–5; and residential mass-political work, 128–39, 144; role conflicts of 141–2; selection and training of, 113–16, 145; and social deviants, 131–3, 137–8, 144–5; and sociological surveys, 140n, 146–7, 159n; speculation of, 140–1; and visual agitation, 126, 144, 146n; and welfare work, 217–18; and youth, 125, 130, 140
agitkollektivy, 114
agitkvartir, 132
agitploshchadki, 132
agitpunkty, 127, 128, 132
Akimov, V. P., 29
Allen, W. S., 45n
'anti-parasite' legislation, 68n
Arendt, H., 81
armies, as mobilizing agents, 266–7

army, German, 91, 99, 223, 226–7, 233, 244, 246
Azerbaidjan, 196

Baden, 222n, 223, 224, 238
Baibakov, N. L., 162
Bakunin, M. A., 28n
Barber, B. R., 1
Belgorod, 137
Belyakov, A., 257n
Betreung, 204
Betriebsappel, 52
Bettelheim, B., 87n
block leaders, 99–104, 208, 212, 214. *See also under* Nazi party
block wardens, 80
Boards of Shame, 126
Bolte, F., 28
Bormann, M., 76, 95n, 96, 211n, 213, 232–3; on 'cultural work', 170, 181; on 'death celebration', 178; and SD, 244–5, 247, 248n
Brauchtum, 176, 201
Brezhnev, L. I., 65n; on free time, 188n; on party, 17–18, 108n, 109n, 110–11; on party reporting, 262n; on propaganda, 36–7
Brigades for Co-operation with the Militia, 67
Bureau for Civil Ceremonies, 193
business associations, German, 73n

call evenings, 92
cemetery festivals, 198
Central Control Commission, 253
Chelyabinsk, 159
Chernyshevsky, N. G., 28
Chief Organizer of Festivals, 193, 220
citizens' letters, 217
Civil Registry Office (ZAGS), 200
collective farmers, 106

281

collectivization, 252, 255
Coming-of-Age Festival, 199
commemoration ceremonies, 197–8
Committee of People's Control, 65n, 259
Communist Customs' Council, 193
Communist Labour Brigade, 196
Communist Manifesto, 26–7
Communist party: activism of members, 107–12, 129; Brezhnev on, 17–18, 109n, 110–11; Central Committee, 23, 34, 36, 127, 128, 143n, 146, 253, 261; central departments and sections, 36, 54, 113, 115, 148, 159 257n, 262; Conference (18th) 119n; Congresses, (2nd) 29, (8th) 24, (10th) 8, (13th) 108n, (20th) 35, 70, (21st) 35, 66, (22nd) 35, 69, 109n, (23rd) 150–1, (24th) 17n, 110, 262n; district committees, 156; 'growing role' of 15–17; Khrushchev on 16, 18, 109n; Lenin on, 8, 13, 15, 19–21, 27–9, 109; local leaders as patrons, 216–17; and mass organizations, 61–5, 266; membership, 48, 105–7, 109–10; party groups, 70–1, 81, 156; political studies programme, 34n; primary organizations, 69–71, 129–130, 156, 266; Programme (1961), 16–17, 34, 182; shop organizations, 70–1, 80; Statutes, 61n, 69,, 70, 108n, 124n, 129
comrades' courts, 65–6, 68–9, 131, 137–8
Conference-Seminar of ideological workers (1966), 148, 150n, 151
Conscience Books, 126
Constituent Assembly, 23n, 44
Constitution, Soviet, 19, 61–2
CPSU, *see* Communist party
Custine, Marquis de, 271

Darmstadt, 230
Darré, W., 172, 181
defeatism, Nazi leaders' fear of, 247–50
democratic centralism, 11
Dietrich, O., 25
Dmitryuk, A., 159
Doenitz Government, 247
Donetsk, 145, 147

DOSAAF, 64

Egypt, 267
elections: Nazi, 44, 86; Soviet: 21n, 44, 126–7
electors' clubs, 127
elitism, 25–6
Ellul, J., 167n
Engels, F., 26–8
Estonia, 190, 195, 198
Extraordinary Congress of Peasant Deputies (1917), 23n

Family Chronicles, 196
family circles, 256
family evenings, 178–9, 184–5
foreign broadcasts, restrictions applied to Nazi leaders, 258
Flensburg, 236
foreign newspapers, control of subscriptions to of Nazi leaders, 248
Frankfurt, 230
Freiburg, 231
Frick, W., 15
Friedrichs, H., 76, 97n
Fuehrerprinzip, 11

Galen, F. von, 211n
Georgia, 197
Gestapo, 102n, 103, 227, 230–1, 239, 243
German Home Guard, 73, 75–6
German Labour Front (DAF), 52, 72–3, 74n, 77, 80, 99, 171, 223, 232, 248n
German Women's Union, 73, 75
Giesler, P., 15
Goebbels, J., 175, 179n; on commemoration ceremonies, 177; on defeatism, 239, 237–9; and foreign broadcasts, 47n; on masses, 10; on Nazi programme, 41; on party, 14, 243; on propaganda, 33–4; public confidence in, 243, 347n; on public opinion reports, 246–7; on word-of-mouth propaganda, 91–2; and WHW, 208–9
Goerdeler, K., 42n
Goering, H., 75, 77
Gorlovsk, 160
Groups for the Protection of Public Order, 67
Grushin, B. A., 58n

Hadamovsky, E., 61
Harvest Festival, 172
Hess, R., 77, 102, 224n
Hessen-Nassau, 222n, 230, 233, 241
Heydrich, R., 243n
Hilgenfeld, E., 205, 207, 211n
Himmler, H., 76, 232, 243n,, 246–7, 249
Hitler, A., 26, 172, 211n, 212, 248n; on 'cult activities', 176; on dictatorship of the *Volk*, 19; on ideology, 41–2; on masses, 9–10, 20–1, 40n, 42n; *Mein Kampf*, 9, 46, 76n; on organization 11, 72, 78; on party, 12–14, 18, 20–1, 234; on party recruitment, 84n, 95n; on public opinion, 247n; and WHW, 208
Hitler Youth (HJ), 73–5, 77, 91, 94, 236
houseboards, 212
household index, 101–2
Houses of Civil Ritual, 194

ideology, 38–43
Ilyichev, L. F., 65, 136
indirect propaganda, 52, 167–70
Nazi: and communal recreation, 171; and 'counter-ceremonies', and 'cultivation of customs', 176; effectiveness of, 179–82; and 'family evenings', 178; and 'life celebrations', 176–8; and 'morning celebrations', 174–5; and mourning ritual, 173–4, 177–8; and public holidays, 171–2; and religious traditions, 172–3
Soviet: and amateur groups, 185–6; and 'civil confirmation', 199; and commemoration ceremonies, 197–8; effectiveness of, 201–3; and family ceremonies, 194–5; and Komsomol, 190, 192–3; and leisure, 182–4, 187–9; and 'new traditions', 190, 202n; and public holidays and festivals, 189–0, 196–7; shortcomings of, 199–201
information sections, 257n, 259. See *also* public opinion reporting, Soviet
informatsionnaya svodka, 251. See

also public opinion reporting, Soviet
Inland Service, *see* SD
interest articulation, in Soviet Union, 62–4
International Labour Day, 171
Italy, 91
Izhevsk, 261

Jews, Nazi opinion reports on, 228, 232, 240–1

Kalinin, M. I., 21n, 204
Kaltenbrunner, E., 232, 243–5
Kazakhstan, 188n
Keitel, W., 213n
Khabarovsk, 200
Kharman-toi, 197
Khrushchev, N. S., 66, 68n; on control, 65; criticisms of, 36; on party, 16, 18, 109n; and propaganda, 35–6, 53–4
Khudaiberdyev, Ya., 197
Kiel, 237
Kiev, 185n
Kitzingen, 236
Komnata politicheskoi agitatsii, 132
Komsomol, 61n, 65, 67, 129, 186–7, 189–90, 193, 199–200, 219–20, 259
Kordt, E., 102n
Kornhauser, W., 265
Krasnodarsk, 146, 160
Krasnoyarsk, 187
Kuibyshev, 128, 136
kulaks, 253
Kuryanov, M. S., 147, 151, 152n, 160–1
Kyffhaeuser Bund, 76

Lassalle, F., 28n
Latvia, 190, 195, 198–9
Left Opposition, 40
Leibholz, G., 1
Leipzig trial, 41n
leisure, 168–70, 182–4, 187–8
Lenin, V.I.: on agitation, 108; critics of, 29; and masses, 6–8, 15, 20–4; on NEP, 41n; on party, 8, 11–13, 15, 19–21, 27–9, 109; on propaganda, 24, 34–6, 40n; on revolutions, 20, 22–4; *What Is to be Done?*, 8, 28n
Leninism, 6–8

Leningrad, 67, 146, 194, 200
Ley, R. 10, 39, 72, 77–8, 80, 179n, 232, 248n, 249
life celebrations, 176–8
'lightening bolts', 126
Linz, 213
Lohse, H., 238
Luxemburg, R., 29

Mainfranken, 211, 236
Marchenko, A., 143n
Marcuse, H., 263
Marx, K., 26–8
Masherov, P. M., 36, 201
mass organizations, Soviet, 61–5
mass society, 263
Mensheviks, 29
Merriam, Ch., 264
Meyer, A., 211n
mobilization, 5, 30–1, 43, 50, 81–2, 265–7
Model Kolkhoz Charter, 153
Moldavia, 134
morale reports, *see* public opinion reports, Nazi
morning celebrations, 174–5
Morozov, M. A., 36, 118, 132
Moscow, 112n, 113n, 148, 160, 185, 197
Mundpropaganda, 89–93, 266
Munich, 225, 232

Nazi party: activism of members, 88–95, 98–9; affiliated organizations, 72–9; 'call evenings', 92; cells, 80, 92; Chancellory, 204, 209, 213, 223–4, 226–7, 233–4, 243–4, 246; and Churches, 94; and elite groups, 84–5; functionaries, 74, 77, 87n, 93; Goebbels on, 14, 243; *Heil Hitler!* salute, 87, 96; Hitler on, 12–14, 18, 20–1, 84n, 95n, 234; local group, 80, 92, 101; membership, 48, 83–4, 95; as movement, 13; Office for Civil Servants, 211; Office for Peasants, 238; 'old fighters', 84; primary organization (*Block*), 74, 79–81, 266; projected purge, 95n; rallies, 88, 98; Reich Directorate, 74; Reich Propaganda Office, 90, 174–5, 179, 238; social composition, 85–6

Negri, Pola, 226
Nieder-Oelm, 227
Nikitin, K. I., 144
Nikolaev, K., 163
Nizhny Tagil, 112n
NKVD, 81, 107
Norder-Dithmarschen, 230
'Nordic' sculpture, 167
Novomoskovsk, 261
Novosibirsk, 132, 192
Novruz-bairam, 197
NS-Beratungsstellen, 212
NS-Cultural Project, 179
NSDAP, *see* Nazi party
NS-Flying Corps (NSFK), 73–5
NS-League of German Technology, NSBDT), 73–4
NS-League of German University Teachers, 73–4
NS-League of Teachers, 73–4
NS-Motor Corps (NSKK), 73–4
NS-People's Welfare (NSV), 73, 80, 98, 205–8, 211
NS-Reich Warriors' League, 73, 76
NS-War Victims' Care (NSKOV), 73, 205n
NS-Women's League, 73–4, 80, 93, 214n
Nuikin, A., 192

Oberdonau, 223, 243
Odenwald, 241
Odessa, 132, 196
Offenbach, 241
Ohlendorf, O., 244, 247
oktyabrina, 188
Okulov, A., 200
Omsk, 165, 260
opinion leaders, 139–40
Ortega y Gasset, 263
Osipov, G. V., 56n

Palaces of Happiness, 194
Palsmane, 198
Park of the Newborn, 194
party informators, 259, 261
Party-State Control Committee, 65n
'patronage' of Soviet party organization, 130
Pavlov, S. P., 57n, 186–7
Pennants of Fame, 126
people's controllers, 65
people's guards, 65, 67–9, 129, 131

Perm, 183
Petukhov, A., 202n
plant community, 45
Plekhanov, G. V., 32–3
Plot of 20 July 1944, 91
Political Situation Reports, *see* public opinion reporting, Nazi
politinformators, 266; criticism of, 161–4; deployment of, 156–7; 157; effectiveness of, 157–9, 161, 164–6; functions of, 152–5; introduction of, 148, 150–1; and leading personnel, 164–6; number of, 151; official claims for, 159–60, 164; and party organizations, 156–7; social composition of, 157; specialization of 155–6
Populism, 28–9
Potemkin villages, 210, 233
propaganda
 Nazi: conception of, 33–4; conditions of, 43–8, 266; demonstration effect, 83, 95; Goebbels on, 33–5; Hitler on, 33n, 39, 46; and ideology, 38–43; and Jewish question, 40; Ley on, 39; mass rallies, 50–1; Ministry of, 209, 235n, 247; oral agitation, 50, 90–3, 96–7, 266; party responsibility for, 48; Propaganda Rings, 92; 'propaganda with emphasis', 103
 Soviet: Brezhnev on, 36–7; Central Committee decree (1960) on, 34, 36; conception of, 32–3, 35–8; conditions of, 43–8, 266; criticisms of, 36–7, 54–5; emphasis on economic production, 36–8, 51–2; fusion with agitation, 34–5; and ideology, 34, 37–43; Khrushchev on, 35–6; Lenin on, 24, 34–6, 40n; mass media, 50, 54; and Party Programme, 34; party responsibility for, 49; and party studies, 34n; Plekhanov on, 32–3; post-Stalin changes, 53–5; and sociological research, 55–60.
 See also agitation, agitators, indirect propaganda
public holidays, Soviet, 189
Public Opinion Institute, 57
public opinion polls, Soviet, 57–8, 221

public opinion reporting
 Nazi: assessment of, 248–50; and the Churches, 227, 241; contents of, 225–9; criticisms of propaganda measures, 228–9, 240; Goebbels on, 246–7; 'hostile elements', 228; importance of, 224–5, 229; limitations of, 229–33, 235–9; operating procedures, 222–4; and Party Chancellory, 223–4, 226–7, 233–4, 236–7, 243–4; radicalism of, 241–2; and SD, 223–4, 230–2, 239, 242–9
 Soviet: contents of, 251–2, 256–7, 259–60; contrast with Nazi, 252–5; criticisms of, 257–8; importance of, 256; and modern technology, 262;; and 'non-staff activists', 258–9; operating procedures, 259–61; recent publicity, 256; and secret police, 251–2, 255–6

Rakhmankulov, M., 113
red weddings, 188
Reich Air Defence League (RLB), 73, 75
Reich Defence Council, 47n
Reich Food Estate, 73, 75, 99
Reich Labour Service (RAD), 73–5
Remembrance Day, 171–2, 175n
residential councils, 131
Rheingau-St Goarshausen, 241
Riga, Kirov Borough, 260
Right Opposition, 40
Ritter, G., 42n
Roehm, E., 83
Rohland, W., 242n
Rolls of Honour, 126
Rosenberg, A., 39, 174–5, 176n, 211n, 213n
Rostov, 260
RSHA, 81, 224, 244–5. *See also* SD
Rutkevich, M., 60n

SA, 72, 74, 76n
Samarkand, 260
Satire Windows, 126
Sauckel, F., 95n
Schacht, H., 249n
Scheringer, W., 41
Schirach, B. von, 212n

Schleswig-Holstein, 222n, 226–7, 233, 236–8
Schwarz, F. X., 75
Schweitzer, J. B. von, 28
SD, 223–4, 230–2, 239, 242–9. See also RSHA
Seehaus Service, 248n
selective exposure, 135–6, 158
Seldte, F., 76n
Shchelokov, N. A., 145n
Shvets, I., 257n
Smolensk Archives, 251
Smolensk Scandal, 253
sobranie, 52
socialist realism, 167
Socialist Revolutionaries, 252
sociological research in Soviet Union, 55–60, 112n, 134, 140n, 146, 158–9
Solzhenitsyn, A., 191n
soviet *aktiv*, 65
Speer, A., 51n, 242n
SS, 72–4, 77, 81
Stahlhelm, 76n
Stalin, I. V.: on ideology, 42; on mass organizations; on 'moral-political unity', 19–20; and nature of Soviet politics, 268; on party, 15–16, 17–18, 20, 62, 108n; and party recruitment, 105–6; and propaganda, 40n, 53; on 'victory of socialism', 19
Stalingrad, 230
Stalino, 128
Stennes, W., 41
Stepakov, V. I., 54, 148, 150n, 151
Stepanov, V., 16
Sterlitamak, 162
Stormarn, 237
Strasbourg, 236
Strasser, O., 41
Strength through Joy, 171, 179n
Stuermer cases, 100
Suederdithmarschen, 241
Sumgait, 196
Sunday readings, 185
Sverdlovsk, 136, 163

Tadjikistan, 185
Taganrog, 159n
Tallin, 198

Tatar ASSR, 259n
Tkachev, P. N., 28
Tolkunov, L., 158
Tocqueville, A. de, 263, 271
totalitarianism, 1–4; and mass support, 30, 263–4; survival of in Soviet Union, 267–71; and terror, 81, 268; and 'voluntary compulsion', 264–5
trade unions, Soviet, 65
Transbaikal, 200
Trotsky, L. D., 29, 40n
Truman, D. B., 58
Tula, 138, 261
Turkmenistan, 197

Udmurt ASSR, 261
Ukraine, 160
Uledov, A. K., 58n
Urban, G., 87n
Urgut, 260
Utikal, G., 87n
Uzbekistan, 111, 218

Vienna, 212n
Vladimir, 113
V-Maenner, 239. See also SD
Volk, 6–7, 19
Volkssprechtage, 212
voluntary compulsion, 340–1, 43
Voronezh, 219
Voroshilovgrad, 113

Waffen-SS, 98–9
Wagner, A., 225
Wagner, R., 238
wall newspapers, 126
welfare collections, Nazi, 208–11, 215–16
Winter Help Project (WHW), 102, 206, 208–9, 211, 216
'withering away' of the state, 16, 68

Yaroslavl', 113
'Yellow Peril', 92
Young Communist League, *see* Komsomol

Zhdanov, Yu., 187n
Zolotukhin, G., 160
Zyryanovsk, 195n, 196n